A CASEBOOK FOR MANAGEMENT INFORMATION SYSTEMS

McGraw-Hill Series in Management Information Systems

Gordon B. Davis, *Consulting Editor*

A CASEBOOK FOR MANAGEMENT INFORMATION SYSTEMS

THIRD EDITION

Henry C. Lucas, Jr.

Graduate School of Business Administration
New York University

McGraw-Hill Publishing Company

New York   St. Louis   San Francisco   Auckland   Bogotá   Caracas
Hamburg   Lisbon   London   Madrid   Mexico   Milan
Montreal   New Delhi   Oklahoma City   Paris   San Juan
São Paulo   Singapore   Sydney   Tokyo   Toronto

This book was set in Optima by The Graphix Group, Inc.
The editor was Christina Mediate;
the production supervisor was Diane Renda;
the cover was designed by Infield, D'Astolfo Associates.
Project supervision was done by The Graphix Group, Inc.
R. R. Donnelley & Sons Company was printer and binder.

**A CASEBOOK FOR MANAGEMENT
INFORMATION SYSTEMS**

3 4 5 6 7 8 9 0   DOC/DOC   9 9 8 7 6 5 4 3 2 1 0

ISBN 0-07-038948-9

Library of Congress Cataloging in Publication Data

Lucas, Henry C.
    A casebook for management information systems.

    (McGraw-Hill series in management information
systems)
    Includes bibliographical references.
    1. Management information systems—Case studies.
I. Title. II. Series.
T58.6.L8 1986   658.4'0388   85-11651
ISBN 0-07-038948-9

To Scott and Jonathan

CONTENTS

ANALYSIS OF SYSTEMS

PREFACE

This third edition of the casebook contains many changes from the first two editions. In response to feedback from instructors, this edition offers cases that are in general shorter than the previous editions. There are also several very brief cases that can be assigned for reading and discussion in class rather than for preparation in advance.

The cases are grouped into three sections:

1 Management issues. The purpose of this section is to illustrate some of the problems of managing a business in an increasingly technological environment.

2 Systems development. The cases in this section deal with the design of systems. Several can be used as design projects during a term.

3 Analysis of systems. This section is new to the text; it contains reports of very extensive investigations of three major systems and raises both design and management issues.

The cases in this book are designed to supplement two texts, though they are suitable for use in other contexts as well. The two books are *Information Systems Concepts for Management* (3rd. ed. forthcoming) and *The Analysis, Design and Implementation of Information Systems* (3rd. ed.), both published by McGraw-Hill.

The first section of the casebook offers cases which illustrate the problems of managing technology. Firms are finding it important to use information processing technology competitively. In order to use the technology strategically, a company must be able to manage information processing. The cases in this first section raise issues of how a firm can use technology as a part of its competitive strategy, how to establish policies for the control of microcomputers in the organization and how to manage the information services department in general.

The second section of the casebook is dedicated to problems of systems analysis and design. The best way to learn about systems development is to design an application. It is difficult to arrange a real design exercise for students and a case offers a reasonable substitute. SDB Corporation and the Center for Child Development A, B, and C cases are suitable for individual or group design projects in a course. The other cases in this section can also be assigned as design projects or treated as problems in how to approach design, e.g. UFWOC A.

The final section of the book is new in this edition; it contains the analysis by the General Accounting Office of three major governmental computer applications. The investigations are thorough and suggest a number of design and management problems. Students can be asked to comment on the problems in these systems, what might have been done differently and what they would recommend now. The GAO reports have been edited and most of the recommendations contained in the original reports have been eliminated so that students can develop their own analyses.

Much of the material discussed in classes on information systems is abstract. I have found cases to be an invaluable adjunct to lectures; they serve to make many of the concepts discussed in class real and help to develop the analytical skills of the student. The purpose of this casebook is to provide a selection of cases that the instructor can use in a variety of ways to improve students' understanding of the key issues in the design and management of information processing in an organization.

I would like to express my thanks for the many useful comments and suggestions provided by colleagues who reviewed this text during the course of its development, especially to Ed Baylin, Concordia University; Stuart Miller, Vanderbilt University; and Robert Minch, Purdue University.

Henry C. Lucas, Jr.

A CASEBOOK FOR MANAGEMENT INFORMATION SYSTEMS

MANAGEMENT ISSUES

AMERICAN HOSPITAL SUPPLY: THE ASAP SYSTEMS

Index Systems

The ASAP systems used by American Hospital Supply for entry of customer orders are widly cited as a (perhaps, as *the*) example of the use of information technology for strategic advantage. This note provides a brief description of the series of ASAP systems that American Hospital Supply has introduced and of the environment in which those systems are used.

This case study presents a background on the market for hospital supplies and instruments in 1975, just before the introduction of the initial ASAP system followed by American Hospital Supply's arguments for the need of such a system (as revealed in recent sales literature). It details the four ASAP systems that have been introduced as of this writing. Finally, the note considers environmental changes that have occurred since the ASAP introductions and describes sales literature and public relations used to promote the benefits of the ASAP systems.

All of the information presented was obtained from public sources. The background information was taken from a (disguised) case about a manufacturer of hospital instruments.[1] (Details of the disguise do not interfere with the usefulness of that material for the purposes of this note.) The remaining information came from sales literature and other publications by American Hospital Supply and from published articles.

BACKGROUND

As of 1975, the time of the Newport Instrument Division (NID) case, there were 7000 hospitals in the United States. The 1800 largest hospitals (200 or

[1]*Newport Instrument Division* (Harvard Business School, Case 6-576-035).

3

more beds each) accounted for 50 percent of the market for medical equipment and supplies. Equipment and supplies were also sold to laboratories,
individual physicians, and to others. The case presents 1972 data showing 68
percent of the dollar volume of manufacturer's sales of equipment and
supplies flowing through distributors (local, regional, and national with 30%,
17%, and 21% shares, respectively); 27 percent sold directly to health care
institutions; and the remainder through miscellaneous channels (such as
drug stores).

The case describes a complex buying process within hospitals. Often, it
was difficult to determine who in fact made the purchase decision. The
primary contact by a salesperson (from a distributor organization or from a
manufacturer organization that sold direct) was generally with a doctor,
nurse, technician, or pathologist. The hospital administrator might ask for
advice or input from department heads or purchase committees. For especially large purchases, the hospital's board and various government agencies
might also become involved. The government role was increasing as agencies
tried to help control costs of health care and to avoid aggregate overcapacity
among health-care institutions within the same geographic area.

Historically, distributors had been strong in selling the thousands of relatively straightforward supply items required by hospitals. Distributors emphasized their ability to provide the desired assortment of products and to give
customer service in delivery and in other regards.

Many of the items required by hospitals were essentially supply commodities (such as syringes or disposable hospital gowns). The supplies and equipment market also included instruments—some rather simple and others
highly sophisticated. The NID case cites a study showing that 75 percent of
the medical instrumentation sold in the United States in 1974 went direct; in
general, only less expensive, more standard instruments were sold through
distributors. The case suggests skepticism on the part of manufacturers about
the ability of the distributor's salespeople to sell sophisticated instruments.

At the same time, the case emphasizes that some distributors wanted to
participate in the market for sophisticated instruments. It explains that the
largest distributor (which the case calls Medical Supply Corporation) was
working hard to obtain product lines from manufacturers. That distributor
was also building its own manufacturing divisions (which sold their products
through the distribution division). The case states that MS was obtaining
approximately 40 percent of its sales dollars from products it manufactured.

THE NEED FOR ASAP

Recent (1984) sales literature from American Hospital Supply describes the
need for a system to reduce hospital ordering and inventory costs. The
remainder of this section reproduces the text from the first part of a sales
brochure.

The endless shuffle...is an expensive shuffle.
The shuffle of determining what, when, and how many to order; the shuffle of

paperwork, purchase orders, and invoices; and the shuffle of receiving, storing and delivering products is endless—and expensive—much more expensive than the unit cost of each item reveals. For every dollar you spend on the unit cost of an item, you can expect to pay up to one additional dollar acquiring and storing that item.

The cost of acquisition. Think of it as money tied up in paperwork. The cost of acquisition is the cost of people, supplies, and time necessary to:

- Determine the need for a product
- Gather product information
- Process the paperwork
- Place the order
- Receive the shipments
- Distribute the items to the end-user

The cost of an average purchase order is $25 to $50—approximately 75 percent people and their time, and 25 percent supplies.

The cost of inventory. Think of it as money on the shelf. The holding cost of inventory is generally considered to be 27 percent of the unit cost of an item. Inventory is a large, nonspendable asset which:

- Earns nothing
- Must be counted and controlled
- Can be obsolete, outdated, lost or improperly appropriated

A costly inventory within the hospital is the elusive "department" or "shelf" inventory.

- It is not entirely visible
- It is usually controlled by the end-user rather than materials management
- It is usually not subject to physical inventory count
- It is often larger than the visible storeroom inventory

Inventory also has a heavy impact on the cash flow system within the hospital. High inventory and low productivity can lead to low cash flow, reduced operating revenues, and decreased working capital.

THE ASAP SYSTEMS

The first Analytical Systems Automated Purchasing (ASAP) system was introduced by an American Hospital Supply division in 1976. Over time, ASAP was used by all six distribution divisions at American Hospital Supply. Systems improvements created ASAP 2, ASAP 3, and in November 1983, ASAP 4. Each successive system built on and expanded the capabilities of its predecessors.

ASAP 1 provided automated order entry either through a touchtone phone (and 7-digit product numbers) or through a wand that could read bar codes (either from the sides of packages or from a catalog of the codes). Some of the early versions also used prepunched plastic cards to provide automated dailing of preset orders. As of this writing, ASAP 1 was still used by some small hospitals or single departments within larger hospitals.

ASAP 2 contained the order input capabilities of ASAP 1 plus the ability to accept orders from a deck of computer cards and a card reader. ASAP 2 also added a teleprinter that could be used either to input orders or to obtain a printback of an order for verification. Printback (in a fixed standard format) was useful to help catch errors.

ASAP 3 added several features to customize the system to a particular hospital's needs. The system allowed users to create computer files of purchase information to reduce the amount of input subsequently needed to send the order. A user might create a *standing order file* for regular orders of routine items. The file would contain the list of items and quantities as well as information about the timing of orders. A user could also establish *repetitive files*, listing items that were ordered as a group (although they might not be ordered regularly). Such files could contain economic order quantities (EOQs) to determine reorder decisions for individual items. Users could also create *basic files*, or more complete lists of items. On any specific order the user would select some, though generally not all, of the items in the basic file. EOQs could be included for the individual items.

ASAP 3 also provided customization of output. Customers could specify their own purchase order formats (which would be programmed by American Hospital Supply). They could thus obtain ASAP purchase orders in the same formats as their other purchase orders. Further, ASAP 3 inputs were automatically separated by American Hospital Supply's computer into the sets of items processed by each of the company's six distribution divisions. Customers received copies of purchase orders and invoices from each of the divisions.

ASAP 4 provided a computer-to-computer link from the hospital computer to the American Hospital Supply mainframe. It was appropriate only for hospitals using computerized materials management systems. ASAP 4 linked directly to such systems, providing for automatic ordering (subject, of course, to override) as the materials management software determined needed purchases. (The actual physical link involved telephone communication between machines.) Before ASAP 4, hospitals had to take information from their computerized materials management system and rekey it into a teleprinter for transmission.

Each hospital placed its ASAP 4 orders at prearranged times of the day. The system was not designed for emergency orders. The original ASAP 4 system linked to mainframe computers within hospitals. The first system was installed in late 1983. American Hospital Supply had also announced plans to introduce a system for microcomputers during 1984.

Customers did not pay for the use of any of the ASAP systems or for the necessary software customization (which might take up to 8 hours). Sales people were not charged for software customization; however, the sales force was otherwise compensated entirely on the profitability of their accounts, with no base salaries. All costs (including their automobile costs and the costs of computer terminals) were borne by the sales people (from their gross commissions).

It took time for competitors to respond to the ASAP systems. The first response came two years after the ASAP introduction. Initial response was difficult in part because the competitors had to computerize their own inventories in order to offer a computerized system to their customers. As of this writing a hospital can order from many different suppliers via teletype. At the same time, however, competitors have continued to lag (significantly) the successive ASAP enhancements.

ADDITIONAL DEVELOPMENTS

Important additional developments have occurred in the American Hospital Supply's market since the first ASAP introduction. Perhaps the most significant is a major change in the way the United States government reimburses hospitals for costs of treating Medicare patients. Previously, hospitals had been reimbursed on the basis of the actual costs they incurred in serving those patients. According to Karl D. Bays, Chairman of American Hospital Supply, "...the cost-plus system didn't offer any incentive to watch costs and be more efficient." Federal legislation signed on April 20, 1983 provided for a change (over a 4-year period) to what was called a prospective payment approach based on diagnosis related groups (or DRGs).

DRGs were developed at Yale University initially as an aid in reviewing and predicting the length of patients' stays in the hospital. The basic DRG idea was to create major diagnostic categories (MDCs) and subgroupings (DRGs) that identified patients with sufficiently similar conditions to produce similar patterns of length of stay, treatment, and consumption of hospital resources. The initial project was intended to help review and manage capacity utilization. A revised system of DRGs was later developed as a tool for predicting the amount and type of resources that would be used in treating patients. The system used in the 1983 legislation contained 469 DRGs.

Under the new reimbursement system, payment to a hospital would be based on national and regional costs for each DRG—not on the hospital's own costs. Moreover, the national and regional averages would be updated over time, so that if hospitals improved their cost performance overall, they would be subject to stricter DRG-related payment limits. For the phase-in period the hospitals would be compensated by a fraction of their cost-based rate and the complementary fraction of the DRG-related rate. Over that period, the fraction based on the DRG rates would increase to 100 percent.

This fundamental change in reimbursement was making hospitals substantially more conscious of costs—including inventory and ordering costs. It was creating increased interest in materials management and in systems like ASAP.

Another important development in the health-care industry that was also heightening concern about costs, was the growth of alternative forms of health care. In part because employers and third party insurers were increasingly concerned with controlling the costs of care, there was substantial interest and growth in health maintenance organizations and other alternatives to the traditional health-care institutions. Hence, for the first time many hospitals felt they faced competition in their business; they felt the need for improved management (including control of inventory costs) to avoid pricing themselves out of the market.

PROMOTION OF ASAP

American Hospital Supply promoted the ASAP systems as tools for productivity and cost containment, and in fact used a theme of productivity in much of its overall marketing. For example, in early 1984 the firm staged a product exposition called "Productivity through Technology," that displayed many of the products it handled. The exposition emphasized equipment to produce high quality clinical analyses at low cost; only one of many booths contained information about ASAP and one of many seminar presentations considered the ordering systems.

The American Hospital Supply newsletter for customers discussed both the new reimbursement scheme and increased competition in health care. It regularly stressed the importance of productivity. For example, the spring 1983 issue listed some measurement criteria for health-care productivity: orders per person hour, materials management expenses over total revenues, inventory dollars over revenue dollars, and inventory transactions per employee. The winter 1983 issue noted that "Under prospective payment, a high priority will be placed on developing an information system that captures and integrates clinical, financial, and operational data. To monitor performance, hospitals will need to accumulate historical DRG information and statistical, cost, and revenue data by DRG to monitor and control case mix."

The remainder of this section gives an example of sales literature specifically addressed to ASAP. It quotes most of the remainder of the "endless shuffle" sales brochure quoted in an earlier section.

> *ASAP ends the endless shuffle.* The American ASAP System is a complete, automated order entry system, designed to provide rapid order entry, order confirmation and ensure efficient product delivery. It puts an end to the endless shuffle while supporting effective materials management and aggressive cost containment.
>
> *The end of costly acquisition.* The American ASAP System can reduce your cost of acquisition by:
>
> - Reducing order errors
> - Decreasing time-consuming paperwork
> - Supplying quick order confirmation
> - Providing critical materials management information rapidly
>
> *The end of costly inventory.* The American ASAP System can reduce your cost of inventory by:
>
> - Ensuring fast, efficient delivery
> - Providing analytical reports that allow more effective inventory management
> - Supplying information that assists in the establishment of optimum inventory levels

The beginning of more cost effective materials management. The American ASAP System encourages innovative materials management supporting:

- Standardization through identification of duplicated product types
- Centralized purchasing control
- "Stockless" purchasing for significant inventory reductions

Aggressive cost containment...with ASAP. Let the benefits of the American ASAP System become important components of your purchasing program.

The ASAP network provides effective inventory control through the use of management reports and the ASAP usage report.

Immediate reduction in the cost of acquisition can be significant.

Reduction in inventory holding costs can be as high as 40 percent.

Inventory impact on cash flow can be significantly reduced.

Automated purchasing saves time, eliminates paperwork, and ensures faster delivery.

The system within a system. The American ASAP System was developed by American Hospital Supply Corporation. Years ago, AHSC recognized the importance of efficient delivery systems and overall reduction of hospital costs. Today, we demonstrate our continued commitment to cost containment by offering the American ASAP System and the corporate system of resources it accesses.

ASAP is your direct link to the resources and capabilities of American Hospital Supply Corporation.

ASAP is your hot line to American Hospital Supply, Dietary Products, Hospitex, McGaw Laboratories, Scientific Products and V. Mueller.

ASAP is responsive, personal service from 3500 sales and over 600 customer service representatives.

ASAP is selection at its finest—88,000 products from 5000 suppliers.

ASAP is quick, consistent service from 90 local distribution centers and 200 delivery trucks.

ASAP is the end of the endless shuffle....

FINAL COMMENTS

The reader may find it interesting and useful to consider some additional questions about ASAP:

1 What impact do you think ASAP has had and will have on other distributors?

2 What impact do you think ASAP has had and will have on other manufacturers of medical equipment and supplies?

3 What do you guess were American Hospital Supply's expectations for ASAP when the first system was introduced?

4 How should American Hospital Supply Corporation use, modify, and enhance ASAP in the future?

5 What constitutes a strategic use of information technology? What is the difference between a strategic use and a more mundane use? What is the difference between a strategic use and a collection of mundane individual uses?

HAWKINS AND SHERMAN PERSONAL COMPUTER POLICY

Henry C. Lucas, Jr.

Hawkins and Sherman (H&S) is a large manufacturer and marketer of household products. In 1982 the company reported gross sales of $2.4 billion and an after-tax profit of 8.6 percent of sales. The company was founded seventy-five years ago and has expanded primarily by the acquisition of smaller, family held firms. All mergers and acquisitions are "friendly," and often existing management stays on to run the new subsidiary of H&S.

Corporate headquarters is relatively small since the individual divisions (companies) are autonomous. Headquarters responsibilities include a finance function, corporate marketing, and a corporate information systems group. This latter group is headed by Sam Newman, Vice President of Systems and Administration. He reports to Charlie Smith, Senior Vice President of Finance. Each division has a manager of systems who reports either to the divisional vice president of finance or, in some cases, the division president.

Some of the companies have their own mainframe and/or minicomputer installations, while others make use of three Consolidated Computer Centers. These centers had proven to be a cost effective way to provide batch, on-line, and timesharing computing services.

The corporate information systems group reporting to Sam Newman operates primarily as consultants to the divisions. This group also undertakes the development of special applications which are transferred to the divisions. Most of these special applications are programmed in APL and involve extensive computations such as financial or marketing analyses. (All APL applications were designed so that they could be executed from any terminal, not just an APL terminal.)

Charlie Smith believes strongly that users should not program: "It just isn't economical for a $50,000 a year manager who is an expert in finance to spend days writing a program that a professional programmer could complete in a few hours."

Sam Newman has become increasingly concerned about the proliferation of microcomputers at Hawkins and Sherman. "I don't know how we are going to support this deluge of different hardware and software. Eventually everyone is going to want to be on a network, or at least be able to access data from the mainframes. My staff can't possibly handle interfacing and software for twenty vendors' micros."

Sam and Charlie had several meetings on the question of micros and finally Sam sat down to draft a computer policy statement. He wanted to be sure that personal computing was treated as intended; that is, a flexible tool for the user, not requiring a systems study or a lot of analysts and programmers. "We've finally recognized that there are applications where there just isn't any payoff in doing a large system for multiple users. The personal computer can handle them nicely."

A number of issues were of concern to Sam as he developed the draft.

1 It appears that the mainframe is considerably more economical than a personal computer. Why don't users want to take the option of a terminal instead of a PC?

2 Can we standardize on a single brand of microcomputer, or will users insist on different machines out of personal preference or some special software package?

3 Charlie Smith does not want users to write programs, yet that is one of the whole selling points of personal computers. The user does not have to make a formal written request, wait for priorities to be assigned, and then go through a systems study. Anyway, how can we define programming with a personal computer? Is entering data from a spreadsheet programming? Sure, writing a system in BASIC is programming, but where do you draw the line?

4 How do we exert some quality control on personal computers? Everyone takes the output printed by a computer as fact, yet if the application is developed by a user, we cannot be sure that things like data editing and error checking have taken place. We also obviously can't validate the output to be sure the calculations are correct.

Sam prepared the draft memorandum and policy statement which follows. While he feels that it will probably work, he is a little uneasy about several parts of the policy. He particularly does not look forward to having the responsibility of approving each request in the firm for a personal computer.

Can you make recommendations to help Sam Newman and H&S manage personal computers in the firm?

DRAFT

The following draft of the proposed company policy for personal computers identifies application areas for which personal computers will be permitted; defines the approvals required; establishes a data base policy and hardware/

software standards; and affixes responsibility for implementation of the policy.

This policy draft is being issued for review prior to the next information systems directors' meeting. When the draft has been finalized and the policy has been issued, acquisitions of personal computers will be carefully controlled for the following reasons:

1 While personal computers unquestionably can be effective tools for a wide variety of applications, the cost of each PC must be considered an add-on to our present companywide computer equipment costs. During the past ten years, the company has invested significant financial resources to build and maintain the computer capacity required at the Consolidated Computer Centers to support the computing needs of the staff and operating divisions. The CCCs have proven to be an effective approach to providing batch, on-line, and timesharing facilities. Equipment costs at the CCCs currently exceed $5,100,000 annually. It is virtually impossible to reduce these costs through the acquisition of personal computers. Therefore, each personal computer must be justified, not as an alternative to existing computer facilities, but as additional expense and purely on a stand-alone basis.

A productivity advantage must be proven since, for the company, there is definitely a cost disadvantage. For clarification, an analysis of timesharing replacement costs and incremental costs for a typical timesharing user (which is clearly less than the cost of a personal computer) is attached as Exhibit 1.

2 Personal computers are still in an early stage of evolution. While state-of-the-art technology will always be a moving target, it is anticipated that particularly significant advancement in hardware and software capability will be announced in the next few months. It is expected that these advancements will facilitate the integration of personal computers into the planned corporate communications network and will provide software solutions that will improve the usability of the new systems (see Exhibit 2).

Significant reductions in prices are also expected because of manufacturing efficiencies and increased competition. Similarities to what happened to prices in the calculator and digital watch businesses are evident.

3 Communications capabilities that will permit personal computer compatibility with the current and planned corporate network have been announced but are not yet available for use. It is expected that within the next six months these capabilities will be fully tested and understood.

4 The most prevalent reason found for installing personal computers is to support financial modeling packages such as VisiCalc and DSS:F which have been successfully installed at some divisions. The users of these packages believe that they have provided productivity benefits and improved the quality of analysis work. However, these packages often require an extensive amount of time from professional people to perform data entry work. Also, because of a lack of edit and control software to support the data entry activity, accuracy of the output might be subject to question.

EXHIBIT 1
Timesharing replacement costs.

	Annual Cost
CPU Replacement	
Current 3033N Configuration	$610,000.00
—Supports 400 active users currently	
—Estimated maximum users supported are 650	
Possible Future CPU Upgrade is IBM 3083J	840,000.00
—Estimated maximum users supported are 1,300	
Incremental CPU Cost Per Additional User	350.00

$$\frac{\$840,000 - \$610,000}{650} = \$350.00$$

	Annual Cost
Disk Replacement	
Personal Computer Hard Disk (5 MB)	Purchase 2,000.00
IBM 3380 Annual Cost Per 5 MB	50.00
CRT	
3278-2 with Twelve Program Function Keys	1,000.00
Incremental Cost-Typical Timesharing User	
CPU	350.00
Disk Space	50.00
CRT	1,000.00
	$1,400.00

Integration of financial modeling packages with packages that support data entry/data base, graphics, and word processing would permit the use of clerical people to input data, provide improved editing, and additional capabilities to enhance analysis work. Also, a capability to extract from data bases located in the existing mainframe for use with financial modeling packages would significantly reduce data entry and improve data accuracy. All these capabilities are expected in the next generation of software (some have been announced) to be available by the summer of 1983.

We expect that within the next six months most of these issues will be clarified. During this time, specific responsibility must be established in each division to oversee the selection, justification, and implementation of personal computers. Meanwhile, specific uses of personal computers will be handled on a case-by-case basis.

Work continues on the development of recommended hardware configurations and a standard software list (see Exhibit 3), which we plan to issue with the finalized policy.

EXHIBIT 2
IBM Personal Computer minimum suggested configuration.

This configuration will support local processing and limited asynchronous communications with mainframe computers. CRT (3270) emulation cannot yet be effectively supported.

System Unit with 128K Memory. Memory required for effective use of applications packages for spread sheet calculation, word processing, etc.

Two 320KB Diskette Drives. To support data retention needs.

Monochrome Display. Green (80 x 24).

Matrix Printer with Graphics. For printed output, non-letter quality. 80 CPS.

Asynchronous Communications Adapter and Modem. For teletype communications with computers.

Optional

Color Display. Replaces monochrome display. Used primarily for graphics.

Daisywheel Printer. Replaces dot matrix printer. Used when letter-quality print is needed.

Vendor	Description	Retail Price
IBM	System Unit with 64K Memory, 1-320K Diskette Drive and Keyboard	$2,405.00
IBM	Second 320K Diskette Drive	650.00
IBM	Monochrome Display	345.00
IBM	64K/256K Memory Expansion (with 64K)	475.00
IBM	Matrix Printer with Graphics	595.00
IBM	Monochrome Display and Parallel Printer Adapter	335.00
IBM	Serial Adapter	150.00
Hayes	Smart Modem (300 baud)	279.00
	TOTAL	5,234.00

PERSONAL COMPUTER POLICY

Hawkins and Sherman has been actively pursuing opportunities to increase effectiveness and productivity through the use of data processing, decision support, and office automation technologies. In addition, planning is nearly completed to integrate these technologies through telecommunications. The main objective for the planned information network is to provide the company with computing and communication resources to support the availability, analysis, and timely flow of information.

Personal computers have developed to the point where they should be considered as an additional processing approach, along with batch, on-line, and timesharing for solving problems and meeting information processing

---

EXHIBIT 3
Preliminary IBM Personal Computer standard software list.

	Retail Price
Operating System/Languages	
—DOS with Advanced BASIC	$ 40.00
—STSC APL (being evaluated)	595.00
—UCSD P-System with PASCAL (being evaluated)	625.00
—IBM Macro Assembler	100.00
Financial Modeling	
—VisiCalc	200.00
—Multiplan (being evaluated)	250.00
—DSSF (being evaluated)	1,200.00
Word Processing	
—Easywriter	175.00
—Easywriter II (being evaluated)	350.00
—Wordstar (being evaluated)	495.00
Data Base	
—VisiFile (being evaluated)	300.00
Communications	
—IBM Asynch Support	60.00
—IBM SNA Support (to be evaluated)	1,000.00
Data Entry (to be evaluated)	
Graphics (to be evaluated)	

---

needs. However, the selection of the most effective approach should be based on a careful assessment of the system requirements to understand its relationship to other systems, data base needs, transaction volumes, and need for communication. Some guidelines to be followed in selecting the most appropriate approach are:

Batch. Typically used when data bases are large, transaction volumes are high, and immediate results are not required. This form of processing is usually the least expensive.

On-line. Typically used when data bases are large, transaction volumes are high, immediate results are needed, and response times must be consistent and fast.

Timesharing. Typically used when data bases are small, transaction volumes are light, and immediate results are necessary. Also used for decision support applications with on-going usage that require development languages that support quick response to user needs.

Personal Computers. May be useful as an input or communications device to access existing timesharing applications; for stand-alone applications where the amount of data required is small and the complexity of calculations to be performed is limited, and where software packages are available which eliminate or minimize the need for programming. Applications categories where personal computers have been successful are spread sheet manipulation, financial modeling, graphics, data entry, and word processing. In all these application areas, software packages are available which have eliminated the need for original programming.

STATEMENT OF POLICY

1 The use of personal computers will be considered in the following areas:

    a As a communications device (terminal) to access applications and data from Corporate Computer Centers (CCC) and other company and non-company computers.

    b As an input device for collecting and editing data for entry to company computers for processing.

    c To support stand-alone applications that utilize corporate or division data which were extracted from official company data bases.

    d To support stand-alone applications in those cases where the personal computer approach has been determined to be the most effective when compared to batch processing, an on-line system, or timesharing.

2 Data from company/division files can be used on personal computers for analysis purposes. *Company/division information must not be maintained on personal computers.* It is the responsibility of the vice president, systems and administrative services, and corporate controller to designate the information considered a company information resource. It is the responsibility of the division information systems director and controller to designate the data considered a division information resource. It is also the responsibility of the division information systems director to review all proposed data bases located in personal computers to ensure compliance with this policy.

3 The acquisition of each personal computer and software must be approved jointly by the information service director, division controller and user department manager at the acquiring division. Initially, all personal computer acquisitions must then be approved by the vice president of systems and administrative services.

4 Division information systems departments should develop a support function with responsibility for:

    a Evaluating the personal computer as an appropriate solution to an identified problem or need.

    b Assisting users in implementing and using personal computers.

    c Administering training programs and education to ensure effective use of personal computers.

    d Ensuring that use of personal computers is consistent with standards and guidelines.

5 Corporate, in conjunction with the divisions, is responsible for:

    a Approving all personal computer acquisitions.

    b Evaluating hardware and software.

    c Developing hardware and software standards.

    d Negotiating prices and establishing master agreements.

    e Ordering and maintaining an inventory of hardware and software to meet division requirements. This is to obtain maximum discounts on a companywide basis.

    f Arranging equipment maintenance and service.

    g Establishing standards to ensure effective communications.

    h Coordinating the development of needed software.

6 Hardware must be the IBM Personal Computer. A minimum configuration has been identified (see Exhibit 2) and will be updated as appropriate. Other vendor equipment, which might be required in certain functional areas, such as research and development, must be approved by the vice president of Systems and Administrative Services.

7 Software should be selected from the Standard Software List, which will be supplied and supported by corporate. Exceptions must be approved by the vice president of systems and administrative services.

8 As with other terminal equipment, personal computer communications with corporate computer centers and other company computers must be approved by the appropriate information systems director. Access to specific company data bases must also be approved by the information systems director.

9 Programming is not permitted on the personal computer unless specifically approved by the appropriate information systems director.

10 Personal computer use at a company location must be approved by the user department manager, information systems director, and the controller, regardless of who purchased the equipment.

11 The personal computer user, his department manager and information systems director are responsible for compliance with H&S internal control standards, including security, back-up, recovery, documentation, and proper fixed-asset control.

12 Software must not be copied in violation of any copyright laws.

GENERAL FOODS
INFORMATION SERVICES
DEPARTMENT [1]

Ed Schefer, vice president of Information Services, looked back at the accomplishments of the Information Services Department (ISD) over the past year with considerable satisfaction. This time last year ISD lacked a policy on personal computers so that any that were brought in were brought in ad hoc or in an uncoordinated manner. At that time, there were only ten authorized personal computers in General Foods (GF). Today there are over seventy.

Since last summer ISD has, with unanimous support from the functional units and divisions, established the Personal Computer Placement Advisory Council to help the user departments find profitable opportunities to exploit personal computers. Further, ISD has started the Executive Development Program with the purpose of helping to acquaint the senior management of General Foods with the potential opportunities presented by these new tools. Finally, and perhaps most important, last week, June 7, ISD opened its own Computer Store where General Foods' functional units and divisions can look at and experiment with personal computers to become more familiar with them before acquiring one for their department. In addition, the Computer Store provides classes to employees on how to use these new tools.

Ed Schefer realized that it was extremely important for ISD to strike the appropriate balance between encouraging the user to seek appropriate profitable opportunities for personal computers and controlling what could

[1]Copyright © 1982 by the President and Fellows of Harvard College

This case was prepared by Leslie R. Porter as the basis for class discussion rather than to illustrate either effective or ineffective handling of an administrative situation. Reprinted by permission of the Harvard Business School.

grow into an extremely expensive passing fad. Ed felt that at least now they had a workable policy but he knew there was much left to do.

COMPANY BACKGROUND

In the early 20s, several food processing firms, most notably, Maxwell House coffee business and Jell-O gelatin desserts business, joined forces with the Post cereals business to form General Foods (GF). By 1982, with net annual sales well past the eight billion dollar mark GF had become one of the world's leading producers of packaged grocery products. Many of its brand names are household words, such as Maxwell House, Sanka, Jell-O, Post, Bird's Eye, Tang, Shake 'n Bake, and Gain's. Of this $8 billion in sales 70 percent came from the United States market; however, the international market is increasing in importance.

After an abortive effort at diversification in the late sixties, General Foods settled into a decade of slow, steady growth, mainly achieved through careful planning and cost control. By the end of the seventies, they realized they were losing market share with their main products such as coffee, and that if General Foods was going to maintain its position of dominance in the coming years it would have to develop a more aggressive policy toward growth. To this end in 1980 it reorganized into four sectors, giving each sector head increased responsibility and authority.

Packaged Convenience Foods   This is the largest of the four sectors with net sales accounting for 40 percent of GF total net sales. Employing a matrix form of organization it has six product group divisions in addition to the four function support groups. The functional support group services not only the product divisions of Packaged Convenience Foods but also the two divisions of the Coffee and Food Services sector. Thus all the products sold by these two sectors as well as many of the products sold by the International Operations sector are produced in the twenty General Foods plants that report functionally through this sector. Each of these plants is operated as a cost center and may produce several of GF's products.

Coffee and Food Services   Coffee is viewed at GF as their flagship product and they take great pride in the fact that Maxwell House is the nation's best-selling coffee. In addition to coffee, this sector is also responsible for the Food Services Products Division which deals with institutional clients who purchase many of GF's products.

International Operations   This sector is becoming increasingly important as GF strives to increase the volume of its sales. Broken down into four geographical regions, each region has profit responsibility for the area it serves. In addition to the products GF manufactures in the United States, the international operation also manufactures and sells products that are unique to the region served. While the regions share a marketing and development function, each region has its own administration support function, such as personnel, with the heads of these having dotted line relationships to their functional counterpart in the United States.

Oscar Mayer Of the four sectors, Oscar Mayer is the most autonomous and least integrated into the GF corporation. With its headquarters in Madison, Wisconsin, Oscar Mayer has been left essentially intact since it was acquired in May 1981. As of yet, it shares none of the corporate functional support resources, though the heads of its functional support units do have a dotted line relationship with their corporate counterpart in White Plains.

For GF to change its orientation toward growth they recognized that more than the organizational structure had to change. As James Ferguson, chairman and CEO, asserted:

> We are encouraging their aggressive stance, one that's oriented toward growth. All of us must be willing to take prudent risks to attain it.
>
> It boils down to what you might call the "culture" of a company. And we are changing our corporate culture—by articulating goals, increasing risk levels. By doing so, we have established the kind of environment in which aggressiveness and risk will be rewarded, recognizing that people may fail once in a while.
>
> The ultimate responsibility lies with the people running the business. We have told our various sectors: "You tell us how you can do your job better, and we'll support you." We find we are gaining their wholehearted commitment to this cultural change, because it's fun and rewarding to build a business.

To emphasize this change away from cost control to growth, GF added two new operating goals. First, each sector must generate volume growth that is greater than the growth of the aggregate market. Thus, each sector must meet its own specific growth targets. Second, each sector must accelerate its investments in new and existing businesses. These investments must add value to GF in that they produce incremental cash returns and generate growth in earning.

INFORMATION SERVICES DIVISION

In the late 1970s GF became concerned about the effectiveness of their information services function. An external review of this function reported:

> To a considerable extent, the facilities planning responsibility is fragmented throughout the various information services organizations within the corporation. As is frequently the case when facilities planning is performed and controlled on a decentralized basis by people who have other full-time responsibilities, facilities decisions appear to be made on a reactive rather than on a carefully planned basis. The overall result of the decentralized planning process is a diverse picture of hardware, facilities plans of varying quality, unnecessarily high costs to satisfy processing requirements, and significant barriers to the use of common systems. As was found in the project team's review of the existing systems plans, there is no

comprehensive corporate facilities plan which defines the long-range strategic direction that the company plans to follow in providing operational support for its future information requirements.

The study concluded that GF ranked relatively low in the area of information systems when compared to other major consumer goods companies of similar size and sophistication.

In 1978 GF had sixteen data centers located throughout the country. The corporate offices had two centers, one in Battle Creek (360/65) and the other in White Plains (360/65, 370/158). In addition, each of the SBUs and plants had some data processing capability. The distribution, sales and service division had four regional centers each with either an IBM 370/138 or 370/125. Food products division had a 370/138 in Dover and their plant had System 34s. Pet Foods' beverage and breakfast foods and Maxwell House plants all had some degree of data processing support.

Just as there was a proliferation of equipment throughout GF there was also a proliferation of applications and approaches to these applications. For example, in the marketing function there were twenty-six different systems for sales tracking and analysis, thirteen systems related to call reporting, and ten systems for sales forecasting. The main reasons cited for this proliferation of duplicate systems were incompatibility of hardware and a general lack of knowledge of what other divisions were doing.

Despite the large number of systems installed, very little was provided to management to help them in increasing sales or reducing cost. The information they received was often neither timely nor in a useful format. In interviews with the user at the time, comments like the following frequently surfaced:

- I know the information is available in our current systems but I can't get it in the format (or within the time frame) that I need it.
- This report has information which I consider critical, but it is so difficult to dig it out of the details, that it's not worth the effort.
- Yes, I get that (voluminous) report once a month. My secretary files the new one, throws away the old one, and I seldom, if ever, reference it.
- We collect the data on a daily basis, but when I see it on a report, it's ten days old and no longer actionable.
- If we could state plant costs on a comparable basis, we could make those decisions with more confidence.
- That other function collects the information at the level of detail we need it, but we don't have access to the detail.

By 1978, the expenditures for data processing had grown to over $35 million. The review of the information services function concluded that there was a real need for more centralized control of this resource, with this centralized control having three primary advantages. First, there would be large savings by centralizing the hardware in White Plains and only distributing processing capability to those plants that do have unique needs for local processing. Further, those plants that do require local processing capability, should all use the same hardware to facilitate the sharing of software. Second, there would be significant saving through centralized control of software development. This saving would accrue through reduced redundancy and more cost-effective development made possible through a larger development group. Third, centralizing would allow those responsible for the information resources to focus on the development of software that would have the greatest advantage to the corporation as a whole and would support the corporate strategic objectives.

Jim Tappan, group vice president who had the responsibility for planning and development, as well as information services, saw ISD supporting the corporate strategic objectives in two ways. First, by providing better and more timely information, ISD supported the goal of building GF's base businesses. Second, ISD needed to take an active role in helping the divisions and function departments in meeting the strategic objective of controlling and reducing the corporate administrative costs.

By 1982 most of the recommendations arising from that 1978 review had been implemented. The information services department was a centrally directed function, with a corporate staff that managed the business information systems for the coffee and food services sector, packaged convenience foods sector, the domestic divisions, and all corporate functions. In addition, it had the responsibility for coordinating the international operations' systems activity worldwide. Oscar Mayer at that time still had its own MIS function though it had a dotted line relationship with ISD management. By this time ISD budget had grown to over $50 million.

ISD had the responsibility not only for data processing support, but also management science support and telecommunications. To provide this as well as the systems support ISD was divided into five groups (see Exhibit 1).

Business Systems and Client Services   This group is the focal point for the department's support of clients. It is composed of two units, Business Systems and Client Services. Business Systems is responsible for identifying opportunities to improve business performance through the strengthening of business systems, for developing an integrated portfolio of strategic systems and a practical implementation plan for that portfolio, and for satisfying division and sector system needs.

Business Systems staff include among their roles: assuring commonality of business information, translating business solutions into data processing designs, determining the feasibility and economic practicality of systems solutions to business problems, and providing overall project management to most systems projects.

Client Services is staffed by client service managers, each assigned to a sector or a division, and each responsible for assisting the client in developing and executing systems plans. The client services manager helps his or her client to identify business problems, explore alternatives, and determine which are the most appropriate systems solutions; and arranges for support from other information services in achieving solutions. The client services unit provides feedback from the business units which helps to insure the practicality and the effectiveness of the department's services.

Information Systems   This group is responsible for working closely with Business Systems in the design, programming, and implementation of systems. It consists of three professional, technically oriented units: Systems Development, System Services, and Information Management.

Systems Development has primary responsibility for technical design, programming, and implementation of large-scale systems which have been identified as strategically important and as supporting the major business thrusts of the corporation.

Systems Services has responsibility for the support of all currently operating GF systems. Additional responsibilities include development of certain systems (process control applications and others); management of field data centers at manufacturing locations; and support of time-sharing applications.

Information Management focuses on the integration and management of the corporation's data. Included in its responsibilities are data base design, data resource management, and support and performance-monitoring of the GF data base environment.

Information Systems presently employs over 300 programmers and other professionals. Approximately 150 of these professionals are permanently located in the seventeen plants which have data processing capability while the remaining 150 are split more or less evenly between new Systems Development and Systems Services.

Information Facilities   This group has functional responsibility for GF information processing facilities and provides a service-oriented operation across the corporation. The group manages the corporate data processing center and all voice and data network facilities. Within this group are specialists in hardware, systems software, and telecommunications.

In 1982 this equipment at GF included an IBM 370/158 and a 3033 operating in an MVS environment supporting their transaction oriented systems. GF's general-purpose time-sharing needs are run with two IBM 4300 running CMS. At that time seventeen of their twenty-three plants supported local processing and the sending and receiving of data with System 34s, which were to be replaced with System 38. While these machines were owned by the plants, the staff (seven to nine supporting operations, data entry, and programming), as discussed earlier, reported to Information Services.

In addition, eighteen of the twenty distribution centers have IBM Model 34s for order entry. These machines have no support staff. There are also four region centers, one of which has an IBM 370/138 and the remaining three have IBM 370/135. These machines were scheduled to be replaced with System 34s.

Chairman & CEO
J.L. Ferguson

President & COO
P.L. Smith

Group Vice President
J.C. Tappan
- VP-Planning
  R.A. Kiath
- VP-Information Services
  E.A. Schefer
- VP-External Dev.
  A. Haas
- Internal Dev.

Senior Vice President
&
General Counsel
P.J. DeLuca
- Secretary
  A.G. Perkins
- VP-Urban Affairs
  L.A. Archer

Senior Vice President
&
Chief Financial Officer
I. Engelman
- VP & Treasurer
  D.M. Brush
- VP & Controller
  J.B. Hoeppner
- General Auditor
  Auditing & Security
  E.G. Hakula
- VP-Tax
  R.C. Schaub
- Dir., Investor Relations
  D. Rickart

Senior Vice President
Administration
A.J. Schroder
- VP-Consumer Affairs
  P. Kohl
- VP-Personnel
  C.R. Blundell
- Public Affairs
  A.J. Schroder

Exec. Vice President
President & CEO
Oscar Meyer
J.M. Hiegel

Vice President &
Exec. V.P.–Oscar Meyer
R.L. Tolleson

Group Vice President
Coffee and Food Service
R.L. Seelert

Vice President–Group Ex.
President
Food Service Prod. Div.
B. Laragh

President
Maxwell House Division
R.L. Seelert

Executive Vice President
President
Packaged Convenience Foods
D.J. Keller

Group Vice President
PCF Business Divisions
W.F. Dordelman

GM-BEAPD
E.R. Fenci

Vice Pres. &
GM-Beverage Div.
R. Sansone

VP-Breakfast Foods Div.
W.H. Korab

VP-Desserts Div.
I.P. Rosow

GM-Main Meal Div.
C. Bowen

Vice Pres. &
GM-Pet Foods Div.
R.L. Cobb

Vice President
Group Executive-Operations
H.A. Golle

Vice President
Group Executive-Sales
K.E. Fulton

Vice President
Group Executive-Purch.
Mats. Mgt. & Distrib.
P.A. Korn

VP-Marketing Staffs
F.K. Mitchel

Dir. Marketing Research
J.R. Andrews

Executive Vice Pres.
International Oper.
(4/4/82)
E.R. Shames

Group Vice President
President-GF Europe
J.M. Keenan

Vice President
President-GF Canada
R.S. Hurlbut

Vice President
President-Asia Pacific
G.D. Wollert

Vice President
President-GF Latin Am.
D.A. Smith

Vice President
President-International
Marketing Development,
Marketing & Admin.
J.H. Whitcomb

Vice President-Far East
J.B. Tharp

Vice President
Technical Research
A.S. Clausi

Chairman's Committee

- Long Range Strategy
- Diversification
- External Affairs

Operating Committee

Daily Running of the Business

EXHIBIT 1
General Foods Corporation
Corporate Management
July 1982

Finance, Planning, and Administration This group is responsible for developing the department's strategic and financial plans, operating policies and procedures, and standards; for assurance that all systems developed conform to standards; and for training and development programs to help increase the skills of all information services people.

It is also in charge of developing office systems for the corporation (automating secretarial/clerical activities, electronic mail communications, work simplification studies, and other projects).

International This is a complete systems management function responsible for coordinating all international operations systems activities and for integrating international operations plans and objectives into overall information services strategy. It also assists in the transfer of technology and applications between the systems organizations of GF's domestic operations and the various GF international companies.

PERSONAL COMPUTERS

Over the past several years Ed Schefer had become increasingly concerned about determining the appropriate role for personal computers with General Foods. He participated with the research board as well as other industry groups in numerous discussions on the role of these devices. In the summer of 1980, Ed acquired a Radio Shack Model III for ISD to be used by the staff to determine their overall potential. By the summer of 1981, it was clearly evident that there was significant interest within the user departments of GF in personal computers. Food Service Products Division already had one which ISD had installed as an experiment 6 months earlier, and they were very happy with the productivity gains they had achieved through the use of its spread-sheet program. In June, Sal Andreoli had returned from a tax conference where he met with an old friend who had an Apple computer. Sal became convinced that he could meet many of his needs through the use of a similar Apple computer. The system he had just spent $11,000 for ISD to develop, and which was costing him $300 to $400 per month to run, certainly was not doing the job. He had just received an ISD estimate that it would cost another $13,000 to redo the system. So, rather than spend the additional $13,000, he couldn't see why he should not spend $7000 and try using an Apple. His friend had assured him that the applications were straightforward and he would even come up and set it up for him in an afternoon. After ISD had received Sal's proposal to forego the new system in favor of acquiring an Apple, they met with Sal on numerous occasions to make absolutely certain he understood both the limitations of the Apple as well as the potential problems he could expect to encounter.

Up to this time, ISD had been somewhat apprehensive about taking a position on personal computers because they really didn't know how they would fit in. However, with the success of the food services experiment and pressures from other departments Ed Schefer decided that ISD could no longer wait to develop its policy toward this issue. The first problem Ed faced, however, was where to place responsibility for personal computers. Bill Kiedaisch, director of information facilities (see Exhibit 2), felt that personal computers were primarily another piece of hardware and therefore the responsibility for their dissemination and the control of that dissemination should be under facilities. However, Bernie Kopitz, director of information systems, felt that the use of these devices was primarily software driven and therefore the responsibility for them should fall under information systems. Ed, however, felt strongly that the approach taken should not be technology based but user driven. He therefore felt that the responsibility for personal computers should be located in ISD marketing area, that is, client services. To this end he asked Bob Judge, associate director of client services, to synthesize the information collected to date and come up with a proposal for General Foods.

Bob presented a proposal stating that ISD should aggressively support the introduction of personal computers. As he saw it they fit into three basic areas. First, they were useful as a stand-alone productivity tool to help people do their jobs better. Second, as a prototyping tool where they could be used to develop working models of large systems. Thus, ISD could work with users to create the models of the desired system, get the bugs out, and make certain that the system met the users' needs. This would have a beneficial impact both in the user departments and in ISD. Third, as an intelligent terminal to access data on the mainframe. The concern, therefore, should not be on the number of personal computers placed, but where they are placed. If they are placed in an inappropriate location they could be counterproductive because of all the distraction available for these machines. For this reason, Bob felt that it was important to have top management involvement in their place-ment. In addition, Bob proposed that they have an area in GF where the potential user could come and work with personal computers to gain a better understanding of what they could and could not do. Schefer agreed with Bob's proposals and authorized him to implement them.

Bob first secured the involvement of senior management. He met with the heads of every functional unit and every division to explain what ISD was doing and to get from that person the name of a representative from their unit or division to serve on the Personal Computer Placement Advisory Council (PCPAC). The PCPAC would meet once a quarter to recommend policies with regard to personal computers, thus providing a forum for the dissemination of information back to the individual units and divisions. In addition, the unit's representative on PCPAC would be a required signature for any placement request sent to ISD for a personal computer, and this, it was felt, would provide the unit head or division president with an assurance that in his area this thing was being controlled. All the unit heads and division presidents agreed and within a week each had provided the name of the

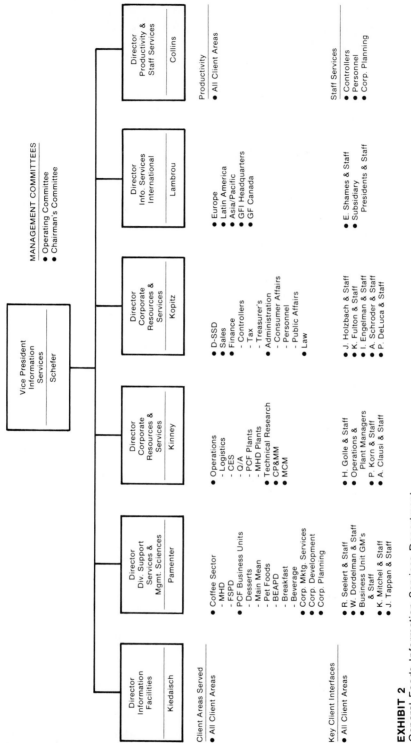

MANAGEMENT COMMITTEES
- Operating Committee
- Chairman's Committee

Vice President Information Services
Schefer

Director Information Facilities
Kiedaisch

Director Div. Support Services & Mgmt. Sciences
Pamenter

Director Corporate Resources & Services
Kinney

Director Corporate Resources & Services
Kopitz

Director Info. Services International
Lambrou

Director Productivity & Staff Services
Collins

Client Areas Served
- All Client Areas

- Coffee Sector
  - MHD
  - FSPD
- PCF Business Units
  - Desserts
  - Main Mean
  - Pet Foods
  - BEAPD
  - Breakfast
  - Beverage
- Corp. Mktg. Services
- Corp. Development
- Corp. Planning

- Operations
  - Logistics
  - CES
  - Q/A
  - PCF Plants
  - MHD Plants
- Technical Research
- CP&MM
- MCM

- D-SSD
- Sales
- Finance
  - Controllers
  - Tax
  - Treasurer's
- Administration
  - Consumer Affairs
  - Personnel
  - Public Affairs
- Law

Productivity
- All Client Areas

Staff Services
- Controllers
- Personnel
- Corp. Planning

Key Client Interfaces
- All Client Areas

- R. Seelert & Staff
- W. Dordelman & Staff
- Business Unit GM's & Staff
- K. Mitchel & Staff
- J. Tappan & Staff

- H. Golle & Staff
- Operations & Plant Managers
- P. Korn & Staff
- A. Clausi & Staff

- J. Holzbach & Staff
- K. Fulton & Staff
- I. Engelman & Staff
- A. Schroder & Staff
- P. DeLuca & Staff

- Europe
- Latin America
- Asia/Pacific
- GFI Headquarters
- GF Canada

- E. Shames & Staff
- Subsidiary Presidents & Staff

EXHIBIT 2
General Foods Information Services Department

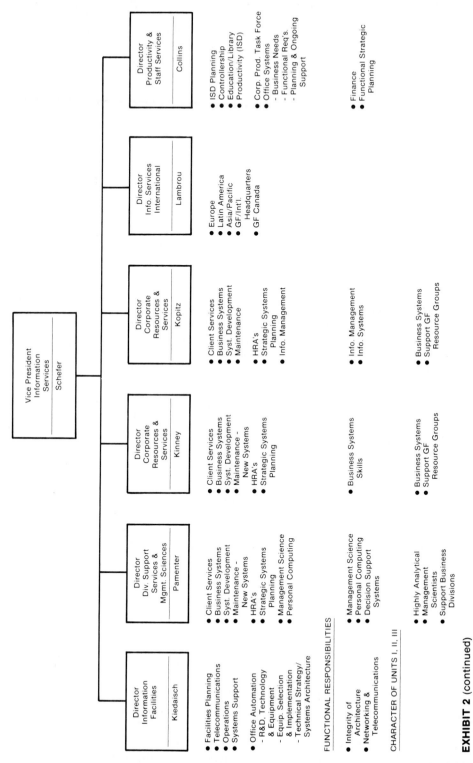

Vice President Information Services — Schefer

Director Information Facilities — Kiedaisch
- Facilities Planning
- Telecommunications
- Operations
- Systems Support
- Office Automation
  - R&D, Technology & Equipment
  - Equip. Selection & Implementation
  - Technical Strategy/Systems Architecture

Director Div. Support Services & Mgmt. Sciences — Pamenter
- Client Services
- Business Systems
- Syst. Development
- Maintenance - New Systems
- HRA's
- Strategic Systems Planning
- Management Science
- Personal Computing

Director Corporate Resources & Services — Kinney
- Client Services
- Business Systems
- Syst. Development
- Maintenance - New Systems
- HRA's
- Strategic Systems Planning

Director Corporate Resources & Services — Kopitz
- Client Services
- Business Systems
- Syst. Development
- Maintenance
- HRA's
- Strategic Systems Planning
- Info. Management

Director Info. Services International — Lambrou
- Europe
- Latin America
- Asia/Pacific
- GF/Int'l. Headquarters
- GF Canada

Director Productivity & Staff Services — Collins
- ISD Planning
- Controllership
- Education/Library
- Productivity (ISD)
- Corp. Prod. Task Force
- Office Systems
  - Business Needs
  - Functional Req's.
  - Planning & Ongoing Support
- Finance
- Functional Strategic Planning

FUNCTIONAL RESPONSIBILITIES

- Integrity of Architecture
- Networking & Telecommunications

- Management Science
- Personal Computing
- Decision Support Systems

- Business Systems Skills

- Info. Management
- Info. Systems

CHARACTER OF UNITS I, II, III

- Highly Analytical
- Management Scientists
- Support Business Divisions

- Business Systems
- Support GF Resource Groups

- Business Systems
- Support GF Resource Groups

EXHIBIT 2 (continued)

29

appropriate individual. While in some cases this individual was the unit head or division president himself, in other cases the person nominated was a person in a responsible management position usually on the staff of the unit head or division president.

In addition to the creation of PCPAC, Bob felt it was very important to raise the overall level of consciousness of GF as to the capability of the personal computer, especially with senior management. It was well accepted that there was a growing gap in the understanding of senior management in the potentials of system technology. Bob felt it was important to the future of GF that the top management of the company understand not only the capabilities of these machines but, more importantly in the broader context, understand where these systems can impact the functions they manage. To facilitate this, Bob proposed the establishment of an executive development program. In this program the function heads and division heads would be loaned a personal computer to take home for 120 days. They would be given a structured set of exercises to follow to build their confidence with the device. The final project required the participant to put up two applications; one from his job, and one from his home.

Lastly, Bob proposed the creation of a computer store within GF. This store would provide interested employees hands-on experience in working with one of three personal computers. He decided that the store should stock Apple IIs, IBM Personal Computers and Radio Shack Model IIIs. Further, it would stock a wide array of software designed to support the business functions. Additionally, the store would provide classes in the morning for interested employees to better prepare them to use these devices. GF negotiated favorable purchasing contracts at a number of computer stores in the area and also arranged that GF's employees could purchase personal computers for their own use at the same discount.

In October, Sal Andreoli's tax department received their Apple and by the following spring every group within the tax department had some application on the Apple using either VisiCalc or a DB Master, a data base package. In fact, the Apple was being used over 160 hours a month and it was usually necessary to reserve it in advance. As Sal pointed out:

> These things are really cost efficient because they remove all that grunt work from a person's job. I feel I'm using my job time better. I look at it as job enrichment for those who work for me for their jobs are becoming more meaningful. People are staying late or coming in early just to get access to the computer because it means that much to them.

By the end of June, the proposals defined in General Foods' strategy statement for implementing GF/ISD's policy on personal computers (Exhibit 3) were almost completely implemented. PCPAC's representatives had approved the purchase of over seventy personal computers. Twenty of GF's senior management were involved in the executive development program, and all had their personal computers at their homes. All were enthusiastic about the opportunity of gaining exposure to this new technology and were

EXHIBIT 3

GENERAL FOODS INFORMATION SERVICES DEPARTMENT

Strategy for Implementing GF/ISD Policy Personal Computing

I TOP DOWN DIRECTION

GF management will set the direction on placement of personal computers in their respective units. Information Services will support all unit heads in this process by implementing and managing the ongoing aspects of our executive development program on personal computing.

A Executive Development Program

1 Inform unit heads of the current technology, capabilities, and trends from a business perspective.

2 Review the GF/ISD process for providing appropriate guidance and support to assist users in the effective use of this technology.

3 Involve senior management in determining the extent to which their organizations should pursue the personal computing option.

4 Assist unit heads in selecting an appropriate delegate to act as that unit's representation on the advisory and placement council.

B Advisory and Placement Council

The Personal Computer Advisory Council will meet on a quarterly basis for the purposes of constructively reviewing and discussing policies, processes, activities, and uses of personal computers across GF. The activities of this group will result in periodic reports to senior management on the status of personal computers in the company.

The council is a forum to foster understanding within GF and to insure consistent communication of policies progress and plans. The make-up of the group will consist of representatives from each functional area and division appointed by the unit head.

II FACILITY SUPPORT

Information Services will maintain a support facility that will assist units in the placement and use of personal computers. The facility will consist essentially of the following:

A Personal Computer Center

1 A facility designed to serve the units educational needs, demonstrate equipment (current Apple, IBM, TRS-80), software and selected applications, and counsel users and potential users on the myriad of tools and packages available.

2 This center will provide GF units with a single contact and coordinating point for obtaining purchases at the best possible price, ensuring maintenance and service contracts are in order, and provide trouble shooting/problem solving service to the units.

B Loan Program

Accompanying the executive development program is a loan program of personal computers for up to 120 days. This program is managed through the computer center and is designed to increase management's awareness and understanding of how technology based information processing and tools can impact their operation, via hands-on activity.

convinced that there were many applications for it in the various functions that reported to them. Andrew Schroder, senior vice president of administration, felt there were a number of issues that the personal computer helped address. Schroder noted:

I'm not a financial executive. My responsibilities are government relations, consumer affairs, public relations, and corporate personnel. I picked up my computer last Friday and have only worked on it over this past weekend. So far I'm halfway through the chicken farm exercise which involves setting up tables for dealing with inventory issues. I'm about at the point where I wonder whether this is really what I, in my particular capacity, need. However, I'm beginning to get some feel for how one goes about interacting with a computer and I think that will be helpful. Whether I need to get very much further with the chicken farm exercise is another question.

There are some principles here which I would certainly support. One of the issues I've felt strongly about is what we in General Foods are doing about making certain that the learning experience doesn't stop when an individual enters the workplace. So in the broadest form, what this is, is an opportunity for us to continue learning. This would avoid putting ourselves in the unfortunate situation where massive learning has been acquired by our newer entries but is not being understood by the more senior levels of our organization.

A second issue which is applicable to my function, is learning firsthand what are the capabilities of personal computers in terms of managing the knowledge mass that we have got to handle in our part of the business. I can't think of any more interesting issue of technology, new technology, busting onto the scene than the notion of the personal computer, which provides the capability in the office or in one's home of keeping pace with this information. Again a chicken farm exercise must not be an end in itself but a means to something else. I see the exercises as a means to understanding the computer as a tool for monitoring more effectively the news, either media or congressional events. I'm going to be increasingly interested in ways that it can be harnessed for my particular purposes. Putting together a P & L for a hypothetical business again had better be a means to some other more appropriate end, for as an end in and of itself it is going to grow old very quickly.

On June 7th Bob's Byte Boutique, as Bob's computer store had become affectionately called, opened. The store had a classroom with ten Radio Shack Model IIIs and a large screen TV. Because Bob had chosen to restrict the class size so that each student had a machine to work with, each class could only accommodate eight students. The classes were so successful that they quickly became booked up for two months in advance. Bob charged the student's sponsoring department $25 a student. The charge was intended to provide a minimum amount of inconvenience, thereby, it was hoped, limiting the enrollment to those that had a serious interest. Further, it had been hoped that those who enrolled in the class would feel obliged to attend given that their department was going to be charged whether they came or not. The computer store was open from 12 noon to 4:30 for anyone to come and experiment at no charge.

While everyone in ISD management was extremely supportive of Bob Judge's effort in raising the general level of computer literacy within General Foods there was some disagreement as to what would be the total potential benefits. For instance, there was an agreement between Bernie Kopitz and Bill Kiedaisch that the interest in personal computing was based, to a large extent, on a general misunderstanding as to the capabilities of these machines. Thus, this provided an excellent educational opportunity which was well worth the expense. As Ed Collins, director of planning, finance, and administration said:

> The installation of these seventy or so personal computers provided an excellent cost-effective opportunity which was well worth the investment of $350,000. Even if you assumed two dollars of personal time for one dollar of computer cost, the cost to GF was only one hundredth of one percent of GF's net revenue. Besides, very few new individual systems could be developed for under $350,000.

Bill Kiedaisch emphasized the importance of this educational aspect of GF's personal computer policy as follows:

> The person coming in the door who says, "Gee, I've never had a computer before but now I can use it," sees a lot of potential benefit that probably will not materialize. People like CMS with its broad range of software; capability to share data; and this is what they need to solve their problem. They can use vehicles like VisiCalc but eventually they are going to say "how do I get the general ledger data into my VisiCalc model, message it, and put it back?" This opens up the whole broad issue of centralized data management. Further, there is just as much discipline required in programming a personal computer as there is in programming a Cray computer. As people bump against these limitations they are going to take a different point of view and eventually these things are going to collect dust. However, we have to let the people get hands-on experience if they are going to begin to understand the benefits and the limitations of personal computers. That's what we are looking to achieve.

Bernie Kopitz added for emphasis:

> A minority of these computers will stick to the ribs but the majority will fall off and collect dust. That's what is really underlying our basic philosophy in setting up the computer store. Let them try it and get it out of their systems rather than going out and buying a computer for anyone who is interested. Just because their sixth grade child can sit at a micro and program it, they come in here and say, "I can do everything for myself with only a one-time cost of a few thousand dollars. I don't have to pay you to do what I need. I'm going to try it." We give them one of these things to try for a while and most of them will come back. They will realize they can't do everything that they want.

In discussions with ISD's senior management several concerns were raised on the introduction of personal computers. First, Bill Kiedaisch felt that rather than being a productivity aid the personal computer could actually be counterproductive:

> As far as productivity is concerned, this is where I feel we have the biggest trap. Unless you have a vehicle like VisiCalc where a person sits down and becomes productive immediately, who says how much time managers waste trying to program these things. You can't take a guy who is supposed to be forecasting sales and let him get enamored with the hardware and software. He's not going to be doing his job.

Another problem of concern often expressed was the potential for departments to develop systems on their personal computer upon which they become operationally dependent. These systems, in all likelihood, will not be adequately documented and thus when the person who developed them is promoted, or worse, leaves GF, there is the danger that the department could be unable to function at its full effectiveness. While ISD strongly discourages the development of such systems, they believe once the user has a machine it is really out of ISD's hands. As Bernie stressed:

> Let him not back up his system, let him not document it, that's his prerogative. That's how he saves his money. If he wants all those things, he may as well pay us to do it.

As Bill pointed out earlier, there is also the problem of data security and access. To cope with the problem of data access, in general, ISD had already formed the data access center as part of the information management group. This center is staffed with people knowledgeable on all of GF's data bases, and it is their responsibility to provide the data to the user in whatever form the user needs in a timely manner. This data could be provided in printed reports or in files in the data interchange format (DIF), which can be accessed by personal computers. This data access center with its extensive data dictionary provides the interface between the data and the users. It is at this point that ISD management feel that they can at least control who has access to what data. Further it is ISD policy that all updates to this data be done on GF's mainframe. Thus, when a user needs to work with the most current data, they can simply download the data from the mainframe to their personal computer. This approach limits the user's responsibility for the security of the data as the files of record are the data files stored on the mainframe.

Ed Schefer was well aware of the potential problems such as data and program security, inappropriate use of management and employee time, and excessive expenditure of corporate funds for something that ultimately would not be used, but he felt that there was such a significant potential for productivity gains that it was essential that the opportunities presented by the personal computers be pursued aggressively. He hoped that this policy would serve to strengthen the relationship between the users and ISD. Further, he hoped that this relationship would give ISD the credibility needed to provide the guidance that would help prevent the user from falling into any of the potential pitfalls.

EUROEX LTD.

Index Systems

The chairman of the board, Walter Big, slammed his hand down on the desk. "No," he said, "EuroEx is *not* a conglomerate. It is a multinational company in many businesses and the job of the managing directors is to make sure those businesses are profitable. Anyway," he went on, "I don't see what all this has to do with information systems."

Tom Prince and the professor left the room. Their project to determine what executive information system (EIS) the managing directors needed was breaking down, and they were not sure how to rescue it. "Let's go back to the beginning," said the professor, "and review how we got to this point."

EUROEX: BACKGROUND

Under its new chairman, EuroEx had been consolidating and restructuring in the last three years. Mr. Big had taken over from a predecessor who had taken advantage of the company's cash position to make several acquisitions into new businesses. Several of these ventures were not profitable and consequently the company's financial performance had been poor for the past several years.

The company's origins were in extractive industries (hence its name). These included mining bauxite, which began in Guyana and was now worldwide; copper mining in Zaire; and limited gold and diamond mining in South Africa and Rhodesia. Extraction had been extended to refining and sheet production in the aluminum area, and because EuroEx had experience in managing large mining projects, it had entered the construction industry in developing countries. The late 1960s and 1970s had been a period of acquisition into other businesses. For example, excess computer capacity had been formed into a computer services company, which was then enhanced by the acquisition of several computer timesharing and software companies in Europe and North America. By the late 1970s the poor return to shareholders required that a change be made from expansion to control.

During 1980–1981, the company undertook a significant reorganization. With annual revenues of $10 billion from operations in fourteen countries, EuroEx decided that its desired restructuring and profitability improvement would only be accomplished by an increased focus on its lines of business. Mr. Big's predecessor had therefore decided to organize the company using a matrix structure consisting of fourteen country affiliates and five businesses.

EUROEX: ORGANIZATION

The chief executive of each of the five businesses had worldwide responsibility for his business; the chief executive of each country affiliate had responsibility for all of Euro Product's businesses in his country. The business organization met at the managing director level; each managing director had responsibility for a business and region of the world (consisting of country affiliates). Support functions and head office operations were also organized to report to the managing directors. As of the summer of 1983, the managing directors and their responsibilities were (see also the organization chart in Exhibit 1):

Mr. Maiti. EuroEx Mining, European Region, Corporate Finance and Control

Mr. Ruff. EuroEx Refining, Middle East and Africa, Corporate Planning

Mr. Byte. EuroEx Computer Services, North America, Management Services

Mr. Dubois. EuroEx Aluminum Sheet, Asia, Engineering

Mr. Gross. EuroEx Construction, Latin America, Research and Development

These managing directors met every Monday morning from 10 a.m. until 12 noon. Their agenda generally consisted of a formal presentation from one of the businesses (generally requesting capital funds), followed by an informal discussion of events and people. The governance of EuroEx was centered in this Monday morning meeting; its agenda and its minutes were carefully managed by the board's secretary, who worked closely with the chairman to have the minutes accurately reflect the attitudes of EuroEx senior management.

EUROEX: SYSTEMS

With the need to restructure, consolidate, and rationalize the unprofitable businesses, early attention had been given to financial control. As corporate

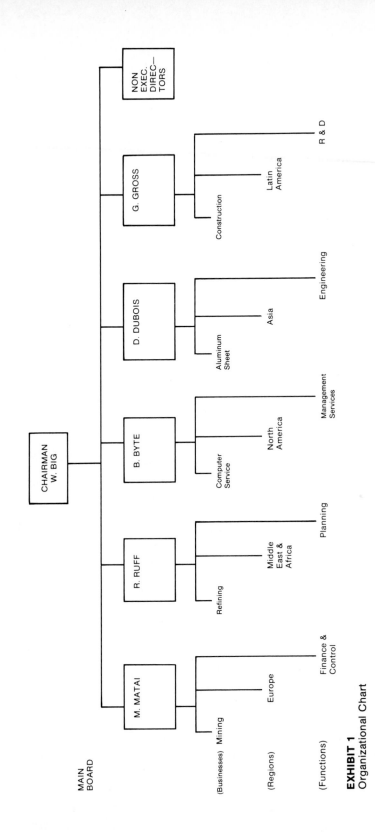

EXHIBIT 1
Organizational Chart

controller, Tom Prince had implemented a number of sensible control systems throughout EuroEx, and he was able, thus, to provide the managing directors with reports on operations and variances from plan on a regular basis. The control system was built up through the structure of the businesses so that, for example, the chief executive of the Refining Company and his chairman, Mr. Ruff (also a Main Board member), both received reports on operations of the Refining Company.

Further, a planning system was in place. An annual strategic planning cycle, using large-scale simulation techniques, produced alternative scenarios for managing directors to pick annually.

Tom Prince took his job seriously. After twenty years with EuroEx, mostly in marketing positions, he knew that he had a good chance of arriving on the Main Board before the end of his career, and had been put in the position of corporate controller to give him some experience with the workings of the head office. He knew that a major part of his job was to provide information to the managing directors to help them run EuroEx. He also sensed that the managing directors had an underlying dissatisfaction with the information they were receiving; financial control, it seemed, was not enough. However, they did not seem to be able to tell him what else they needed. Tom had formed a committee consisting of the senior person in each of the staff functions—planning, tax, treasury, information services, personnel, public relations, and so on. "The task," he said to the committee, "is for each of us to decide what we think the managing directors should know on a regular basis to help them run this company. The current information systems are not supporting the managing directors, and we have to improve them."

The committee worked hard on the project. From time to time it gave the managing directors a brief report at their Monday morning meeting. The managing directors pointed out that, while they thought this was a very important project, it was not something that they should be expected to spend much of their valuable time on—better to leave such things to the experts. At the end of six months, the committee's report recommended that the thirty-six reports currently received by the managing directors should be expanded to fifty-four, with twenty-one of the existing reports being modified, none of the existing reports being given up, and eighteen new reports being produced. These new reports would be available over the course of the next eighteen months at a development cost of $1.8 million. The managing directors complimented the committee on the completeness of its work and the comprehensiveness of the report. Their only advice was that, although they were not experts in such matters, on the whole they felt it might be better to use IBM equipment.

Looking back on it, Tom Prince thought it was this last comment that derailed the project. Despite the fact that he had received approval to continue along the lines that he and his committee had recommended, Tom stopped the project. He started looking for someone who could help, and after many conversations, and some research into the literature and attendance at a conference, Tom hired the professor as a consultant to assist him in defining the information needs of the managing directors.

THE PROJECT: PHASE O

Initially, the professor came for a week to answer the following questions:

- Is the perception that the managing directors need different information a valid one?
- Will our current project satisfy their information needs?
- If not, what should we do?

The professor met two managing directors, three directors (including two who were chief executives of businesses), and three general managers from staff departments. At the end of the week he reported back to the committee that:

- The managing directors did, indeed, appear to have a need for information that was unfulfilled and unarticulated.
- The roles of the managing directors needed to be better defined before their information needs could be understood.
- The current project would not result in satisfaction since it was merely an extrapolation of current circumstances, providing no insight into the needs to be satisfied.
- A "tops-down" approach should be initiated involving a significant commitment of the managing directors' time to identify what, in their view, was important to the accomplishment of the objectives of EuroEx and therefore should be monitored and supported by information systems. The top two levels of management (managing directors and directors) should participate in this definition.

Because this recommendation implied a significant commitment by the managing directors, Tom Prince's committee could not make a decision on it. After two months of discussion and informal lobbying, the proposal was put before the managing directors, who approved it.

THE PROJECT: PHASE I

With a team of four people drawn from University faculty, the professor interviewed the chairman, the managing directors, the directors (which included all the chief executives of the businesses), and the heads of the staff functions, chief executives of two of the country affiliates, and three general managers in home office functions. In each two hour interview he asked:

- What is your mission?
- What are your objectives?
- What are the things that must go right (and must not go wrong) for you to accomplish your objectives?

Then, in the second part of the interview, he asked:

- What is the mission of EuroEx?
- What are the EuroEx objectives?
- What are the things which must go right (and must not go wrong) for EuroEx to accomplish its objectives?

The results of these interviews were aggregated into two composite statements. The first reflected, in the opinion of the professor, the composite view of the managing directors. The second reflected what appeared to be the composite view of the directors.

The professor then conducted workshop sessions to obtain signoff of each of the groups on their consensus view of the mission, objectives and critical success factors for EuroEx. As a result of these workshop sessions, the managing directors approved their consensus view (Exhibit 2) and the directors approved theirs (Exhibit 3).

EXHIBIT 2
Managing Directors Revised Composite

Mission

Maximize profitability as a multinational resource extractor to provide a stable, superior return to our shareholders while operating as a responsible employer and corporate citizen. Separate businesses should be profitable and should contribute more to all shareholders' return than they could as independent companies.

Objectives

1 Reconstruct the current business portfolio with separate strategies and objectives for each business, then balance cyclicality and geographic risk by building the new businesses.
2 Have high quality management worldwide.
3 Manage the totality of the EuroEx efficiently.
4 Achieve financial robustness with strong earnings and sound balance sheet, at least to maintain dividend value in real terms.
5 Contribute to the societies in which we operate and act responsibly in the environment.
6 Exploit technology in order to strengthen existing businesses and find new commercial opportunities.

Critical Success Factors

1 Manage costs, profitability, cash flow and capital.
2 Continuously monitor political, economic, and environmental trends in all the countries in which we operate; continue relationships with their leaders.
3 Communicate a clear long-term view of business prospects and plans to the management of EuroEx.
4 Understand the businesses well enough to monitor risk and allocate resources according to corporate goals.
5 Develop people for positions of greater responsibility.
6 Understand our markets and our competitors.

EXHIBIT 3
Directors Revised Composite

Mission

Provide a long term return to our shareholders while operating as a responsible employer and corporate citizen in natural resources and technology or market-led industry.

Objectives

1 Clarify accountabilities within the matrix management structure.
2 Manage the corporate portfolio of businesses to improve profit and reduce risk; sell unprofitable businesses.
3 Be profitable and robust enough to take opportunities and withstand unexpected demands.
4 Keep our competitive advantage in mining.
5 Improve competitive ability in non-mining businesses.
6 Reduce corporate overhead.
7 Contribute to the societies in which we operate and act responsibly in the environment.
8 Exploit technology in order to strengthen existing businesses and find new commercial opportunities.

Critical Success Factors

1 Communicate clearly how matrix accountability is to work in the EuroEx culture.
2 Motivate people to manage costs, profitability, cash flow, and capital allocation in acquisition and divestment of assets.
3 Exercise influence and avoid problems in the environment and political context within which EuroEx operates.
4 Control financial resources carefully.
5 Recruit top quality international people with key skills and assure strong management succession.
6 Understand our markets and competitors.
7 Find new opportunities to compete with technology.

THE PROJECT: PHASE I REPORT

At this point the professor made a progress report to the managing directors at their Monday morning meeting. He reminded them that the purpose of the critical success factors interviewing had been to define the role of the managing directors by identifying the things which were really important for them to attend to. He pointed out that there were some differences between their view of their role, and the view held by the directors and chief executives of the businesses who reported to them. He also made some observations, as an outside observer, about the objectives and critical success factors they had defined for EuroEx:

• None of the objectives or critical success factors gave a clue as to what businesses EuroEx was in. He suggested that EuroEx was, in fact, a financial conglomerate with no product or market linkages.

- The objectives seemed vague and lacking focus on desired end results.
- Noticeably absent from the critical success factors identified were concerns about customers or products. Was this an accurate reflection of the concerns of EuroEx senior management?

In general, the professor reported, each business seemed to have a clear understanding that its job was to be profitable, but he wondered whether the collection of those businesses—the totality of EuroEx—had any existence. As a group of companies, EuroEx seemed to lack focus, definition, and direction. The EuroEx preoccupation with making the matrix organization work, and with restructuring the businesses was inward looking; the professor said that EuroEx reminded him of a ship in dry dock refitting for an unspecified journey to an unknown destination. The roles of the managing directors under such circumstances seemed rather unclear, since the business of EuroEx was being run by the chief executives of the businesses.

As one managing director, Mr. Gross, later put it, "subsequent discussions induced a mild neurosis in the organization." Various directors and managing directors felt compelled to write memos with their analysis of the situation; most of these memos contained the author's prescription for what managing directors of EuroEx *should* have as their role. The chief executive of EuroEx Refining broadcast that while, of course, he was very happy to have *his* managing director, Mr. Ruff, monitoring the refining business, he understood that some of his peers in other businesses resented the intrusion of *their* managing directors.

Tom Prince got a call from the chairman's secretary. Would he and the professor be good enough to see the chairman at 10:00 on Tuesday morning?

The chairman began the meeting by saying that he had found the critical success factors interviews most interesting, and that he believed great value would come out of the meetings in which critical success factors had been discussed, and that EuroEx's senior management had gained clarity on what was important to the successful achievement of their objectives.

He went on to say that the difficulty the directors found with the matrix organization was something which, in his opinion, would sort itself out over time.

While he appreciated the professor's observations about the lack of mention of customers or products in the objectives and critical success factors, he suggested that these concerns were defined within the objectives and critical success factors of the businesses. He made it clear that he did not find the "dry dock" analogy particularly useful. Nor did he find particularly appealing the notion that EuroEx was a "conglomerate." As for the role of the managing directors, they were "his men" and he expected them to be responsible for the profitability of the organization.

But the main reason he had asked them to see him was because he was himself somewhat confused with their approach. What, he wanted to know, did this have to do with executive information systems?

PACIFIC COOPERATIVE

Henry C. Lucas, Jr.

INTRODUCTION

David Martin hung up the telephone in his office at Pacific Cooperative and reached for his calendar. A partner of the Coop's CPA firm had just made an appointment for the end of January. The purpose of the meeting would be to discuss the recommendations of the CPA's Management Services Department for improving information processing procedures at Pacific Coop. Martin wondered what kind of improvements would be recommended. He had been uneasy with computer operations ever since his accounting firm had suggested that problems existed in the computer area.

BACKGROUND

Pacific Coop is a San Francisco Bay Area cooperative food wholesaler owned by 145 independent stores. The members of the cooperative join to obtain the benefits of economies of scale in purchasing and distribution. The food industry on the retail level is intensively competitive and there is little customer loyalty. Shoppers are influenced by low prices and convenience, primarily in store location. After World War II major food chains began a rapid expansion which included the purchase of many smaller independents.

Pacific Coop was founded in the Bay Area during this turbulent period in grocery retailing by fifteen stores. Over the ensuing years, it has grown to include the 145 current members. The Coop had 1984 sales of $675 million. In 1983, Pacific Coop moved all of its operations, including the office and warehouse into a new, one-square-block building in Oakland, California.

MEMBERSHIP

Members of the cooperative buy shares and invest an amount of capital in the coop equal to two weeks' average purchases. A board of directors is elected by members to supervise the activities of the coop. The members influence the coop through the board and through membership on various committees. For example, a new products committee meets semi-monthly to decide on new grocery items to be stocked by the warehouse.

The cooperative strives to make a reasonable profit which is returned to member stores as a patronage refund. The refund calculation is complex because a different percentage is returned for each type of sale, for example, grocery, meat, dairy. Pacific Coop's firm of certified public accountants determines the actual formula to be applied to each year's refund.

New stores applying for membership in the coop have to meet strict standards, particularly with regard to location. To protect existing members, new members have to be located a certain distance (currently one mile) from existing stores. The Pacific Coop sign is displayed prominently in each store, though the store also displays its name as an independent, for example:

NORRIS BROTHERS
A Pacific Coop Store

The bulk of the stores are independents, but there are three or four chains of ten to thirteen stores each. A large store has a volume of sales in the range of 3000 to 6000 cases a week while a small member might move only 600 cases.

OPERATIONS

The cooperative divides its products into the following categories:

Grocery
Meat
Dairy
Fruit and Produce
Drop Shipments

Grocery, fruit and produce, frozen meat, and certain dairy items are ordered and distributed through the Pacific Coop warehouse in Oakland. Only dairy items with a relatively long shelf life are found in the warehouse, for example, cheeses. Perishable dairy items like milk are delivered directly to retail stores. "Drop shipments" is the name given to merchandise sent directly to the store, but ordered through the coop. Fresh meat is handled as a drop shipment; the meat at the warehouse is usually refrigerated in boxes or frozen (such as turkeys).

Retail stores order grocery deliveries each week and the warehouse fills the orders. The stores are required to purchase exclusively from Pacific Coop. Fruit and produce, meat, and most dairy products are ordered more frequently than once a week because of spoilage. Retailers are billed each week and payment is due by the next week.

DEPARTMENTS

The major departments in Pacific Coop are shown in the organization chart in Exhibit 1.

Purchasing

The supply cycle begins in the purchasing department, which is headed by Bob Atherton. Buyers receive a weekly inventory status run from the computer department showing stock status and the last four weeks of movement plus average movement for each item. Inventory status reports are produced more frequently for fruit and produce, and dairy because of their rapid turnover. Buyers use these stock status reports to determine order quantities and reorder points.

Exhibit 1
Pacific Cooperative Organization Chart

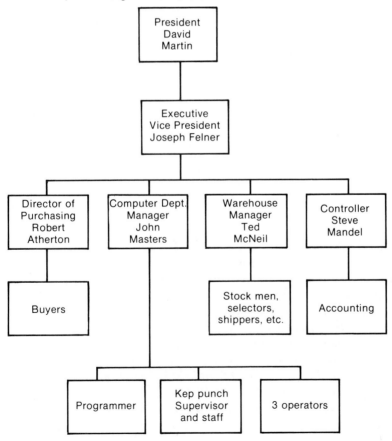

As Bob Atherton put it, "We are in business to serve our members; we strive for no stockouts, though we usually run around 1 to 2 percent stockouts because of bad forecasting on our part or delays in shipments. Our basic rule of thumb is to have two weeks' supply in inventory and one week rolling (that is, in transit)."

A buyer added, "I like to key on seasons. Sales of the product last year at this time are important." The buyers specialize by commodity, for example, there is a candy buyer, dairy buyer, etc. There are six buyers in the grocery area, two in fruit and produce, three in meats, and two in dairy. The buyers try to set up shipments from the different suppliers to take advantage of full car loads and price breaks for volume orders. The chief grocery buyer said: "Sometimes I buy to have more than two weeks' supply in stock because I get a good deal on a box car of merchandise."

Another buyer said, "The real trick is to be familiar with food manufacturers and their representatives. The company's habits are our best basis for forecasting. Some goods like fresh fruit from the San Joaquin Valley arrive in a few days and a rail shipment from the midwest may take several weeks."

After deciding to place an order, the buyer uses a preprinted form prepared by the computer to write the order. The original copy of the order goes to the food vendor. A copy of the purchase order is kept by the buyer for his own reference and another copy is sent to the receiving area in the warehouse. A final copy is used to verify accounts payable bills from food vendors.

Bob Atherton also stated that "we have to protect our stores. We plan specials well in advance and order extra merchandise to cover the anticipated higher volume due to the sale."

Naturally one role of the buyer is to obtain the best price. During rapid fluctuations in prices, continued price changes are authorized by purchasing (Bob Atherton must approve each change). The new prices are used to update the computer inventory file for billing purposes.

Warehouse

The warehouse staff has two functions: one to receive merchandise and place it in its proper location and the other to select orders and ship them to member stores. Most deliveries arrive in the morning and about 95 percent of the time they arrive on schedule. Pacific Coop averages about fifty trucks unloading a day. The trucks and rail cars are unloaded as quickly as possible and all merchandise is placed on wooden pallets which are stored in pre-assigned "slots" in the warehouse.

A copy of the purchase order, filed in the receiving office, is used to check in shipments. Prior to the arrival of merchandise, the warehouse staff prepares large signs with slot numbers on them to be fastened to the pallets. Fork lift drivers take the loaded pallets to the appropriate slots. These drivers are also responsible for keeping the bottom rack full of goods for the selectors. The warehouse is arranged by product, and fork lift drivers specialize in certain rows. Thus, the drivers become very familiar with the products in their territory.

Selectors use a powered dolly to move pallets through the warehouse. A selector also usually has a group of rows to which he is assigned. The computer system prints orders in sequence by slot so the selector can move in one direction through the warehouse without retracing his steps.

The selector loads the pallet with the items ordered to form a "cube" of the precise dimensions to fit through the back door of a delivery semi-trailer truck. Missing items are noted on the picking list ("scratches") and a copy of the list is returned to the computer department for billing purposes. (Bills cannot be prepared on the basis of picking lists as originally printed by the computer because there is often a discrepancy between book inventory on the computer file and physical inventory in the warehouse.)

There are two selecting shifts and the night shift is the busiest. Day orders are usually split among several selectors to be filled in parallel. At night, one selector might select a whole order and even load the truck. There is a set delivery schedule for each store. Pacific Coop contracts with a trucking agent and does not operate its own fleet of trucks. However, because of the substantial volume of the coop, the trucks are painted with Pacific Coop signs on them.

The warehouse supervisor offered this example of the service orientation of the coop, "If we are out of stock, the fork lift driver searches for the item. He gets an inventory report three times a week. I even look for missing items occasionally. (Items are sometimes misplaced or excess goods are placed in an overflow slot away from their designated position.) We get 'short sheets' from the computer which list stores and items they want that the computer says are out of stock. We watch incoming shipments and if the item arrives, we hustle it over to the order pallet being picked for the store. We know the shipping schedule to stores pretty well because we are relatively small. Shorts are a pain in the neck, but the stores love us for keeping stockouts low."

Controller

The controller, Steve Mandel, is responsible for all financial and accounting operations. The coop requires financing for inventories and for routing operations. There are also many accounting transactions since suppliers must be paid on a regular basis and stores are billed weekly.

Steve said, "The routine goes pretty well—we aren't too big and everyone cooperates. We get good, reliable service from data processing. Johnny Masters has been here 25 years and he delivers the output. I worry a little bit about control because we seem to have a lot of punched cards and my staff spends too much time checking computer output."

Computer Department

Background   The computer department is at the heart of the transaction processing activities necessary to keep Pacific Coop running. The current executive vice president, Joe Felner, set up the first IBM 604 machinery in 1957 and brought Johnny Masters in from accounting to help him.

The major objective of the first system was to keep track of inventories, and this remains the most important computer function today, though now there are other applications including:

Order entry
Inventory status
Grocery catalog
Accounts receivable
Accounts payable
Physical inventory
Payroll
Purchase order printing
Weekly sales report
Patronage refund
Warehouse productivity

Recently Dave Martin, Pacific Coop president, had become concerned over the operation of the computer department. A report from the coop's accounting firm indicated that there were some control problems in the department, particularly regarding backup and system documentation. The accountants also felt that the computer was being underutilized.

Martin asked Joe Felner to prepare a report for him on the current status of operations in the computer department so he could review it with a management services representative of the accounting firm. Felner readily agreed since he had been the "founder" of the computer department, though since becoming executive vice president five years ago he had been kept busy by problems with the new warehouse. He observed now, on an equivalent rental basis, the computer department budget exceeded $200,000 per year.

Equipment   From the 604, Pacific Coop progressed to an IBM 305, 1401, and a 360 model 30. When the 370 was announced, Pacific Coop purchased a model 135. In 1981, Pacific installed an IBM 4341. The current configuration represents an investment of over $500,000.

Pacific Coop also owns an IBM System 7 which is dedicated to meat, dairy, and produce ordering. Store representatives phone the System 7 and use a touch tone pad attached acoustically to the phone to enter orders for these perishable items. After ordering during a scheduled time period each day, the orders are processed in batch mode on the 4341. The new phone system uses a package program developed by a grocery wholesaler in Pennsylvania and replaces the old approach of phoning orders to keypunch operators. As one retailer put it: "I suppose the phone orders save the coop and us some money, but it sure has been tough getting my produce man to push all of the little buttons and listen to the tones."

The 4341 is currently running under the disk operation system (DOS) with two to three partitions depending on the job. A spooling package is used to put reports on a disk and print them later during other processing.

A great deal of time was spent when the 370 came in, converting programs to COBOL from Autocoder which ran on the old 1400 series equipment. For many years, the computer department produced few new applications; instead all resources were devoted to the conversion process since so many programs were running in emulate mode.

One purpose of bringing in the 4341 was to move toward more on-line processing. Users had requested a number of on-line applications. For example, if the entire inventory could be updated on-line, it would mean that receivings could be entered by the warehouse and that picking lists would be more up-to-date. (See the discussion of the inventory application below.)

Even with the addition of one more programmer, progress toward implementing on-line systems was slow. First, the staff installed CICS, an IBM telecommunications monitor that serves to control the communications network and the interaction between the computer and remote terminals. CICS was installed fairly easily, and then the staff turned its attention to developing on-line applications. It is this development process that has been moving slowly.

As the new programmer said: "everyone around here is used to thinking in batch processing terms. This place is a little too inbred; it would help if the staff got out to see what other companies are doing."

Applications   The most important application at Pacific Coop is the order cycle, from entry through billing. The computer processing involved in this order cycle is illustrated in Exhibit 2. Preparing orders for the warehouse has priority over all other processing and orders are run several times a day. Orders for the different inventories are run at different times, for example, grocery, dairy, fruit and produce, etc.

An order book is printed for the stores showing the merchandise currently stocked by the warehouse. Four decks of mark sense cards are sent to each member grocer every week. These cards are prepunched with the store number on them and fit on rings on one side of a loose leaf binder with the order book on rings on the other side. One line in the order book corresponds to one line on a mark sense card. Store personnel order by darkening the quantity desired on a mark sense card line aligned with the item line in the order book, so by turning one page and card, the individual ordering keeps the cards coordinated with the order book. While the process does not represent the most modern technology, it has been used successfully for a number of years. The order decks are dropped off by the grocer in Oakland for processing.

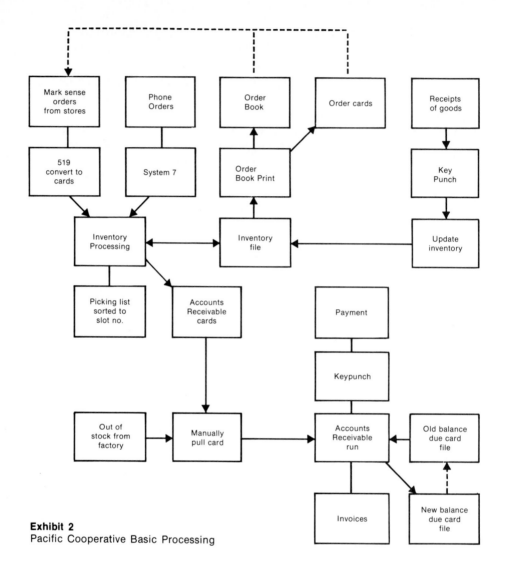

Exhibit 2
Pacific Cooperative Basic Processing

On the average there are about 1300 to 1500 items on a weekly order. When the order decks are received at Pacific Coop, the computer department runs the mark sense cards through a 519 interpreter which produces a standard punched card. The punch cards (or the file of orders from the System 7 for meat, dairy, and produce) are used to print picking orders for the warehouse. Before any picking order is run, however, the inventory file is updated with receipts of goods so the information on stock status will be up to date.

The picked orders are sorted into slot number sequence by store for the warehouse selectors. The computer also prints a recommended price sticker

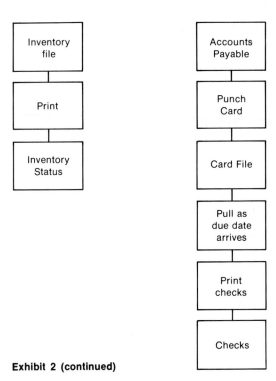

Exhibit 2 (continued)

for the items. Grocers can select which price category they wish to use, for example, low, medium, and high. Prices for each product in that category are then printed on the stickers which are affixed to the cases picked. At the same time the order is selected, the inventory file is updated to show that the merchandise has been picked and an accounts receivable card is punched and placed in a manual card file.

An inventory status report is also prepared and distributed as a part of the inventory system. This report is watched closely by the buyers and is used in the warehouse as well.

Accounts receivable at Pacific Coop runs about 10 to 15 million dollars while inventory averages $20 million. The average inventory turnover is one to two weeks for grocery items, though fruit and produce turn over in a few days. The accounts receivable manual card file is processed by the computer regularly to produce reports for control and verification. If an item has not been picked in the warehouse because it is out of stock, the picking list copy returned from the warehouse notifies the computer department of the out of stock condition. The accounts receivable card is pulled from the card file and destroyed (or if a partial shipment, a new card is punched manually).

Weekly the accounts receivable file is updated on the computer to reflect receipts. Prior balances, receipts and new accounts receivable cards are run to produce invoices. The invoices are created separately for each type of order (for example, meat, produce, etc.) and then sorted by store before printing so they can be mailed in a single envelope.

For accounts payable, a card is punched by the keypunch section for each payable. Daily balance runs are made on these payable cards. As the due date for a payment draws near, the cards are pulled and used as input to a computer run which generates checks. There is also a run of scheduled and outstanding checks, though there is no check reconciliation by computer.

The payroll system has been a real problem at Pacific Coop. It was programmed on a contract basis by a software house which failed to provide an adequate product. A number of different staff members at the software vendor worked on the system and it ended being written in some three different computer languages! Errors and user resistance problems at Pacific Coop resulted in an eighteen month implementation period.

There are also a number of other small applications including sales reports, warehouse productivity reports by selector, preprinting of purchase orders, etc. At year end, the computer department also runs refund checks after the refund is calculated by their CPA firm. Every six months a physical inventory is taken and the book inventory on the computer files is adjusted to correspond with actual inventory balances. There may be up to six physical counts before the inventory figures are accepted. Duplicate copies of critical files are made regularly and stored in a fireproof vault in the building.

A typical day's processing might have the following schedule:

A.M.

6:00-10:00	Process orders to give warehouse at least 12 by 7 a.m.
10:00-11:00	Run receiving for dairy and grocery
11:00-11:30	Process dairy orders and print the dairy inventory status report
11:30-12:00	Run other receiving and begin meat orders

P.M.

12:00-12:45	Process more grocery orders
12:45- 1:30	Run accounts payable and drop shipments
1:30- 2:00	Process dairy orders
2:00- 2:30	Run receiving and adjustments
2:30- 3:15	Process fruit and produce orders
3:15- 5:00	Run more grocery orders
5:00- 6:00	Program testing

Several new applications are planned by the computer department. The general ledger is an application that has high priority. Pacific Cooperative has also been thinking about trying to provide computer services for some of its member stores. The coop has a print shop which has been making a good profit by printing all signs and special advertising for members. Johnny noted that "several of our members are big enough to have their own minicomputers or to use a service bureau for payroll and accounting work. Given the extra time available on the computer off-peak shift, we should be able to do this processing more cheaply."

The IBM representative for the account also pointed out that one reason for acquiring the 4341 was to be ready for point-of-sale systems. These systems utilize electronic scanners in the stores or electronic cash registers. The central computer maintains an in-store inventory and prepares reorders for the warehouse automatically. While a complete system alone would probably be too expensive for a member store, Pacific would be in a good position to offer point-of-sale service to all member stores.

Joe Felner had also thought several times about investigating an inventory control package. "Our present inventory system is not too sophisticated; we basically keep track of what we have. I know there are some packages which have mathematical models to help in forecasting and recommending reorder quantities. However, Bob Atherton is really opposed to such systems. He says they remove human judgment which is necessary given the complexity of the buying decision and that people he knows with packages say they don't work. I would still like to investigate it to be sure we are not missing an important opportunity."

CONCLUSION

David Martin discussed the status of the computer department with the management service representative of his accounting firm. The consultant, after interviewing the computer staff and users, confirmed the accuracy of the material presented above. He now wondered what to recommend at the planned January meeting to improve the coop's information processing activities.

ABZ ELECTRONICS: PART A

Henry C. Lucas, Jr.

Hal Watson stopped pacing the floor of his fourteenth-floor office in mid-town Manhattan and returned to his desk once more. He stared again at the interview notes that had just been typed by his secretary. Two months before he was contacted by an old friend, Martin Holiday of ABZ Electronics, who asked him for some advice about information processing at ABZ.

Hal is a senior partner in Homes and Watson, a consulting firm specializing in information systems. During the last two years the firm supplemented its work in the technical area with studies for senior level managers. Now Hal prefers to enter the organization at the level of the president or chairman of the board.

I've observed that most problems with computers generally start with top management; most senior level managers today have had little exposure to computers. They haven't encountered computing in their education and seem to have trouble managing it.

Top management is uncomfortable with the technology because it is not like other specialties in the firm. For example, a manager who came up through finance understands the production process in his industry; the accountant can relate to the R & D lab because the products that come from it are similar to those already produced by the firm. Also, one can see something; information processing is more abstract.

Hal Watson went to school with Martin Holiday, the Chairman of ABZ. Their careers diverged after that; Holiday joined a large firm that made electric motors and Watson started work with the management services division of a major accounting firm. After five years with the accounting group, Watson and a colleague, Ted Homes, formed their own consulting company. The firm grew rapidly to over fifty professionals and a number of supporting staff members.

Hal had not heard from Martin Holiday for several years when he received a phone call two months earlier requesting a meeting. Martin solicited help from several sources; different consulting firms offered advice, but none of it appealed to Martin. He asked Hal to conduct a quick study at ABZ because they were committing resources to a major new system and Holiday wanted to be sure that it would work.

Specifically he raised the following questions and asked Hal to make recommendations:

1 ABZ has sales of about $130 million per year and has been growing at a rate of 20 percent per year compounded. ABZ will spend $4 million this year on computing including salaries, supplies, etc. Is that too much money? How much should ABZ be spending on information processing?

2 What kind of processing should ABZ have? Should there be small mini-computers at various locations or should the firm continue to operate a large, mainframe computer?

3 ABZ is about to implement the IBM COPICS system for production control; is it the right system for the company and is ABZ prepared to use it?

4 What does ABZ need in information processing capabilities to be a $250 million a year company?

ABZ

ABZ Electronics is a west coast manufacturer of resistors, devices that are used in almost all electronic circuits and electrical products. The firm is a leader in the industry and sells to all of the major manufacturing companies in the world. Orders come directly from the manufacturers and from various distributors.

ABZ has four plants and is opening a small manufacturing facility in Japan. Two large plants are located in California; the largest is in the San Fernando Valley and a smaller, more specialized plant is located in Santa Clara, near San Francisco. The headquarters for the firm is Phoenix, Arizona. Two foreign plants are located in Taiwan and Uruguay.

Because resistors are small and of relatively low value, the volume of production is quite high. Next year production plans call for one billion resistors to be produced by ABZ worldwide. The average value of a unit is 14¢ and the price range is from 2¢ to $20.

There are several different product lines and there is a definite sequence of operations, some thirty-eight are required to produce a resistor. While the operations are sequential, the production process resembles a job shop more than an assembly line. There are many different options for scheduling production. Maintaining control when there are millions of items produced a day is a major task. One of ABZ's competitive advantages has been its development of specialized machinery to automate the most labor-intensive parts of the production process.

MANAGEMENT STRUCTURE

A simple organization chart of ABZ is shown in Exhibit 1. Martin Holiday is chairman and president; reporting to him are four vice presidents. The marketing vice president is Michael Faraday and the sales vice president is Steve Amps. Barry Levine is in charge of production; the four plant managers report to him. Bob Ziegler is the vice president of finance and the corporate director of MIS; Fred Edison reports to Ziegler. Half of the corporate officers are located in Phoenix; Amps and Levine are at the San Fernando plant.

The corporate MIS staff is located with the main computer facility at San Fernando. Fred Edison has a staff of four managers: Gary Boltman handles technical services and Terry Cambridge is in charge of development of systems analysis and design; Carl Karstens handles the operations of the data center while a new employee, Larry Larson, is in charge of education, user training and documentation. Larson joined ABZ only six months ago; prior to that time he was a systems engineer with IBM.

COMPUTING AT ABZ

The corporate MIS facility at San Fernando has an IBM 3031 computer with four million bytes of main memory. Because the firm has moved up rapidly in computing with the addition of new on-line applications, the 3031 is running DOS/VS as the operating system. Current plans are to acquire an attached processor for the 3031 and to convert to MVS in order to take better advantage of the 3031 and its attached processor. The 3031 system runs inefficiently with DOS/VS and processing capacity is tight. There is demand for greater on-line availability, for example in shipping, and yet there is barely time during the period at night when there is no on-line processing, to complete the required batch work.

The corporate facility also handles all processing for Santa Clara, which has a line printer plus remote job entry capabilities.

The plant in Uruguay has its own computer, as does the facility in Taiwan. Both of these locations run systems that were originally developed in San Fernando. There is some communications among these foreign plants and the United States, but it is minimal.

INFORMATION SYSTEMS

ABZ has had a poor history of information systems. Until two years ago all applications were batch. Users did not receive anything useful from the

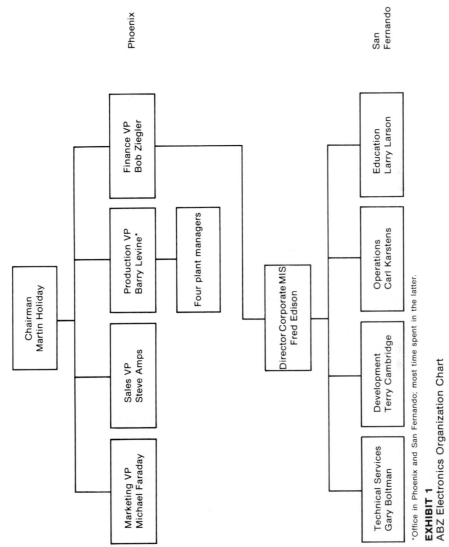

Phoenix

San
Fernando

Chairman
Martin Holiday

Marketing VP
Michael Faraday

Sales VP
Steve Amps

Production VP
Barry Levine*

Finance VP
Bob Ziegler

Four plant managers

Director Corporate MIS
Fred Edison

Technical Services
Gary Boltman

Development
Terry Cambridge

Operations
Carl Karstens

Education
Larry Larson

*Office in Phoenix and San Fernando; most time spent in the latter.

EXHIBIT 1
ABZ Electronics Organization Chart

57

systems and there was little incentive to cooperate in the design of new systems. At that time an Applications Transfer Team (ATT) was formed with the support of IBM to develop a plan for processing at ABZ. When the team was formed, Fred Edison was in the production control and scheduling area; he was chosen to be the major user representative on the team. The team concluded that ABZ should develop a production scheduling and control system using the IBM package COPICS as the framework for its system.

Management accepted that recommendation and made Fred Edison the new director of the corporate MIS function, a major upgrade for the existing data processing department. While the ATT study recommended a new and elaborate production control system, Edison recognized that it would take too long to install such a system. He began to hire the staff that reports to him now and to develop some relatively fast solutions to critical information processing problems at ABZ.

> In retrospect, we made some mistakes, but there was just so much to be done that we had to take action. Our major problem is with users; we are pulling them along kicking and screaming into modern computing. They have more now than ever and yet they still complain a lot. I have ulcers and high blood pressure....
>
> Few people look at the progress we have made in the last two years. Remember that two years ago there was only batch processing. Now we operate on-line and process 60,000 transactions a day through 150 terminals.
>
> Yes, we made some mistakes. We decided to buy an existing order entry system developed by one of the tire manufacturers; the system had to be extensively modified to fit our environment. While we had good help from some users, there are a number of people who should have been more involved. Had they spent time before the installation rather than after, we would not have had so many problems.

Hal asked him to explain.

> Well, when the system came up we lost all track of orders for three days. The plant manager now admits that if he had taken the time to study and understand the system beforehand, he could have caught 90 percent of the problems. This is just a symptom of what we find with most users—a lot of complaints and very little willingness to get involved. The other thing that kills us is maintenance and enhancements along with special emergency jobs.

With that, Fred reached into his desk and found a memorandum that showed for the last month that there were 132 requests for changes or enhancements with an estimate of 7000 worker hours of time required to accomplish them.

> We have responded well in emergencies, but then we're criticized for letting other things slip. This year we decided that it was necessary to add a charge for scarce materials to our contracts. The price of the components used in resistors was rising so rapidly that we had to price contracts at shipment rather than on the receipt of

the order. This meant some complicated programming to measure quantities, enter costs, and compute the price. We had one month to do the job.

Because it was done fast, there were some errors. In one instance we failed to bill about half a million dollars which we could have invoiced. We went back to the customers and reclaimed some of it, but how embarrassing! This little incident took the attention away from a really outstanding job done by the MIS staff to get the system up and running in such a short time.

MAJOR APPLICATIONS

Hal Watson's interviews highlighted major applications at ABZ. The MOLS or manufacturing on-line system is key to production scheduling and control. Planners allocate capacity to each product line and the computer examines orders as they are entered. The order entry clerk either takes from existing inventory, or leaves it to the program to schedule production. The computer rolls production forward and schedules it for each of the product lines. When there are problems that the program cannot handle, it prints an exception report which a planner examines and juggles production to rectify.

An on-line order entry system has made a tremendous difference in the accuracy of order input. The system leads the order clerk through the entry process. A key component of this system is the substitution subsystem. ABZ has allowed itself to create new products whenever a slight variation on an existing resistor is ordered. Instead of having a few hundred standard items that differ only slightly, for example, in the markings on the outside, the firm now has something like 20,000 different products. Many of these products have identical electrical characteristics and another can be substituted for what is ordered. The substitution subsystem looks for items that are similar so that existing stock can be used if desired delivery times cannot be met for the item actually ordered. The order entry clerk has the knowledge of what the customer will accept and is the key to using this function. Fred Edison felt that some of the clerks did not take full advantage of this powerful feature of the system.

The locator system operates in batch mode and is extremely important. Eventually it will be replaced by IBM 8100 computers on the factory floor. For the present, production control is exercised through a large package of punched cards that move with each order through the factory. At various stages the cards are sent to the computer where a locator report is prepared showing where the item is in the production process. The thirty-eight operations required to produce a resistor are represented by twelve major sites in the locator system. A new system will expand this number to thirty-eight, making it easier to pinpoint production status and product location. There are thousands of moves each day and a system like this is necessary to keep control in the factory. The resistors travel through the factory in trays, each containing one lot of work in process and a stack of punch cards for input into the locator system.

INTERVIEW RESULTS

Hal Watson reviewed his interview notes as he tried to organize his thoughts about ABZ and develop recommendations for what the firms should do.

Production

Watson had several interviews with production management, and scheduling and control; several of the managers in the marketing area also pointed out problems in the production area.

The first area of difficulty was with yields; if yields are too low in the manufacturing process then scrap cost is high and planning is adversely affected. Difficulty comes in the planning area because the standard yield is assumed when putting an order into production; less than that yield means that too low a quantity will result from production.

The San Fernando plant manager had formerly been with a manufacturing firm with a different type of computing. Each plant had a Hewlett Packard minicomputer tied to a central IBM mainframe. The plant manager had an MIS staff of four working for him.

He asked Hal the following questions:

Why shouldn't I have my own computer in the plant; why does the MIS department report to Phoenix even though they are physically located at my plant?

Do you think we should get rid of the IBM mainframe and go to a series of distributed minicomputers? My service was a lot better at my former employer than it is here.

We never seem to get answers to our problems. I must have ten or fifteen requests in to the computer department; it takes forever to get a response.

The plant manager indicated that he had spent very little time looking at the new COPICS system.

I'm having my industrial engineers spend the weekend studying a part of the new system. They want me to sign the approval for the 8100 which we will use to begin direct data entry from the factory floor. However, I have some real concerns about it. Right now there are thousands of moves a day out there; my expediters work from a printed report. As I understand the new system, the expediter will go to a CRT and copy down the information. How long will that take? We have twenty-digit part numbers and another long number to identify the lot. I've asked engineering to tell me how long it will take someone to write this information down and find the material compared with how it is done now.

Part of Hal's interview requested information from each person on their perceptions of the COPICS system and their own knowledge of it. Watson was disturbed because it was clear that the plant manager and the vice president of production did not appreciate the details or the changes that might be created from installing this system.

Watson had one group interview (due to time constraints) with the manager of raw materials procurement, the production control and scheduling staff, and the raw materials inventory manager. The simplest COPICS modules for materials requirements planning had just been installed. Hal was disturbed because the two managers who were responsible for the functions impacted by the new system did not seem to understand it. They did not have faith in the system's ability to solve their problems nor did they seem to have a grasp of exactly how it worked.

Early discussions with Fred Edison led Hal to believe that the COPICS system would create a major conceptual change in the production process, yet this issue was not raised by the production group. Currently ABZ planned each order beginning at the first production stage. However, since the first three or four manufacturing processes were virtually identical for different products having the same resistance, occasionally semifinished items were diverted to a new order with higher priority or an earlier promise date.

Several people in production and marketing suggested that the company needed to move toward a work in process inventory of semifinished components. Then the first few operations would be scheduled independently of finished goods; the work in process inventory would decouple production of semifinished from finished product. The COPICS system, according to the MIS department, supported this type of a concept. Watson was not convinced that the production staff understood that this feature was present or that there would be significant implications for scheduling and control when it was implemented.

Marketing and Sales

The reaction in the marketing and sales areas was similar to that in production. Feelings were expressed that the MIS area was unresponsive and that it took an inordinate amount of time to make changes. The sales staff was particularly unhappy with the order entry system. There are problems continuing with it beyond the first debacle during its installation. For example, to move from one function to another the operator must return to the first menu. In some instances, to check on the status of inventory or an order, the operator must log off one system and onto another (partly for security reasons).

Sales had submitted a request for what they called "function jump," the ability to move from one function directly to another. When Hal was discussing MIS with the vice president of sales and his assistant, they had just received a status report on the twenty changes they had pending. The only explanation opposite function jump was "Cancelled." Clearly, the MIS area had some distance to go to become more user oriented. (Later Hal raised this problem with Fred Edison and found out that the MIS staff had investigated the work required and found it excessive given present priorities. Edison admitted that they should not have communicated in that fashion to sales.)

A marketing manager at headquarters mentioned to Hal the large number of problems created by having so many different products. "We've let the spec engineering people take the easy way out; they simply create a new product any time a customer comes to us and asks for something a little different. I would be willing to bet that 300 products constitute something like 80 percent of our U.S. sales. There is no need to have over 20,000 different products—some of these differ only in the color of paint used for the final markings."

Corporate MIS

Hal spent almost a day with various members of the corporate MIS staff. He discussed user problems with Larry Larson, who had been trying to help with education and bringing users more into design efforts. Larry commented:

> We really could use more understanding at all levels of management and users about what is involved with systems. I don't think half of our users get the full potential out of our systems. I know that many of them do not understand the impact of a system on their functions, for example, I'm worried about COPICS.
> We also have not been successful in getting management into the planning process. As a result, we seem to operate here in a reactive mode. It would be nice to be in a position to have a plan and to have a certain amount of resources allocated to maintenance and enhancements. If this allocation were approved, then changes from it could be forecast and we would know what emergency requests do to the plan. A good example is the price escalator clause that cost us a month of intensive effort. We did the job (with a few costly errors due to the rush), but it set us back a month on COPICS. We have a hard time getting people to understand that it is natural to have slippage if an unexpected request virtually ties up the department for a month.

Hal's meeting with Terry Cambridge of development echoed the same theme. Terry remarked that the schedule was too tight for COPICS implementation. (In fact, only one person of all those Hal interviewed, thought that the schedule was realistic. Terry said, "We also have not been successful in drawing the user into the design process. Go talk to Barry Levine or the plant managers and they will tell you that user involvement is needed and that they realize this should have a high priority. Then, ask them to give you someone from their operations to work on a system and the answer is entirely different."

Hal also talked with Gary Boltman about the technical problems of MIS. Gary indicated that they had real capacity problems; management keeps getting upset when we ask for more CPU power. "What they don't realize is that when we said the 3031 would last us for five years everything then was batch. Sure we knew that certain applications were coming on-line, but nothing like what we have now."

Hal was concerned about the timing and the resources required for the MVS conversion, some four or five worker years in the current MIS budget. Gary said that they were trapped. "The 3031 doesn't have the horsepower to do all we are trying to accomplish; a large part of the problem is running DOS/VS. That is why we need to move to MVS. I've ordered the attached processor, but we won't get full benefit from it because DOS/VS can't schedule both processors efficiently."

Hal asked him if there were an alternative machine and Gary replied:

Well, we could consider a 3033S which has about twice the power of the 3031. The nice thing about it is that it is a uniprocessor—we will get all that power and it should help us when things are really tight, like when we are half DOS and half MVS. It is more expensive, but it would give us the capacity we need to do the MVS conversion at our leisure. Once we've started MVS, we can't really turn back or delay things. Then we are committed to get away from DOS and onto MVS.

Hal finished his interviews with another session with Fred Edison. Hal reviewed his discussions and found that Fred was in general agreement with his observations. Fred also mentioned how difficult it was to hire qualified individuals given the intensively competitive market in San Fernando.

We're competing with aerospace and a lot of other electronics firms. Our personnel procedures are so bureaucratic that it takes a long time to contact a potential applicant. Everyone that we have recruited has been outside of normal channels.

We've had a mixed experience on the issue of user involvement. I finally got so frustrated doing MOLS that I just built the system based on my knowledge of production control and scheduling. No one has the inclination or will take the time to spend on a systems project. We have tried steering committees and they just don't work. I can't seem to get management attention for any of these problems.

Headquarters

Hal also spent a day in Phoenix meeting with the executive committee which consists of the chairman and all vice presidents. He interviewed each man individually, concentrating on Bob Ziegler since MIS reports to him.

Bob expressed frustrations similar to those Hal had heard from Fred and others in MIS. "We've done a lot of things for this company, but no one seems to recognize that; all we hear are complaints about service. Yet when we ask for some help no one has time. Our users prefer to design systems after they have been installed.

"We've had plenty of resources. I can't complain about failures to approve expenditures on computers and equipment. Sometimes I think we may be a little too tight on authorizing new positions. I suspect that our staff is not the best, either."

Hal responded, "I asked Fred for some background on each individual on his staff; you're correct in that they are not at the top educationally or from the standpoint of work experience. However, I'm impressed with their dedication and with what has been accomplished in a relatively short period of time."

"I hope that you can do something to help us. I'm worried about COPICS: we can't afford what happened with the order entry system. This time we could completely stop the factory."

CONCLUSION

Hal Watson finished reading his interview notes for the second time and dropped them on his desk. "There are a lot of problems here, but what is the most important?" he thought. Watson had two weeks in which to prepare recommendations for Martin Holiday. "My biggest fear is the COPICS system; I see millions of resistors strewn around the factory with production completely out of control. I wonder if ABZ could ever recover from such a disaster...." Hal picked up a pad of paper and began to make an outline of the key problems he had discovered preparatory to formulating recommendations to help solve them.

ABZ ELECTRONICS: PART B

Henry C. Lucas, Jr.

RECENT EVENTS

In 1982 Gary Boltman became the new director of MIS; Fred Edison became production control manager. During the period from 1981 to 1982 ABZ constructed a new data center to house a 3033S that replaced the 3031. MIS work during this period concentrated on the move and in design work on COPICS.

Overall management of ABZ underwent some changes, too. Tom Dolan, a former vice president of sales, who had retired, returned as executive vice president. The vice president of finance, Bob Ziegler, retired and was replaced by Martin Grundy. Tom Dolan moved Gary Boltman into a direct reporting relationship with him after a year in which Gary reported to the manager of the San Fernando division.

Dolan also reorganized all of ABZ into three profit centers. Each of the major divisions became responsible for its own "bottom line," and each division manager became a vice president of the corporation. (To encourage cooperation, management bonuses were computed on overall company, rather than division, performance.) By early 1984, the reorganization plan was complete.

EVENTS IN MIS

With a great deal of effort and a number of problems, MIS and users implemented COPICS in all but one location where it did not appear appropriate. Boltman observed that "we have COPICS in, but none of the users understands how to use it as a Materials Requirements Planning System (MRP). It's basically a locator system that replaces a lot of punched cards with on-line terminals."

MIS was successful in establishing a corporate MIS steering committee consisting of top corporate officers, Tom Dolan and each of the division vice presidents. The committee worked well in setting overall priorities for systems development. For example, the group placed a high priority on getting terminals into distributor locations that would be directly connected to the ABZ order entry system. It was the consensus of the group that these terminals would make it easier for distributors to order ABZ's products and would increase sales.

MIS also set up a series of user committees to provide guidance on the needs of the divisions. These committees met occasionally, but had problems focusing on the longer term. They tended to get bogged down in the details of present problems, despite the fact that a separate maintenance committee met regularly to allocate resources to maintenance requests.

CURRENT PROBLEMS

By the end of 1984, operational systems were running fairly well. There was still a large maintenance backlog, but more programmers had been added and an attempt was being made to reduce the number of outstanding requests.

The most serious problem facing ABZ with its systems was a growing dissatisfaction and distrust of the central MIS effort. A lot of these problems were due to the explosion of hardware and software alternatives to the traditional, mainframe systems approach. Vendors contacted local managers with ideas for cost-saving systems. The local managers, who are not information systems professionals, were easily convinced that an investment of from $5000 to $300,000 would easily be returned by a new application.

A good example of this type of proposal came at the Santa Clara plant, where the quality control manager decided that a Hewlett Packard minicomputer would improve the performance of his area and reduce staff. In fact, he justified the $250,000 purchase by stating that sixteen people would be eliminated in data entry and computation because of the new system.

Gary Boltman only saw the request for capital investment shortly before the order for the machine was to be placed. He raised a number of questions, all of which were overlooked as the machine was approved. Dolan argued "these people coming to me with requests for computers are producing; they make profits and it is hard to say that they can't have a device that will help them."

The lack of a professional staff created some problems and even the quality control manager admits that the HP system has turned out to accomplish less than they had hoped. Boltman mused, "everyone is so anti the mainframe, yet I wonder what we could have done for them with $250,000 more invested in the mainframe."

AN ACQUISITION POLICY

Due to the HP incident described above, plus the growing number of requests for microcomputers, the Executive Steering Committee agreed on a policy that the firm would purchase only three brands of microcomputers, HP, IBM and Apple. The computers should be approved by Boltman, who would try to negotiate purchasing agreements with the vendors. The choice was limited in order to reduce the requirements for support and to provide some level of compatibility. All of the managers agreed to adhere to the policy.

Unfortunately, the policy was widely violated. A good example was the Apple production control system developed in a user area for a new plant in Mexico. The system used a Corvus disk and several Apple II computers. The Apples processed production data in stages; when one finished its job, the data and results were passed to the next Apple, using the hard disk as the buffer.

MIS wanted to develop a common system for plants like the new one in Mexico. Dolan felt that the firm would not grow through large plants, but that there would be many small facilities that were highly specialized. Boltman worried about the cost of hardware and software if a different system was approved for each plant.

"The Apple system has been a real thorn in the side of MIS. We looked negative for opposing something innovative. The users developed this toy system and now the plant depends on it. At least they could have used newer micros than the aging Apples. It just is not a forward-looking solution that we can use other places for the next five to ten years," argued Boltman.

The general perception among management was that the Apple system was the best new system in years. Dolan said, "this is our biggest success, and the fact that MIS had nothing to do with it has raised a lot of requests by users to go it alone, too. An audit team found a few control problems in the application, but otherwise, it works better than the mainframe."

THE PLAN

Despite the presence of the steering committee, the MIS situation was not improving. More and more requests were coming for micros and minis; a number of computers appeared without anyone from MIS being aware of it.

Dolan, who felt MIS was low priority because he had to integrate two small companies just purchased by ABZ into his operations, finally realized that something had to be done. His solution was to call on MIS to come up with a plan for the next five years. Where should ABZ go? What is a reasonable architecture for systems? What kind of organization structure should MIS have given the recent changes in the structure of ABZ itself?

Boltman said, "at least we have an assignment now to try a plan. Somehow we have to give users freedom to be creative while at the same time not lose so much control that computing turns into chaos. We can't afford to let users at each plant buy different hardware and pay for different software to do the same job. How do we encourage and control information processing at the same time?"

ASSIGNMENT

Prepare a plan for computing at ABZ. Your plan should include at a minimum the organization structure for MIS, the mechanisms for supporting end-user computing, and an explanation of how information systems will be coordinated across the company. You should also consider the broad outlines of a hardware and software architecture for the firm and a policy statement on the acquisition of hardware and software by the local operating units.

HEIDELBERG CHEMICALS

Andrew Grindlay

I guess I'm on the steering committee to protect the interests of the Agrichemicals Division. We can't seem to get service out of the data processing department and although it has not hurt us much yet, we have had to do some manual data manipulation because we could not get our systems changed. We would like eventually to have our program modified to let us get the reports we need by entering the data in the same form as we receive them. But the systems people have been too busy developing the on-line system for the industrial division; they haven't had time for us. At the monthly steering committee meetings I keep pressing for more service for Agrichemicals.

Miss Fabian was not complaining. She was simply responding to the question of why she was on the data processing steering committee. She was an operations analyst in the Agrichemicals Division of Heidelberg Chemicals Inc. and was responsible for preparing reports for management and for government bodies on the chemicals purchased and sold for various agricultural purposes. These chemicals included fertilizers, animal food additives, veterinary supplies, pesticides, and insecticides.

THE COMPANY

Heidelberg Chemicals Inc. was a wholly-owned subsidiary of a German chemical firm. Located in Boston, it sold approximately $30 million in chemicals each year. The company did no manufacturing, although it did some blending and packaging of products which it purchased in bulk.

The German parent also owned another company, Pennsylvania Chemicals Inc., which sold approximately $100 million per year. A second kindred company of Heidelberg's, Bedford Dye Inc., was located in New Bedford, Massachusetts, and did much of the chemical manufacturing for small firms such as Heidelberg. The total of the sales of all three American subsidiaries represented approximately 6 percent of the worldwide sales of the eighty affiliated companies.

Heidelberg Chemicals Inc. was managed as two operating divisions, Industrial Chemicals and Agricultural Chemicals, usually referred to as Agrichemicals. 1979 sales of the Industrial Division amounted to $12 million and for the Agricultural Division, $18 million. A third division, Administration, cut across both of the other two and was responsible for all financial and administrative matters for the whole company.

The two operating divisions performed mainly a marketing function but they also took responsibility for warehousing their products and some blending and repackaging. Each of the three divisions was headed by a vice president who, as one of his many duties, sat on the data processing steering committee.

COMPUTING AT HEIDELBERG CHEMICALS

The company started processing data in 1960 on unit record equipment rented from IBM. George Lake was retained at that time to run the equipment and to supervise the newly-hired keypunch operators. Later, the unit record machines were replaced by an IBM 360/20 card system, which in 1971 was replaced by a Univac 9300, and in February 1980, by a Univac 90/30 computer. The Univac 90/30 had 160,000 bytes of memory, six disk drives, a card reader, a printer, and a video terminal which was located in the computer room and used by the programmers.

Over the years systems had been developed for all three divisions of the company by programmers who had been hired by Mr. Lake. One of them, Don Patton, joined the firm in 1968 as a programmer/trainee. Since he had no training or experience in computing he was sent to IBM courses to learn RPG and COBOL. In 1970 he was made systems and programming manager, reporting to Lake who in turn reported to the vice president of administration.

About two-thirds of the programs in use were written in RPG, a simple, easy-to-use language with rather limited capabilities. The remainder were written in COBOL, a more powerful but more difficult language. The company payroll was not processed on Heidelberg Chemicals' computer. Instead, it was done by one of the large banks at an agreed price per check.

Data processing grew within the Heidelberg Company, and in 1974 Robert MacDonald was employed as vice president of administration. He was given responsibility for the systems and data processing. In 1979 there were eight people in the department: Lake, Patton, a programmer/analyst, a programmer, a supervisor of data entry and control, two data entry clerks, and a computer operator. The supervisor of data entry and control also served as a backup computer operator. About 60 percent of the two programmers' time was used to maintain and enhance existing programs.

Shortly after he was appointed, MacDonald received a letter from the data processing manager at the parent company in Germany, outlining the company's policy on computing. It was policy, the letter said, to charge out all system development and all computer operations costs to the operating divisions. Further, within two years annual systems and data processing costs including a space charge of 15 percent of actual expenditures, should be held to no more than 1 percent of sales. Finally, MacDonald was urged to meet with his counterparts from the two other United States subsidiaries, both of which had machines of their own, to explore the possibility of the joint use of a single computer.

On receiving the letter, and having had no experience in systems and data processing, MacDonald formed a steering committee to help him manage it. He asked the other two vice presidents to serve, along with Lake, Patton, Hill, who was the Industrial Chemicals marketing research and planning director, and Fabian, the operations analyst in the Agrichemicals Division. Mr. MacDonald was chairman. At one of the early meetings, MacDonald presented a statement to the committee outlining the role of data processing in the company. This statement had been drafted initially by MacDonald and presented to the firm's management committee (the president and the three vice presidents). The management committee saw two different drafts of the statement before approving the third one. This final version was presented to the steering committee in December, 1974 and approved without change (see Exhibit 1 for the statement as finally approved).

At the meetings of the steering committee, Patton customarily presented progress reports on the various systems under development and on maintenance and enhancements to existing programs. Other members suggested new systems or modifications to old ones; the committee decided on priorities and recommended additional resources where appropriate. For example, in 1978 when Patton and Lake thought it was time to replace the Univac 9300 computer, they presented a proposal to the steering committee which authorized Lake to issue a Request for Proposal (R.F.P.) to computer vendors. When he and Patton had selected the Univac 90/30 from the several proposed, the steering committee approved the acquisition and the vice president of administration wrote to the parent organization in Germany for authorization. The main reason given to justify the new equipment was that the Industrial Chemicals Division had asked Lake to develop an on-line order entry system for them which would require a computer with greater capabilities than the one they had. In addition, the existing computer was becoming unreliable and was taking longer to repair when it did fail. In 1977, for example, it was unavailable during scheduled operating hours for a total of 345 hours.

The data processing officials at the parent company wrote a long letter to

EXHIBIT 1
Heidelberg Chemicals Inc., The Computer Services Department Mission

The mission is intended to develop and maintain a systematic approach in the provision of EDP services with which the user will concur and identify.

1.0 OBJECTIVES OF EDP DEPARTMENT

1.1 Prime Objective:

To satisfy the company's need for management decision making and monitoring tools through the provision of timely, accurate, and usefully presented information.

1.2 Secondary Objective:

To maintain optimum operational efficiency in the areas of:

—hardware utilization
—technology (software development, upgrading, and maintenance)
—personnel (capability and upgrading)

1.3 These objectives must be achieved at an optimum cost benefit to the company measuring up to the Heidelberg Group standards if possible and desirable.

2.0 RESPONSIBILITY

It will be the responsibility of company management (through the management committee) to oversee the benefits of EDP and approve priorities. The operational aspects remain the responsibility of the Administration division.

3.0 USER NEEDS

The company makes use of computer services through satisfying various user needs. User needs are:

(a) To identify the business environment based on information which the user has generated.
(b) Receive timely, accurate, and useful information regarding the user's position relative to past performance, current objectives, and future plans. This information will be useful for the user to:

—take advantage of opportunities
—act promptly on problem areas
—manage day-to-day operations efficiently and effectively
—make future plans

4.0 COMPUTER SERVICES DEPARTMENT NEEDS

The satisfactory provision of services to the user is the specific responsibility of the department through the use of specialized personnel and equipment. To service user needs, the department must be able to identify its operations according to the following functions:

(a) new applications
(b) maintenance/review of existing applications, basic data, programs, and internal computer systems
(c) on-going operations (production of established applications for the users)

To obtain maximum efficiency, the EDP resource (personnel and equipment) must be coordinated with user needs by means of:

(a) an annual EDP operating plan. This must be completed in sufficient detail in order to develop an operating budget for the coming year.
(b) five-year resource plans to accommodate long-term requirements. These plans would be revised annually at the completion of the annual operating plan.

5.0 PLANNING AND RESPONSIBILITIES

In order to arrive at these plans, the following requirement responsibilities are necessary.

(a) It will be the user's responsibility to develop a list of required projects specifically for the following year and generally for the next five years.

(b) It will be EDP's responsibility to further develop with the user an agreed upon detailed description of current proposed projects as specified by procedures.

(c) It will be EDP's responsibility to secure such a list in a timely fashion and match time/cost requirements with current capabilities.

(d) The user's needs will be coordinated through an EDP steering committee.

(e) The proposed project list will be reviewed for overall priority and finalized by the management committee for inclusion into an operating plan.

(f) It will be EDP's responsibility through the EDP steering committee to develop and secure agreement on a project timetable within the limits of EDP capacity.

(g) The EDP steering committee will be responsible for reviewing the progress of projects and/or operations from the user's point of view as specified by procedures.

(h) It will be an Administration division responsibility to plan and provide the requirements of EDP facilities and manpower for the short- and long-term needs of the company.

(i) It will be the EDP manager's responsibility for efficient and effective operations in all aspects of that department.

(j) The Administration division will develop costs of the various elements of (a) established EDP productions, (b) new project development costs, and (c) maintenance costs.

(k) It will be an Administration division responsibility to develop an equitable EDP cost charge-out system and to monitor it with the users.

December 13, 1974

MacDonald asking for additional information. They wanted to know the reasons for the 345 hours of downtime in 1977 and also requested a project plan for the development of the on-line order entry system. They wanted to know, too, why Heidelberg had rejected the IBM System 34 in favor of the Univac 90/30. They pointed out that an affiliated company, Bedford Dye Inc., had a small System 34, tended by one person, and strongly urged MacDonald to try to work with both Bedford Dye and Pennsylvania Chemicals to coordinate their data processing activities and perhaps share computing resources. They also wanted to review any final contract with a computer vendor before it was signed by Heidelberg and urged MacDonald to try to negotiate more flexible terms for a broken contract, a lower price, a maintenance guarantee, and a provision whereby Heidelberg would incur no maintenance charges for the first three months of the installation.

There followed a period of several months of negotiations between the data processing officials in Germany, MacDonald and Univac, with Lake and Patton providing most of the contact with Univac. Finally the order was placed and the contract signed.

THE ON-LINE ORDER ENTRY SYSTEM

Under the order entry procedure then in use, when a customer telephoned an order to Heidelberg Chemicals, a clerk at the order desk searched through a tub file of cards to find the customer's card to get credit and shipping information, and then searched through an inventory tub file to learn if the required products were in stock. As there were approximately 1000 items in stock, it usually took a few seconds to find the correct card before being able to accept the customer's order. The card showed not only the quantity on hand but also the price and other relevant product information. After accepting the customer's order the clerk wrote the quantities in pencil on the appropriate cards, and then prepared a shipping order. Later, after the goods were shipped, this order was returned to the order desk where another clerk went back to the inventory cards and wrote in pen the actual quantities shipped and a new balance on hand. When a shipment was received from a supplier, the card was updated. If, on scanning the inventory card, the order clerk discovered that they were out of an item, before telling a customer, he or she checked a third tub file containing purchase orders, to be able to tell the customer when a new supply was expected. While this procedure sometimes took only a few seconds, it occasionally kept the customer waiting on the telephone for several minutes. An on-line order entry system, the vice president of Industrial Chemicals felt, would reduce the average time it took a customer to place an order.

Six clerks worked in the order desk area answering the telephones, checking card files, and updating records as goods were shipped or received. They enjoyed their work and thought the system worked well. When asked if they thought a computerized system would improve things, in unison they said "no." Several suppliers they occasionally called had computerized systems and the clerks reported that these calls invariably took longer than calls to noncomputerized suppliers.

A video display terminal had been purchased by the company in anticipation of the development of an on-line order entry system. It had been located in the room where the six clerks worked. Although it had a plastic cover over it and was not yet being used, the clerks viewed the terminal as a threat to their customary way of doing things. They had been told that a new system was being developed, but they had not been told how it would be used or what the effect would be. They heard in the employee cafeteria that one of the arguments used to justify the development of the on-line system was the plan to eliminate one, and perhaps two, of the six jobs.

To develop the on-line order entry system, Lake and Patton had visited Pennsylvania Chemicals Inc., a much larger but similar company, to learn how orders were processed there. They learned that Pennsylvania Chemicals had spent a half million dollars for the design of an on-line order entry system and was in the process of writing the programs to make it run on a large IBM 370/158 computer. This machine was several times larger and faster than the Univac 90/30 at Heidelberg Chemicals. Lake and Patton decided, however, that with the design specifications developed for Pennsylvania Chemicals they would be able to draw flow diagrams and write the programs for an on-line order entry system of their own. It would not be so large nor so complex as the other company's, but they would still require an additional 230,000 bytes of memory on their Univac. The steering committee authorized the additional memory at a rental of $10,000 per year, as well as the purchase of two video display terminals which would cost $3000 each. There would be no additional cost for programming because Patton and one of the programmer/trainees who was already on staff would do the necessary work. To speed up the work, Patton decided not to draw flow diagrams, but to write the COBOL code directly from the detailed specifications provided by Pennsylvania Chemicals.

THE STRUCTURE OF THE ON-LINE ORDER ENTRY SYSTEM

When complete the on-line order entry system would consist of five modules:

1 The purchase order module would allow the direct entry of all purchase orders to a purchase order file containing complete information on all orders which had been placed on suppliers and which had not yet been delivered.

2 The customer file module would allow the customer file to be updated with new information on address changes, credit information, sales, balance outstanding, and unfilled orders.

3 The product module was designed to introduce new information into the product file about the products, both raw material and finished goods, carried by the company. This included chemical composition, names of suppliers, product code number, and other information that would be used in a sales catalogue carried by a salesman.

4 The formulation module maintained a file that contained complete information on the ingredients of all of the end products blended by the company.

5 The inventory module was to keep a running count of all items stocked, showing both the quantities on hand and quantities on order, but not yet delivered.

Some of the information to be used by the new on-line system was already stored in computer files, but these files would be converted to use the file structure required by the information management system provided with the Univac 90/30. Patton said he planned to write a program to make the conversion. He also planned to run the new on-line system parallel with the manual system for a few months until he was sure the new one worked properly, at which time the manual system with all its tub files would be abandoned.

EXISTING SYSTEMS

The Univac 90/30 was used for two main purposes. The first was to provide analysis of sales information to the marketing people in both of the operating divisions of the company. The division vice presidents received monthly reports giving sales by product, by salesman, by customer, and for the whole division. Costs were also provided, as were net profit figures.

The other major use of the Univac was to transmit data on the price and chemical composition of the various raw ingredients of the Agrichemical products to a computer in Rochester, New York. Information was also sent on the finished products to be sold by the Agrichemicals Division. The computer in Rochester, owned by a computer service firm, processed the data in what was called an optimizing model and returned to Heidelberg Chemicals' Univac the most economical mix of ingredients to meet the product specifications. The model was written in the FORTRAN language and required a much larger computer than the Heidelberg machine. The total cost of this service was $7000 per year.

The procedure used to access the Rochester computer started in the Agrichemicals Division office where a clerk prepared sheets containing the pertinent information. These sheets were then taken to the computer room at Heidelberg Chemicals where a keypunch operator prepared punched cards which were read by a card reader and the information stored on one of the Univac disks. Later Fabian sat at a video display terminal in the Agrichemicals Division office and called the keypunched information onto the screen of the terminal, correcting errors and changing the way it was organized. When she was satisfied that the information was correct, she typed a command on the keyboard of the terminal, and the entire file was transmitted by telephone line to Rochester, where it was stored on a disk awaiting its turn to be processed. Later, when the processing was complete, the results were returned by telephone line to the Univac and were printed on the system's line printer.

Fabian, who was responsible for this use of the computer by the Agrichemicals Division, said that the service was excellent. The computer at Rochester gave her fast turnaround and had not had a malfunction in all the time she had used it. Occasionally the telephone connection between the two computers was troublesome, but other than that, the system seemed to work well.

The one thing she did not think was very good was the fact that she had to perform an edit function on the data before sending to Rochester. She had asked George Lake if he would have a programmer modify the program on the Univac which created the file from cards so the data would be in the correct format and sequence for Rochester, but Lake said he did not have any people available to do it right then. He suggested she wait until the on-line order entry system for the Industrial Chemicals Division was complete. Fabian offered to make the change herself because, although she had never learned RPG, she had taken a course in FORTRAN and believed that by studying the manuals she could learn enough about RPG and the Univac's operating system to make the necessary changes. Lake declined her offer to help.

THE CHARGEOUT SYSTEM

At the beginning of each year Lake estimated the usage of the computer for the year and calculated a price per cpu hour which would cover his total computer cost. People and data entry machines located in the area occupied by the operating divisions were paid for directly by those divisions.

Patton and his two programmers kept track of the time they spent on the development of new systems and, where a system could be identified with a division, their time was charged to that division. In 1980, the rates charged the divisions were:

Computer Time	$429.59 per cpu hour
Data Entry	18.11 per hour
Systems & Programming	$29.94 per hour

Each month Lake sent a list of divisional charges to the accounting office which adjusted them proportionally to make the total charged to the three divisions equal to the total of all expenditures incurred to operate the data processing department.

When asked about the effect of this charging out on the division decision makers, Lake was unsure of any. He said that no user manager had ever come to him to ask why the charges were what they were, although occasionally at a steering committee meeting someone would say something like, "With all this money I am paying for data processing, why can't I get better service?" Lake went further to say that the only reason he knew of for having a charge-out system was because the parent company in Germany wanted them to.

THE WORD PROCESSOR

Because the Agrichemicals Division was required to submit numerous reports to various government bodies, the manager of Quality Assurance and Reports, Dwight Ladd, requested approval to get a word processing system. The request was forwarded by the vice president of Agrichemicals to the president, who sent it to MacDonald for action. MacDonald was not opposed to the idea of a word processor; indeed, he had for some time been thinking of getting one for the entire company. He was a little reluctant to order one for just one division, however. He was also concerned about the organizational authority over the proposed machine. He had an office manager who looked after typewriters, photocopiers, stationery, and so on, and he wondered if this man should be asked to take responsibility for the word processor. After all, it was just a big brother to the typewriters with storage capability, of which the company had many, all in the jurisdiction of the office manager.

He thought too that perhaps Lake, manager of the Data Processing Department, should be asked to take responsibility for it. Although no decision had been made on which word processor was to be purchased, MacDonald knew that some models were stand-alone, while others, for about the same price, could be coupled to the Univac, providing for greater capability. It somehow seemed that if it were to be coupled to the computer, it should be the responsibility of the data processing department.

Finally, he considered the possibility of letting the Agrichemicals Division take responsibility for it; they had requested it and they would be the major users. Further, if it "belonged" to Agrichemicals, it would not show up on the financial statements as data processing. MacDonald was having trouble keeping data processing expenditures below the 1 percent of sales target set by the parent organization. While he was contemplating the question, his secretary placed his afternoon mail on his desk. Right on top was a memorandum from the vice president of the Agrichemicals Division explaining that he had seen a demonstration of a word processor connected to a Univac 90/30 with the same configuration as Heidelberg Chemicals, and he wanted permission to lease one for five years at $15,000 per year out of Agrichemicals' funds. It had 2000 bytes of storage, a printer, two diskette drives, and two video terminals. Although it would be the responsibility of the Agrichemicals Division, the vice president said he would be willing to make it available to the other two divisions.

C-I-L INFORMATION RESOURCES: MANAGING COMPUTER RESOURCES IN A MULTIDIVISION COMPANY

Andrew Grindlay

In late 1983, C-I-L's Data Processing Steering Committee was presented with a proposal for the installation of a large IBM computer. At that time the company had several computers: some made by Burroughs Corporation and some by Digital Equipment Corporation. A few of the computers were located centrally, with the remainder in the business units. Over the prior few years the professional systems people in the divisions and wholly-owned subsidiaries had been gradually replaced by nontechnical, experienced business personnel who, as systems coordinators, were to identify and provide leadership for systems projects. Systems analysis, design, and programming would be carried out by functional specialist teams from the center assisted by users who would lead and manage projects.

THE COMPANY

C-I-L Inc. was a subsidiary (73.2% owned) of Imperial Chemical Industries (ICI) in the United Kingdom. It manufactured and sold chemicals, explosives, and fertilizers across Canada, and sold chemicals in the United States. In total the company owned and operated thirty manufacturing plants and twenty warehouses. It was managed by a president and four senior vice presidents, each of whom took responsibility for one or more of the seventeen subsidiary companies, six operating divisions, and eleven corporate functions.

C-I-L Inc. employed approximately 6800 people, of whom about 450 worked for one of the corporate functions at the head office in Toronto. An organization chart is shown in Exhibit 1. The subsidiary companies, some of

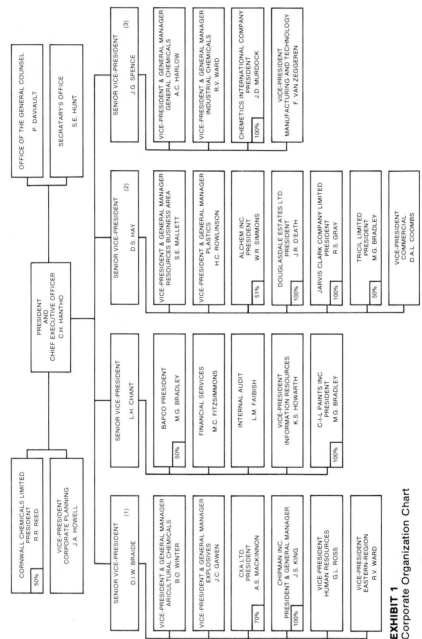

EXHIBIT 1
Corporate Organization Chart

CORNWALL CHEMICALS LIMITED
PRESIDENT
R.R. REED
50%

VICE-PRESIDENT
CORPORATE PLANNING
J.A. HOWELL

OFFICE OF THE GENERAL COUNSEL
P. DAVIAULT

SECRATARY'S OFFICE
S.E. HUNT

PRESIDENT
AND
CHIEF EXECUTIVE OFFICER
C.H. HANTHO

SENIOR VICE-PRESIDENT (1)
D.I.W BRAIDE

VICE-PRESIDENT & GENERAL MANAGER
ARICULTURAL CHEMICALS
B.O. WINTER

VICE-PRESIDENT & GENERAL MANAGER
EXPLOSIVES
J.C. GAWEN

CXA LTD.
PRESIDENT
A.S. MACKINNON
70%

CHIPMAN INC.
PRESIDENT & GENERAL MANAGER
J.S. KING
100%

VICE-PRESIDENT
HUMAN RESOURCES
G.L. ROSS

VICE-PRESIDENT
EASTERN-REGION
R.V. WARD

SENIOR VICE-PRESIDENT
L.H. CHANT

BAPCO PRESIDENT
M.G. BRADLEY
50%

FINANCIAL SERVICES
M.C. FITZSIMMONS

INTERNAL AUDIT
L.M. FAIBISH

VICE-PRESIDENT
INFORMATION RESOURCES
K.S. HOWARTH

C-I-L PAINTS INC.
PRESIDENT
M.G. BRADLEY
100%

SENIOR VICE-PRESIDENT (2)
D.S. HAY

VICE-PRESIDENT & GENERAL MANAGER
RESOURCES BUSINESS AREA
S.E. MALLETT

VICE-PRESIDENT & GENERAL MANAGER
PLASTICS
H.C. ROWLINSON

ALCHEM INC.
PRESIDENT
W.R. SIMMONS
51%

DOUGLASDALE ESTATES LTD.
PRESIDENT
J.R. D'EATH
100%

JARVIS CLARK COMPANY LIMITED
PRESIDENT
R.S. GRAY
100%

TRICIL LIMITED
PRESIDENT
M.G. BRADLEY
50%

VICE-PRESIDENT
COMMERCIAL
D.A.L. COOMBS

SENIOR VICE-PRESIDENT (3)
J.G. SPENCE

VICE-PRESIDENT & GENERAL MANAGER
GENERAL CHEMICALS
A.C. HARLOW

VICE-PRESIDENT & GENERAL MANAGER
INDUSTRIAL CHEMICALS
R.V. WARD

CHEMETICS INTERNATIONAL COMPANY
PRESIDENT
J.D. MURDOCK
100%

VICE-PRESIDENT
MANUFACTURING AND TECHNOLOGY
F. VAN ZEGGEREN

NOTE: (1) Overall responsibility for relations with governments and with the business community in the eastern region.
(2) Overall responsibility for relations with governments and with the business community in western Canada.
(3) Overall responsibility for relations with governments and with the business community in Ontario.
% Indicates C-I-L ownership.

80

which were wholly owned by C-I-L, and some partly, were headed by presidents. Each of the operating divisions was managed by a general manager who was also a vice president of C-I-L Inc. The twenty-three subsidiaries and operating divisions were referred to as "businesses" and, from a management perspective, were all treated in much the same manner. The subsidiaries did, however, tend to have a greater degree of autonomy than did the divisions. (See Exhibit 2 for a brief description of the businesses.)

1982 was a difficult year for C-I-L, with earnings dropping from $54.3 million in 1981 to $15.3 million in 1982. Earnings in 1983 were expected to reach $24 million on sales of $1.1 billion.

CORPORATE ORGANIZATION STRUCTURE

The company was attempting to achieve a balance between providing autonomy for decision making to the division and subsidiary managers, yet at the same time retaining central control over functions that they believed needed it. Although several of the businesses had their own warehouses, there was some sharing of warehouse space and cost.

Project engineering and some specialized engineering services were centralized. A new plant, or the expansion of an existing plant, was designed and developed by the corporate engineering staff, often with assistance from engineers in the division or subsidiary or from the ICI headquarters.

Transportation was partly centralized. The corporate transportation people negotiated rates with carriers and determined how goods would be shipped; the businesses did the shipping. The company had over 1800 railway cars under lease which were used to haul chemicals and other products across the country. These cars were shared among several divisions. C-I-L had an arrangement with a Chicago firm, Kleinschmidt Inc., whereby C-I-L provided Kleinschmidt with a list of the numbers of all of its rail cars and received daily information from Kleinschmidt on the movement of the cars throughout North America. The information was fed electronically from Chicago into one of C-I-L's computers in Toronto, from which C-I-L's transportation people could give customers daily updates on when to expect their shipments.

Purchasing for the divisions was mainly centralized. The corporate purchasing people negotiated contracts with major suppliers and then the divisions bought from the approved sources. There was local purchasing of minor items by the divisions. Most of the subsidiaries did their own purchasing and negotiated their own contracts.

Information systems was partly centralized. For many years C-I-L Inc. had had large central computers in which transaction-driven systems resided. A few of the businesses had their own computers, but systems design tended to be centrally controlled.

The one function which was highly decentralized was marketing. Each business had its own marketing staff and sales force and operated independently of the others. There was, however, a corporate function called "com-

EXHIBIT 2

THE BUSINESSES

The divisions

Industrial Chemicals (710 employees. Sales - $260 million)

This division manufactured and marketed chloralkali products including chlorine, caustic soda and solvents and marketed sulphur products such as sulphuric acid and liquid sulphur dioxide. Most of Canada's basic industries utilized these commodity chemicals as essential raw materials. Because the products were sold in bulk in large quantities transportation costs were a key factor in the price to customers and consequently critical as a sales determinant. The head office of the division was located in Montreal, Quebec. The division had six manufacturing facilities in total: two in Quebec, and one in each of Ontario, New Brunswick, Alberta, and British Columbia. Computing for this division was done in the batch mode on the corporate Burroughs B7700 computer in Toronto and on one of the centrally located PDP 11/70s.

Explosives (1200 employees. Sales - $217 million)

The Explosives Division served two-thirds of the Canadian commercial explosives market with all types of commercial explosives. It employed an extensive sales and technical support staff in twenty-five offices which advised buyers of commerical explosives and blasting accessories on up-to-date techniques and equipment. With its head office in Toronto, it had manufacturing plants in Alberta, Ontario, and Quebec. This division had some of its computing done in the batch mode on the C-I-L B7700 computer and the balance done on another of the PDP 11/70s at the C-I-L computer centre.

Agricultural Chemicals (580 employees. Sales - $180 million)

The Agricultural Chemicals Division's principal products were urea, ammonium nitrate, phosphate, and anhydrous ammonia. Most of the chemicals produced, such as explosives and nylon manufactures, were sold to Canadian industrial users, with the balance sold to large fertilizer distributors, blenders, and individual farms in eastern Canada, with some sulphur-coated urea fertilizers being produced for the home gardener. Some products were exported, mainly to the States around the Great Lakes. The division was noted for establishing its Agromart System of on-the-spot blending facilities to serve farmers. At these fifty outlets farmers could purchase fertilizers, agricultural products, and supplies, as well as services such as soil analysis and crop planning. Many of the Agromarts had Apple microcomputers which they used to help their customers to calculate their fertilizer requirements and plan their crops. This service was considered by C-I-L to be a valuable sales aid. The Agricultural Division's head office was in London, Ontario and it had nine interrelated plants at Courtright, Ontario. The division had a PDP 11/70 computer which was used mainly for order processing and for transmitting information to C-I-L Inc.'s Burroughs B7700 computer in Toronto. The managers in the division made extensive use of the sales information generated by the PDP 11/70 computer and found the machine to be very helpful in regular sales monitoring and at budget preparation time. The division also used financial models for planning.

General Chemicals (160 employees. Sales - $125 million)

The General Chemicals Division sold a broad range of low volume but important bulk and packaged chemical products to a wide variety of industrial consumers across Canada. General Chemicals had three packaging facilities from which it supplied 200 product lines to 4000 customers in 30 different industries. It had no computing equipment of its own but used the B7700 and PDP 11/70s at the corporate office in Toronto. It had a plant in Cornwall, Ontario.

Plastics (530 employees. Sales - $114 million)
The Plastics Division had two operating groups: polymers, which was responsible for the manufacture and sale of polyethylene resins, and films, which made and sold films for industrial packaging. The headquarters of this division was in Toronto, with manufacturing plants in Alberta and Ontario. It too used the B7700 and one of the corporate PDP 11/70s, mainly for order processing and for accounting at its two plants.

C-I-L Resources Business Area
This was the smallest division and was formed to administer the company's interest in the petroleum, gas, and oil field service industries in western Canada. It was based in Calgary and employed twenty people. It sent its data to the corporate's B7700 for processing.

Wholly-owned subsidiaries

C-I-L Chemicals Inc. (110 employees. Sales - $90 million)
C-I-L Chemicals was a marketing and distribution company which was formed in 1975 to serve the U.S. chemicals market when C-I-L acquired a distribution company in Detroit, Michigan. It was a major reseller of sulphur and chloralkali products in addition to explosives, plastics, and agricultural chemical products. It had a manufacturing plant in New Jersey and sulphuric acid terminals in Michigan, Ohio, and Illinois. It had a VAX 11/750 computer and two systems people.

C-I-L Paints Inc. (445 employees. Sales - $65 million)
This subsidiary produced and sold industrial paints to other Canadian companies, mainly in the automotive and farm implement industries. It had no computing facilities of its own but used the corporate B6900 and B7700 for its total computing requirement. Its head office and plant were

in Toronto a short distance from the corporate head office.

Chipman Inc. (180 employees. Sales - $60 million)
Chipman Inc. had developed and introduced a wide variety of pesticides supplied by ICI in the U.K. and by U.S. manufacturers. The company had brought about many advances in pesticide and herbicide technology. Its head office was at Stoney Creek, Ontario. The company had plants in Ontario, Alberta, and Quebec. It had two systems people and a Burroughs B1955 which was used mainly for order processing, sales accounting, and inventory control. It also fed data into the corporate B7700 for further processing. Chipman had developed plans to introduce Materials Requirements Planning using a packaged system on its B1955 computer.

Chemetics International Co. (240 employees. Sales - $53 million)
Chemetics sold chemical process technology worldwide in the form of fully engineered systems and specialized equipment. Its head office was in Vancouver, B.C. with engineering offices in Vancouver and in Toronto, Ontario. It had a PDP 11/44 computer and one systems professional.

Jarvis Clark Co. Ltd. (320 employees. Sales - $50 million)
Jarvis Clark was Canada's leading designer and manufacturer of mobile underground mining equipment and manufactured some construction equipment. The company's head office and plant were in Burlington, Ontario. It had parts and service centers and agents across Canada and in many other parts of the world. The company had a Hewlett-Packard 3000 Model 44 computer, which it used mainly for plant and material scheduling. Its Information Systems Department employed 18 people.

Party-owned subsidiaries

The other twelve subsidiaries were partly-owned by C-I-L Inc. Most had computing equipment of their own and a few relied on C-I-L for some of their data processing.

mercial" which oversaw the marketing activities for the entire corporation as well as taking responsibility for the company's TV studio, public affairs, market research, and government relations.

CORPORATE PLANNING

A central planning group, headed by Mr. John Howell, Vice President for Planning, was responsible for overall corporate strategy and for assisting the businesses in writing their business plans. The length of the planning cycle varied across businesses; those in the more volatile industries revised their plans every six months, and those in the more stable markets reviewed and revised their plans every two or three years. In the agricultural chemicals division, for example, a three-year strategic plan was prepared annually and submitted to the corporate objectives and plans committee. After the plan had been discussed and, if necessary, revised, a more detailed one-year financial plan for the next year was written and submitted. Recently, there had been a shift in the content of the plans from financial orientation to business strategy.

Mr. Howell expressed the view that a change was coming in the way the businesses in C-I-L were managed. He said:

> There will be far greater clarity of the strategy the business managers will follow. For one thing, we will witness a change in product policy. In the past we have sought new markets for our products. In the future, we will have to concentrate more on developing new products for recognized market opportunities. We need a mechanism to make this change in management culture happen. It will not occur by itself. Should we change the organization? Should we change the people? However it is accomplished it will bring with it enormous demands on the Information Systems group who will be expected to provide quick and easy access to computers for information and analysis.

INFORMATION SYSTEMS CONSULTANT RETAINED

In the mid 1970s several of the C-I-L businesses and corporate functions had their own information systems people and did their own computing. They were allowed to acquire machines and hire programmers as they saw fit. Some of the businesses were well advanced in their use of computers, whereas others lagged behind their competition. Most of the C-I-L systems were batch-oriented and ran on a large Burroughs computer.

In 1978, in order to get an overall review of their information systems, C-I-L retained the consulting firm Nolan, Norton and Associates, which recommended, among other things, that a data processing steering committee be formed, and that each division and corporate group be asked to prepare a three-year systems plan. The committee was formed in the following year and the three-year plans were requested.

KEITH HOWARTH APPOINTED

In 1981, Keith Howarth was seconded for a two- to five-year period from C-I-L's parent company in the United Kingdom, Imperial Chemical Industries (ICI), reporting to C-I-L's Senior Vice President of Finance, Mr. L. H. Chant. Mr. Howarth had had extensive experience in information systems with ICI. When he arrived in Canada, he "placed a firm hand on the tiller" and set about moving the systems activity to a higher level of significance in the company. He initiated the practice of purchasing software whenever possible rather than writing it in-house. He would only approve the inside development of a system after the market had been thoroughly explored for an existing system that might be adapted to serve C-I-L's needs. Two years after his arrival Mr. Howarth was made a vice president, still reporting to Mr. Chant. He was also a member of the president's council, a group consisting of the four senior vice presidents at the corporate level and the heads of the divisions and major subsidiaries. He received approval to change the name of his department to Information Resources (IR).

At the time of Mr. Howarth's arrival, C-I-L had a data processing center which contained two Burroughs computers, a B7700 and a B6900. Later, a B5900 was added, as well as four small Digital Equipment Corporation PDP 11/70s. Then two VAX 11/780s were transferred from C-I-L's Engineering Department to IR.

The general ledger system ran on the B7700. All of the divisions and several of the subsidiaries used it. The explosives division used an on-line order entry system on one of the PDP 11/70s which was connected to the B7700 and fed data into the general ledger. The system had been developed within C-I-L. Agricultural chemicals had its own PDP 11/70, which it used to run its on-line order entry system, a system which had been derived from the explosives system. The agricultural chemicals computer was also connected to the B7700 and transmitted sales and purchase information to it each evening. The other divisions did all of their computing in the batch mode on the B7700.

Two of the subsidiary companies, C-I-L Paints Inc. and Bapco (partly-owned), used the corporate B6900 computer. Another subsidiary, Chipman Chemicals Inc., had a Burroughs B1955 of its own but did some of its computing on the corporate B7700. The other subsidiaries did almost all of their computing on their own equipment.

Some of the subsidiaries had their own information systems people because these groups had existed at the time the subsidiary was acquired. Theoretically any business head could still form his own information systems groups or buy computing services outside the corporation. He would be required, however, to discuss this with Mr. Howarth first. Jarvis Clark Company Limited, a wholly-owned subsidiary, had an information systems department with eighteen people who reported through an IS manager to the president of Jarvis Clark. Mr. Howarth had no direct authority over this IS group, but if he observed something going on in Jarvis Clark of which he disapproved he would first speak to that firm's IS head. If he was not satisfied, he would then speak to the president of Jarvis Clark. In effect, Mr. Howarth had a major say in information systems activity throughout the whole of C-I-L.

THE EXECUTIVE INFORMATION SYSTEM

One system which the senior corporate officers found particularly useful was the executive information system. It ran on one of the VAX computers and processed financial information assembled specifically for the executives. Financial data was transferred electronically to the VAX from the Burroughs B7700 and other information was keyed in. Each month the corporate controller made a presentation to the operations committee making extensive use of computerized on-line graphics. (The operations committee included the president and the four corporate senior vice presidents meeting biweekly to review company operations.) The controller specified his graphs at a terminal and had multicolor transparencies made on a photographic device connected directly to the computer. He also had "hard copies" of the graphs made on paper for the executives to take away for later study. With his terminal the controller could choose from among an almost unlimited array of financial information and presentation styles. The president kept a complete set of the hard copy graphs in his briefcase and used them in discussions with division and subsidiary heads. Each of the senior vice presidents and the president had a terminal in his office with which he could access additional information or display data in different ways at his leisure.

IR ORGANIZATION STRUCTURE

Information Resources had six people reporting to Mr. Howarth (see Exhibit 3 for an organization chart). Mr. Peter Goodwin managed a group of systems analysts who helped the users in the businesses to define their systems needs and to search for a suitable software package to do the job. If changes to a package were to be required, Mr. Goodwin's people specified the changes and then formed the core group of a user-managed project team responsible for all aspects of the project including implementation.

Martin Young supervised a team of system designers and programmers who received the changes requested by the analysts and did the necessary design and programming. This group spent about 50 percent of their time maintaining existing programs. They also set programming and documentation standards, implemented productivity tools, and developed project controls.

One problem was the time it took to satisfy an unanticipated request for information, especially if the data required was stored in separate files in the computer. For example, one of the members of the corporate purchasing department wanted to know how much was paid to a certain supplier in the first quarter of 1983, and also how this compared to the first quarter of 1982.

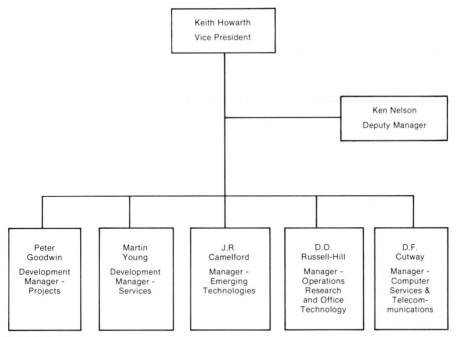

Exhibit 3
Information Resources Organization Chart

Since only current information was kept on line, in order to answer the inquiry, a programmer from Mr. Young's group had to analyze the request to ensure that he or she understood it, write a program in a language called Extracto, test the program, and compile it. Then the tape containing the 1982 data had to be mounted on the Burroughs B7700 by a machine operator and the Extracto program run. The time required to do all this varied from a couple of days, if a programmer was readily available, to about one month. Consequently the members of the purchasing department found it easier to rely on their suppliers for that type of information, a practice which they considered less than satisfactory.

THE DATA PROCESSING STEERING COMMITTEE

A data processing steering committee (DPSC), consisting of six executives, had been formed in 1980 but had grown over the years as more and more people wanted to be included. In 1983 the membership was:

L. H. Chant, Senior Vice President (Chairman)
J. G. Spence, Senior Vice President (Vice Chairman)
B. O. Winter, Vice President and General Manager, Agricultural Chemicals Div.

J. C. Gawen, Vice President and General Manager, Explosives Div.

H. C. Rowlinson, Vice President and General Manager, Plastics Div.

A. C. Harlow, Vice President and General Manager, General Chemicals Div.

R. V. Ward, Vice President and General Manager, Industrial Chemicals Div.

D. A. L. Coombs, Vice President, Commercial

F. Van Zeggeren, Vice President, Manufacturing and Technology

J. A. Howell, Vice President, Corporate Planning

M. E. Johnson, Controller

K. S. Howarth, Vice President, Information Resources

K. L. Nelson, Deputy Group Manager, Information Resources (Secretary)

The role of the DPSC was stated as "the establishment of an overall data processing strategy and plan for C-I-L; . . . it was to consider and recommend to the operations committee the appropriate system development and related activities." In actual practice, however, according to one of its members, the DPSC served more as an educational vehicle, informing the members of what was going on. Another member said it served as a brake. The committee met quarterly, at which time it reviewed proposals for new systems and heard progress reports of systems under development. It did not ask the businesses to write systems plans; rather, it responded to proposals submitted to it.

In March 1983, the control manager of Jarvis Clark Company Limited appeared before the DPSC with a proposal that his firm replace its three small, old computers with one larger, modern machine, an HP 3000, on which it would do material requirements planning and inventory control. The capital cost was expected to be $569,000 and the increase in operating cost, $171,000. The DPSC did not approve the request and three months later the president of Jarvis Clark appeared before the committee requesting approval of a slightly smaller HP 3000 costing $482,000 with annual operating costs expected to increase by $90,000. That request was approved.

In line with the Nolan, Norton and Associates proposal of 1979, Mr. Howarth urged the businesses to continue their own steering committees and many of them did so. Then when a manager, usually the control manager, in one of the businesses wished a new system, he or she would discuss the need with the head of the business and the people in information resources and, if they all agreed, a proposal would be submitted to the user's steering committee. If the committee approved it, the proposal would be submitted to Mr. Howarth's department. For expenditures estimated to be $100,000 or less, Mr. Howarth, with the business head, would make a decision on whether or not to proceed. Proposed systems costing in excess of $100,000 would be presented to the corporate steering committee along with recommendations from Mr. Howarth and the business head. Any expenditure above $500,000 would subsequently be submitted to the corporate operations committee for approval.

This process was different from the authorization procedure used for other capital expenditures for which a division vice president or a subsidiary president could approve a capital expenditure of up to $200,000.

MICROCOMPUTERS AND WORD PROCESSORS

In 1983, the DPSC approved a set of guidelines for the acquisition of micro-computers and word processors. Thereafter, users could only acquire IBM, Digital, or Apple microcomputers or Digital word processors and then only after the user's management had approved the cost/benefit analysis and IR had agreed that the equipment to be acquired would indeed do the job.

A catalogue of existing personal computer software in C-I-L was created and maintained, with copies sent to each division, subsidiary, works location, and corporate group. As well, bulk purchase and maintenance agreements for microcomputer hardware and software were signed.

To encourage senior executives to learn how to use a microcomputer, Mr. Howarth arranged for a Digital Equipment Corporation Rainbow to be delivered to the homes of three of the corporate vice presidents.

IR also established a user service center that provided assistance and in-struction on microcomputer use to existing and potential users. The center was staffed full time by a member of the operations research group in IR and contained several of each of the three brands of microcomputers that had been approved. As well it contained an Apple LISA which turned out to be the most popular machine in the center. In all there were 15 microcomputers in the center. Some of the machines were connected to one of the VAX computers and some to the Burroughs B7700. A user, if he or she wanted access to data stored on one of these larger machines, asked a programmer in the user service center who then wrote a program to download the data to a microcomputer. Users were not allowed direct access to the corporate files, nor were they allowed to send any data to the large computers, such as for backup purposes.

INFORMATION SYSTEMS PLANNING

A few of the C-I-L businesses included information systems in their strategic plans. They all, however, included in their annual budgets any costs expected to be transferred from the information resources department during the forthcoming year for running and maintaining existing systems and for new development work. Mr. Howarth, when he prepared his annual information resources plan, included all systems activity and hardware purchases for all the businesses. The IR plan then went to the DPSC where, if approved, it was presented to the C-I-L objectives and plans committee, which had the same membership as the operations committee but met for a different purpose. At that point the plan represented the blueprint of the systems work to be undertaken for the entire corporation.

When asked about systems planning for his division, the Vice President of Explosives, Dr. J. G. Gawen, said:

> I do not feel that I know where we in Explosives are going with systems. My Control Manager suggests areas he thinks should be mechanized and if I agree he then talks to Keith Howarth's people and they develop a proposal. But we have no long range systems plan. The computer contains a great deal of information about our explosives business but most of it is not really useful for managing. To get approval to develop systems which would be of help in managing we would have to demonstrate a financial payoff on some basis such as return on equity. This is not always possible, especially since some of my managers do not see the need to use the computer for management purposes.

Mr. Howarth also expressed some concerns. He said:

> Our applications portfolio is out of date and C-I-L is not taking advantage of productivity gains which are available from the current state of information technology. At the moment we do not have the facilities to provide the rapid access to data which the modern manager requires. We can achieve maximum organizational flexibility if our systems are capable of decentralized operation from a central host. We can achieve minimum cost by installing very advanced operational systems which can not likely be justified by a single division.

Mr. Howarth's five-year information resources (IR) strategic plan said, in part,

> It is becoming increasingly evident that all information processing and communications resources should be consolidated under one authority to avoid duplication or competition and to improve the quality of equipment acquisition decisions.

Believing that a strong central IR department was essential in C-I-L Inc., Mr. Howarth had earlier received the agreement of the data processing steering committee that, over time, the systems managers should be removed from the businesses which had them, to be replaced by system coordinators. These coordinators would not be data processing professionals but would be people who knew the businesses. It would become their responsibility to identify potential computer applications and to manage software development projects. IR would supply the analysts and programmers; the businesses would supply the leadership.

Mr. Howarth saw the roles of IR and of the users as quite distinct. The role of IR, he believed, should be to:

- Provide leadership to the businesses in the use of information technology to obtain maximum competitive advantage.
- Define the corporate information strategies in conjunction with the businesses.
- Monitor activities across the company.
- Operate the central computers.
- Build data files.
- Control standards.

- Find productivity tools and introduce them as appropriate.
- Ensure that the systems software such as the operating system, telecommunications software, and the database management system, were functioning properly.
- Run the transaction-oriented systems such as payroll, general ledger, order entry system, and the goods acquisition system.
- Provide tools for inquiry of data files.
- Provide leadership in finding suitable application programs and make whatever modifications were required to satisfy users' needs.
- Provide systems analysis and programming services for the users.

The responsibilities of the users, in his view, should be:

- Problem definition.
- Application systems project leadership, implementation, and funding.
- Data entry.
- Report printing.
- Writing and using programs on microcomputers.
- Writing and using programs to retrieve data from the large computers.

THE GOODS ACQUISITION SYSTEM

For some time the purchasing department had expressed concern over the fact that they had little control over the $800 million spent annually on commodity purchases. Each business did its own purchasing in those days and there was only limited bulk buying. The central purchasing group believed that a better computer-based system would permit them to combine orders and deal with the suppliers on much larger volumes as well as keep better track of inventory.

A project team consisting of representatives of purchasing and IR was established to find a new procurement system. After scanning the market carefully, the team concluded that a system called Goods Acquisition System (GAS), which ran on IBM computers, would, with modifications, be suitable. GAS was being used by several ICI divisions in Europe and by some ICI affiliates in South Africa. The team recommended that an IBM 4341, a medium-sized, modern computer, be acquired and GAS installed on it. The benefits to C-I-L were estimated to be of sufficient magnitude that GAS and an IBM 4341 could be justified.

THE ORDER PROCESSING SYSTEM

In mid-1983 the Industrial Chemicals Division and the General Chemicals Division asked IR to develop or find an on-line order processing system for them. A project team with representatives from the two divisions and IR was formed. There were several on-line order processing systems in use in C-I-L at that time, all running on different computers. C-I-L Paints used a system running on the central Burroughs B6900 computer. Agricultural Chemicals ran an on-line system, which was a modification of one developed by C-I-L for the Explosives Division, on a PDP 11/70. As well, the Plastics Division had a modified Explosives Division system, also running on a PDP 11/70, but it was different from those of both Agricultural Chemicals and Explosives. None of these three was as advanced technically as the Paints system. Any of them could, however, with effort and money, have been modified to meet the needs of the two chemical divisions.

The project team, after an intensive search of the market, located an on-line order processing system running on an IBM 3031 computer at an ICI subsidiary in Australia, as well as on a Hitachi computer in South Africa. The system was close to what was wanted by C-I-L Inc. for the two chemical divisions but would require some modification. The team investigated the possibility of getting an IBM 3031 to run this system and found that, although this machine was of older technology, it would do the job and could be justified on economic grounds. The members of the team recognized, however, that the order processing system is the hub of a company's data processing; many other systems, such as invoicing, production scheduling, general ledger, and accounts receivable, feed from it. It made sense to the project team, therefore, to think of doing all of the computing for the two chemical divisions on whatever computer was acquired to run the order processing system. The IBM 3031 was not really large enough for that, however. The next larger IBM machine available at that time was the model 3083E, a state-of-the-art computer, but it was so much larger and more costly that it could not be justified on the basis of the computing of the two chemical divisions alone. It would only be economical if the work of some of the other businesses could also be done on it. If, for example, all divisions did their order processing on an IBM 3083 and thereby shared its cost, the machine and the program with its modifications would be economical. There would, of course, have to be some customization of the order processing program for each division but this could be accomplished by building custom modules in the program. Also, if the Goods Acquisition System (GAS) being proposed for purchasing were to be run on the IBM 3083 instead of getting an IBM 4341 to run it, significant additional savings would result.

In late 1983, Mr. Howarth presented to the data processing steering committee a proposal that an IBM 3083E computer worth $3.8 million be acquired and that the Australian on-line order processing system become the standard for all of C-I-L, with the divisions being converted first and the wholly-owned subsidiaries later. There would then be one order processing system with special modules written for each business. As well, the goods acquisition system for purchasing would be run on the IBM 3083. "Eventually," Mr. Howarth said, "the businesses will do all their computing, with the exception of that for process control and engineering, on a central IBM machine operated by IR."

The proposal to centralize computer operations in C-I-L would, Mr. Howarth knew, meet with some resistance from the division general managers. With the exception of Industrial Chemicals and General Chemicals, most of the divisions were quite content with their current order processing systems and would see no need to change. Besides, with the new computer and all the programming to be done, the divisions' data processing costs would likely rise with no apparent benefits to them.

THE CASE OF PRINTCO FROM BEHIND THE TERMINAL: THE INSTITUTIONAL ORGANIZATION OF COMPUTING IN ORGANIZATIONS[1,2]

Rob Kling and Suzanne Iacono

PRINTCO is a medium-sized manufacturing firm of approximately 800 employees which designs, makes, and markets three types of medium-speed dot matrix line printers for the minicomputer and small business computer marketplace. They started shipping printers in 1975 and during the late 1970s maintained a fairly constant demand of 12,000 to 15,000 printers a year, despite market fluctuations. During the 1980s the firm has undergone tremendous growth, outperforming the competition, so that they are now the largest producer of dot matrix line printers.[3] In addition, an entirely new line of miniprinters was ready to go onto the market in early 1982. As a result of this recent growth and expanding operations, they acquired seven new buildings

---

[1]The case presented here is part of a larger research project in which field studies were undertaken at four manufacturing organizations with automated manufacturing computing systems. Material Requirements Planning (MRP) Systems were the core modules of the manufacturing computing systems in each of the organizations.

[2]Our data from PRINTCO are based on forty-four detailed interviews which were conducted with forty respondents in a variety of roles in different departments and at different levels of authority. Interviewing started with the central users and proceeded outward toward more peripheral users over an eighteen month period. We determined that we had completed interviewing when no other names were mentioned as people who had significant interactions or input into the manufacturing computing system.

[3]1982 sales were $65 million; 1981 sales were $50 million; 1980 sales were $37 million.

For ideas on analyzing cases like PRINTCO, see Rob Kling and Walt Scacchi, "The Web of Computing: Computer Technology as Social Organization," in *Advances in Computers*, edit by M. Yovits, vol. 21 (New York: Academic Press, 1982), pp. 1–90.

to accommodate increases in manufacturing and office space preferences in 1982.

PRINTCO did not have a data processing department when it started computing in 1975 on an IBM System 32. An accounting manager programmed all the financial systems. Data was entered by accounting staff who needed the output. The Material Control Department did not have an MRP* System for handling inventory and purchased material requirements. Instead, they did a simple explosion progression, gross-to-net, on the computer.

However, as PRINTCO grew, the manufacturing staff started having problems of inventory buildup. With their rudimentary inventory and scheduling system, the material controllers couldn't phase the timing of purchased parts properly or reschedule these purchases when manufacturing demands changed. In 1977, all the corporate officers attended a week-long seminar taught by one of the "gurus" of MRP systems. They became convinced that an MRP system would solve their problems so they purchased a package from a local vendor. They also created a data processing department which consisted of a manager/programmer and two data-entry staff.

The Manufacturing Division started hiring material control staff with MRP experience. The firm sent their managers and supervisors in material control, production control, purchasing, marketing, and accounting to seminars to learn about MRP. By 1978, the effects of the new MRP system were being felt: PRINTCO's staff were able to keep their inventory at acceptable levels and they could make timely adjustments to new forecasts.

Between 1975 and 1978 they had upgraded from an IBM System 32 to an IBM System 34. They had seven local CRTs in data processing and four terminals around the firm. Data processing had grown to include four programmers, one analyst, and the manager. A separate operations department, which worked two shifts, was added.

In 1979, a Marketing Master Production Scheduling (MMPS) system linking marketing's forecasting with the master scheduling process was brought up. Staff in marketing and manufacturing were in conflict as to the methods that would be used for ascertaining a production schedule. Manufacturing argued that marketing overforecasted and caused problems in production. This effort took two and a half years of meetings and negotiations with managers and staff in the two divisions before they could develop a satisfactory system for all.

The firm became more competitive in the marketplace by attempting to please new OEM customers with the addition of individual specifications in

---

*A material requirements planning (MRP) system is based on the fact that the demand for materials, parts, and components depends on the demand for an end product (here, a specific type of printer). At scheduled intervals, there is an "explosion" process driven by a master production schedule which determines purchased parts requirements and their due dates. Sufficient lead time is given so that parts will be available in production when needed but not so far in advance that there is costly inventory build up. The power of this system is its ability to take into account the dynamics of time and quantity for the production of many different but somewhat similar end items.

the printers. While they were still manufacturing three basic types of printers, many of them were unique configurations due to individual specifications. The timing of purchased parts became even more critical at this stage in the evolution of their manufacturing processes.

The manufacturing staff became troubled with MRP system problems that they did not anticipate. They were most bothered by the inability of the MRP system to track revision levels (the cut-out date of an "old" part and the cut-in date of the "new" one). The system only picked up the latest revision level for each part and would explode requirements so that all printers would be assembled with all parts at the latest revision level. These simultaneous multiple revisions in a product coexisted for reasons of cost, convenience, or reliability. Some revisions might be absolutely necessary to implement for all printers immediately (for example, in the case of a newly discovered unreliable part). Other parts might be phased in only when the old part ran out in stock.* Manual workarounds in the form of documentation and comment lines on reports had to be instituted in order to handle this situation. This presented problems because it caused extra work, and also because it increased the probability of error in purchasing the correct parts and building printers.

One of the senior material planners at PRINTCO reported that he wouldn't be needed if they had complete and accurate data; a clerk could do his job. Senior planners have the experience and the skill to identify which data are inaccurate. However, since the MRP system is dependent on completely accurate data, great efforts were expended to increase the level of accuracy to an acceptable level. The material manager reported that there were behind-the-scenes activities that keep the data accurate. These activities include staff education on the importance of timely updating of transactions and daily inventory counts. The stock manager reported that to arrive at a point where they had 79 percent inventory accuracy, required consistent training of the stockroom staff. They expected to attain 90 percent accuracy at their next bi-yearly inventory, due to their increased efforts and experience with daily inventory counts. At some point, attempts to increase data accuracy even further become too costly and not worth the time and effort. The data have become "socially acceptable" or trusted to be usable.

Another chronic problem existed in the purchasing department—the inability of the department to update the past-due dates of purchased parts in a timely manner. When purchased parts are late, the new arrival dates must be input into the MRP system to accurately reflect reality. Part of the problem was an insufficient number of clerks to do the job. A recent hiring freeze meant that no new clerks could be hired. Additional pressure was put on the existing clerks, but they were working in a backlogged situation in which

---

*Any single part might be up to revision level G, for example, in engineering, and only up to revision level C in production due to D and E being phase-in revisions. If another revision, say revision level H, is necessary immediately, a condition then exists where the part has been revised up to level H, but the manufacturing group has never implemented revision levels D, E, and F.

immediate crises were the high priority work and took precedence over some of the more routine updates. As a result, the past-due purchased parts records were not accurate and up-to-date. These errors reverberated throughout the system and users in other departments had to discipline themselves to double check data and not base decisions on computerized data alone. Since it was known throughout the organization that these errors existed, purchasing was generally seen as a weak link in the manufacturing computing operations. A general belief existed that the purchasing organization had to be restructured and tightened. (Eventually the purchasing manager was fired and the organization put under the direct control of the material vice president.)

Since they also lacked other manufacturing computing system modules such as allocation lists, lot-sizing, planned orders, and capacity planning, a group of senior officers (the senior vice president of manufacturing, the vice president of material control and his managerial staff, the data processing manager and his boss, the vice president of finance) started searching for more sophisticated MRP software. After six months of investigation by this informal committee they found a package that satisfied their preferences. It ran on a Data General minicomputer rather than on their IBM System 34. Because they wanted the software, they also decided to purchase the required hardware, a DG S350 Eclipse. The committee justified this decision by arguing that the DG S350 Eclipse had more capacity and could support the thirty terminals that they eventually wanted to install around the firm.*

The conversion was scheduled to be finished in one year, but it took much longer than was originally anticipated. The senior vice president of manufacturing reported that the committee neglected to follow through with a schedule after they made the decision to do the conversion. As a result, a year and a half later they were no further along in deriving any benefits from the new system than there were at the beginning. Morale was low in data processing; numerous problems seemed unsolvable: support for their system was not locally available and users around the firm were tired of waiting indefinitely to satisfy their preferences. The major data processing effort was always on the conversion and there was still no end in sight.

A data processing steering committee was formed to start guiding and directing the data processing manager, who was characterized by the senior vice president of manufacturing as being on a "downward spiral." The steering committee consisted of the senior vice president of manufacturing, the vice president of material control, the data processing manager, and the vice president of finance. They put the data processing manager on schedules, but it soon became evident that the conversion project was a failure. They needed someone to carry out the decision to dump the project, and started searching for a new data processing manager.

After six months of searching and interviewing, the steering committee

---

*The hardware cost $200 thousand, the software cost $30 thousand, and modifications cost between $50–100 thousand.

finally hired a data processing manager. He was their second choice, and even though he didn't have a strong technical background, they felt he had strong managerial capabilities which could benefit the department. Not surprisingly, one of the first decisions of the new data processing manager was to stop the conversion project. The members of the data processing steering committee were resigned to the loss of their investment in the software and the sale of the hardware. The data processing manager and the steering committee decided that they would continue working with the IBM System 34. They would enhance the MRP system as they could and possibly lease another System 34 if it was needed. They upgraded the disk and added core to the System 34. They added additional ports so that thirteen employees could log on simultaneously. The manager instituted several formal arrangements for data processing requests from users, and derived priorities for departmental work both for the short and long run from the direction and advice of the committee.

Despite the long and arduous work invested in hiring the new manager, the data processing steering committee was not satisfied with his progress. He focused his primary energies on the purchase of new and better computing equipment, an IBM System 38, and was not interested in starting the MRP system enhancement on the System 34. The steering committee wanted to see some improvements with the MRP system on their present equipment since they believed that they had been standing still for too long. Conflict between the manager and the other steering committee members heightened over time until he was fired after ten months.

The steering committee members did not want to search for another manager outside the firm. They promoted the manager of engineering services to be the operations services director, a new title for the data processing manager. Almost immediately, they decided to buy an IBM 4331 and then found MRP software which would satisfy their preferences.*

The major purpose of the conversion project had been to satisfy the preferences of manufacturing staff. Users in other departments had been instructed that they would have to wait until the new MRP system was up and running before their data processing requests could be fulfilled. Because the conversion project took longer than was anticipated, staff in other departments began searching for other ways to fulfill their computing preferences.

Several departments obtained microcomputers from test equipment cast

---

*The entire firm was reorganized in 1982. The Data Processing Department was moved from finance to manufacturing and was renamed Operations Services. The senior vice president of manufacturing was retitled senior operations vice president. His organization was expanded by the inclusion of operations services. The vice president of material was retitled manufacturing vice president and the three plant managers were put directly under him instead of under the operations senior vice president, as they had originally been. Thus, his organization was also expanded. The director of operations services was located at the level of the other vice presidents under the operations senior vice president. The director's organization was expanded to include six specific groups with managers or supervisors reporting to him. The members of the data processing steering committee who had been "successful" in coming up with solutions to data processing problems were rewarded in that their organizational reach was expanded.

off by other departments and upgraded them into usable computing equipment. This was possible because of the availability of skilled staff to perform these tasks. Because of the problems with the data processing department, the steering committee allowed departments to purchase additional LSI-11s out of their capital funds. Soon there was an installed base of about six to ten LSI-11s scattered around the organization. One staff member in test equipment became the informal expert in operating, programming, and using the microcomputers.

The data processing steering committee did not become aware of the proliferation of decentralized computing arrangements until late in 1981. They began counting the number of LSI-11s currently in use in the organization and were shocked to learn that there was over $1 million worth of microcomputing equipment dispersed throughout the organization. The data processing steering committee wanted to control this proliferation of microcomputers. They brought the LSI-11 informal expert into their group and created a new LSI-11 steering committee under their auspices.

PRINTCO

Develop a plan for PRINTCO to exert control over its data processing operations. The plan should include the following components:

1 How does information processing fit with the goals and objectives of the firm?

2 How can data processing best support the business?

3 What are the hardware and software needs? How will they change over time?

4 What are the high priority applications for the firm?

5 How should PRINTCO set priorities and choose new applications to undertake?

6 How should maintenance requests be handled?

7 How should management control the ongoing operations of computers in the firm?

8 What is the best organization structure and reporting relationship for data processing at PRINTCO?

9 What committees might be appropriate for helping to manage information processing?

SYSTEMS DEVELOPMENT

AMERICAN PRESIDENT LINES, LTD.: THE CMS-I DECISION (A)

On Saturday, December 5, 1981, a four-person study team from American President Lines, Ltd. (APL) gathered for its final meeting in Hong Kong, halfway around the world from APL's Oakland, California, headquarters. After visiting eight APL ports of call in Asia, the team needed to decide whether it favored centralizing or decentralizing the company's equipment tracking and management system. The team's recommendations would be presented to APL senior management on Monday. For its final deliberations, the team had been joined by four other people: a consultant who had worked closely with APL top management in the past, the company's vice president for information systems, its director of equipment management, and a representative of the vendor which supplied most of APL's information services.

The audience would be larger than the team had expected, because several APL managing directors and vice presidents who had not initially been invited to the presentation had decided to attend. Part of the widespread interest in the team's report arose from the appearance of a contradiction between the centralized solution favored by some, and APL's announced corporate commitment to a decentralized organizational structure.

Pat Morrison, vice president of APL's information systems department (ISD), had been on the job for less than six months. He was now in Hong Kong to discuss an issue which had achieved such high visibility within the

Copyright © 1982 by the President and Fellows of Harvard College
This case was prepared by Michael Vitale under the direction of James Cash as the basis of class discussion rather than to illustrate either effective or ineffective handling of an administrative situation. Reprinted by permission of the Harvard Business School.

company that its outcome could have a significant impact on users' overall perceptions of ISD.

Bill Hubbard, the senior vice president for operations who would preside on Monday, wanted to reach a decision before the study team left Asia. The question of centralization versus decentralization had been discussed within APL for years, and attempts had been made to develop both kinds of systems to handle equipment tracking and management. Recognizing that there were good arguments on both sides of the question, but feeling that continued vacillation would be counterproductive, Hubbard thought that the time for a decision was at hand.

For the study team, the December 7 presentation would be the culmination of a month of steady travel and hard work. Until now, they had not taken a formal vote on which type of system to recommend. Several members of the team had strong reservations about each of the options which had been developed in the course of their study. In less than 24 hours, the three secretaries who had been asked to come in on Sunday would arrive to begin typing the team's final report.

COMPANY BACKGROUND

APL, a wholly-owned subsidiary of the Natomas Company, has annual sales exceeding $500 million and operates scheduled ocean cargo service between the Pacific Coast of the United States and twenty-three ports in North and South Asia (see Exhibit 1). APL's routes are among the most competitive in the world, served by some twenty major carriers, including the national flag fleets of Korea, Hong Kong, and Taiwan. Although the amount of freight shipped between the United States and Asia has increased significantly in recent years, shipping capacity had grown even more rapidly, leading to a highly competitive market. In 1980 APL had about 11 percent of the containers that travel its routes and operated below capacity both westbound and eastbound.

The company transports the majority of its freight in large containers which can be hauled on a special truck chassis or on a specially-designed railroad flat car. In 1981, seventeen of APL's twenty-two vessels were full containerships which carried all of their freight in containers stowed in their holds and stacked on their decks. At that time APL owned approximately 28,000 containers, 11,000 chassis, and 550 motor generator sets, having a total replacement value of approximately $350 million, and could obtain additional equipment on short-term leases when needed. In 1980, APL moved slightly more than 136,000 loaded containers and thousands of empties.

The company's ports of call varied widely in the amount of traffic handled. San Pedro, California, and Seattle, Washington, two of APL's North American gateways, handled about 55,000 containers each, while Oakland, the third gateway, handled about half as many. Among APL's Asia ports, Yokohama, Keelung, Hong Kong, and Kobe each loaded and discharged more than

25,000 containers. Singapore, Manila, and Kaohsiung handled between 7500 and 10,000 containers, while Bombay, Dubai, Jakarta, and Surabaya each handled fewer than 5000.

APL grew through a series of mergers and consolidations dating back to 1848. Its predecessor was acquired by the United States in 1938 and was renamed American President Lines, Ltd. In 1952, management and ownership of APL was assumed jointly by the Signal Company and a group which later became the Natomas Company. In 1954, in a final consolidation on the road to APL's current structure, APL and American Mail Lines (AML) combined to offer freight and passenger service throughout the world, retaining the APL name.

Natomas had in 1956 approximately $3 million in cash, a listing on the New York Stock Exchange, extensive land holdings, and the remnants of its declining intitial business: four gold dredges. At this time, APL was seeking funds for expansion and the acquisition by Natomas of a controlling interest in APL seemed mutually beneficial. During the 1960s, earnings from APL operations helped offset marginal performance in gold dredging and facilitated redirection of the parent company's interests from minerals development to energy, and petroleum in particular. By 1972 Natomas' oil earnings had surpassed earnings from consolidated shipping operations.

While oil profits rose, APL's net income dropped steadily from its 1960 level (see Exhibit 2). From 1970 to 1972, APL moved rapidly toward containerization, which some of its competitors had pioneered in the mid-1960s. By the mid-1970s APL's poor performance led Natomas management to move toward divestiture of the ailing shipping company. Dorman Commons, president and CEO of Natomas and CEO of APL, asked instead whether additional investments or operating changes might improve APL's results. Moreover, Commons decided that Natomas should determine APL's market value before offering it for sale. Natomas hired a Boston-area consulting firm, Temple, Barker & Sloane, Inc. (TBS), to evaluate APL. TBS was asked to estimate the shipping company's current market value, and to identify any short-term investments which might improve this value.

The TBS 1977 report recommended that APL not be sold, and suggested some operating changes at APL which could make the firm more profitable without a large additional investment by Natomas. Natomas took a more active role in APL management, and began to view APL as a transportation company, not merely as a shipping line. Natomas management wanted broadly-experienced general managers as APL leaders. In 1978 Commons moved W. B. (Bruce) Seaton from Natomas to the presidency of APL and hired W. B. (Bill) Hubbard to manage operations. In January 1980, Brandt Brooksby, vice president of finance at Natomas, moved to APL as senior vice president of finance and administration (see Exhibit 3).

This new management team began to make tactical and operational changes. Round-the-world service was eliminated, allowing APL's ships to be redeployed into the Pacific Basin, the largest and fastest-growing market in

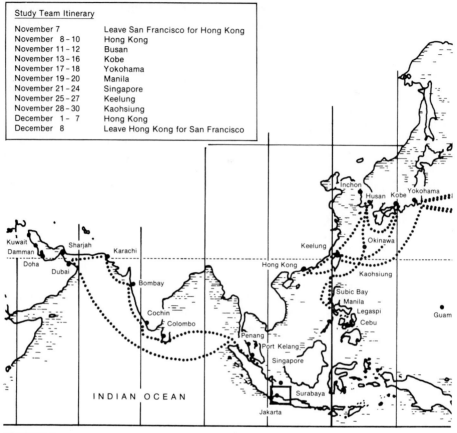

Study Team Itinerary

November 7	Leave San Francisco for Hong Kong
November 8–10	Hong Kong
November 11–12	Busan
November 13–16	Kobe
November 17–18	Yokohama
November 19–20	Manila
November 21–24	Singapore
November 25–27	Keelung
November 28–30	Kaohsiung
December 1–7	Hong Kong
December 8	Leave Hong Kong for San Francisco

EXHIBIT 1
Routes, American President Lines, Ltd.

the world. The functionally centralized organization which had prevailed before 1977 was decentralized in order to provide greater flexibility and sensitivity to local markets. The company remained a series of cost centers, with neither costs nor revenues allocated to individual units. Local managers worked within financial budgets and headcount quotas established in Oakland. "What managerial autonomy really meant," one observer commented later, "was freedom of speech—it was now O.K. to complain about the restrictions from Oakland."

Gaining a significant local presence in overseas ports was intended to help the company attract and train aggressive young managers, as well as bringing APL closer to its customers. Local managers were encouraged to make decisions at the lowest possible level and were given a significant degree of operating autonomy. Most of APL's country managers in Asia were expatriate Americans who were generally regarded as sharp, aggressive leaders. APL's

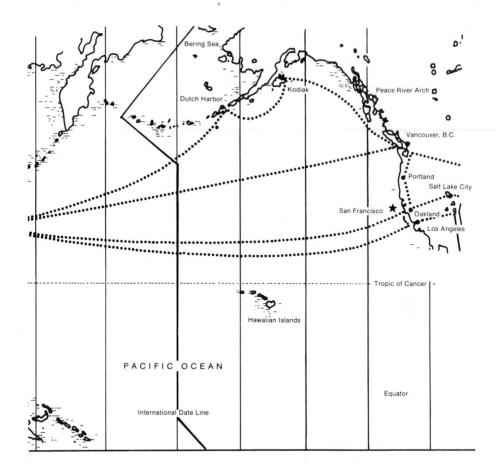

North American managers were encouraged by company policy and by top management to serve two- to five-year tours of duty in Asia. Bruce Seaton, in particular, regarded such job rotation as very beneficial in promoting cross-cultural communication and understanding within the company. APL's senior management made frequent visits to the company's Asian ports.

APL hired specialists from throughout the transportation industry and began the development of an integrated land-sea container shipping network. This "intermodal" system soon became one of the most advanced in existence. At the same time, APL successfully implemented efficiency measures which dramatically reduced its operating costs. APL's earnings between 1977 and 1981 exceeded those of the previous thirty years combined.

Rates for much of APL's cargo were established by Transpacific rate conferences in which most major shipping companies participated. In exchange for an operating subsidy from the U.S. Government, APL bought American-made vessels, had them repaired in American shipyards, and staffed them with American crews. APL had higher costs, even with the subsidy, than

EXHIBIT 2
American President Lines, Ltd. and Subsidiaries.

Five Year Summary of Operations and Financial Review

For the Years Ended December 31	1980	1979	1978	1977	1976
	(Dollars In Thousands)				
Operating revenue	$576,299	$498,614	$417,001	$359,883	$293,665
Operating expenses	528,174	416,079	350,756	324,022	280,041
Operating income	48,125	82,535	66,245	35,861	13,624
% of operating revenue	8%	17%	16%	10%	5%
Operating-differential subsidy	67,489*	33,919	26,561	29,257	36,828
Gain (Loss) on disposition of ships	492	(3,967)	(210)	(2,633)	4,450
Income before depreciation, interest and administrative expenses	116,106	112,487	92,596	62,485	54,902
Administrative and general	28,096	22,950	13,556	10,111	8,558
Depreciation and amortization	28,879	22,909	20,765	20,948	20,066
Interest expense	11,488	8,045	9,080	9,632	10,423
Income before income taxes	47,643	58,583	49,195	21,794	15,855
Provision for income taxes	(3,400)	(3,986)	(3,000)	(3,418)	(2,750)
Cumulative accounting change		3,420			
Net income	$ 44,243	$ 58,017	$ 46,195	$ 18,376	$ 13,105
% of operating revenue	8%	12%	11%	5%	4%
Revenue tons in thousands	7,026	5,872	5,267	4,947	4,125
Capital expenditures	$102,133	$108,206	$ 19,358	$ 16,741	$ 15,577
Working capital provided from operations	$ 72,978	$ 80,758	$ 70,223	$ 41,284	$ 33,548
Financial position at year end:					
Cash and temporary investments	$ 38,843	$ 47,684	$ 66,180	$ 56,965	$ 25,324
Working capital	$ 2,563	$ (6,482)	$ (6,036)	$ 16,112	$ 9,061
Property and equipment, net	$345,955	$273,331	$205,700	$209,219	$216,606
Total assets	$572,972	$454,590	$368,819	$343,690	$320,238
Long-term debt, including current portion	$210,704	$134,122	$120,336	$140,166	$142,988
Stockholders' equity	$252,795	$208,552	$165,535	$133,075	$121,590
Employees at year end	2,643	2,591	2,328	2,012	2,121
Number of active ships:					
Containerships	17	17	15	15	17
Breakbulk	5	5	5	5	5

Note: Effective January 1, 1979, APL changed its method of accounting for operating revenue and expenses. 1978 net income would not be significantly different if reported under the revenue loaded method. The effect of the change in accounting method on net income for years 1976 and 1977 is not determinable.

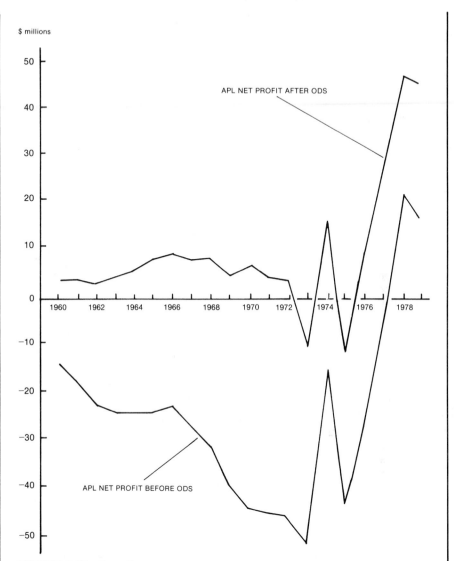

EXHIBIT 2 (Continued)
APL Net Income After and Before Operating Differential Subsidy, 1960–1979 (*American President Lines*).

   Certain reclassifications have been made on the Consolidated Statement of Income for 1978 and on the Five Year Summary of Operations and Financial Review for 1976 through 1979 in order to conform to the 1980 presentation. The reclassifications have no effect on the previously reported net income or retained earnings.
   1976 data has also been restated to give effect to leases capitalized in 1977.
*Includes prior year subsidy adjustments totaling $25.0 million in 1980.
   Like most U.S. ship lines, APL received an Operating Differential Subsidy from the U.S. Maritime Administration. In return, APL accepted regulation of its trade routes, used American crews, and purchased U.S.-built vessels.

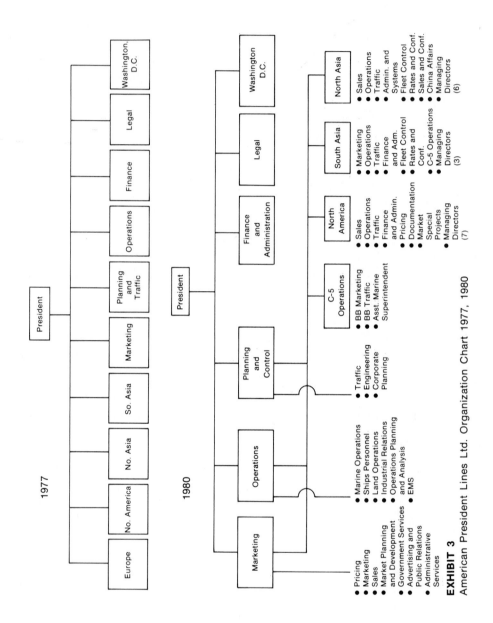

EXHIBIT 3
American President Lines Ltd. Organization Chart 1977, 1980

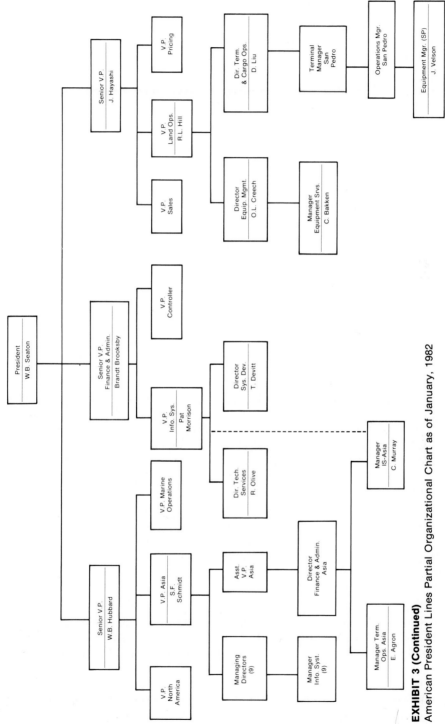

EXHIBIT 3 (Continued)
American President Lines Partial Organizational Chart as of January, 1982

foreign lines, and did not anticipate ever becoming a low-cost competitor. The company competed by offering superior service, including its complete intermodal service and weekly sailings. APL also attempted to focus its marketing on shippers of high-revenue cargo.

INFORMATION REQUIREMENTS FOR EQUIPMENT TRACKING

Bill Hubbard described the special information needs of a maritime company.

> When you consider the large number of different organizations potentially responsible for a shipment, the problem becomes non-trivial. It has been our experience that most of APL's customers want to deal with only one organization, so we are forced to monitor the location and movement of a container regardless of whose possession it may happen to be in—the railroad's, a trucker's, a dock agent's, etc. Since we are not and can never be the low-cost competitor, the quality and efficiency of our service is a key success factor.

Brandt Brooksby added:

> Any company must have basic administrative support systems, and we are no different. But there are two critical information requirements for APL which are unique for our industry and competitive thrust. We must know where our containers are, and where they should be going; and we must know what merchandise is in a given container.

To address the question of service, Hubbard hired Rick Hill, with whom he had worked at another shipping company, and made him responsible for APL's West Coast operations. In January 1978, Hubbard and Hill hired Larry Creech and gave him overall authority to manage APL's "equipment"—that is, its collection of owned and leased containers, chassis, and motor-generator sets. Creech had risen rapidly in his former company, where he had worked for Hill, holding nine different positions, including worldwide director of perishable cargo, between the time he joined the company in 1966 and the time he grew bored and decided to leave in 1977.

At the time Creech arrived, APL's information services were being provided by outside suppliers, mainly Electronic Data Systems, Inc. (EDS). Creech analyzed the eleven equipment-management reports which EDS was producing for APL. At a meeting with the EDS sales representative, Creech threw copies of nine of the reports into a wastebasket, declared them to be useless, and refused to pay for them in the future. The nine reports, which had been produced as part of APL's Container Management System (CMS), were no longer generated; EDS' charges to the equipment-management area dropped by 80 percent as a result.

"I believed CMS would work," Creech said later, "but I thought it needed fixing. I felt that the situation was out of control. Anyone could request a new report, or a change to an existing report, and EDS would do it. Since we were paying EDS for programming time and for computer time, they had no incentive to control the changes." Creech ordered EDS to make no further modifications to CMS without his personal approval, then he completely evaluated the system. Two years later, Creech was receiving only six equipment management reports, including redesigned versions of the two which had escaped the wastebasket. Creech felt at that point that APL's equipment reporting system gave the company a significant competitive advantage.

Beyond identifying problems with the EDS reports, Creech recognized the need for tighter equipment control and better tracking. He insisted that he personally sign all leases for additional equipment, and he hired and trained a staff to manage the equipment APL already had. Equipment costs, which were one-third of APL's operating expenses in 1978, fell to 9 percent by 1981.

INFORMATION SERVICES AT APL

Following the 1954 merger of American Mail Lines and American President Lines, the company continued to operate two separate data centers. The original AML center, in Seattle, used Burroughs equipment, while APL had IBM gear in Oakland. In 1967, the AML center acquired the Container Management System (CMS) software package from the Port of Seattle. CMS, a batch system designed to run on Burroughs hardware, was modified somewhat for AML's needs and then installed in the Seattle data center. Major enhancements, including conversion to on-line operation, were designed and initiated in the early 1970s. At that time APL's competitors were working on similar systems.

By early 1975, APL's management had become increasingly frustrated with the political and technical difficulties of combining the company's two data centers and hired Electronic Data Systems (EDS) of Dallas to provide information systems resources on a facilities management basis. Under EDS, the changes to CMS which had been underway were completed on the Burroughs hardware in Seattle. The modified package was then converted to run in the EDS environment, which consisted of IBM operating software, some special EDS modules, and IBM hardware. EDS closed the APL data centers, and the APL in-house information systems staff was reduced to a liaison group.

As part of its 1977 review of APL for Natomas, TBS was asked to evaluate CMS. Bud Mathaisel, the TBS staff member responsible for studying CMS, found that widespread acceptance and use of CMS was being delayed by the system's rigid screen formats and weak data editing; that the accuracy and timeliness of CMS data were poor, despite the time and money which had been spent on modifying the software; and that CMS was implemented only in North America, while traffic—and problems—were increasing most rapidly in Asia. Mathaisel said, "The exclusive use of CMS in North America was like using a magnifying glass and precision surgery for an area of the world which was not the real trouble spot."

Mathaisel recommended that a completely new system, which he called "CMS-II," be developed over the next several years. Centered around a database containing information about shipments, vessels, and containers, CMS-II would provide equipment management capabilities as part of an integrated management information system. CMS-II would be used for booking cargo, accounting and billing for that cargo, and equipment scheduling as well as for container management. Packaged database management software would be used to access the central file. Meanwhile, the company should reestablish an in-house data processing department and should undertake some immediate modifications to the existing system, which was thereafter called "CMS-I." APL accepted the TBS report, and shortly thereafter the company hired an information systems director and chartered him to implement TBS' recommendations.

Beginning in 1978, modifications to CMS-I were made by EDS personnel. Mathaisel had gathered a list of suggested changes during his meetings with CMS-I users; other suggestions came from APL management and from EDS itself. The enhanced system remained centralized, but on-line data entry and inquiry were simplified through new user interfaces. All existing CMS-I reports were redesigned, and standards for testing and documentation were established. APL's North American offices installed additional CRTs and printers for use with CMS-I. Programming and operating personnel were located in Oakland; other APL offices in North America were at this time not allowed to have their own computers.

CMS-I eventually became the standard system used by APL to manage and control its equipment in North America. The system contained a record of each container, chassis, and motor-generator set owned or leased by APL. Equipment acquisition, allocation, tracking, and disposal were all handled through CMS-I. The basic data on each piece of equipment included its type, size, identification number, and ownership. As equipment moved through APL's intermodal network, CMS-I recorded its origin, destination, current location, and status; the position where a piece of equipment was stowed was also recorded if it was at sea. APL's North American offices entered equipment movement data via CRTs, while data from Asia was sent via telex to Oakland, where it was entered into CMS-I.

CMS-I had been designed to track container status in North America move by move, but once a container reached Asia CMS-I kept track only of the country in which the container was located. (For example, CMS-I would record that a given container was in Japan, but not whether it was full, empty, damaged, at a shipper's site, or so on. Indications of the latter activities were available for containers in North America.) This design had initially seemed appropriate in light of the relative simplicity of APL's Asian operations, but it meant that CMS-I could not be used in Asia for detailed container tracking, as it was used in North America.

Meanwhile, APL's emphasis on decentralized operations and the generally difficult telecommunications environment in parts of Asia had led some of the company's Asian ports to develop independent information systems using IBM System 34 computers. There was little consistency among these information systems. For equipment management, Hong Kong and Singapore had completely automated systems, while Korea and the Philippines used cards to track equipment and the computer to produce summary reports. In Japan, Kobe used a computer system and Yokohama a manual system, while in Taiwan there were two manual card systems for containers and a computer-based system to track chassis. Even the automated systems required a great deal of manual intervention, and the information produced was designed for operational rather than analytical use. There were no uniform standards for software or documentation, and each of the local equipment tracking systems had a unique set of features and limitations. Several locations had reached the capacity of their first System 34 and had requested authorization to obtain another.

The head of APL's rejuvenated information systems department was aware of the shortcomings of CMS-I in Asia, but he did not believe that enhancing the system was worthwhile. He felt that CMS-II, which would be able to do the tracking needed for Asia as well as for North America, would be finished within three years. An in-house technical evaluation of CMS-I in 1978 determined that the system could not be used as part of CMS-II; its pre-data-base design and the use of nonstandard file access and teleprocessing techniques made CMS-I an unsuitable base for a system which was expected to last well into the next decade. Further investment in CMS-I did not seem appropriate given the older system's expected lifetime.

As a followup to its 1977 report, APL asked TBS in early 1980 to reevaluate CMS. This time Mathaisel found a widely-used, well-supported system which formed the backbone of APL's North American operations. On the other hand, little progress had been made on CMS-II. A state-of-the-art distributed system using a central computer in California and System 34s in Asia and North America had been designed. The equipment to support it had been ordered and in some cases shipped. But Mathaisel's evaluation soon convinced him that this new system would never work. The design called for a hierarchically distributed system in which an unofficial central file, maintained on a mainframe host computer, would be updated from official files distributed to the System 34s. However, many of the details which had been deferred during the macro-design phase turned out to have a major impact on the cost and performance of the planned system. Issues of data synchronization, integrity, and consistency had not been addressed. Particular problems would arise when operations were interrupted, for example by a communications line failure. The severe shortage of trained technical staff, including people to maintain computer hardware, in much of Asia also raised questions about the distributed approach. The design for CMS-II, an ambitious attempt to move APL from its traditionally cautious approach toward information technology to a state-of-the-art system, was abandoned and work began afresh.

Ultimately the controversial design of CMS-II, and a number of other issues which caused concern among APL management, brought about the departure of the head of ISD. Mathaisel became acting vice president in charge of APL's Information Systems Department. He set out to rebuild ISD's somewhat demoralized staff and to continue APL's move to in-house facilities. He hired the head of the EDS team working at APL to take charge of software development, and a long-time IBM employee to manage technical services, including operations. Pat Morrison was hired as vice president in mid-1981. After eight years with IBM, Morrison had founded a Dallas-based service bureau which designed and operated a world-wide reservation system for a major hotel chain and a rental car company. Morrison's department had been without a full-time leader for some sixteen months. (See Exhibit 4 for an ISD organizational chart.)

By late 1981, APL had a new, large data center in San Mateo, some thirty miles from Oakland. The center, which was staffed largely by employees of a facilities management firm, contained two IBM 3033 computers and a network control center for APL's data communications. CMS-I was still running at EDS, but plans were underway to move the system to the APL center, whether or not CMS-I was extended to Asia. Once there, the software would be maintained during 1982 by EDS staff members. The move was intended to save APL money and, more importantly, to increase its control over an application which was seen as increasingly critical to the company. After the San Mateo facility was opened, EDS was retained to maintain and enhance eight applications, including CMS-I, which the vendor had written. APL planned to be completely independent of EDS for computer processing by the end of 1982.

CMS-II was scheduled for initial field testing in mid-1982, and the CMS-II project leader anticipated replacing CMS-I by 1983 or 1984. Data on container movements in Asia was now being telexed to Hong Kong and Singapore, where operators at terminals entered it directly into CMS-I; a pair of 9600-baud lines connected Hong Kong to Oakland. An interface between CMS-I and the Bill of Lading Information Processing System (BLIPS) enabled APL to track a shipment based on information about the freight, as well as on information about the container.

CMS-I FOR ASIA

The development schedule for CMS-II was slowed by reevaluations of earlier decisions about hardware and data base management software, as well as by changes in priorities for various parts of the new system. As a result, some of APL's headquarters staff proposed that CMS-I be modified to meet Asian needs as well as North American, then used in Asia until CMS-II became operational. Rick Hill, who by late 1981 had become APL's vice president for land operations, noted that CMS-I gave North American managers early warning of problems and opportunities arising from equipment distribution. For example, in anticipation of an excess of inbound containers a regional manager might be able to find marginal outbound freight to fill some of the excess containers, which would otherwise have to be shipped out empty.

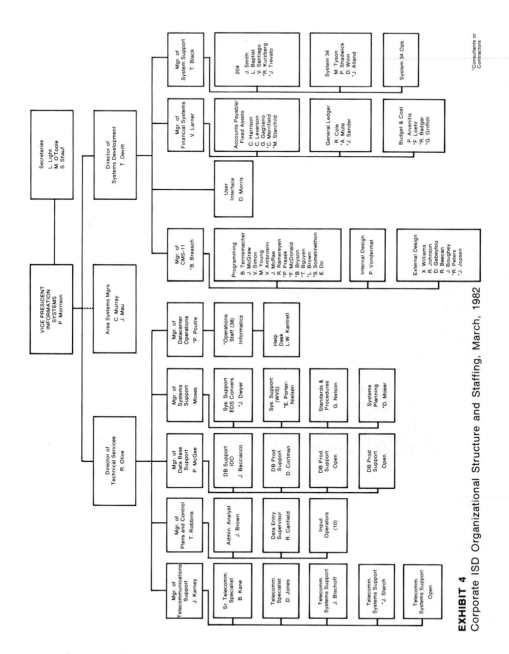

EXHIBIT 4

Corporate ISD Organizational Structure and Staffing, March, 1982

*Consultants or Contractors

117

Without CMS-I, an Asian manager was much less likely to see this kind of situation developing in time to turn it to the company's advantage.

Larry Creech, who as director of equipment management reported to Hill, noted that extending CMS-I to Asia would also provide APL headquarters with an important planning tool by making assets more visible on a real-time basis, both to the company's managers and to its bankers. This, he believed, would lower APL's borrowing costs. Creech insisted that it was essential to have up-to-the-minute information available on-line at all times. Moreover, the telecommunications network required for CMS-I could serve as a means of communication with APL's far-flung ports, some of which were not yet reached by a voice-grade telephone line. Creech pointed out that even in APL's decentralized environment some things, such as the format of a bill of lading, were absolutely standardized. Container tracking was a totally *internal* function, and the Asian environment posed no fundamentally new problems. Creech argued that an equipment management system should be seen as a corporate service, provided to the ports in the interest of companywide coordination, and not as a means of centralized operational control.

In contrast to headquarters managers such as Hill and Creech, APL's Asian managers were generally opposed to the expansion of CMS-I. Some countries and regions had developed equipment tracking systems on their own, and although these systems could not communicate with each other or with APL's central computer, they were tailored to meet local needs. In many cases, locally-developed systems were heavily integrated with other key applications, such as cash collection, sales reporting, trucker authorizations, and container maintenance and repair. These integrated systems adequately met local needs, and the additional work required to install and use CMS-I would bring few direct benefits in return. The Asian managers took considerable pride in their systems, which APL and Natomas management had in the past described as "very effective" and "state of the art," and viewed them as proof of the virtues of the company's emphasis on decentralization.

Asian managers also objected to the costs of running CMS-I, which would be assessed against their budgets. They noted that in many parts of Asia clerical labor to track equipment manually was far less expensive than a telephone line to Hong Kong or Singapore. Communications between ports in Asia could be handled adequately, according to some managers, by APL's existing low-speed teletype network. Although they had not been kept up to date on recent modifications to CMS-I, many Asian managers had reviewed the system in 1979–1980 and felt that it would not meet their needs.

Pat Morrison viewed the situation as a "classic" centralization versus decentralization struggle. He did not wish to become involved at such an early stage of his tenure with the company. Morrison therefore waited for direction from the ISD Steering Committee. (Chaired by Brandt Brooksby, who attended and led its monthly meetings, the committee included Morrison and five of APL's six senior vice presidents.) The committee asked Morrison to prepare an economic justification for the expansion of CMS-I to

Asia. He declined, on the grounds that ISD's proper role at APL was to provide service, not to justify new application systems or to act as a referee when contention arose between user departments.

Bill Hubbard felt that he should take a leadership role in the company's decision making on CMS-I, and wanted to get an independent assessment of required changes and potential impact of the modified system. Morrison proposed that Bud Mathaisel spend six weeks in the early fall of 1981 travelling to each of APL's Asian ports, gathering the necessary data. Mathaisel was interested in helping APL develop a general methodology and framework for addressing similar situations in the future. He therefore suggested the formation of a study team consisting of himself, an Oakland user of CMS-I, an Asian user, an EDS representative, and Larry Creech.

When they learned about the proposed study, APL's Asian managers requested that the team be augmented with employees from their part of the world. After numerous tentative membership lists were prepared, a four-person team was chartered to carry out the study:

Chuck Bakken, age 42, had been with APL since September, 1978. Bakken had worked for Creech at another shipping line and now reported to him at APL. As manager of equipment services, Bakken served as a liaison between equipment operators in the field and the information systems group. Bakken was generally regarded as APL's most expert user of CMS-I, which he described as "my whole thrust in life."

Earl Agron, age 32, joined APL in 1974 after graduating from the U.S. Merchant Marine Academy and receiving an M.B.A. from Northeastern University. He had worked in operations in New Jersey and Oakland, and was currently the manager of equipment control for north Asia. Agron had both administrative and operational duties, including the repositioning of containers and the implementation of equipment leasing decisions.

Joe Velson, age 30, was the equipment manager in APL's terminal in San Pedro, California. He reported to the local manager of operations, who in turn reported to the terminal manager. Velson had day-to-day responsibility for equipment movements in San Pedro.

Chuck Murray, age 35, was APL's Asian information systems manager. He had worked for APL for four and a half years, the last three in Asia. He reported to Richard Powell, the vice president for finance and administration in Asia, who also was located in Hong Kong. Murray had dotted-line relationships to ISD in Oakland and to the local data processing managers in Asia. His role was to coordinate local and corporate goals in order to facilitate effective and efficient systems development. He spent about 50 percent of his time travelling to the Asian ports, and met with the Asian data processing managers as a group three times a year.

The team was to travel around Asia for about three weeks, ending in Taiwan in late November. There they would meet with Creech and Mathaisel, who were to remain in the United States until then. They would be joined by EDS team leader Dave Bilodeau, and by Michael Diaz, APL's Taiwan manager.

After gathering information in Taiwan, the entire group would move on to Hong Kong, where they would be joined by Pat Morrison and Bill Hubbard.

THE STUDY

The study team made extensive formal plans for the methodology of their work. They sent a memo to Asian managers describing the purpose of their visit and the CMS-I system as it then existed. The team also distributed to each manager a detailed questionnaire to be filled out in advance and to be used as a guide for their interviews. The team agreed to share note-taking duties on a rotating basis. At night they would review their notes and the questionnaire to see what questions should be asked on the following day. Before leaving each country, the team would write a report about that location's needs and preferences.

The team began in Korea, where they spent the first day looking at the container yard, the offices, and other physical facilities. The next day Chuck Bakken introduced the team to a group of local employees and described the purpose of their visit; Bakken continued to play this role, which he later described as "the colonel," throughout the study. When the team asked for questions, there were very few. The Koreans seemed to agree that extending CMS-I to Asia was the best course, but the team sensed that they had not uncovered their hosts' true feelings about the matter. In their hotel that night, the team decided that their presentation had intimidated the Koreans. In subsequent visits to other ports, the team wrote "NO DECISION HAS BEEN MADE YET" at the top of the blackboards or flipcharts used for their presentations.

The team's Korean experience soon developed into a pattern. They spent the first part of each visit on a tour of the physical facilities to identify any constraints which might be imposed by unique local conditions. Later Chuck Bakken opened and moderated a discussion with the local staff, at the end of which the team would ask for a recommendation for the type of equipment management system that would best fit that location's needs. Without exception, the local staffs recommended the System 34.

The team was particularly interested in talking with the data processing manager and the equipment control supervisor in each port. Like all of APL's Asian staff below the country manager level, the local data processing managers were English-speaking Asians. Each reported to the vice president of finance and administration for his or her country, with a dotted-line relationship to Chuck Murray and a close working relationship with the country manager. Typically the data processing staff included one to three programmers assisted by operators and data entry clerks, although in some cases the data processing manager performed all of these tasks. The difficulty of finding and retaining staff varied from country to country, but in most areas personnel were at least as scarce as in the United States.

The equipment control supervisors had to balance the needs of local customers, the regional manager, and Larry Creech's staff in Oakland. "Without a worldwide information system, there are lots of games that people can play with containers," one observer remarked. "For example, 'I plan to use those containers right away!' 'Those containers are out at customer sites being loaded,' or even 'Those need repair.' If CMS-I is extended to Asia, the Oakland staff will know exactly how many containers are in each port and what their status is."

Until recently, the equipment control supervisors had reported to Creech, with a dotted-line relationship to the local manager. The company's decentralized operating philosophy had led it to a reorganization, after which the equipment control supervisors reported directly to the local managers, with a dotted line to Creech in Oakland.

Members agreed that for the most part the team got along extremely well. "Occasionally someone would start to rant and rave," Bakken commented later, "but the next morning he would apologize and things would be back to normal. There were no recriminations or personality analyses." Members of the group, particularly Velson and Agron, discussed their somewhat different philosophies of equipment management and control, but the team did not attempt to reach a consensus before the end of their trip. The team managed itself democratically, although Bakken as the oldest and longest-term employee played the leading role during presentations and meetings. Looking back on his interaction with the team during the final portion of the study, EDS' Dave Bilodeau described the group's style as "professional, with a lot of interaction and teamwork."

ALTERNATIVES

By the time the team reached Hong Kong, the options seemed clear: (1) APL could extend the current version of CMS-I to Asia; (2) one of the locally-developed System 34-based packages could be modified as necessary; or (3) a combination of centralized processing via CMS-I, modified to provide files to the local System 34s, and decentralized processing, using the local System 34s, could be adopted. (See Exhibit 5 for a diagram of the final option.)

In all cases, the system was to be installed in Taiwan, Hong Kong, Japan (two ports), Singapore, Korea, and the Philippines. The first installation was to take place three to six months after the decision, the next three installations within nine months, and the final installations within a year. One-time costs were estimated at $81,826 for the System 34 approach (option 2), $260,762 for a modified and extended CMS-I (option 3); recurring annual charges were estimated at $478,044 and $969,948, respectively (see Exhibit 6). The higher costs for the CMS-I approach were due to increased needs for software development, training, data communications (including an additional backup telecommunications line to Korea), and processing.

The team reported, "CMS-I does not require the performance of functions or the capture of data that could not be required by any standard equipment

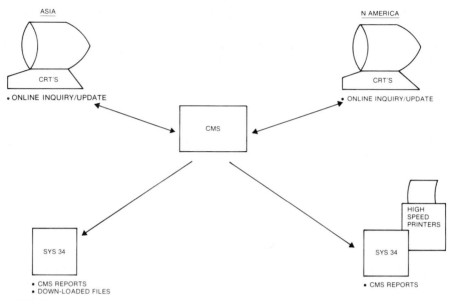

EXHIBIT 5
Equipment Control Schematic of Downloading CMS-I Data to Regional System 34

management system." Response time at a CRT for a CMS-I system was not expected to be significantly different from response time for a System 34 system, and with the addition of backup lines a CMS-I system was expected to be "almost as reliable." The use of a CMS-I system would not result in the reduction of any local hardware. Any standard system would require some changes in procedures at the Asian ports, but under the assumption that a computer-based system would replace manual systems the study team concluded that, overall, many redundant record-keeping steps could be eliminated.

The first option, use of the existing CMS-I, was rejected because that system did not have all the functions and reports required by the Asian regions, and because CMS-I was down for maintenance on Monday mornings, a crucial part of the Asian operations schedule. Other alternatives, including a so-called Asian solution using IBM 4300-series machines to replace some of the System 34s, were discarded as too time-consuming. APL was about to launch the first of three new C-9 containerships, the largest ever built in the United States. With its load of over 1200 containers, the C-9 would place new demands on all of APL's information systems. In addition, APL had heard that Japan was about to begin enforcing an existing law which restricted the height of containers allowed on the country's roads. Bill Hubbard felt strongly that the importance of meeting this deadline was too great to risk trying any completely new approaches, such as developing a system based on the IBM 4300 series. The study team also identified the loss of the

EXHIBIT 6
American President Lines, Ltd. Definition of an Equipment Management System.

A Types of Equipment

  1 Containers - All Types
  2 Chassis
  3 Motor Generators

B Characteristics of the System

  1 Timing
    a Regions in real time
    b Corporate and Area Daily
  2 Context Checking (Edits)
  3 Uniformity throughout APL
    a Data Elements
    b Approach

C Functions

  1 Equipment Acquisition and Disposal
  2 Tracking
  3 Inventory
  4 Allocation
  5 Management (in addition to above)
    a Utilization
    b Budgeting
    c Forecasting
    d Cost Control
  6 Interface
    a Booking
    b Yard Control
    c Documentation
    d Vessel Operations
    e Accounting
    f Planning Tools (e.g. M204 Utilization Model)

12/1/81

Equipment Management System Alternatives For Asia

Comparison of Singapore S/34 and CMS-I
Against Identified Requirements*

	Singapore System	CMS-I
A Types of Equipment		
1 Containers - All Types	X	X
2 Chassis		X
3 Motor Generators		X
B Characteristics of the System		
1 Timing		
a Regions in real time	X	X
b Corporate and Area Daily		X
2 Context Checking (Edits)	X	X

EXHIBIT 6 (Continued)

	Singapore System	CMS-I
3 Uniformity throughout APL	Asia only	X
a Data Elements	Asia only	X
b Approach	Asia only	X

C Functions

	Singapore System	CMS-I
1 Equipment Acquisition and Disposal	Asia only	X
2 Tracking	Asia only	X
3 Inventory	Asia only	X
4 Allocation (Dispatch Control)	X	X
5 Management (in addition to above)		
a Utilization (cntr days)	Asia only	X
b Budgeting	—	—
c Forecasting	—	—
d Cost Control	—	—
6 Interface		
a Booking	X	X
b Yard Control	—	—
c Documentation	Developing	
d Vessel Operations	X	
e Accounting	—	—
f Planning Tools (e.g., M204 Utilization Model)		X

D Specific Data

	Singapore System	CMS-I
1 Type	X	X
2 Location (APL Terminal)	X	X
3 Size (Length)	X	X
4 Height	X	X
5 Container Identification Number	X	X
6 Activity (by date, retained forever)	By country	X
a Load and Discharge	"	X
b In/Out	"	X
c In Yard	"	X
d CFS	"	X
e M&R		
—Status	"	X
—Description of Damage/Condition	"	
f Interline		
—Loaded	"	X
—Inbound	"	X
—Outbound	"	X
—Empty	"	X
g On/Off Lease	"	X
h Relay	"	X
i Domestic	"	X
j Intermodal (Rail)		X
7 Ownership	X	X
8 Origin		X
9 Destination	X	X
10 Yard Location		X

11 Stow Location	X	X
12 Shipper Consignee	X	X
13 Seal Number		X
14 Motor Carrier	X	X
15 CSC		X
16 License Number	CLS	CLS
17 Reefers		
—Commodity	X Booking	X Booking
—Temperature	X Booking	X Booking
18 Link to Associated Equipment		X
19 Tare Weight		X
20 Load Weight		X Booking

*Specifications developed by study team, December 1, 1981.

Costs (Asia only)
Comparison of New S/34 and Modified CMS-I Systems
TOTAL (U.S. dollars)

	New S/34	Modified CMS-I
Hardware		
CPU	$10,914	$ 2,183
CTL/CRT	3,681	10,536
CRT	3,082	3,963
PRT	7,418	9,155
Total Monthly	$25,095	$ 25,837
One Time	$ 600*	$ 800*
LINES		
Intl	$ 3,462	$ 9,141
Domestic	6,934	12,460
Modems	4,346	5,118
Inp		2,273
Total Monthly	$14,742	$ 28,992
One Time	$31,262*	$ 57,962*
SYSTEM DEV		
PGM/Test Total (One Time)	$30,000*	$120,000*
TRAINING		
People (One Time)	1 x 8 man mos	2 x 8 man mos
Travel (One Time)	$20,000	$ 82,000
HEADCOUNT		
People	one	one
PROCESSING		
Transaction	—	$ 26,000
TOTAL RECURRING		
Total One Time	$39,837	$ 80,825
(sum of items marked *)	$81,862	$260,762

ongoing savings which would come about from more effective asset utilization as an important reason for installing a standard computer-based equipment management system in Asia in the next six to twelve months.

The study team arrived in Hong Kong on Wednesday and began checking and reverifying its cost estimates and other figures. The group took no votes and made no commitments prior to its Saturday meeting. Pat Morrison speculated later that the team's decision evolved during their Wednesday–Saturday discussions; he felt that his presence had "zero influence" on the outcome. The team developed a set of specifications for an equipment management system for Asia (see Exhibit 6) and determined that the System 34 software developed in Singapore was the best of the locally-developed systems according to the specifications. The Singapore system was then compared against the CMS-I alternative (see Exhibit 7).

As the team's final discussion approached, Pat Morrison tried to remain an observer rather than an active participant. When challenged about ISD's ability to deliver telecommunications services, Morrison acknowledged the difficulty of the Asian environment but claimed than an ISD-managed system could easily improve on prior performance. Dave Bilodeau also played a backup role, providing estimates as needed of the cost and feasibility of proposed changes to CMS-I.

Bill Hubbard, on the other hand, had become steadily more involved as the report date drew nearer. As part of an already-announced reorganization, Hubbard would as of January 1, 1982, become responsible for APL's operations in Asia as well as in North America. Some of the regional managers who would report to Hubbard as of January 1, 1982, would be attending the December 7 presentation, and Hubbard wanted to reach a decision by consensus if possible. He also wanted both to demonstrate a participative style in keeping with APL's decentralized philosophy and to set a decisive tone after the changes in direction which had taken place during the company's development of an equipment tracking system.

EXHIBIT 7
American President Lines, Ltd.
Equipment Management System
          Alternatives for Asia—CMS-I Benefits and Limitations

A Tangible Benefits

- Equipment savings approximately 4–7% due to improved turn time.
- Reduction voice and telex telecommunications costs (elimin 520.04 telex)

B Intangible Benefits

- **Equipment Management**

  —Standardization would permit easier review of aggregate activity, faster decisions by management, less time reconciling differences on a worldwide basis.

—Uniformity also reduces training burden, permits transfer of staff more readily on a worldwide basis.

—Advance data on incoming loads on a worldwide basis.

—Direct tie to Budget and Utilization Model, a valuable planning tool.

—Permits consistent review of performance against goals.

—Automatic data synchronization.

—Supplemental data available in categories such as: aging, turn time, exact location, to/from, size of trailer pool, etc.

—Known, documented, tested system.

—Real time data editing/validation at or close to source.

- **Marketing**

  —Enhanced capabilities in freight tracing: status checks and inquiries on shipments.

  —Improved competitive posture, customer service.

  —Booking functions available.

- **Documentation**

  —Direct access to Eastbound BLIPS.

  —Reduces efforts in verifying and correcting data.

- **Operations**

  —Telecommunications and information dissemination assists in vessel operations.

- **Systems**

  —No increased demands on S/34 computers above what Regions have or should have for processing loads on equipment management (may offload, in fact).

  —Enhancements/modifications available to all users; lower system maintenance costs (collectively among all systems).

  —Phasing in or integrated worldwide MIS (CMS-II).

  —Reduced system integration problems (don't have to interface multiple, different systems).

C Limitations

- Duplicate input required for tie to other Asian computer systems, e.g., booking, on a local basis.

Equipment Management System
                Alternatives For Asia—S/34 Benefits and Limitations.

A Tangible Benefits

- Lower initial network investments.
- Lower processing costs.
- Reduction voice and telecommunications costs (elimin 520.04 telex).

B Intangible Benefits

- **Equipment Management**

  —Standardization would permit easier review of aggregate activity, faster decisions by management, less time reconciling differences.

  —Uniformity also reduces training burden, permits transfer of staff more readily.

  —Advance data on incoming loads.

  —Permits consistent review of performance against goals.

  —Supplemental data available in categories such as: aging, turn time, exact location, to/from, size of trailer pool, etc.

  —Real time data editing/validation at or close to source/only within a Region, not among Regions.

EXHIBIT 7 (Continued)

—Tailored to local needs, conditions, or precedents.
—Availability geared to local time requirements, not to U.S.

- **Marketing**

  —Improved competitive posture, customer service.
  —Booking functions available.

- **Documentation**

  —Reduces efforts in verifying and correcting data.

- **Operations**

  —Telecommunications and information dissemination assists in vessel operations.

- **Systems**

  —Continuity with pre-existing systems requiring data.
  —Priorities for development or enhancements under local control.
  —Improves local control over problem resolution (application, hardware).
  —Enhancements/modifications available to all users; lower system maintenance costs (collectively among all systems).

C Limitations

- System 34 cannot communicate on a real-time basis with CMS-I, posing serious edit and control problems.
- Impossible to keep data synchronized among Regions, Areas and Corporate.

Equipment Management System
Alternatives For Asia—Assumptions Used in Developing Costs
for New S/34 and Modified CMS-I Systems.

—Additional CPUs (S/34) are required for S/34 EMS alternative in Japan and Taiwan.

—25% of Korea, Hong Kong, the Philippines, Singapore S/34 cost is included for S/34 EMS alternative.

—25% of the cost of currently installed international lines are included in S/34 EMS alternative.

—One time line costs for S/34 and CMS-I are for purchase of modems required by Korea.

—In the CMS-I alternative, 5% of S/34 CPU will be used for down loading CMS-I files to S/34 and producing reports.

—CMS-I and S/34 system development costs are based upon ISD and EDS estimates.

—CMS I processing costs are based upon 260,000 transactions per month at $0.10 per transaction.

—S/34 training cost requirements are less than CMS-I due to local people who are capable of training.

SUMMARY

As the date of its final meeting approached, the team was well aware of the diverse opinions and strong emotions which they had encountered during their trip. Each member viewed equipment management from a somewhat different perspective, and each would interact in a different way with whatever system was ultimately installed in Asia. They were aware that some of their fellow employees, particularly in Asia, viewed the entire study as a sham designed to sugar-coat a predetermined decision. Above all, the team understood the importance that had become attached to the decision within APL, and the impact which it could thus have on the company's success and on their own careers.

SDB CORPORATION—
BLOOMINGTON PLANT

Lee Gremillion

It was a typical rainy Indiana summer morning as Joan Wrenn, programmer/analyst for the Consumer Electronics Division of SDB Corporation drove from CED headquarters in Indianapolis to the Bloomington Television Assembly Plant. As she drove, Wrenn reflected on last week's meeting with her boss. She had been given her first independent project since she joined the CED Information Systems Group eight months before. During that eight months Wrenn had worked as a junior team member on several plant systems projects, and had become strongly attracted to production and logistics support systems. Thus, she was especially pleased with the assignment she had just received.

The Friday before, Don Buse, manager of manufacturing and materials system design and Wrenn's boss, had called her in and given her a copy of a memo from the materials manager at the Bloomington Plant. In this memo (Exhibit 1), Bloomington management had requested that Management Information Systems undertake an analysis of the trailer traffic control system at that plant. With literally hundreds of truck trailers moving in and out of the plant daily, the operation had become a complex and expensive one, and plant management was beginning to question whether it might be handled more efficiently and cost effectively. Buse had told Wrenn that this project seemed appropriate for her, given her background (an operations management major in her M.B.A. program) and her interest in plant systems.

"Putting in the on-line receiving and goods stores system in Bloomington has sort of turned materials management around down there," Buse commented. "Now they're looking for ways that the computer can help them out, where before, they were pretty passive toward systems. One thing to

130

EXHIBIT 1

To: M. R. Lawson, MIS

From: G. Sieving, Bloomington Plant   Date: 1/21/80

Subj: MIS Project—Trailer Traffic Control System

As we agreed in our meeting last week, I am following up with a formal request for MIS services for analysis of our trailer traffic control operations. Initial and broad objectives for this analysis would be

1 Improved utilization of tractors and drivers.
2 Improved information for the receiving functions to advise them of loads ahead of them to help control detention and help with material availability status.
3 Improve information available regarding empty trailers available for outbound loading.
4 Ability to respond to carriers' inquiries regarding empty trailers or availability of outbound loads.
5 Information to enable detention audit.

Undoubtedly, some additional advantages would be uncovered during the analysis. At this point, of course, we don't know if any MIS system for traffic control could be cost-justified. To give an idea of potentials involved, however, consider that tractor and driver expense is $20 per hour; 12 drivers are involved; detention during the last two years averaged $6,000 per month.

John Kagan should be the person to contact if one of your people is assigned to this project.

G. Sieving
/s

cc: J. D. Kagan

---

watch out for though—since the receiving and goods stores systems went so well on a stand-alone minicomputer, they just naturally assume that that's the approach we would take with a traffic system. Make sure you keep an open mind as you investigate this. Let's shoot for a preliminary report in about two weeks."

SDB CONSUMER ELECTRONICS DIVISION

SDB is one of the world's largest corporations, and operates a variety of businesses, including the manufacture of consumer, industrial, and military electronics devices, broadcasting, publishing, vehicle leasing, and food processing. The Consumer Electronics Division (CED), headquartered in Indianapolis, is the largest of SDB's divisions, with worldwide sales in excess of $1.5 billion, and over 20,000 employees. CED's major products include color and black-and-white televisions, video tape recorders and players, and, as of early 1981, video disk players.

CED plants are scattered around the United States and several foreign countries, but practically all final assembly operations for color televisions and video disk units are located in the plant in Bloomington, Indiana, fifty miles southeast of Indianapolis. Components from plants as far away as Taiwan are shipped to the Bloomington facility, which assembles them into finished sets which are shipped directly into the distribution channels. This plant produced the first commercially available color television set, and, for a number of years, produced all the color television sets sold in the United States.

Management Information Systems (MIS) functions for CED are largely centralized and headquartered in Indianapolis. The division data center, a large UNIVAC installation, services the worldwide plants of the division, including Bloomington. This data center maintains the operations data base, one of the most advanced manufacturing data base systems in the country, which supports all factory operations in the division. All the division's remote sites, including those outside the country, are connected to the data center via a complex data communications network. In addition, most sites have at least some processing distributed into local processors, mostly minicomputers.

TRAILER TRAFFIC CONTROL AT BLOOMINGTON

Wrenn's first appointment in Bloomington was with John Kagan, traffic administrator for the facility. Kagan described the traffic situation in Bloomington, and the way the current control system worked.

> Trailer movement in this plant is the function of the dispatch office, which reports to me. Currently, we're moving over 200 trailers per day to and from the loading docks. The dispatchers not only direct all these moves, but they also keep track of the location and status of all the trailers on site. That's typically between 150 and 250 trailers. I think you'll probably want to start by spending some time in the dispatch office.
>
> Then I imagine you'll want to see how the drivers work, too. Right now, we've got twelve drivers and rigs who do nothing but shuttle trailers around within the yards. These drivers work for Electronics Transfer, Inc., an outfit out of Indy. SDB just has a contract with ETI for both driver and tractor, and we're now paying about $20 per hour for a driver and rig.
>
> Trailer moves are actually requested by the dock foremen, when they want materials, or empty trailers for loading. You'll want to see what they do, too. I'll arrange for you to go out to the dock with one of them and observe their operations. Of course, he'll probably give you an earful about how good it used to be.

Kagan went on to say that the dispatch function had been initiated only three years before. Previously, the yard drivers were assigned to particular dock foremen, who directed their movements. As the plant volume, and therefore the number of drivers, grew, it looked to traffic management as though central control of local trailer movements would be more efficient. Kagan admitted, however, that central dispatch was not without problems.

> For one thing, we're still using a lot of drivers to keep things moving—there are twelve now, and we'll probably have to add some more when the video disk line gets cranked up. Even so, the dock foremen and materials people continually complain about how long it takes to move a trailer. And it seems like we ought to be able to reduce the trailer detention penalties—$6000 a month is enough to make plant management take notice. On the bright side, though, this is an area where we don't have to worry about the union—if we can figure out how to get by with fewer drivers, we can sure get rid of some of them. At any rate, I'm really glad to have MIS looking into this.

In response to Wrenn's question, Kagan explained that detention penalties were charges levied by the owners of trailers which SDB kept on its premises beyond a standard turnaround time. The rates for the penalties were fixed by tariffs, and ranged from $20 to $50 per day. (The longer a trailer was detained, the higher the daily penalty.) Some detention was inevitable, Kagan explained, since SDB in effect used trailers as temporary warehouses, but he suspected that some of it was simply due to oversight. Kagan finished the meeting by arranging for Wrenn to spend a day in the dispatch office. Wrenn also got a map of the Bloomington facility (Exhibit 2), and descriptions of the trailer parking lots and docks (Exhibits 3 and 4) from Kagan before she left.

THE DISPATCH OFFICE

The dispatch office operated from 6:00 a.m. to 4:00 p.m. Monday through Friday, so at 6:00 Wednesday morning Wrenn was at the guard shack to meet Harvey McClain, one of the dispatchers. Before going to the dispatch office, McClain obtained the night arrival log from the guard. He explained to Wrenn that drivers who arrived with incoming trailers while the dispatch office was closed checked in with the guard station, which was always open. They then dropped their freight bills through the mail slot in the dispatch office, and parked the trailer wherever there was an empty space. Over a weekend, there could be as many as 100 such arrivals. His first job, therefore, was to check the freight bills against the guard's log, and prepare cards for the new trailers.

As he worked up the new trailers, McClain explained to Wrenn how the trailers were tracked. Trailer location and status were contained in a card file which the dispatchers maintained. There was one card (Exhibit 5) for each trailer on the premises, containing the trailer number, arrival date and time, contents, freight bill number, current location, and destination. At 7:30, one of the drivers came in with an inventory of the trailers on the lot, from which McClain got the locations of the new trailers. About that time, the telephone started ringing frequently with movement requests, and the dispatching got underway.

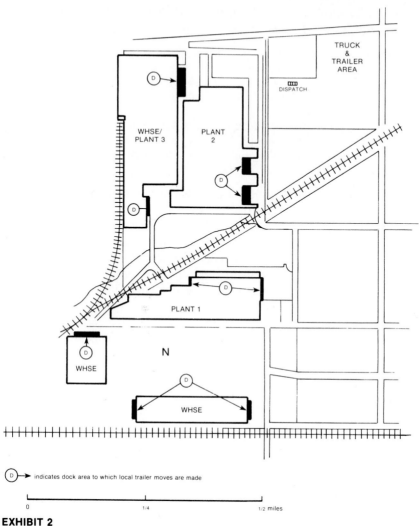

 indicates dock area to which local trailer moves are made

EXHIBIT 2
SDB Bloomington Facility Layout

For most of the rest of the day, Wrenn merely sat out of the way and watched. McClain and the second dispatcher, who had come in at 6:30, were too busy to spend much time talking with her. By watching and asking an occasional question, however, Wrenn was able to follow what was happening.

Requests for trailer movement were made by foremen of the various docks via the "hotline" telephone which connected the dispatch office and all the docks. When a request was made, the dispatcher would enter the dock, trailer number, and delivery location onto the dispatch log sheet (Exhibit 6). He would then look on the card for that trailer for the current location,

EXHIBIT 3
Trailer Parking Lots Description

Lot	Capacity	Type Trailers	Destination
1 (blacktop)	130 (-8 for tractor parking, trash, etc.)	inbound matl (45) finished goods (30) empties (50)	ND, SD, GLN, AHE Dock #1, Dock #2, IW, outbound
2	50–60	empties	outbound empty, GLN, GLS, AHW
3 (employee parking for overflow)	30	empties	outbound empty
North fence (directly across from North Dock)	20	various	North Dock, Dock #2

which was also entered on the log sheet. The next step was to give the move order to a driver. This was usually done when a driver called in (via CB radio) to report that a previous move was completed. Once the assignment was made, the dispatcher entered the driver number and dispatch time on the log, put the destination location on the card for the trailer, and returned the card to the rack. When the dock called to have a trailer removed, the procedure was much the same, except that the dispatcher told the driver where in the lots to drop it.

Wrenn noticed that during most of the day the dispatchers had a backlog of requests waiting for assignment. Occasionally, they would call a driver to ask if he was ready for another move, but most often assignments were made when the driver called in. When someone called on the telephone to ask about the status of a request, the dispatchers searched through the log sheet for the answer. On occasion, when there was only one dispatcher available to handle the telephone and radio, calls would come on both simultaneously. In such a case, the radio was usually ignored.

At 2:15 p.m. McClain turned to the preparation of the evening report. This report listed and categorized the status of all trailers on the grounds and was delivered to the central traffic office by 3:00 p.m. A copy of the report (Exhibit 7) went to all the dock foremen the next morning. McClain explained that the dock foremen were supposed to use the report to verify freight bills and to reduce trailer detention penalties. Since the report showed all the trailers ahead of a certain dock in order of their arrival dates, the foremen

EXHIBIT 4
Bloomington Facility Dock Description

Dock Name	Location	No. Holes	Lot Feeding Into It	Activity
1 North Dock (ND)	Plant 1	10 (1–10)	1, no. fence	Receiving: tubes, components, misc.
2 South Dock (SD)	Plant 1	6 (12–17)	1, no. fence	Receiving: chassis, cabinets (from Juarez, Taiwan)
3 Grimes North (GLN)	Grimes Lane Whse	9 (23–31)	1, 2 (empties)	Receives finished goods to ship out later (holding)
4 Grimes South (GLS)	Grimes Lane Whse	8 (32–39)	2 (whse trailers)	Rec: cabinets, tubes, components, hold for shuttle to plant 2
5 Apple Hill East (AHE)	Plant 3	10 (40–49)	1	Rec: cabinets, tubes, components
6 Apple Hill West (AHW)	Plant 3	15 (51–65)	2	Shipping: finished goods
7 Dock *1	Plant 2	8 (81–88)	1	Receiving: tubes, cabinets
8 Dock #2	Plant 2	5 (89–93)	1, no. fence	Receiving: components from Juarez, misc.
9 Indiana Whse (IW)	Indiana Whse	12 (69–80)	1	Receiving: tubes, cabinets, packing materials and anything else having no place to go because of lack of space

would be able to select the "oldest" trailers with the right material, or the oldest empties, when making a request.

As trailers arrived during the day, the dispatchers would receive the paperwork from the drivers, tell them where to drop the trailer, and create a card for it. In addition, they would pull and annotate the card for each trailer leaving the premises. Wrenn counted sixty-five arrivals and fifty-nine departures. She also noted that the dispatch office handled over 500 telephone calls and 300 radio messages during the course of the day. At 4:00 p.m. when the office closed, she checked the log sheets and found that 205 trailers had been

TRAILER NO.			DATE IN		
SDB 41625			5	28	80

L
T ☐   T _____
L   L

PRO. NO. 29714628

COMMENTS _Indnpls_

Cabinets ; to AHE

6/3; to DOCK ; 6/3 empty

	IN MORNING	OUT NOON	IN NOON	OUT NIGHT	IN EXTRA	OUT EXTRA	
MON							MON
TUES							TUES
WED			2:17				WED
THUR	10:40						THURS
FRI							FRI
SAT							SAT
SUN							SUN

DATE OUT		
MO.	DAY	YR.
6	4	80

IBM B14740

EXHIBIT 5
Trailer Card. Trailer current location was indicated by the position of the card within the rack in the dispatch office. When the trailer was moved, the card was likewise moved.

moved. Of these, forty-eight had been moved between 3:00 and 4:00 p.m. McClain explained that this was normal, since the foremen usually liked to get trailers positioned for the start of work the next day.

THE DRIVER'S DAY

Wrenn's next step was to go out and spend a day riding in one of the tractors observing the activities from the driver's point of view. At McClain's suggestion, she joined his friend Deremer Valdeau one morning at 7:30 and climbed into the cab of his tractor. Valdeau seemed amused at the idea of a "woman

DISPATCHING SHEET

DATE: 6/10/80

DOCK	TRAILER NUMBER	PRESENT SPOT	DELIVERY SPOT	DRIVER DISPATCH	TIME	REMARKS
ND	GR 258	10(ND)	240(L-1)	1	10:05	
ND	B-12	L-3	10(ND)	7	10:06	
IW	B-10	230(L-1)	74(IW)	6	10:10	
SD	SDB A541	15(SD)	L-2	4	10:12	
IW	TP 241505	GR	73(IW)	11	10:17	HOT
D2	Mc 45763	90(D2)	47(AHE)	1	10:26	
D2	B-5	91(D2)	213(L-1)	8	10:27	
IW	B-35	74(IW)	L-3	2	10:28	
IW	E-37	L-1	74(IW)	3	10:29	
IW	B-7	GR	75(IW)	7	10:30	
SD	SDB 2748	17(SD)	L-1	10	10:33	
SD	SDB 4514	L-1	17(SD)	10	10:34	
SD	T97	219(L-1)	18(SD)	9	10:35	
D1	T20	L-2	88(D1)	6	10:38	
D2	SDB 4548	94(D2)	L-1	4	10:42	
IW	T9	72(IW)	L-2	5	10:44	
IW	B12	L-2	72(IW)	5	10:44	

EXHIBIT 6

DISPATCH TRAILER RECORD

DATE 6/13

PAGE 10

TRAILER	DATE	AHEAD OF DOCK	CONTENT	TRAILERS AT DOCK	EMPTIES
45530	6/7	AHE	Indpls cabinets		
CRT207	6/8	D#1	Jasper cabnt		
46681	''	''	Mont. cabnt		
8226	''	''	''		
40718	''	''	''		
T1304	''	''	Indpls cab.		
45201	''	''	Jasper cab,		
48112	''	''	''		
48431	''	''	''		
T1201	''	''	Indpls. cab.		
T1465	''	''	''		
T1620	''	''	''		
44210	6/9	''	Jasper cab.		
44200	''	''	''		
Grif179	''	''	Alma		
Grif5026	''	''	''		
42105	''	''	Jasper cab,		
8310	''	''	Mont. cab.		
MCL201	''	''	Alma		
West 247	6/10	''	Indpls cab.		
47572	''	''	Jasper crb		

EXHIBIT 7
Evening Report Prepared by Dispatchers

engineer" riding around with him, but was generally pleasant and willing to talk about his equipment and how he did the job. Activity started immediately, as he was dispatched to move a trailer at 7:35 a.m.

The first few moves were uneventful. Valdeau would drive his rig to the parking space where the trailer was located immediately upon receiving the dispatcher's call. He would attach the trailer to the truck, drive to the appropriate dock, back in, detach the trailer, clear the dock, and radio back to the dispatcher that he was finished. After each of the first five runs, he immediately got a new assignment. After the sixth run, however, Valdeau remarked that he was "getting ahead of himself," and, instead of radioing the dispatch office, drove to an area of the parking lot where several tractors were parked. Here he discussed the fortunes of the local sprint car racers with other drivers for about twenty minutes until dispatch called him to see if he was ready for another move. He replied that he was, and, after several more minutes of conversation, started out in the tractor again.

This time the trailer wasn't in the space dispatch had given him. Apparently unconcerned, Valdeau began searching up and down the rows of trailers for the one with the correct number. After about five minutes he located it in the corner of an adjacent parking lot. Wrenn asked why the location dispatch gave was so wrong.

"Well, you know they go out and find all the trailers first thing in the morning," Valdeau replied, "and, for a while, dispatch knows where they are. After all the boys have been moving them around for a while, though, what the dispatcher has isn't right anymore. You know, it sort of snowballs—once you put one trailer in the wrong spot, it bumps another one, and then that one bumps another, and, first thing you know, lots of trailers are in lots of wrong slots. But we can usually find them in five minutes or so." Wrenn asked if they reported back to dispatch when they put a trailer in a slot different from the one assigned. "Naw, they don't have time to keep track of that," was the reply.

By the lunch break, Valdeau had moved fourteen trailers, stopping several times to chat with fellow workers. During lunch, Wrenn looked over some old correspondence concerning traffic control, one piece of which alluded to an efficiency study performed in 1972. This study had apparently concluded that a reasonable standard for a truck and driver would be about thirty-five moves per day. Clearly, Valdeau was not going to make that, and she asked him about this when they started up after lunch.

"Rate busters" was Valdeau's appraisal of the 1972 study. "Twenty-three, maybe twenty-five moves, that's the standard here. Any more than that, and what you've got is a rate-buster." Since this answer was liberally sprinkled with obscenities and deprecations, and since the subject seemed to inspire Valdeau to some truly aggressive driving maneuvers, Wrenn dropped the subject. During the remainder of the afternoon, Valdeau completed nine more moves, two of which were "paperwork runs" to take freight bills from the dispatch office to the docks. Wrenn made a copy of Valdeau's log for the day for her documentation (Exhibit 8).

ON THE DOCK

Wrenn spent the afternoon of the next day on the dock of the main warehouse at the Bloomington plant. This warehouse, which covered three acres and employed nineteen people, was one of the most active unloading areas.

DAILY LOG

DATE: 6/14/80   DRIVER: Valdean

	TRAILER	LOCATION FROM	TO	SEAL #		TRAILER	LOCATION FROM	TO	SEAL #
1.	E-28	9(ND)	90(D2)		23.	SDB2172	3(ND)	246	
2.	SDB 2746	91(D2)	2(ND)		24.				
3.	GR 193	9(ND)	230		25.				
4.	West 35547	240	88(DI)		26.				
5.	E 30	10(ND)	210		27.				
6.	SDB 2605	110(NF)	2(ND)		28.				
7.	Mc 40730	86(DI)	110		29.				
8.	Mc 45689	77(IW)	AST		30.				
9.	B-8	261	77(IW)		31.				
10.	B-7	74(IW)	85(DI)		32.				
11.	B-9	90(D2)	15(SD)		33.				
12.	GR 211800	15(SD)	8(ND)		34.				
13.	Mc 45689	L-2	AST		35.				
14.	FR 45051	250	77(IW)		36.				
15.	—	DISP.	ND		37.				
16.	—	DISP	SD		38.				
17.	Mc 40569	7(ND)	AST		39.				
18.	Et 8308	8(ND)	GR LOT		40.				
19.	Mc 42632	6(ND)	210		41.				
20.	Mc 45791	82(DI)	2(ND)		42.				
21.	Et 7941	92(D2)	8(ND)		43.				
22.	Et 8427	15(ND)	AST		44.				

EXHIBIT 8

She spent the time mostly watching and talking with Orvis Wampler, the dock foreman. Wampler determined from computer reports and from production personnel what materials were required for the day. Working from the freight bills and a little black notebook, he would call the dispatch office to request that specific trailers be moved to the dock, or that empties be removed. At each call, he would record in a log the trailer number and contents, and the time of the call. Wrenn noted that very seldom was there a delay in getting through to the dispatch office. Time to get the trailer to the dock, however, was quite variable—during the afternoon, delivery lag was anywhere from ten minutes to one and one-half hours.

Wampler was less than enthusiastic about the current trailer traffic control. He stated that the previous system, in which he as a dock foreman had his own drivers and tractors, was much better. Keeping the assembly lines running, he told Wrenn, was by far the most important objective in this whole operation, and one that the current system didn't always satisfy. To support this contention, he gave Wrenn a copy of a memo from materials management pointing out this problem (Exhibit 9).

Finally, Wrenn asked Wampler what he did about avoiding detention penalties. "Well, to the extent that it's practical, I try to look on the traffic report and find the oldest trailers and move them," he answered. "But frankly, that's not my problem—my job is to make damned sure that no line goes down from lack of materials. Detention penalties aren't diddley-squat

---

EXHIBIT 9

   To: R. M. Smith, Materials Management

From: R. Taylor, South Dock   Date: 10/10/79

 Subj: Trailer Dispatching

With the increased activity on the south dock, we are not getting adequate trailer moves on a timely basis. We are waiting up to one hour for moves to support both our unloading and production activity.

The latest incident involved trailer # RCA 2623 which was called into the south dock at 8:35 a.m. and the trailer was placed at 9:50 a.m. At the same time trailer #T-193 was called out empty and the move was not made until 9:40 a.m. This resulted in two chassis assembly lines being down for twenty minutes. Trailer #E-37 is being used as a shuttle for cabinets from Indiana Warehouse to the south dock. This trailer was called in at 8:50 a.m. and was not placed until 9:50 a.m. This resulted in the instrument line being down for 37 minutes.

We handled over 400 trailers at the south dock in September. This is 800 moves or an average of 38 moves per day. The first seven days of this month we have averaged 24 trailers or 48 moves per day and we are still building up a backlog of trailers.

It is imperative traffic initiate some method to move trailers, not only at the south dock, but at all docks. This indirectly effects all docks in the complex.

R Taylr

R. Taylor

rjm

cc: J. D. Kagan

compared to a line going down, so I put my effort into making sure that the right material moves, not that certain trailers move."

BACK IN INDIANAPOLIS

On Friday morning Wrenn was back at her desk at MIS headquarters in Indianapolis with a pile of notes and photocopies of documents she had amassed during the week at Bloomington. She decided that the best thing now would be to stop and review and organize the information she had already gathered to help determine what to do next. She was pretty certain that trailer traffic control could be improved, but didn't feel ready to make any specific recommendations yet.

She had barely started to work when Don Buse called. When she told him what she was doing he suggested that she join him for lunch and brief him on the project. Wrenn protested that she didn't have it tied down well enough to present yet, but he insisted. "I don't expect any sort of final report or definite recommendation, or anything like that. But you have been scratching around down there for a week, and ought to be able to at least give me an idea of what the general situation is. See you at noon."

CENTER FOR CHILD DEVELOPMENT—CASE A

Sue Conger

INTRODUCTION

CCD is a not-for-profit social service agency that provides counseling and education to children. The center is funded by federal, state, and city programs. It has been serving its community since 1946 and is currently located in New York City.

This document defines current information processing at the Center for Child Development (CCD) based on interviews with one or more representatives of each functional area. The center wants to identify functions that would benefit from automation, and have recommendations made for manual and/or automated changes to the workflow to alleviate some problems and to facilitate accomplishment of their goals. To focus attention on CCD's desires and concerns for computerization, directional statements were developed by the executive director. These are included as Exhibits 1A and 1B.

The staff of the CCD clinic is organized into seven functional areas; each area is responsible for one or more key activities as identified by the executive director. The area and their key activities are:

Business Office
    Accounting
    Medicaid Billing and Reconciliation
    Payroll
    Employee Time-Keeping for Monthly Reports
Administration
    Intake Scheduling
    Visit Recording

EXHIBIT 1-A
Information Processing And The Center

General

The Center for Child Development desires to undertake a study leading to the specification of an information processing system that will:

1 Improve the efficiency of handling new clients.
2 Maximize the effectiveness of professional resources.
3 Provide for the creation and maintenance of accurate, consistent, and complete patient records.
4 Support the creation of statistical and financial reports required by outside agencies and center management and staff.

An initial overview statement, "Proposal for the Use of Computers at the Center for Child Development, Inc." is attached to this document. It represents a conceptual starting point for discussion and planning.

The system suggested by the overview document is an on-line multi-terminal system containing some aspects of an office automation system, some aspects of an on-line small data base system, and some aspects of a traditional batch system. We believe that the functions required are available from a wide range of computer systems or services. The center requires guidance in understanding the costs associated with different available alternatives. The feasibility of the intended applications have already been well established.

The center is operating under the following constraints that translate into rough requirements for a computer system.

1 It must predict costs at all phases of investigation, implementation, and operation accurately. Consequently, a fixed price relationship with a specification of deliverables is very important to the center.
2 There will be no professional computer staff of any type. Consequently, information processing systems used by the center must be effectively operatorless and programmerless. We must know, as part of a feasibility study, what kind of preparation and installation effort is involved in the use of selected software.
3 Any networking or interconnection facility must not involve costs associated with rewiring the building.
4 A fully functional computer system may have to evolve over time. Any initial configuration must evolve gracefully. Graceful evolution does not permit changes in data representation and interface beyond those needed for the new function.
5 There must be provision for failsoft operation, and a plan for manual failsoft operation must be part of a systems proposal. High-availability configurations should be part of a systems proposal.

These constraints and requirements are by no means unusual in environments of first-time small users such as the center.
In particular we wish to avoid the following mistakes:

1 Acquisition of a system without a full understanding of its evolutionary problems and limitations.
2 Acquisition of a system without an appreciation of the quality of the service associated with it, the costs of such service, the reputation and reliability of the vendor, the nature of hardware and software warranties.
3 Acquisition of a system without regard for the quality, performance, availability, portability, of systems and applications software.
4 Acquisition of a system without a full appreciation of the effort required to make the system operational, establish and maintain its data, establish and maintain its function.

5 Acquisition of a system whose availability characteristics will disrupt the operation of the center.

6 Acquisition of a system whose usability characteristics will cause resistance from the user population.

What CCD Needs from a Vendor or Consultant

1 Analysis of applications in sufficient detail to estimate required processing power, memory sizes, storage space, computer configurations and interconnections.

2 Recommendation for phase-in of applications functions and consequent growth of system. This should include recommendation for phased configurations.

3 Identification of an appropriate software environment including names of software elements and characterization of price, installability, availability, and performance characteristics.

4 Description of an operational environment and the impact of the information processing equipment on the working environment of CCD staff.

5 Identification and description of any network or interconnection facility associated with various computer system configurations.

6 Development of a list of reliable vendors for systems elements and systems service.

7 Development of an estimate for the costs involved in moving from feasibility study to installed system. The price of the implementation.

8 Recommendation of the basis for implementation if options seem to exist. Identification of possible turnkey contractors, and other sources of professional support throughout the development phase.

9 Specification of training for user populations and phased plan for cut over to the system.

In general, the finished report should be usable as the basis for approaching vendors. The gap between feasibility study and implementation must be minimal. CCD desires to be able to determine its ability to progress and the pace of its progress based upon this report without expenditure on additional studies.

EXHIBIT 1-B

PROPOSAL FOR THE USE OF COMPUTERS
AT CENTER FOR CHILD DEVELOPMENT, INC.

A QUESTIONS

1 Do we need 4 interconnected micros? A mini with 4 terminals? One micro with considerably improved manual systems?

2 Where should the terminal(s) be located to promote efficiency?

3 Is there available software to meet our needs, if now how much time would be required of a systems analyst to develop programs for us?

B PROPOSED USES FOR A COMPUTER

1 Intake secretary (clinic)
   a Record referral dates
      —identifying information on child
      —source of referral and date
      —presenting problem, etc.
   b Give referral source
      —next available appointment with whom

—appointment for orientation meeting

—registration in parent discussion groups

  c Obtain information from pertinent outside resources

2 Reception desk

  a Receive monthly appointment schedules from therapists

  b Log kept appointments

—walk-ins

—cancellations

—no shows

  c Collect fees (or if client is new, refer to administrative office for fee setting)

3 Record room (clinic)

  a Maintain master file of all clients enrolled in clinic; complete client referral sheet and inserts

  b Receive and file all reports generated by therapists or clients:

—psychiatric evaluation

—family history (from social worker)

—psychological evaluation

—pediatric evaluation

—intake and case review conferences on child and/or families

—initial treatment plan

—comprehensive treatment plan

—quarterly summaries

4 Day school

  a Maintain records on children referred to the school and disposition

  b Maintain records on each child enrolled in school (same as record room in clinic)

  c Initiate an individualized educational plan on enrolled children semi-annually and monitor child's progress in accordance with plan

  d Maintain attendance records for enrolled children daily

5 Statistical reporting

There are a number of statistical reports that must be generated monthly, quarterly, and annually. Among these reports are the following:

—Two monthly statistical reports for New York City Department of Mental Health;

—Monthly day school attendance records for board of education;

—Monthly financial claim for New York City Department of Mental Health;

—Monthly financial claim for board of education;

—Monthly internal statistical posting ledger;

—Local 1199 Drug & Hospital Union monthly report;

—Quarterly accruals and budget modification reports for New York City Department of Mental Health;

—Maintain up-to-date personnel records: Vacations, time worked, sick leave, etc.

This profile has not included information about the fiscal office as this function is common to all businesses.

C EXPECTED RESULTS

By automating many of our functions, the following is expected:

1 Service clients more efficiently re: appointments, waiting lists, timely referrals, and reevaluations

2 Enable agency to develop program plans accurately, based on existing client data

3 Enable agency to analyze trends in referrals

4 Allow for more accurate analyses of staffing patterns and needs

5 Permit analysis and manipulation of client data for research purposes

6 Generate reports on a more timely basis

7 Higher productivity from existing staff because many of their current functions will be taken over by computer

Client Reports Update
Monthly Reporting
Cash Receipts Recording
Fund Raising
Personnel
Social Work
Remedial Therapy
Psychology/Intake Evaluation
Psychiatry/Clinical Activities
Medicine

The entire organization is managed by an executive director. There are twenty-seven full-time and sixteen part-time employees in the clinic. A CCD organizational chart is provided as Exhibit 2. The center also supports a day school which is not included in this discussion.

The center provides counseling for an average 600 clients per year; the target audience for service is children between the ages of 3 and 18 and their families. Each client has at least one visit to the center per week. An overview of the client "life cycle" for the clinic is provided as Exhibit 3.

For each visit, once a person becomes an active client, he/she sees at least the receptionist and a therapist once per week. Visits to other therapists are possible depending on the circumstances. For each person seen, manual records of the visit are developed and eventually used to generate monthly reports for New York City, New York State, and the federal government.

The amount of paper generated for filing and subsequent visit recording and reporting is over 300 pieces per day. As the number and type of services increases, this number will increase. It is desirable to provide a higher level of service to each child and to serve a higher number of children; however, it is equally desirable to maintain overhead staff at current levels. Growth has become constrained because of manual processing limitations. CCD currently has no computers for word, text, or data processing. Payroll, the only automated process, is provided by an outside service.

The objectives of automating the administrative functions of the clinic and school are to increase the organization's informational processing capacity and to increase the accuracy of the information processed. With a capacity increase, growth in services will not require an immediate increase in support staff; increased accuracy reduces error potential and potential funding problems.

CURRENT ENVIRONMENT—CCD CLINIC

Intake Processing

The intake clerk receives referrals from schools, teachers, other social agencies, or other sources. About 75 percent of the referrals are from formal agencies via the telephone. Another 10 percent are walk-in clients who request assistance, the remaining 15 percent are from agencies via the mail.

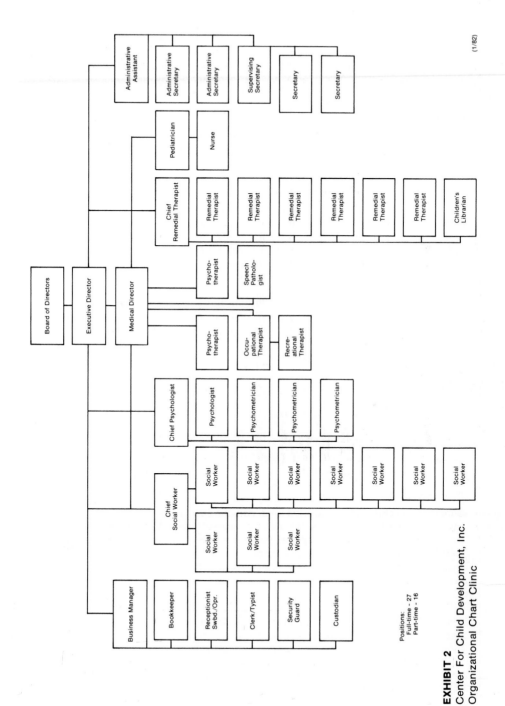

(1/82)

Positions:
Full-time – 27
Part-time – 16

EXHIBIT 2
Center For Child Development, Inc.
Organizational Chart Clinic

EXHIBIT 3
Center For Child Development
Client Life Cycle

Overview

Clients have a series of intense contacts with CCD during the testing and admittance or intake process, and, generally, once a week thereafter. Follow-up diagnosis is performed at regular intervals.

Intake Processing

A series of meetings, usually during the first visit, occur:

Mother (or Parent, or Guardian)—Administrative Secretary
Mother—Social Worker
Child—Psychiatrist
Mother—Social Worker, Psychiatrist.

At the first meeting, any fees to be paid by the family are discussed, a fee schedule is agreed to, and any fees are documented via a fee schedule form.

The next two meetings are usually simultaneous: mother-social worker and child-psychiatrist. The social worker obtains a family history which is documented via a number of forms. The psychiatrist conducts a psychiatric evaluation, and performs any blood tests that may be necessary. The psychiatric information is documented on a number of forms.

In the final session, the mother meets with both the social worker and the psychiatrist, who jointly recommend a treatment program for the youngster. Therapies recommended might include a number of types of individual, group, and/or family counseling. This sessions' outcome is assignment of the child to a program of therapy and up to seven other types of assignments including:

- Day School
- Cognitive Training
- Educational Counseling
- Loss and Bereavement Counseling
- Diet Counseling
- Group and/or Family Therapy

Variations of this visit may take place. For instance, if family therapy is likely, the group meets with the psychiatrist.

Other Visits

During the second, and possibly the third, visit, the child meets with the psychologist, who administers between four and ten different types of tests and inventories. If remedial reading is indicated, the psychologist may recommend that the child be seen by a remedial therapist. Results of the psychological tests are documented via a number of forms and are discussed with the child's therapist before any treatment sessions are held.

Subsequent Visits

After the intake processing is complete, the child begins weekly (or more frequent) sessions with the social worker and other clinicians assigned to the case. The principle form of therapy is play therapy performed by a social worker.

In addition, if medication was recommended by the psychiatrist, monthly visits for medication are made. The parent is required to participate in the treatment of the child and is seen by the therapist on a regular basis.

Periodic Contacts

A pediatric exam is conducted annually. Other quarterly and annual updates to the files on client progress are made. Case reviews are required by the New York City contract every two years, but are held more frequently if there are treatment issues to be discussed. The social worker, psychiatrist, case coordinator, and chief social worker attend these sessions.

On a two year cycle, all initial testing is redone to update the files on each child. Several tests, such as the Wechsler exam, may be administered at the discretion of the psychologist.

New admissions and clients in treatment two or more years are documented in an annual utilization review required by New York State to determine the continued suitability of clients to CCD. An alternate form of therapy is planned if movement from CCD is indicated.

Case Closing

Cases are closed (therapy is discontinued) when a child reaches the mandatory age of leaving therapy, when a child discontinues therapy for some reason, or when other therapy (such as hospitalization) is recommended by CCD. The most common reason for case closing (age) is in accordance with CCD policy which states that the ages of children served is three to sixteen. The mandatory age for leaving therapy is eighteen.

The clerk contacts the parents by telephone to discuss CCD procedures and determine their interest in pursuing therapy for their child. If there is interest, the clerk creates a client referral card which is updated with dates for sending and receiving an authorization release form to the parents. Upon return of the authorization form, requests for information are sent to school, committees on the handicapped (if a prior evaluation has been completed), other agencies, hospitals, or centers as appropriate. The purpose of this data gathering is to obtain all pertinent historical information about the client before any CCD work is conducted. As information is received, its receipt is noted on the referral card and an intake file is established.

The contents of the intake file include a referral sheet, all information from external sources, and CCD's own intake processing forms (all blank at this point).

When external agency information is complete, the clerk schedules the parents for a series of four orientation meetings which are held once per week for one month. A mailing list for invitations to the meeting is developed from the current CCD waiting list which averages about 100 to 150 names. (Of those awaiting entrance to the center, 25 percent will drop out after the initial contact, 25 percent will drop out after being on the waiting list for some time, and the remaining 50 percent will eventually become clients.)

The parent orientations are conducted by the psychology department. Orientation is mandatory to a child's acceptance as a client; attendance is reported back to the intake clerk for record keeping.

After orientation is complete, an intake interview is scheduled for the child and parent(s). The clerk creates a master list of intake schedules once per month. The chief social worker makes up a schedule for social worker assignments to intake processing once per month and gives the information to the intake clerk. The selections for intake are on a first-come-first-served basis from the waiting list of names whose parents have completed the orientation meetings, or are sometimes based on a special priority selection based on the immediacy of a child's need. Up to six new clients can be admitted every week. Intake evaluations are conducted on Tuesday and Wednesday.

One to two weeks prior to the meeting date, a meeting reminder is sent to the client and the referring source. A telephone call to verify attendance is made to the parents several days after the mailing.

Cancellations of intake appointments are replaced with the next person from the waiting list whenever possible. If the cancellation is the day of the appointment, or no replacement can be made, a dayschool child who is awaiting evaluation is substituted.

The day of the intake interview, the referral card is updated with the meeting date, and the intake file is given to the social worker assigned to intake that day. The referral card is maintained even though there is no further use for this information planned. Occasionally, when a child's folder is out of the records room, someone will reference the referral card file. These cards are never loaned out. When a case is closed, the intake clerk removes the referral card from the file.

Before the intake clinical evaluations begin, the administrative secretary meets with the parent(s) to determine their ability to pay for therapy. If one or both parents work, a nominal fee is charged for treatment. If the family is approved for Medicaid, a copy of the child's Medicaid card is procured. The fee agreement form documents this transaction and becomes part of the client file.

Clinical Activities

Clinical activities for a client begin with the orientation meetings for the parent(s), continue through intake processing, which is a series of meetings that vary depending on the nature of the problem, and become routine with regular visits to the center for therapy. Record keeping for clients includes recording of short (less than 30 minutes) and/or long (more than 30 minutes) visits, periodic summaries of therapy, and annual client reviews.

Orientation   The orientation meetings are held by the psychology department to prepare the parents for their role in the therapy. The meetings are used as an indicator of parental interest in committing to a therapy regimen.

Intake   A social worker meets with the parent at intake while the child is meeting with the psychiatrist. The social worker collects demographic, family, and social history information. The worker may recommend psychological and remedial evaluations, and so forth, if the child has not been evaluated within the last six months. The worker also conducts the normal intake evaluation.

When intake processing is begun, a decision on accepting a client is made within two weeks and treatment begins. The social work staff perform the main therapies provided by CCD, which are usually individual play therapy, group, or family therapy.

Psychology does not ordinarily treat clients; however, several clients now receive psychological therapy. The documentation of those visits are completed via forms similar to those used in the other departments.

Case Coordination   The primary responsibility for proper treatment and therapy assignment for clients rests with the case coordinators. They coordinate with both external agencies and all CCD internal departments. Case coordinators are psychiatrists and psychologists who report to the chief social worker (CSW). The coordinators receive all recommendations about a client's treatment and further evaluation and do all scheduling and follow-up for further treatment as needed.

At any time, a case coordinator can refer a client for speech (or other) evaluation. The case coordinator sends the referral request to the CSW with an indication of the priority of the request. The CSW forwards the request to the speech therapist based on the availability of the therapist's time (there is only one speech therapist).

Closing and completion of proper case-closing forms is the responsibility of the case coordinator. The forms used are the closing form and the clinical summary of the course of treatment. Information on most recent test results, disposition, and so on, are completed and signed by the coordinator. The closing form is countersigned by the case coordinator's department head.

Chief Social Worker   Upon completion of intake, an intake note is developed by the psychiatrist and the social worker. The note is a narrative account of the diagnosis, recommended treatment, and short- and long-term goals for treatment. In addition, the assignment form is initially developed by the psychiatrist who forwards the form to the chief social worker. The CSW assigns the new client to a therapist(s) and sends the original of the form to the records room to complete the client file records. The form then is sent to the chief psychiatrist's secretary for filing in the client log file.

The CSW monitors treatment by reviewing and signing all comprehensive treatment plans, three-month summary forms, and annual summary forms developed by the social workers.

Remedial Therapy   Remedial therapies are determined based on an evaluation that is requested via case coordinators but which can originate from any client contact. Referral for speech/language evaluation may be made as a result of observations during the psychological work-up. The need for a speech/language evaluation is communicated via a remedial evaluation recommendation form to the case coordinator, who then refers the case to speech therapy as required.

Forms In general, each clinical department uses its own color of forms to easily distinguish between them:

Remedial therapy—pink
Psychology—blue
Medical and Psychiatric—green
Case Coordinators—white
Case reviews and intake—yellow

There are exceptions to these forms colors, which are noted in the discussion below.

Several forms are completed by all people involved in a client's diagnosis and treatment:

- Flow Sheet
- Chart Review
- Daily Summary
- Three Month Summary
- Monthly Statistics

The flow sheet provides case status summary information at a glance. It is signed by each person responsible for the various intake and re-evaluation activities for a specific client.

The chart review is completed by all department chiefs when a case is formally reviewed. Every three months, five cases are selected randomly by each of the four department chiefs. They meet, discuss the status of the client, and document the case aspects reviewed with any comments and further therapy recommendations. Each department is responsible for one or more of the sections of the chart review form.

An annual review of all records is conducted to reconfirm the course of treatment from the original recommendation. The chart review form is also used to document this annual case review.

A daily summary form is used by each clinician to document any significant occurrences and notes on each visit of each client.

The three month summary is based on daily summary progress and provides a quarterly review of each case. The summaries are prepared and forwarded to the chief social worker for review and approval. They are then typed and filed in the client file.

Monthly statistics are provided by each clinician as the basis for development of monthly reports to New York City and New York State by the administrative secretary. The statistics include a count of the type (short versus long) and number of visits by client.

In order to monitor the completion of all the summary reports generated by all the clinical staff, the intake clerk develops a "Status of Dictation" report by clinician. This is a list of clients and the last date of dictation for the case. It is sent monthly to the department heads of social work, psychology, psychiatry, remedial services, and the executive director.

Once remedial therapy is determined, the same daily and quarterly summaries of treatments are completed. In addition, there is a separate assignment sheet for remediation and a reading diagnostic report that supplement the forms used to document treatment.

The assignment sheet is used to document remediation assignment. It is used to track diagnostic testing completion, assignment, closing and/or reassignment. The assignment of a worker is done by the chief of remedial therapy.

The reading diagnostic report is used to document results of achievement and reading tests, to summarize strengths and weaknesses of the child, and to recommend a course of treatment.

In addition to formal forms that are maintained as part of the client files, each clinician keeps 3x5 card files for each client. The psychologists maintain three sets of 3x5 cards to document psychological evaluation, psychological test records, and report completion. In addition, the psychological report is a verbal description of the client's state.

Progress cards are also kept by the individual remedial clinicians to document the progress of a child via test scores. The cards are updated each time testing is redone.

Visit Recording

The therapists and intake clerk send client visit schedules to the receptionist on Friday for the following week. Each day, the receptionist refers to the weekly lists and generates her own daily visit log. The log contains the names of each therapist with the times and names of clients with whom they have appointments listed under the therapists' names.

As clients enter the center, the receptionist uses a log to monitor entry of expected arrivals, and then enters a check next to the client's name to signify the arrival. The receptionist verifies whether or not a fee is owed from the payment card file which he or she maintains, or whether the patient has a Medicaid card. If a Medicaid card is presented, the receptionist copies it and returns it to the client. If a fee is paid, the receptionist collects the fee and completes a receipt, giving one copy to the client. If a fee is owed but not paid, the receptionist notes nonpayment for later entry in the payment card file.

Visit dates, fees collected, and Medicaid information are later recorded in the payment card file. Another check mark next to the client's name on the daily visit log is made to confirm entry of the information on the payment card. If a fee was paid, the money is sent to the administrative assistant along with a copy of the receipt for cash recording.

The following morning, the records clerk picks up the daily visit log from reception, new fee sheets from the administrative secretary, and intake forms and assignment sheets from the chief social worker, then uses this information to post appointments, therapist assignment, and fee assignment on the master client "visidex" card file. For active clients, the date of visit is entered under the therapist's name(s) on the visidex card and the card is refiled. The daily visit log sheets are maintained on file for three years in compliance with legal requirements.

In addition to the recording of visits by the receptionist and the records clerk, each therapist maintains a record of visits and the visit type (short or long).

At the end of the month, each source of visit information is used in month-end reports. The receptionist creates a monthly summary of client activity that summarizes, by client, the number of visits, the amount of monies paid or the Medicaid number, and any balance outstanding. This report is sent to the business office manager, who uses it to estimate the accuracy of the other visit reports.

The therapists summarize their client visits by listing the names of the clients with whom they have had contact, and identifying the number of times and type of visits they have had.

The visidex file is used as the official source of information for Medicaid billings. The business office clerk reviews the file manually and generates Medicaid bills.

The time for the receptionist to develop schedules and log visits is about two hours per day. For the records clerk, all filing and visit recording takes three (or more) hours per day. Therapists spend about two hours each per month developing a summary of visits by client.

Client File Update

The records clerk is responsible for all maintenance of the official CCD client files. There are two principal files: the visidex master client card file and the client file.

The visidex master client file (also known as the visidex file or the master client file) contains any demographic information collected about the client: Medicaid or fee information as appropriate, and visit information by therapist assigned to the client.

The assignment form is used to identify the assignment of therapist(s) to a client. The clerk takes the worker's name from the form and enters it on the back side of the visidex card. The card is then filed in the active client file. The assignment form is returned to the psychiatrist for entry in the client log file.

If a client is new to the center, and intake was the previous day, the records clerk uses the information from the referral form and fee sheet to create a master client card and permanent client file. The new master client card is filed in a drawer marked "Diagnostic and Unassigned." When an assignment sheet is received, the assigned therapist's name(s) is entered on the master client card and the card is refiled in the active client drawer.

The client file is created either at intake or when a client is assigned to a social worker, depending on which is completed first. This is because a child can start therapy before intake is complete when the need is immediate. A client file is a heavy manila folder that contains dividers for:

- Consent Forms
- Activities Therapies
- Speech/Language Therapy
- Psychology
- Psycho-Education (Remedial Therapies)
- Therapy Summaries of Sessions
- Diagnostic Intake/Evaluation

As forms are completed, either during intake or periodically throughout a child's therapy, they are filed in the client file. The center has maintained its historical, or closed client, files since its inception in 1946. A client file is changed from active to historical status when a closing form and therapy summary are received. They are filed in the client file, and the file is filed in the closed client file drawer.

Monthly Reporting

For one week each month, the administrative secretary gathers, collates, and summarizes visit information manually to generate three reports for New York City and New York State. The visit information used is provided by the therapists because, presumably, their records are the most accurate of the three sets kept. The information used in the reports is not checked against the payment card information or the master client card file. The accuracy of these reports is extremely important because they determine actual compliance with the New York City Department of Mental Health contract, which provides the majority of the clinic's funding. In event of an audit, inaccuracies that might be found would result in repayment of funds back to the funding agency and might hamper future funding efforts.

The administrative secretary receives client visit summary information from each clinical department, and also obtains monthly hours scheduled and actually worked for the CCD clinical staff from the business office clerk. Then, the secretary generates two summaries of the information: one of the number of visits by client, and one of the number of visits by parents/siblings. These are two dimensional matrices of clients by clinician with a count of the number of contacts. The count by child is the number of visits; the count for parents/siblings is the number of visits for the group. These counts are used to generate the New York State LS2C report.

Still using the clinicians' monthly summary sheets, a preparatory statistics sheet is developed. This form is a count by clinicians of hours by type of contact: direct—face-to-face client contact; or indirect—case work including writing therapy summaries, telephone, and so on. Categories of therapy, within which direct and indirect contacts occur, include individual, group, family, collateral, chemo-therapy, diagnostic, testing, intake, telephone, tutoring, and volunteer.

The counts of contact types are transferred to the New York City report forms. The secretary then computes the amount of money due to the center based on the number and types of visits.

Recipients of the reports include the government agencies involved, the business office manager, the administrative assistant who maintains the files on the New York City contract, and the executive director. The business office manager uses the reports to validate the amount of money due to the center based on the number and type of visits.

Cash Receipts Recording

Cash and checks are received from clients as they enter the center for therapy and from New York City DMH, Medicaid, donors, The New York City Board of Education, and others via the mail. All receipts are logged by the administrative assistant in the backup cash journal. She then forwards the cash and checks to the business office manager, who maintains the CCD cash journal. At the end of the month, during the closing of the financial books, the two journals are compared and reconciled.

The two journals are kept at the suggestion of the center's accountants, who recommended the duplication of effort to provide a check and balance against any type of defalcation.

Budget and Contract Maintenance

The New York City Department of Mental Health (DMH) contract represents the primary source of funding for CCD's clinical activities. Once the contract is developed, the budget for the clinic is developed to mirror the contract information; the only additional information required is for administrative support-staff salaries and expenses. Because of this relatively minor difference, only the contract is discussed here; and anywhere the contract is mentioned, the reader should be aware that this implies the budget as well.

Contract Development The contract is prepared annually in January through March for the following fiscal year, which is July through June. Quarterly updates to the contract are made to reflect any changes in expectations of clinical activity. New York City requires that each clinician average 960 visits per year to qualify for reimbursement of services.

The contract is developed by the administrative assistant with input from various sources:

• Personnel records and the executive director on current and anticipated salaries
• Business office manager for expenses and fees

• Department heads and prior year reports for number and type of visits anticipated by month

Both direct and indirect time must be estimated. The formula used is 90 percent indirect time for department heads, and 30 percent indirect time for all clinical staff.

Contract preparation time has never been formally measured; it is a part-time activity spread over the three-month period. An estimate is that seven to ten days are spent in contract development by the administrative assistant, the executive director, and the business office manager. Another one to three days is spent by each of the four department heads. The estimate of total person days required in development of the contract is 25 to 42 days.

Two key issues in contract development are security (especially for future salary estimates) and accuracy-of-visit information.

Contract Maintenance   The administrative assistant receives copies of the monthly New York City 54 and 55 reports and all work sheets used in development of those reports from the administrative secretary. From that information, a spread sheet of DMH claims by employee, by month, is developed. Quarterly and annual summations of this information are developed.

Other reports generated are based on actual income received from the DMH:

• Analysis of Visits Generated and Income Collected—this report is submitted to the DMH monthly.

• Comparison of Visits Generated and Income Collected to last year—for use by the executive director in monitoring contract compliance and financial planning.

• Analysis of Fiscal Information from the DMH Claim—submitted monthly to the DMH, this report is by budget line from the contract. Six-month summaries of this information in the form of budget versus actual are generated.

Medicaid

Once per month, the business office clerk reviews the visidex master client card file to obtain Medicaid number and visit information for each client. Based on the visidex file information, Medicaid forms are completed: one per client with up to four visits listed on each form. Most clients have multiple forms produced because they have more than four visits to the center. Each form must be completed in its entirety (top and bottom) in order for Medicaid to process it (the forms cannot be batched by client with only variable visit information supplied).

One copy of each form is kept and filed in a Medicaid—Pending Claims file. The other copies of the forms are mailed to Medicaid for processing.

About four to six weeks after submission of claims, Medicaid sends an initial determination on each claim. Reconciliation of all paid amounts is done by manually matching the Medicaid report information with that from the original claim form. The paid claims are then filed in a Medicaid—Paid Claims file.

Claims that are disputed by Medicaid (almost 90 percent are disputed on the initial report) are researched and followed up with more information as required. The center has a contact at Medicaid, with whom they work closely to resolve any problems.

Most often, the problem is that the claimant has had multiple visits to multiple agencies in one day (for example, to CCD and to a hospital); Medicaid reimburses expenses for one such visit per day. This means that multiple appointments at CCD for a given day will have one appointment reimbursed; multiple claims on the same Medicaid number for the same day are paid on a first-claim-received-first-paid basis by Medicaid.

Medicaid processing and reconciliation is the responsibility of the business office clerk. The total amount of time devoted to Medicaid processing, including time by the business office clerk and temporary help, averages from six to ten days per month.

Fund Raising

Fund raising is performed by a professional fund raiser who works at the center two days per week. She obtains information about prospective donors which is used by the administrative secretary to update a donor card file. Demographic information is sparse and past donation information is not kept on a regular basis.

Selection from the card file for specific campaigns is manual and time consuming. Information on potential donors is also obtained from books listing foundations and other entities that make significant donations to specific causes (library upgrades, automation, and so on). The usefulness of the books is hampered by the fact that their organization is alphabetical by geographic location. To locate specific institutions that fund related activities requires reading each entry to determine the fit of the foundation's interests to CCD's needs.

The fund raiser works with the executive director to develop effective fund raising strategies. The card file and/or the books are manually researched to identify potential donors. Letters for the campaigns and other literature are developed by the fund raiser and typed by the administrative secretary on a memory-writer typewriter. Frequently, information on the demographics of the center's client population is required in developing the proposal; this information must be obtained by manual compilation of the statistics from the visidex file (or educated guessing). Customizing letters or literature on the memory-writer is difficult and rare. Finally, envelopes and other mailing materials are all developed manually. There is no central mailing list of individual donors kept because of the clerical time and expense involved in maintenance of such a list.

Accounting

In general, CCD's accounting is very straightforward and simple; the center maintains a traditional double-entry bookkeeping system. The application areas within accounting include accounts payable; accounts receivable; general ledger; financial reporting; and purchasing and inventory processing. Each of these areas is discussed separately. The CCD school, which is not specifically the subject of this case, does have its accounting and business services provided through these procedures. Where relevant, differences for the school are noted.

Accounts Payable   Payables are approved via a single copy voucher system. The business office manager stamps and signs the item to be paid and identifies the proper general ledger (GL) account number.

There is no tracking of vouchers to prove that all are used and accounted for. The vouchers used are filed monthly in no particular order; the bills for the month are collected and held together with a rubber band, then the bundle is filed by month. The current fiscal year's records are kept on file. There are no vendor files or tracking of expenses by department.

There are three bank accounts from which payments can be made:

Regular account—clinic activities
Special projects account—school activities
Special account 2—fund raising, affairs, and activities not related to daily operations, such as summer and youth programs

The one major monthly payment for dues, benefits, and pension is a union payment. This payment requires a special form (supplied by the union) to identify the payments breakdown. It includes the employee name, union number, amount paid, and the amount of dues paid.

Accounts payable balancing is also performed by the business office clerk and requires cross-footing column totals in the accounts payable journal to the total amount paid. Ledger entries include:

Date
Company (payee)
Check Number
Amount
Federal, FICA, State, City taxes

The major entries are for supplies, materials (therapy), travel, rent, telephone, utilities, Local 1199 (benefits, pension, dues), loss and bereavement special programs, and machine maintenance and equipment leases.

At the end of the month, the closing cycle includes cross-totaling of columns and rows in the payables journal, and transfer of the total to the general ledger.

Accounts Receivable   Receivables processing is similar to payables processing. The major sources of regular receivables are New York City DMH, Medicaid, and New York Board of Education. Sources of aperiodic receivables are mostly donors. On a daily basis, receivables from all sources are entered in the receivables journal by the business office clerk.

Regular receipts from the DMH and Medicaid are deposited in the regular bank account. Board of education receipts are deposited in the regular bank account for the school. General donations to the center are also deposited in the regular account for the appropriate entity: clinic or school. Donations that might also have conditional usage (such as donations for the library only), are deposited in one of the special bank accounts for special handling.

On a monthly basis, the books are closed by cross-totaling the columns and rows and reconciling any differences. The total receipts are then transferred to the general ledger for final closing.

General Ledger   The general ledger is maintained by the business office manager. This responsibility includes:

• Maintenance of all bank account balances and guaranteeing that expenditures, if conditional, are from the appropriate fund
• Monthly closing of all financial books
• Development of contracts and accounting for expenditures to funding agencies
• Management of bank balances including directing investment activities for excess balances and conditional funds

Posting to the general ledger on a daily basis is for changes in fund accounts and movement of funds from one account to another. During the monthly closing of the books, the balances of the backup and regular cash receipts journals are compared and reconciled. The cash, receivables, and payables balances are entered in the ledger. An income statement, identifying all incoming monies and outgoing expenses, is developed. Then debit and credit accounts are balanced to the asset and liability accounts. Finally, a statement of condition, or balance sheet, is developed.

Financial Reporting   The major financial reports are a monthly Statement of Condition for the board of directors, Budget versus Actual by department (payroll and hours only), and Bank Account balances.

State required reports include quarterly and semi-annual tax information summaries by employee. The state sends the forms, and the business office manager prepares the numbers, which are then typed on the report forms by the business office clerk.

There are other reports for city, state, federal government, and internal uses. The required formats, times, and sources of information are not yet available due to the change of business office managers.

Purchasing and Inventory   The business office clerk prepares and mails purchase orders, or telephones orders to suppliers. Orders for office supplies are generated by the records room clerk, who is responsible for monitoring inventory supply levels. Orders for clinical or medical supplies are requested by the individual clinicians to their department heads. The department managers submit the requests for supplies to the business office clerk.

Follow-up on late orders is informal and usually via a telephone call. Few problems seem present in this system.

When orders are received at the center, the business office clerk and the responsible party, either the department manager or the records room clerk, check off ordered versus received items to verify receipt. The invoices are then initialed by the checking parties and submitted to the business office manager for payment approval.

Personnel/Payroll

Personnel and payroll processing are intertwined because the initiation, termination, and change processing of personnel all impact the payroll system. Both processes must accommodate different types of employee processing for union versus nonunion and full-time versus part-time staff.

The different processes for personnel and payroll are discussed in the following sections.

Personnel As a prospective employee applies for a position at CCD, he or she completes an application form. It is completed with comments on the results of any interviews, and a final resolution on the hiring process. When a new employee starts work, an employee file is established with the application form and copies of tax forms (W-4, union, and so on).

More information is added as vacation, sick leave, or other absences occur. When an absence slip is completed, it is signed/approved by the person's supervisor and forwarded to the business office clerk for factoring into payroll processing. It is then given to the administrative assistant for filing in the employee's personnel folder.

Other forms are added to an individual's personnel file as tax status changes occur, annual reviews are developed, or other changes of status occur.

Payroll Basic payroll activities are:

1 Develop the actual time worked by employee.
2 Receive any personnel actions from the administrative assistant.
3 Complete the Manager's ADP master sheet.
4 Call in the hours worked to Manager's ADP.
5 Receive the checks and a proof sheet back from Manager's ADP.
6 Proof the checks against the sheet and create the check receipt log.
7 Allow employees to pick up their checks and sign the check receipt log.

Payroll is based on time sheets or cards from exempt and nonexempt employees. Sign in is by the doctors, nurses, speech therapist, and most administrative staff. Most other staff members punch time cards for entry or exit from the building. The executive director is the only salaried employee.

Time cards from the reception lobby are retrieved at the end of the month and hours worked are computed. A summary of time worked by employee is developed at the end of the month by the business office clerk. The summary is used by the administrative assistant in developing monthly reports and by the business office in developing the payroll.

Payroll is biweekly for the clinic, and the fifteenth and last of the month for the school. Thus, payroll is a fairly constant activity. The average amount of time spent on calculating and proofing payroll is two days per week.

The business office clerk also notes any changes in deduction information based on new change of status forms submitted for payroll processing. Once all hours to be paid are calculated, the clerk calls the payroll service company, Manager's ADP, with the information. Four days later, the checks and a check register are delivered back to the center.

The clerk reviews the register for the number of hours paid to verify that it is consistent with the number of hours to be paid. She also cross-verifies the amount of pay per person with the amount paid on the checks.

To disperse payroll, the employees visit the business office clerk's desk to pick their checks up. They sign the payroll register to signify receipt of their check. The register is filed in the business office files.

Deductions that need to be accommodated include:

Sick
Holiday
Vacation
Retro-pay
Tax Shelter
Other Earnings
Disability pay
Disability tax
Hospitalization
Other deductions
Union Dues (Local 1199 Hospital and Health Employees)
Miscellaneous
FICA
Federal Tax
State Tax
City Tax
Retirement
Major Medical

Cost of the current service is not completely identifiable today. The payroll costs about $70.00 per payroll: 52¢ per item plus 25¢ to add a new employee, 30¢ to change an employee. Quarterly ledger recaps, W-2s, and payroll cards are extra.

APPENDIX

The following lists contain information on the contents of the various forms used at the Center for Child Development. Only the most important forms are documented.

INTAKE FORMS

Referral Form

Referral Date
Worker Name (referral)
Intake Date
Worker Name (intake)
Child Name
Date of birth
Age
School
Grade
Counselor
Mother Name
   Address
   Zip code
   Phone
Father Name
   Address
   Zip code
   Phone

Guardian
   Address
   Zip code
   Phone
   Relationship to child
Referral source
   Phone
   Address
   Zip code
Rejected because
Received
Report(s) requested from
Received
Medicaid number
Clinic number
Statement of the problem

Intake Card

Name of Child
Name of Parent/Guardian
Medicaid Number
Expiration Date (Medicaid)

Fee Set
Date of fee setting
Diagnostic
Weekly Fee

Authorization for Release of Information

Date
Concerning: child name
To concern/person

Of the organization
Name of signee

Appointment Reminder Letter

Type appointment
Child name
Parent name

Date of appointment
Signee name

Fee Agreement Form

Child name
Date
Name of Insurance/third party
  carrier

Amount fee
Weekly/Monthly indicator
Signee (parent or guardian)

Diagnostic Intake and Re-evaluation Routing Sheet

Name of client
Clinic/day school/both indicator
Date of intake
Date of comprehensive treatment
  plan
Signature area and date occurs
  once per each department be-
  low and once per intake, re-
  evaluation 1, and
  re-evaluation 2-
Departments include:
  Psychosocial
  Psychiatric
  Psychological
  Psycho-Educational
  Pediatric
  Neurological
  Speech-Language
  Hearing
  Case Review

Prior Evaluations (external
  only)
Medication:
  Started date
  Discontinued date
Blood Work
  Initial date
  Follow-ups 1, 2, 3 dates
Date Assigned
Case Coordinator assigned
Date Closed this case coordinator
Date Transferred
Case Coordinator transferred to
Date Closed this case coordinator
Final Disposition (verbal descrip-
  tion)
Outreach Follow-up
  6 months (Verbal description)
  12 months (Verbal description)
  18 months (Verbal description)

Intake Demographic and Family History Form (new)

Case name
Case number
Case Coordinator
Code
Date
Child information
  Name
  Age
  Date of birth
  Sex
  Address
  Apt.
  City
  Zip
  Phone (home)
  Phone (business)

Referral information
  Source
  New/Repeat Intake
  Referral or treatment at other
    agency
  Referral Date
  Intake Date
  Time between referral and
    intake
Demographic information
(may contain description)
  Race 1/2
  Ethnicity
  Language 1/2
  No English indicator
  Religion

Presenting Problem (verbal description)
School Information
   Current School name
   Grade
   Teacher
   Address
   School type
   Held Back
   Grades held back (up to 3)
   Advanced
   Grades advanced (up to 3)
   Special Education student
   Resource Room at school
   Tutoring given this student
   Remediation given this student
   School Report received
   Date report received
   COH Report received
   Date COH Report received
   Academic Achievement (in grade/months format)
      Reading
      Spelling
      Mathematics
Page 2: continues and duplicates the following:
   Case Name

Case Number
Completed by
Date completed
Biological/Surrogate Parents
Genogram (not automatable . . . a diagram of geneology)
Mother/Father information occurs twice, once per parent
   Age
   Race
   Ethnicity
   Language
   Religion
   Mother status (living, etc.)
   Occupation
   Education
   Income
Parental joint status
If parents are living apart, what relation
Children in household and/or siblings:
   Name
   Age
   Sex
   Child of (relationship)
   Living with

There are other forms used in the clinical evaluation during intake; they are not expected to be automated and are not of interest here.

VISIT RECORDING

Daily Appointments Log

Day
Date
Working Information
   Name

Intake/regular
Client information
   Client Name
   Time of Appointment

Client Payment Card (Billing Card)

Last Name
First Name
Middle Initial
Fiscal Year

Medicaid Number
   Family identifier
   Line/person identifier
   Sex

Client Payment Card (Billing Card) (Continued)

Year of birth
Diagnosis Code (NA)
Fee per week
Monthly Visit Information
Medicaid Number
   Issued Date
   Line/person identifier

Birth Year
Sex
Dates of Visits
Amount Paid
Balance Owed (Updated monthly)

Friendly Reminder—Past Due Notice

Name
Address
Amount Due

Monthly Visit Report and Other Client Information Summary

Client Name
Single Visits
Group Visits
Fee Set/Amount
Amount Paid
Amount Owed

Insurance Company (no longer needed)
Medicaid (Y/N)
Last Seen Date
Therapist

MONTHLY REPORTING

Schedules/Actual Hours

Month
Year
Employee Name
Scheduled Hours

Actual Hours
Daily Information
   Day of month
   Number of hours worked

Monthly Contacts of Clinicians

Staff Member Name
Month
Year
Department
Number of hours on-duty
Client Information
   Service Recipient Name
   Familial Relationship (if not
      primary client)
   Scheduled Appointment Dates
   Status
   Group Treatment

Special Testing
Out-Visits to school
   Home
   Other
Number of phone calls
Regular Clinic treatment
   Number of short visits
   Number of long visits
Crisis Intervention
   Number of short visits
   Number of long visits
Remarks

Day School Summary of Treatments/Hours

Child Name
Worker
Visit Information

Day of month
Type of visit

New York City Form # 55

Reporting period from date
  to date
Contract Number
Boro Code
Facility Code
Unit Code
Name of Facility
Type (MH)
Name of Unit
Age of Clients (Child)
Staff hours and numbers of sessions
  by department
  Department
  Direct Service Modality—

Hours and sessions entered
  for each
  Individual Therapy
  Group Therapy
  Family Therapy
  Collateral Contacts
  Chemo-therapy only
  Diagnosis and Evaluation
  Phone Contacts
  Other Direct
  Total
Signature of person completing the
  form
Title
Date

New York City #55 Report

Reporting Period from date
  to date
Contract Number
Boro Code
Facility Code
Unit Code
Name of Facility
Type (MH)
Name of Unit
Age of clients (Child)
Hours distribution by department:
  Department
  Staff Funded Hours
    Direct
    Indirect
    Total Hours Worked

Staff hours not Funded...
  Direct
  Indirect
  Total Hours Worked
Volunteer Staff hours
  Direct
  Indirect
  Total Hours Worked
Total Committed Staff Hours
Total Non-Funded Staff Hours
Grand Total
Name of person completing the
  report
Title
Date

MEDICAID BILLING AND RECONCILIATION

Medicaid Claims Form

Company Name (NCCD)
Invoice Number (Assigned by

Medicaid, preprinted on the
  forms)

Medicaid Claims Form (Continued)

Billing Date (must be within 90 days of service)
Group ID Number (NA)
Location Code (03)
Clinic (974)
Category (0160)
Number of Attachments (NA)
A/V (NA)
Recipient ID Number (client Medicaid Number)
Year of Birth
Sex
Recipient Name
Office Number (NA)
Place of Service (NA)
License Number
Name of Social Worker
Type (NA)
Coding Method (*6 fixed number)
Primary/secondary diagnosis (table look-up)
Emergency (N)

Handicapped (N)
Disability (N)
Family Planning (N)
Accident Code (0)
Patient status (0)
Chap Referral Code (0)
Abort/Steril Code (0)
Prior Approval Number (NA)
Date of Service
Procedure Code (This is a two line entry to identify first the treatment payment on first line and the treatment code on second line.)
Procedure Description
Times Performed
Amount
Ignore Dental...insurance
Name of person completing the form
Date

PERSONNEL/PAYROLL
(Payroll to be added)

Personnel Records: Application Information

Name
Address
Phone
Referral Source
Education
    High School—date, degree
    College, Graduate, Post-graduate—date, degree, major
    Other—date, description
Position applied for
Dates:
    Applied
    Interviewed and comments
    Offer made
    Acceptance
    Start date
Offer amount (*starting salary)
Type pay (exempt, non-exempt, union, hourly)
Type position (full-time, part-time)
Job History
    Dates started-ended

Company Name
Address
Reference
Position title
Duties
Salary
Date information verified
By whom (CCD personnel)
Name of verifying source and position
References
    Personal (2)
    Business (2)
Notify in Emergency
    Name
    Address
    Phone
    Relationship
Withholding Information (variable)
    FICA
    Federal tax
    State tax
    City tax

Union Dues
Union Retirement
   #dependents

Retirement %
...

Absence Slips

Name
Date(s) absent
Reason
Type absence

Approved by (supervisor name)
Signed by (employee name)
Date submitted

Annual Review Forms

Date
Name
Title
Date of Employment
Last Evaluation Date
Professional Achievement (degrees,
   training, papers, typed in free-
   form prose)
Rating Information
   Relationship with Clients
   Relationship with Co-workers
   Attendance and Punctuality

Work Completed on Time
Ability to Work Independently
Ability to Handle Responsibility
Areas of Strength (prose text)
Areas in need of Improvement
   (prose text)
   General Assessment of staff
   member competence (prose
   text)
   Employee Comment
   Name of Staff member
   Name of Supervisor

Payroll Change Form

Effective Date
Employee Name
Social Security Number (if new)
Clock Number (if new)
The Changes:
   Department from/to
   Job from/to
   Shift from/to
   Rate from/to
   Hours from/to
   Other (complete with explana-
      tion) from/to
Reason for the Changes (1 or more
   can be checked) Hired, Re-Hired,

Promotion, Demotion, Transfer,
Merit Increase, Union Scale,
Probationary period complete,
Length of service increase, Re-
evaluation of job, Resignation,
Retirement, Layoff, Discharge
Leave of Absence start date
   end date
Other (text explanation for change)
Authorized by name
Date
Approved by name
Date

CENTER FOR CHILD DEVELOPMENT—CASE B

Sue Conger

INTRODUCTION

The Center for Child Development is a not-for-profit social service agency that provides counseling and education to children. The center is funded by federal, state, and city programs. It has been serving its community since 1946 and is currently located in New York City.

This document defines current information processing at the school run by the Center for Child Development (CCD) based on interviews with the principal, vice principal, and clinical coordinator. The school wants to identify functions that would benefit from automation, and have recommendations made for manual and/or automated changes to the workflow to alleviate some problems and to facilitate accomplishment of their goals.

The CCD School has a full-time principal, administrative assistant, clinical coordinator, and five teachers in addition to several part-time staff who are shared with the clinic. The school averages fifty full-time students in grades two through eight. In addition to attending classes, each student has one or more therapy sessions per week; children who qualify for the CCD School program have some form of emotional handicap or learning disability.

The entire organization reports to the executive director, who is also responsible for the CCD Clinic, a psychiatric agency for children. A CCD School organizational chart is provided as Exhibit 1. The center's clinic is not included in this discussion.

Growth in the school's services is limited because of limited physical space and the individual attention required in the teacher-student relationship. The objectives of automating administrative functions of the school would be

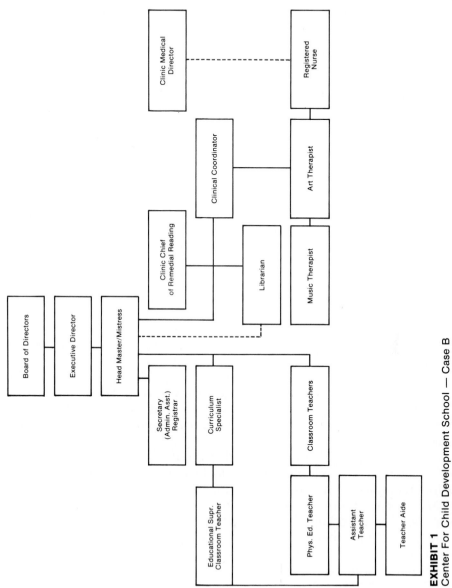

EXHIBIT 1
Center For Child Development School — Case B

to increase the organization's informational processing capacity and the accuracy of the information processed. Objectives in automating educational functions would be to complement classroom instruction with some drill, cognitive skill training, and game-playing to be provided by computers. Support for the school in accounting, billing, and reimbursement from government agencies is handled by the staff of the CCD Clinic and is not included in this case. A level 0 data flow diagram of the functions provided by the school is included as Exhibit 2.

CLIENT INTAKE

All referrals to the CCD School originate with Committees on the Handicapped (COH), of which there are thirty-two in New York City. The committees perform a status review of each case and determine the need for more intensive therapy than is available through existing New York City programs. Intake is heaviest August through October (toward the beginning of the school year); about twenty new students are admitted to the program each year.

The school receives a package on each potential client child that contains psychological, educational, psychiatric, social, and speech and language evaluations. The COH is required to develop a stage one Individual Education Program (IEP) based on the child's historical records, and on their own evaluation. The stage one IEP summarizes the current educational status, weaknesses, and goals for the child. It also identifies special testing styles as required (such as Braille).

Upon receipt of the materials from the COH, the principal screens the material and decides the feasibility of continuing intake based on past programs, openings, and "fit" of the child's problems with the therapy available. The primary handicap must be an emotional handicap (EH), or a learning disability (LD), or a combination of the two, for acceptance at CCD. The ages of school clients range from six to twelve years. Geography is considered but is not an overriding concern during acceptance.

If this initial screening indicates rejection, the COH material, rejection letter, and reason for rejection are sent to the executive director for approval before returning them to the COH. If intake continues, an appointment for child and parent is made. At this meeting, the clinical coordinator completes a developmental workup; the principal determines parent willingness for the child to enter the program and they decide on the appropriate educational program.

Again, rejection may occur at this stage of intake; usual reasons are parental rejection of the program, or a problem that was not mentioned in the original documentation that CCD cannot accommodate.

If intake continues, the clinic coordinator and the principal provide detailed evaluations and a narrative recommendation for acceptance of the child into the program to the executive director, chief psychologist, and

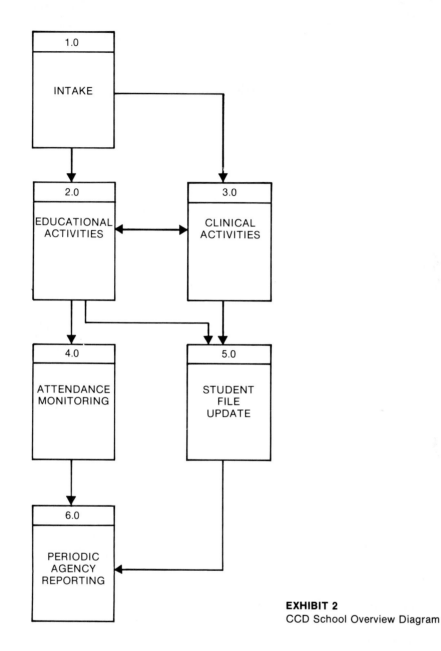

EXHIBIT 2
CCD School Overview Diagram

medical director/psychiatrist. The clinicians write their impressions and suggestions for the proposed regimen of therapy with concurrence by the psychiatrist. The child and COH are notified of the child's acceptance.

The COH obtains a "data bank number" from the New York Board of Education (BOE) computer system. When the data bank number is returned to CCD, transportation, bus route, and starting date are confirmed. The COH also starts the funding process through the BOE Contract Funding System and sends a fund approval request, or form #PHC2, to the state. Upon approval of the PHC2 request, Albany sends funds to the board of education, which in turn reimburses the school for its services. The process takes two to four months from acceptance of a client until CCD begins receiving its reimbursements from the board of education.

A detailed data flow diagram of this procedure is included as Exhibit 3. Information included on the form #PHC2 includes:

Student Information:
  Name
  ID number
  Medicaid Number, if applicable
  Address
  Phone Number
  Grade (placement in school)
  Stanford Binet scores—Reading and Mathematics
  Initial Diagnosis Codes
Child's Regular School Information
  Name and Address
  Borough
  Catchment Area
  School District
Date/Reason of Recommendation to Program
Date of Admittance to Program
Date the student begins attending CCD School
Parent/Guardian Information:
  Name
  Social Security Number, if available
  Address, if different than student's address
  Phone number, if different than student's number
  Work Name
  Work Address
  Work Phone Number

EDUCATIONAL AND CLINICAL ACTIVITIES

The student starts school and attends classes, with individual attention based on the requirements of his/her IEP. Each student has at least one therapy session per week. Currently, there is no use of computers at the school. All instruction is traditional classroom instruction with one-on-one assistance given by teachers and volunteers to the center. Exhibit 4 documents the data flows of this process.

The school staff would like to use computers as educational complements in some areas. They feel that a language that is easy to learn and use, simple word processing, and educational programs would improve the students'

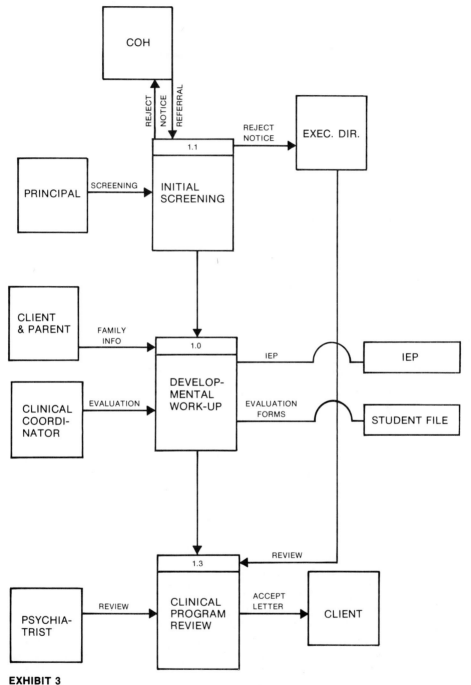

EXHIBIT 3
CCD School Current Intake

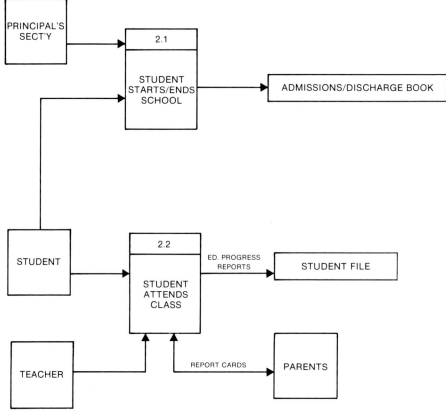

EXHIBIT 4
Current Educational Activities

self-image as well as provide them with some computer literacy. They are unaware of the problems and potentials of computers in education except what they have read in the popular press. However, they are undaunted in their goal to provide some educational computing in the school within the next year. Recommendations on how to initiate educational computing are requested. Funding for exploring and setting up an educational computer program is expected to be approved at the next board of directors meeting.

Every six weeks, report cards are sent home just as in any other school. Report cards contain information such as: student name, grade at CCD, teacher, school year, marking period identification, course name, grade level on which grade is based (students may be graded one or two grade levels different from the actual grade to which they are assigned), teacher comments each period, and parent comments each period. There is also room for parent signatures to verify that they have seen the report cards.

Updates of the child's progress are summarized quarterly and IEPs are updated at least annually. Individual education programs include data on:

student name
date of admission to the CCD program
date of last IEP
signatures of parents and CCD staff
diagnosis codes
progress on up to five subject areas to date
comments for attempts to locate parents for IEP conferences and the disposition of the attempt (for example, phoned on 1/5 at 9:20 a.m.; no answer)
student goals by subject matter, including subject name, current status, current deficiencies, specific educational goals, and scheduled date for goal attainment.

Clinical activities usually include individual play therapy or group therapy. Each child has one or more clinical sessions each week. Clinical activities are documented on the same forms that are used in the clinic. Each form—daily, monthly, annual—contains the name, date of admittance to the program, date of therapist assignment, and notes on progress (or lack thereof) for the period. Goals and notes on discussions with parents are also included. Data flow of clinical activities is included as Exhibit 5. Monthly, quarterly, and annual progress reports are developed for the board of education, CCD management, and the COHs, respectively. This process is diagrammed in Exhibit 6.

ATTENDANCE MONITORING

Attendance monitoring has three facets: entry of student in the school, on-going attendance at the school, and closing of a student file because the student leaves the school. Exhibit 7 documents the data flows of this processing.

On the day the student begins school, his/her name and date of entry are written in the admissions book maintained by the principal's secretary. An attendance card is also created for the student. On a daily basis, the principal's secretary visits each classroom and obtains the names of absent children. Each teacher keeps records on attendance for his/her classes. The attendance card is updated daily. If there are three or more unexplained absences, a NYC407 report is filed with the board of education to notify them of a potential problem.

Possible reasons for discharge of a student include:

- The child begins attending another school
- The child graduates
- The child's age is no longer consistent with CCD policy
- The child drops out
- The family moves

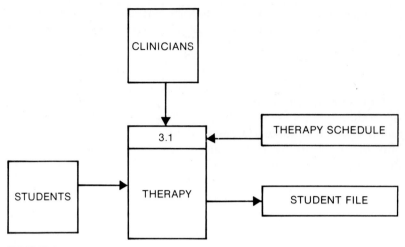

EXHIBIT 5
School Current Clinical Activities

EXHIBIT 6
School Current Reporting

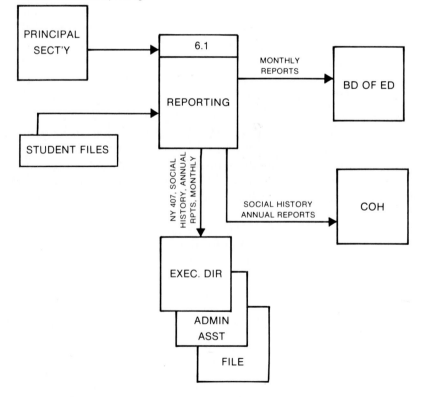

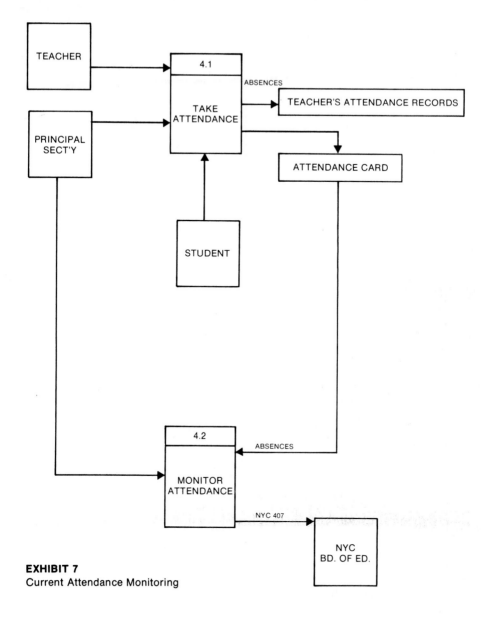

EXHIBIT 7
Current Attendance Monitoring

Information on discharged students is maintained by the secretary in the discharge book. The secretary calls the student's new school, when appropriate, and informs them that the student will be attending as of the discharge date. She then enters the student's name, date of discharge, new school name, name of person with whom she talked, and date of the conversation in the discharge book. COHs are notified as a courtesy. The data flow for updates to the student files is shown as Exhibit 8.

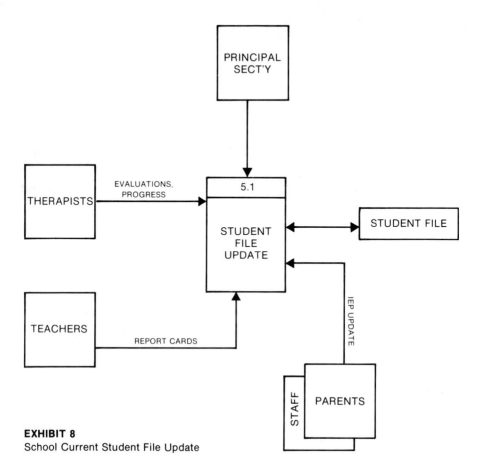

EXHIBIT 8
School Current Student File Update

DISCUSSION QUESTIONS

There are several potential applications that could be developed from the discussion of CCD School.

1 Select one application area; identify all data requirements for that area and reduce the data required to third normal form.

2 For the same application area, identify inefficiencies in procedures that could be improved by automation. Identify redundant files and processes that could be eliminated or reduced by automation. Discuss possible computerized alternatives, recommend a solution, and develop level 0 and 1 DFDs to document the solution that you recommend. Identify the organizational impact and discuss the alternatives for solving the changes to the current procedures that are available.

3 If you did not select educational computing, and your solution would be to purchase a software package, develop a list of the requirements to be accommodated by a candidate software package. (Type of file structure might be one key, multikey, relational, hierarchic, sequential, nonsequential, supporting direct access, etc.)

Categorize the requirements as mandatory or optional for use in a software package selection process. Define backup, recovery, and security requirements that would comply with the legal obligations for privacy of the information.

4 If your solution is to develop a custom application, develop level 2 DFDs and all data file contents (from the third normal form data).

5 If you selected educational computing, what issues must first be decided before the school decides what type of educational computing would be beneficial to its students. Develop assumptions to resolve these issues, and develop a list of requirements for candidate educational software packages.

CENTER FOR CHILD DEVELOPMENT—CASE C

Sue Conger

INTRODUCTION

The Center for Child Development is a not-for-profit social service agency that provides counseling and education to children. The center is funded by federal, state, and city programs. It has been serving its community since 1946 and is currently located in New York City.

The CCD School has a full-time principal, administrative assistant, clinic coordinator, and five teachers in addition to several part-time staff who are shared with the clinic. The school averages fifty full-time students in grades two through eight. Each class has fewer than ten students. In addition to attending classes, each student has one or more therapy sessions per week; children who qualify for the CCD school program have some form of emotional handicap or learning disability.

Because of the nature of the problems with which CCD deals, each student is required, by law, to have an Individual Educational Program (IEP) developed before entering the school and an IEP update every six months thereafter. The information contained in an IEP includes a summary of the students' status in five subject areas, current and previous test scores in math and English, descriptions of educational deficiencies and one or more goals and measures of attainment for each deficiency. Parents and students both participate in the development of the IEP along with the teacher, clinic coordinator, and principal from CCD.

CCD staff would like to obtain computers to provide educational computing as a complement to the classroom instruction the school provides. The teachers cover all regular school topics as well as they can and still address each child's specific problems. Teaching to meet the goals of an IEP is not tolerated.

CCD's teachers and administration realize that, by far, the greatest positive impact of computers in the CCD school would emanate from introducing computing as an aide to the teaching staff. Drills, skill training, programming languages, and game playing are potential areas of automation. The school officials are unsure about how to begin computerizing. They are seeking guidance to help them design a program for educational computing that will get them started, give them evaluation checkpoints, and contingent directions depending on the success/failure of early experiences.

While there are literally hundreds of educational software packages available for purchase, there are a number of issues CCD needs to resolve before evaluating any packages. In addition, based on their definition of their needs, the packages should be carefully evaluated for their real usefulness.

Anticipating this need, some general requests from the staff of the school were for packaged software that:

- Can be used individually while regular classroom instruction continues.
- Packages should be self-contained and not require intervention from teachers or aides. Supervision is not expected to be available.
- Packages should be for individual students; if a package has some unique or exceptional capability that requires several students, it could be considered.
- Drills that allow a student's progress level to be stored and monitored by the teacher.
- Drills that allow a student's stopping point to be stored for start-up another time.
- Drills that allow students to skip a passage with which they are already familiar.
- Software that can be copied for educational purposes at no additional cost.
- If possible, customization of drills by the teacher for a particular weakness of a given student.

In addition to these requests, other issues of concern that were discussed fall into four main categories:

- Program content
- Pedagogical content
- Program operations
- Student outcomes

PROGRAM CONTENT ISSUES

There is a great deal of concern that there will be complex instructions or typing requirements with which the students cannot cope. The content of the materials must be suitable for CCD students. Typing skills required should be minimal. Packages, especially for lower grades 1–3, should have reading requirements consistent with the student's skills.

Content of the materials should fit the student's educational goals as expressed in the IEP for math, reading, geography, English, and so on. If possible, drills and other computer exercises should be tied to the IEP and monitored for progress with reports available for the teachers.

All material should be accurate; it should have been developed by qualified educators with well-defined and documented educational goals. The goals and objectives of the materials should be explicitly stated and clear, when appropriate. There should be teacher's guides. Behaviorist assumptions should be consistent with those of the center; in other words, that children learn best by doing, having closure, experiencing both success and failure (with success predominating), receiving feedback, being able to make and take responsibility for, decisions, and so on. The material should be educationally significant within CCD's priority for teaching computer literacy, educational computing, educational games, drills, and word processing.

Values such as the importance of family, life, and personal responsibility should be consistent with minority life if the package is of the type to have values. Hidden or subtle moral, social, psychological, or cultural values expressed casually, implied, or inherent must be carefully checked for consistency with CCD goals. (Some games might allow killing as a way of winning the game. This is an undesirable value.)

PEDAGOGICAL ISSUES

The feedback provided should be consistent with behaviorist assumptions of the center. For instance, the programs should give positive feedback intermittently when right answers are given. Negative feedback should be accurate ("not quite right" is not correct or as desirable as "sorry, you are wrong"), sincere without being too negative (some packages flash a large red "X" on the screen for wrong answers), and relevant to the problem (one package uses a bird flying across the screen with a message in its mouth). It is desired that receipt of feedback be overridable by the students, and, if possible, customizable by the teachers.

The nature of the learning experience is important. Too many packages that ask progressively harder questions or that lead the student to draw conclusions would become boring. Therefore, a mix of types of learning is desired. Some might lead the student to draw conclusions, some might be show-and-repeat types of drills, some might be fill-in-the-blank (but more interesting) games, and some might have no set format, a form of directed play without a specified outcome. The packages should also be interesting and exploit computer technology through the use of graphics, sound, color, verbal, or numerical capabilities.

OPERATIONAL ISSUES

The programs should be bug-free and contain no unexpected breaks in the processing (undocumented features). The program should be able to shield itself from unintentional errors and, if possible, allow some sort of "undo" capability. The screen should always contain some indication of how to get to the next step of processing or what alternatives are available.

Directions should be clear and directed at two audiences: the teachers and the students. Preferably, the student documentation is on the computer in the form to help facilities. In any case, directions for getting started within the package should be clear and easy to follow.

STUDENT OUTCOME ISSUES

The software should measure how well a student is doing, and, if possible, maintain information for the teacher on weaknesses and strengths that the student exhibits. The packages should include some sort of pre- and post-testing guidelines to allow the school to measure the effectiveness of its program and to measure the effectiveness of the computer learning as compared to noncomputer instruction in the same area.

DISCUSSION QUESTIONS

These questions are intended to be conducted over a two to three week period and in groups. I recommend four-person groups for optimizing the amount of work any one person must do.

1 Identify which form of educational activities you will evaluate. The choice may be longitudinal, one subject from first through eighth grade; or, it may be horizontal and include all subjects for one particular grade.

Identify the particular problems associated with the form of activities you chose. List objectives of the solution, organizational impact expected (in terms of classroom activities: will teachers' aides be required, will computers be in the classroom, will students go to another location for computer use, etc.), and possible alternatives for solving the problems that might arise as a result of the educational computing types you will evaluate.

2 Develop a list of required, desirable, and optional attributes to be used in a software package selection. Determine the amount of disk space needed for the files to accommodate your application. Define backup, recovery, and security requirements (both physical and logical).

3 Develop a list of not more than three potential software packages for each subject/grade that is a candidate for automation at the school. Assume IBM, Apple, Commodore or Atari computers could all be made available depending on the results of this study.

Perform an analysis of the packages based on your list of attributes from #2 above. Select packages and justify their selection. (This might include flexibility, recommendations from users, usefulness for multiple subjects/grades, similarity of hardware environment for all users, etc.)

4 Develop an implementation schedule for the application, assuming the team members are the implementors. Include the amount of training, conversion of student records, and set-up time for customization that will be required.

Determine the total cost of your chosen software packages and the minimum hardware to support the hardware. Include the cost of hardware, memory, software, and any extra programs that will be needed into your estimate of the costs. (Your time is worth $10 per hour.)

Develop a 15 minute presentation to management (the class) on the recommended solution and its organizational impact. Discuss the costs, benefits, and recommended hardware/software environment.

Document the project. Develop a package of answers to all of the above questions, the presentation transparencies and script, and any other applicable information on your recommendations.

GREAT EASTERN BANK: A PORTFOLIO MANAGEMENT SYSTEM

Steve Alter

INTRODUCTION

This case study concerns an on-line portfolio management system (OPM) in the trust department of a large eastern bank. The purpose of this system is to aid portfolio managers in retrieving and analyzing information relevant to portfolio-related decisions. After a lengthy cost/benefit study, the system was developed in close cooperation with bank personnel by a software company which was in the process of installing a similar system in a bank elsewhere.

SETTING

The Great Eastern Bank is a large bank organized in terms of a number of line divisions, of which the trust division is one. The main service rendered by the trust division is the management of security portfolios owned by customers ranging from wealthy individuals to large pension funds. As a fee for this service, the bank receives a fixed annual percentage of the total assets managed. This percentage varies with the type of service that is desired by the customer, being greater for aggressive accounts which require frequent review and smaller for trust accounts which require less time and attention from bank personnel due to the conservative nature of their goals.

The portfolio managers themselves are salaried and do not receive commissions, although their overall performance and experience are reflected in their salaries. The trust division employs approximately fifty portfolio managers, whose major fields in college ranged from business, finance, or economics to engineering or mathematics. Most of these individuals held at least one other job prior to joining the trust department at an average starting age of around 26. What amounts to a two- or three-year apprenticeship at the bank is necessary in order to learn the business well enough to make decisions without review. Many of the portfolio managers spend part of this training period working as analysts in the investment research department. In general, they have a strong commitment to a career in the investment management field. Correspondingly, turnover in the division is quite low.

Four departments in the trust division are important for the system, including investment research; trust and estate; pension; and capital management (see Figure 1).

The investment research department serves a staff function with respect to the other three departments. Its fifteen analysts are responsible for the maintenance of the "approved list," the list of stocks which the portfolio managers may buy for their accounts. In addition, these analysts provide detailed analyses of the prospects for particular stocks or industries. The effectiveness of maintaining separate portfolio management and investment research functions depends in part upon the ability of the investment research group to communicate effectively with the portfolio managers and to receive feedback from them.

Each of the portfolio managers is in one of the other three departments. Portfolio management responsibilities vary from department to department. Portfolio managers in the trust and estate department usually manage a large number of accounts (the average is 160) which are comparatively small. For trust and investment management accounts, the main responsibility is to assure that funds are invested in accordance with (1) the needs of the trust, (2) the investment policy of the bank, and (3) the economic outlook. For estate accounts, additional duties include collecting, conserving, and distributing the estate in accordance with the will. Within geographical regions, there is great competition for new trust or estate accounts. On the other hand, existing accounts tend not to show much movement, largely due to the personal relationship that develops between the portfolio manager and the client.

The pension division handles highly competitive, performance-oriented pension funds. Portfolio managers in this area usually manage only ten to fifteen funds and track their performance very closely. Compared to personally held accounts, pension funds are very large. The direct clients here are pension fund managers who are quite willing to move their accounts to other trust departments if dissatisfied with performance. In fact, some of the larger pension funds have a policy of splitting their capital among four or five trust departments and replacing the worst performer each year with another trust department.

The capital management division provides investment advisory to portfolio management services for the aggressive accounts of wealthy individuals who wish to accept comparatively high risk in order to attempt to obtain high growth or return. Portfolio managers in this area are responsible for approximately thirty accounts.

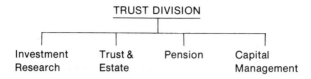

FIGURE 1
The Trust Division of the Great Eastern Bank

The goals of accounts in the various areas differ. Accounts in the trust and estate area tend to be relatively conservative in nature. Traditionally, a "prudent man" rule has applied here, whereby the preservation of capital rather than total return was a primary objective. In these accounts, the discretion of the portfolio manager is often limited by special provisions and requirements. These constraints range from special tax considerations to the client's idiosyncracies and beliefs (for example, that the account should never hold tobacco stocks, or that 30 percent of its holdings should always be in plastics). Capital management accounts are also subject to special provisions and requirements, but tend to be much more aggressive than trust and estate accounts and involve a much higher level of client involvement. Finally, there are the performance-sensitive pension accounts, which are not subject to tax and which allow the portfolio manager greater overall discretion in his or her actions. The point here is that the goals and responsibilities of portfolio management are not homogeneous across accounts and that actions which are appropriate for one account may be totally inappropriate for other accounts.

In general, competitiveness has become an important aspect of the whole portfolio management environment, both in attracting new accounts and in keeping large and potentially mobile pension accounts. Part of the competitive pressure on trust departments has come from the emergence of mutual funds, investment management services, and other new entries into the capital management field. With this heightened competition, the relatively conservative, and even stodgy, image of the banking industry has proved somewhat of a hindrance. Many banks have reacted with a conscious attempt to change their image by demonstrating that while prudent, they can also be progressive, aware, forward-looking, and so on. Although there were many reasons for undertaking the development of OPM, the competitive aspects of the business environment provided two important motivations. It was felt that advantages might be gained both in terms of actual performance and image.

THE JOB OF A PORTFOLIO MANAGER

Activities

The purpose of the on-line portfolio management system (OPM) is to help portfolio managers make investment decisions. In order to understand the impact of OPM, however, it is important to note that decision making is only one of the components of a portfolio manager's job.

An obvious way to think about the aspects of any job is in terms of time allocations. It has been suggested that a typical portfolio manager spent roughly comparable portions of his or her time in customer contact, review and revision of portfolios, and scanning of the security market and related information sources. The time spent on a portfolio review varied from a few minutes to several hours. Without the aid of a system like OPM, most of these reviews involved a significant clerical effort on the part of the portfolio manager and an assistant in producing an adequate picture of current account status, updated from the latest computer-produced review. Pension fund managers typically tried to review their major accounts on a weekly basis, placing a high premium on easy access to current portfolio status and issue holdings across portfolios.

Portfolio managers appear to spend most of their time reviewing and analyzing portfolios, taking care of administrative details, consulting with clients, and obtaining information. Those in different areas had different percentage allocations of their time. For instance, managers in the personal trust area spent more time on client contact and administration than the others.

Several months of observation at Great Eastern Bank reemphasized that different types of accounts require different types of attention. Obviously, someone with ten pension funds will be able to spend more time on each of them than someone else with 160 trust or estate accounts. (In fact, some pension funds are reviewed on a daily basis.) Aside from time considerations, estate, trust, capital management, and pension portfolios tend to have different goals and require different levels of client interaction and administrative work.

Portfolio Theory

For their investment decisions, most portfolio managers make either implicit or explicit use of some of the ideas underlying a growing and rather technical theory of portfolio decision making. This theory assumes that it is possible to quantify the level of risk and the expected level of return for any security. For two securities with equal levels of return, a rational investor should choose the one with lower risk. Therefore, each additional unit of risk should be compensated by an additional unit of expected return. For a portfolio of securities, it should be possible to reduce risk by diversifying across securities whose movements are unrelated. Since it is impossible to diversify away all risk, a portfolio's objectives should include an explicit goal in terms of the tradeoff between high risk and high return versus low risk and low return. Furthermore, portfolios characterized as "growth funds" differ on the basis of risk from those which are "income funds," with the former accepting a higher level of overall risk than the latter. Finally, taxation enters the picture, causing stocks with high dividend yields to be somewhat underpriced for nontaxable pension funds and overpriced for taxable personal portfolios; at the same time, high risk stocks are overpriced for nontaxable portfolios and underpriced for taxable portfolios.

In no way does the above discussion do justice to what has developed into a highly complex and rather elegant normative theory of portfolio decision making. The main point concerning this theory is that many of its underlying notions are included within the thought process of portfolio mangers in spite of the fact that the theory has not developed far enough to permit automatic investment decision making. The basic shortcoming of the theory is that it is primarily concerned with risk versus return calculations, whereas portfolio managers must take into account many other factors such as liquidity, capital gains taxes, personal idiosyncracies of clients, and so on. In addition, neither the goals of most portfolios nor the available security market risk versus return data are sufficiently exact to determine portfolio decisions based on the theory alone, even if the theory encompassed all relevant considerations. Often, in fact, the clients' real goals are not feasible (high return and low risk, high dividends and low capital gains taxes, etc.). Thus, the developing normative theory has helped clarify the nature of the tradeoffs, but has not progressed far enough to allow choices to be made based solely on theoretically-based calculations. This is particularly true for the majority of all portfolios which are taxable and are subject to special arrangements and client needs.

Another very basic problem concerning the applicability of portfolio theory is that the traditional process of investment decision making has tended to be security-oriented rather than portfolio-oriented. In a portfolio-oriented process, decisions are triggered by a perceived discrepancy between the goals and contents of a given portfolio. Based on this discrepancy the decision maker searches for a new portfolio configuration more consistent with the portfolio's goals. In a security-oriented process, decisions are triggered by the general attractiveness of transactions in a given security. The decision maker then searches through the portfolios under his control looking for those whose goals and special requirements would be served by either buying or selling that security. Traditionally, a security-oriented process has been used by large investment institutions, especially since they could execute block purchases at substantial brokerage discounts and could then distribute these purchases among accounts. One of the initial concepts underlying the first version of OPM was that a computer-based system might permit a more portfolio-oriented decision process than was previously possible.

Given the current limitations of portfolio theory and the fact that many decisions are triggered by opportunities related to securities rather than portfolios, it is virtually impossible to rate a portfolio manager's decisions in any objective way. For this reason, the evaluation of portfolio managers is largely subjective. One department head gave the following criteria for the evaluation:

    1 Keeping customers happy; *getting along with* people.

    2 Keeping up to date on investment matters and adhering to the bank and the division investment policies and guidelines.

    3 Interpreting the economy in an appropriate fashion (avoiding cyclical issues as the economy peaks).

Thus, the job of a portfolio manager consists of a number of components, of which investment decision making is only one. Doing the job well certainly requires an acceptable level of portfolio- and security-related performance, but also involves client contact, administrative work, and other activities. The development and use of OPM should be considered within this framework.

THE ON-LINE PORTFOLIO MANAGEMENT SYSTEM (OPM)

General Description

In order to help portfolio managers do a better job, the trust division of the Great Eastern Bank installed an on-line portfolio management system (OPM). This system was developed by an external software company which was in the process of implementing a similar system elsewhere. OPM was envisioned as a flexible, modular system which could evolve over time as the users gained an understanding of the use of computers in the portfolio management process.

OPM is basically a data retrieval and display system. It is used by portfolio managers to help them examine portfolios and obtain information about particular securities. The data base of OPM consists of detailed information about particular securities, listings of the holdings within each account, and a cross reference from each portfolio manager to his accounts. The thrust of OPM is to allow a portfolio manager to examine any account or security and to be able to scan across accounts in a number of ways. This is done by means of a series of basic operators which may be customized by the user to produce the reports needed. The customization is done by means of a menu selection process, although there are default options in some cases.

Some of the operators that are currently available are illustrated in simplified "mock-up" form in Exhibits 1-8. These operators are intended to provide the users with data retrieval capabilities which will put much of the information they use in their decisions at their fingertips. The idea is to allow them to obtain this information quickly and in the form desired. The implicit model underlying the system is that the user can decide what reports are needed, and can generate them by means of a single command customized for his or her purposes. The manager thinks about the results obtained and then requests other reports if additional information is needed (see Figure 2).

Thus, the main problem addressed by the system in its current form is that of data retrieval, that is to say, helping the portfolio manager by providing current information in the form desired without the necessity of extensive

EXHIBIT 1
Directory

The Directory function gives a tabular overview of *all accounts* under the PM's jurisdiction. The table that is generated is sorted by any of a number of fields including account identifier, market value, liquid assets, fixed income, performance, and so on. This sorting feature allows the PM to compare whole portfolios in a number of simple ways in addition to simply listing the portfolios under his jurisdiction.

| | All Amounts in Thousands | | | | | Percent of Total | | | | | | |
Acct. Name	Total Value	Liquid Assets	Common Stocks	Bonds	Part Equity	Liquid	Common	Bonds	Part Equity	Last Trade	Last Look	Acct. Perform
A	01,689	1,014	47,015	22,614	355	1.2	57.6	27.7	.4	04/22	04/22	12.3
B	481	133	230	105	12	27.7	47.8	21.8	2.5	04/22	05/13	10.4
C	137,872	544	97,240	37,015	2,917	.4	70.5	26.8	2.1	05/22	05/28	6.7
D	39,836	2,415	31,412	5,612	0	6.1	78.9	14.1	.0	05/12	05/17	7.1
E	217,015	22,405	142,018	38,412	10,018	10.3	65.4	17.7	4.6	03/03	04/30	8.6
F	1,827	3	976	812	0	.2	53.4	44.4	.0	03/03	04/27	9.6

EXHIBIT 2

Scan

The Scan function allows the PM to view the holdings of a particular security across a group of accounts. The PM slects the security, a sort key, and other information such as whether percentages should be applied to the whole account or just the common stock portion. The report that is produced includes (for each account) units of the security held, unit cost, percentage of that account devoted to this security, percentage of the account within this security's industry classification, the account's cash balance, and so on.

ACCOUNTS HOLDING COMPANY A

	Total Account Mkt Value	Company A Units Held	Company A Unit Cost	Company A Pct Acct	Oil #	Oil Pct Acct	Petrchm #	Petrchm Pct Acct	Jun 23 Price: 50 Account Cash Balance	Reord for 5.30%
Account A	137,871,837	120,500	30	4.4	2	6.6	2	6.6	911,254	25,644
Account B	81,688,794	110,280	28	6.8	4	8.2	6	15.0	315,260	23,600–
Account C	217,014,862	87,240	52	2.0	3	3.2	5	12.7	1,222,087	142,796
Account D	39,835,820	63,100	43	7.9	1	7.9	3	37.7	29,472	20,874–
Account E	26,737,925	30,000	22	5.6	2	5.6	3	29.4	321,354	1,658–
Account F	1,827,396	1,250	32	3.4	2	3.4	2	46.2	417,081	687
Account G	481,134	870	33	9.0	2	9.0	3	12.5	212,065	360–
Account H	46,520	30	53	3.2	1	3.2	1	3.2	1,092	19

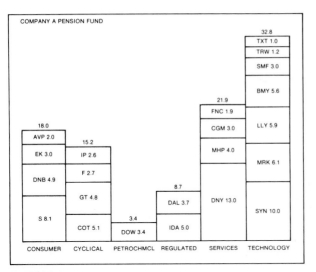

COMPANY A PENSION FUND

| CONSUMER | CYCLICAL | PETROCHMCL | REGULATED | SERVICES | TECHNOLOGY |

Values shown in chart:
- CONSUMER (18.0): AVP 2.0, EK 3.0, DNB 4.9, S 8.1
- CYCLICAL (15.2): IP 2.6, F 2.7, GT 4.8, COT 5.1
- PETROCHMCL (3.4): DOW 3.4
- REGULATED (8.7): DAL 3.7, IDA 5.0
- SERVICES (21.9): FNC 1.9, CGM 3.0, MHP 4.0, DNY 13.0
- TECHNOLOGY (32.8): TXT 1.0, TRW 1.2, SMF 3.0, BMY 5.6, LLY 5.9, MRK 6.1, SYN 10.0

EXHIBIT 3
Groups
The Groups function produces a picture of the distribution of the holdings in an account by broad industry groups. The six broad industry groups that are used include consumer, cyclical, petrochemical, regulated, services, and technology. The display looks like a histogram and gives percentage of the portfolio in each security and in each industry.

EXHIBIT 4
Table
The Table function provides a flexible way for the PM to design his own reports for reviewing the holdings of an account. He types the account name and a list of the data items he wishes to see for each holding. For example, he might wish to see the current price/earnings ratio, the security name, its current market price, five year high and low P/E ratios, value of the holding as a percentage of the account, projected dividends, and so on.

JOHN DOE TRUST FUND

P/E	Security Name	Cur Mkt Pri	Cur EPS Est	5 PE Hi	5 PE Lo	Pct C/S Act	Proj Annl Divd	Yld on Divd
7.4	Company A	22	3.00	15	11	16	1.50	6.74
9.7	Company B	42	4.35	11	8	9	2.40	5.70
10.4	Company C	21	2.00	20	10	3	.40	1.93
10.8	Company D	44	4.00	18	12	10	.80	1.82
12.2	Company E	28	2.10	21	16	12	.88	3.20
17.1	Company F	41	2.40	28	19	8	1.40	3.42
22.9	Company G	41	1.80	28	15	1	.40	1.07
26.0	Company H	91	3.50	31	21	17	.96	1.06
27.7	Company I	72	2.55	36	27	7	1.32	1.83
30.2	Company J	89	2.95	35	24	12	1.20	1.35
41.0	Company K	74	1.80	53	36	5	1.10	1.49

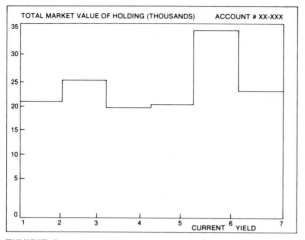

EXHIBIT 5

Histogram

The Histogram function allows the PM to view the distribution of any available data item for all the holdings within an account. For instance, he might want a histogram of the total market value of accounts against their current yield. The menu for Histogram asks the PM to type the data items he wants on each of the axes and to indicate whether he wants percentage or dollar figures.

EXHIBIT 6

Scatter

The Scatter function allows the PM to examine the relationship between two data items which are associated with the securities held by an account. In order to obtain this two-dimensional plot, the PM specifies the account together with the two data items to be displayed. An example of its use would be a scatterplot of current P/E ratio against 10 year average P/E ratio for the holdings in an account.

OPM automatically selects the bounds on the horizontal and vertical axes so that all securities will fit on the display. The PM may also filter the data items so that the only securities that appear are of a certain type or fall within a specified range of data item values.

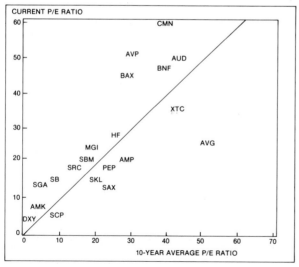

EXHIBIT 7

Summary

The Summary function displays various account summary data, information descriptive of the account, notes on the investment provisions, investment authority, investment objectives, and so on.

The summary report is divided into five general information groupings:

—report heading: people involved, type of account, etc.
—summarized holdings data: total market value, breakdown among categories such as equities, preferreds, fixed income, liquid assets, etc.
—bond maturity breakdown.
—account description: investment provisions and authority, objectives, limitations, retention provisions, nature of investments, etc.
—account long title.

Account # XX-XXX John Doe   **I.O. J. Smith**
Account Type   Irrev Probate   **T.O. J. Jones**
Date Last Tran 04/10/74

			Bond Maturity Breakdown		
Total Mkt Value	2,775,670	100.0			
Equities	2,133,527	76.9	One Month or Less	50,000	7.0
PFDS w/Eq	0	.0	Month to One Year	0	.0
Bonds w/Eq	0	.0	1 to 5 Years	0	.0
			5 to 10 Years	0	.0
PFDS	19,700	.7	10 to 20 Years	0	.0
Fixed Income	618,076	22.3	Over 20 Years	655,000	93.0
			Total Bonds	705,000	100.00
Misc	0				
Liq Asset					
(ex-cash)	4,000	.1			
Prin Cash	365	.0			
Inc Cash	21,132	.7			
Adj Liq Assets	54,365	1.9			

Detailed Investment Provisions --
----

clerical work. By performing these clerical functions, the system frees the user from these time-consuming duties and allows him or her to devote more time to portfolio analysis, customer relations, and other activities.

The Hardware

Technically, OPM is an advanced, state-of-the-art system. Although the operators shown in Figure 2 appear to be reasonably straightforward, the sheer volume of data the system accesses results in highly sophisticated technical design requirements involving CRT terminals, a minicomputer with

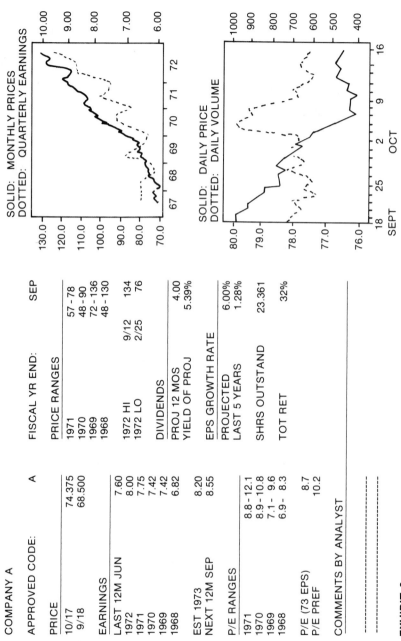

COMPANY A

APPROVED CODE:	A	FISCAL YR END:	SEP

PRICE

| 10/17 | 74.375 |
| 9/18 | 68.500 |

EARNINGS

LAST 12M JUN	7.60
1972	8.00
1971	7.75
1970	7.42
1969	7.42
1968	6.82

| EST 1973 | 8.20 |
| NEXT 12M SEP | 8.55 |

P/E RANGES

1971	8.8 - 12.1
1970	8.9 - 10.8
1969	7.1 - 9.6
1968	6.9 - 8.3

| P/E (73 EPS) | 8.7 |
| P/E PREF | 10.2 |

COMMENTS BY ANALYST

PRICE RANGES

1971	57 - 78
1970	48 - 90
1969	72 - 136
1968	48 - 130

| 1972 HI | 9/12 | 134 |
| 1972 LO | 2/25 | 76 |

DIVIDENDS

| PROJ 12 MOS | 4.00 |
| YIELD OF PROJ | 5.39% |

EPS GROWTH RATE

| PROJECTED | 6.00% |
| LAST 5 YEARS | 1.28% |

| SHRS OUTSTAND | 23.361 |

| TOT RET | 32% |

SOLID: MONTHLY PRICES
DOTTED: QUARTERLY EARNINGS

SOLID: DAILY PRICE
DOTTED: DAILY VOLUME

EXHIBIT 8
Issue
The Issue function displays all the information pertaining to a specified issue on the Approved List in a one-page display. This includes information concerning price, earnings, historical P/E ratios, dividends, number of shares outstanding, total return, and dated comments from Investment analysis which might have bearing on decisions regarding this issue.

DIRECTORY	Table; listed by account; aggregate figures
SCAN	Table; listed by account; holdings of one security
GROUPS	Pictorial; within an account; breakdown by industry and security
TABLE	Table; within an account; listing of all securities with detail
HISTOGRAM	Pictorial; within an account; distribution of one data item over all securities
SCATTER	Pictorial; within an account; relationship between two data items over all securities
SUMMARY	Formatted full page report; summary of an account
ISSUE	Formatted full page report; data about a security

FIGURE 2
Summary of Operators Available on OPM

its own disk, and a large computer which accesses the portfolio and security data base.

The system is used through nine CRT terminals which are physically divided among the three departments of the trust division. There is also one hard copy terminal which is activated by pressing a PRINT button on a CRT terminal. The terminals are connected to a Super Nova minicomputer, which, together with a Diablo disk, provides an interface between the terminals and one of the bank's IBM mainframe computers. The purpose of interposing the minicomputer at this point is to minimize any degradation of the bank's high volume, production-oriented computing capabilities. The minicomputer monitors commands from the terminals. When satisfied that a command is complete, the minicomputer transmits the command to the mainframe. The main computer generates the appropriate report and returns it to the minicomputer where it is stored on the disk. The report the user sees is produced from the minicomputer's disk. In this way, the mainframe is used for the major computational tasks that the minicomputer cannot perform, while the minicomputer takes care of local I/O which would tie up the large computer unnecessarily.

Currently, OPM is in operation only four hours each day. The purpose of this is to limit the load on the bank's mainframe. It is not yet clear when the system will attain full-time use.

The Use of OPM

OPM is used for four purposes: investment decision making, account reviews, administration and client relations, and training.

Investment Decision Making   The initial purpose of OPM was to aid portfolio managers in decision making. It accomplishes this purpose by helping them examine portfolios and obtain information about particular securities. The initial design concept is that use would consist of "terminal sessions" in which the portfolio manager requests a series of reports that help him or her move gradually toward a decision. At each stage in the session, the previously requested reports provide the user with cues and information which help define the direction in which exploration should proceed.

In practice, this search-motivated process of use is employed only rarely. More typically, interaction is not a major factor in the use of OPM even though it is on-line. Often, users begin terminal sessions with very definite purposes in mind and try out several reports until they have generated the information they initially wanted. At this point, they often obtain hard copy which they examine further at their desks. One user usually tries to generate all the hard copy needed for the day in a 10 minute session the first thing in the morning. The on-line nature of OPM allows users to clarify and debug their own requests quickly and to obtain the information wanted without delays and without requiring help from other individuals.

It should be noted that OPM is not the only source of information used in investment decision making. In fact, the primary data base for the trust department is the Trust Accounting System (TAS), a batch-oriented system which existed prior to OPM and which is used to update OPM on a daily basis. The information flow is as follows: When a portfolio manager decides to purchase or sell a security for a portfolio, he or she writes this information on a ticket which goes to the bank's stock trader. The stock trader executes the transaction if a counterpart buyer or seller is found. When the final transaction is booked, it enters TAS, which is used to update OPM later that same night. The lag between the commitment to perform a given transaction and the actual booking of that transaction is around five days (normal trading time for stocks).

Two observations should be made: First, this 5-day lag motivates many portfolio managers to maintain their own manual accounting systems. The managers use monthly prices for account holdings, and to update the prices and the holdings during the month as transactions are executed. Since these manual systems are more up-to-date, OPM is not used heavily for portfolios with recent transactions. One possible extension of OPM would be to incorporate prospective transactions into a temporary data base. This base would allow OPM to represent a portfolio as it should look, assuming that committed transactions are executed.

The second observation is that OPM can be conceived of as an extension of TAS which makes the TAS data base accessible in a decision-related format. Before OPM existed, the only account information available without special clerical effort was a simple listing of the account as a series of securities. Such a listing was not at all conducive to thinking about the account in terms of risk versus return, industry diversification, and so on. One of the main reasons for developing OPM was to transform portfolio accounting information into portfolio decision information.

Account Reviews   The second category of OPM use involves formal account reviews, which are required by law twice in three years, although they are performed more frequently by the Great Eastern Bank. Recently, the account review procedure has been modified by means of a specific requirement that OPM hard copy be used as part of supporting documentation in the review. This standardization of review procedures has led to more thorough account reviews, and to better communication among portfolio managers and senior portfolio managers who review their work. It has also resulted in an increased degree of acceptance among some of the portfolio managers who had been reluctant to use OPM.

Account Administration The third type of OPM use involves client relations and account administration. Here, the main contribution of OPM is that it provides a vehicle for demonstrating to clients that their accounts are under careful scrutiny and for explaining the rationale for the decisions that are taken. OPM is extremely effective in this regard since it generates relevant information without additional clerical work in formats that make sense and relate directly to decisions.

Training The fourth use of OPM is as a training and communication device for portfolio managers. One of the interesting aspects of the portfolio management field is that there are many different ways of looking at any given portfolio. Portfolio managers sometimes develop interesting and original ways of approaching their decision problems. The manipulation capabilities of OPM provide an excellent way of facilitating the communication of these ideas. By starting with a hypothetical portfolio and allowing several portfolio managers to analyze it using OPM, group training sessions can compare and explore the rationales which are used. This is particularly helpful for training new or inexperienced portfolio managers. Another way in which OPM facilitates communication is through the ISSUE function which displays data for use by portfolio managers entered by the investment research department. This function has reduced the circulation of typed memoranda, which often became outdated without the portfolio manager's knowledge.

Other Uses One potential use of OPM involves the possibility of building portfolio manager evaluation routines into OPM. Using such routines, a department manager might be able to compare the performance of portfolio managers in terms of return and the way they maintain their portfolios. This would result in a significant privacy question, since individuals may resent being watched. Furthermore, many portfolio managers prefer to maintain the current subjective process of performance evaluation.

Even if it were determined that OPM should be adopted as a management control tool, it is not clear whether valid comparisons could be made due to the wide range of objectives among portfolios. A portfolio manager handling a large number of portfolios with conservative goals simply cannot obtain the kinds of return which are possible with more aggressive portfolios. The problem goes deeper than this. Often, particular portfolios must be handled in terms of unique considerations such as special tax situations or owner requirements such as keeping a certain stock or avoiding certain industries. Thus, any real performance evaluation scheme has to compare the objectives and pecularities of each portfolio with the manager's actions. Although some of the theory discussed earlier might be relevant to this task, the development of a truly meaningful performance measurement scheme for the managers would be an extremely difficult task.

The differences among portfolio managers in their use of OPM is one of the most interesting characteristics of this system. In terms of sheer volume of usage, some managers use it extensively, others use it occasionally, and some use it only in the mandatory account review procedures. During the technical shakedown phase of system development, these differences were more striking than they are now.

HISTORY OF OPM

The Decision to Develop OPM

The bank officer who is currently the implementation coordinator for OPM read an article in *Institutional Investor* which described a portfolio system being developed for another bank. The officer invited the software company developing that system to visit the Great Eastern Bank and to present a demonstration.

In the spring of that year an initial feasibility study was undertaken. Eventually, it encompassed three phases, the first dealing with all potential functions of such a system, the second with the value of particular functions which seemed most appropriate, and the third with the monetary justification of the proposed system. The trust division recommended development of the system. When a bankwide priorities committee concurred, a contract was signed.

The final cost-benefit included a cost justification based primarily on the need for proportionately fewer portfolio managers as business grew, and also on the effects of the system on developing new business, on improving profits from existing business, and on improving performance in general. As in many cost/benefit studies, there is some question of the extent to which the numbers were the convincing factor, or whether it was mostly an intuitive feeling on the part of top management. Certainly, some individuals were more moved by estimated tangible benefits, while others were primarily interested in intangibles. Regardless of which aspect dominated, the feeling was that the system would help portfolio managers in major ways. In the words of the implementation coordinator:

> The intent was that the mechanics and the ability to examine alternative decisions by a portfolio manager would be facilitated by the system. He would be able to do things he might not ever have done before, plus things that he did do but which took a long time. He could do things with the system that support personnel were

doing; therefore, support personnel could be reduced....We examined the portfolio manager's function and tried to provide him a tool to better perform those tasks that were programmable, not to make decisions as such, but to assist him in evaluating alternative courses of action so that he could make the right decision.

Developing OPM was not the only option considered; several existing on-line portfolio systems marketed by time-sharing houses were examined briefly. The bank concluded that these were inadequate for the task at hand. In particular, these systems had very bad response time and prohibitively high cost. For the kind of system desired, a customized development project was necessary.

The Implementation Effort

Organization   OPM was to be implemented by an external software company for use by up to fifty portfolio managers in three departments of the trust division. These managers have different types of experience, different levels of interests in computer-related innovations, and different views of portfolio decision making.

Given the state-of-the-art nature of the proposal system and the diversity of the people involved, it was essential to formalize the implementation process and to define specific responsibilities related to the project. Within the bank, the officer who had first introduced the concept of OPM was named implementation coordinator. He headed an advisory committee of ten portfolio managers who were responsible for guiding the implementation process. Based on experience in building a similar system in another bank, the technical implementation team in the software company included a team leader and several analysts and programmers. A phased implementation schedule was agreed upon, and work began.

Technical Implementation Issues   If the data bases were small and could be extracted easily from existing systems, implementing the kinds of operators mentioned earlier would not be a great technical challenge. However, with the large portfolio data base that was needed, it was necessary to employ an advanced technical design which interfaced terminals with a large computer through a minicomputer. This kind of technology was relatively new and unproven. Although it was clear that it would be possible to develop software to accomplish this interfacing, such software was not available on an off-the-shelf basis. Underestimation of the difficulty of producing and debugging this software resulted in an overly optimistic project schedule. In an attempt to recoup some of the lost time, OPM was made available to users in a fairly complete, but not thoroughly debugged, version. Although this did help move the user training program closer to schedule, it resulted in a relatively long shakedown period during which OPM went down frequently enough to cause serious user frustration.

Differences in Usage Patterns   As mentioned, the decision to make a partially debugged version of the system available to the users resulted in what was perceived by them as a rather lengthy shakedown period. During this period, differences in OPM usage among portfolio managers were quite extreme. Prior to mandatory use of the system in account reviews, some portfolio managers used it extensively while others never used it.

The portfolio managers who made heaviest use of the system were ten individuals in the advisory group which was responsible for helping to guide the implementation process. These individuals had terminals next to their desks. Even during the period of technical problems, the implementation coordinator felt that these individuals were using the system intelligently and imaginatively. In fact, he noticed the development of a bit of a clique among these heavy users of the system. To them, it became a common denominator in expressing ways to manage accounts. At coffee breaks, members of this group were overheard discussing "what a weird groups report that was" and "what kind of groups report do you like to see?"

Some of the other portfolio managers made little or no use of OPM during this period. Many cited the fact that terminals were not at their desks and that they would have to disturb others in order to use the system. Unreliable system performance was certainly another primary reason for its minimal usage; many individuals became discouraged when the system went down and simply decided to wait until it became fully operational before trying to incorporate it into their work. Managers who used OPM tended to feel frustrated when it did not work.

The following excerpts from notes on interviews during this shakedown period describe user reactions to OPM:

Mr. A of Trust and Estate:

OPM is still viewed as somewhat of a toy. It hasn't reached the point of much usefullness. In any case, it is of no help until you have reached a decision about a stock. At that point you can use Scan.

I use Scan for finding where I hold a particular issue. Table is useful for reviewing accounts. Groups is a fascinating new way to look at an account and to see many new relationships. Scatter is intriguing, but not of much use yet because the research data base is not yet on the system.

OPM is fantastic for impressing customers and communicating with them. Both sophisticated and unsophisticated customers are impressed with the command the bank has over its accounts. I expect that this will be one of its major advantages.

Mr. B. of Trust and Estate:

To sum up the impact of the system in a word, it is *flexibility*. There is an important clerical time saving in keeping track of accounts and in finding which accounts do or don't hold any given issue. Further, it lets you know where you can act immediately and where you need approval (where you have to consult the owner). It gives you the latest information on fundamental numbers for an issue and an ability to look at an account in many different ways.

OPM will be a good marketing tool. Most customers are impressed, particularly the most knowledgeable ones. The customers have more confidence. On the telephone I can say, "we bought Disney last month and you have a 7.2% gain," instead of just saying that I think there was some gain.

Mr. C of Pension:
I have attempted using the system twice. The system failed on both occasions. Also, the scope has bad lighting and I have trouble reading it.

Mr. D of Capital Management:
I have made no use of the system beyond initial training. I will not experiment with it until I can do this without inconveniencing someone else.

Mr. E of Capital Management:
I have extremely active accounts where the customers want to make money and like to be involved in the investment process. The great advantage of this system is its speed. It gives me information I need to react quickly. It saves time and allows me to manage more money. It is an excellent selling tool which can be used to show the customers that I have a competitive edge. Hard copy is important because it is something I can give to customers.

Mr. F of Trust and Estate:
As long as other information sources and standard paperwork is around, I will use this system mostly for special situations such as giving hard copy reports to customers.

Encouraging Use   One of the main steps taken in promoting the use of the system was to require OPM outputs as a standard part of the periodic account reviews mandated by law. Instead of merely saying that some OPM reports must be included, several specific account-review procedures were carefully developed. These procedures contributed to communication by providing a common frame of reference for account reviews. The procedures also served the function of demonstrating to reluctant users that the system was now available and could become institutionalized as part of the portfolio-management process. Furthermore, this action served notice that management genuinely expected portfolio managers to make good use of the tools that had been provided.

Training meetings were held to help managers who knew how to obtain information from OPM into skilled users who could employ OPM effectively in analyzing and managing portfolios. Typically, these sessions involved several portfolio managers who were enthusiastic users of OPM and others who had not displayed as much interest. By demonstrating and discussing the use of OPM in analyzing hypothetical portfolios, these enthusiastic users not only provided ideas and hints for the others, but also generated a form of peer pressure that the others get on board via OPM. This combination of teaching and peer pressure proved successful in encouraging more uniform use of the system among the portfolio managers, although there remain those who are not yet heavy users. To facilitate further use of OPM as a vehicle for training and communication, a special terminal with a large screen display will be installed in a conference room. This will allow ten or twenty portfolio managers to participate in the same discussion session.

In addition to building on the experience with peer teaching and mandatory use in account reviews, other steps toward increased usage are either in progress or in planning. The simplest of these is merely obtaining more CRT terminals in order to make system use more convenient.

Another way of encouraging expanded use is through the development of a number of extensions of the system, some of which are now being implemented. Earlier changes in OPM tended to involve adding new data fields or modifying the formats of some of the function outputs. The newer extensions are at a more conceptual level and involve an evolution toward the use of explicit models and toward more direct use of portfolio theory. When these initial extensions are completed, managers will be able to set up and manipulate composite or hypothetical portfolio configurations by a trial and error process. This will allow them to think more easily about the impact of potential decisions.*

Another possible extension would allow OPM to monitor portfolios by comparing their status to some normative model of what their status should be, given portfolio objectives. When deviations occurred, the manager would be notified. This kind of function requires a system of encoding a portfolio's status, objectives, and special requirements, which has not yet been developed. This would not entail shifting the responsibility for running portfolios to computers; rather, the computer would simply warn the manager whenever certain simple deviations occurred. It would then be the manager's responsibility to take any appropriate action.

Yet another extension of OPM which is complicated, although conceptually feasible, is the incorporation of tax considerations relevant to each portfolio. Primarily, this effort entails a major expansion of the data base, which currently contains only the book value of all holdings. The problem with book value is that capital gains tax is based on the difference between selling price and buying price. A given portfolio may own two lots of stock "x" which were bought twenty years ago at $10 per share and one year ago at $200 per share, respectively. Under these circumstances, it might be advantageous to sell stock from one lot, but not from the other. Thus, the first step in incorporating tax considerations into OPM would be to expand its data base and to decide what new operators would be appropriate for processing the data. The data base expansion would be a major task since the data currently exist in the form of handwritten cards. Since it might be impractical to keep all of this data on-line, an alternative design would maintain this information on tape and allow requests to be serviced on an overnight basis.

---

*The usage of OPM doubled in the four months following the installation of a hypothetical portfolio function.

Finally, it is possible that special OPM functions or usage procedures will be developed to help in managing particular types of accounts. For instance, a pension fund manager with ten accounts can keep track of them almost day to day, and might be helped by specific information concerning the effect of buying or selling particular securities on the total return of a pension fund portfolio. At the same time, a trust-fund manager handling 200 accounts with a wide range of customer objectives might make extensive use of procedures (mentioned earlier) for keeping track of whether his or her other accounts were meeting objectives and for triggering actions.

THE MICROFICHE INDEX SYSTEM

Debra Slotoroff

In 1976, Bill Johnson, of the XYZ Corporation Payroll Department, became concerned about the time-consuming and labor-intensive task of maintaining documents on corporate personnel. As a result of the current process, a backlog of paperwork occurred and the payroll specialists, Johnson's subordinates, have had little time to perform their other duties. Armed with his own research, Johnson, along with his supervisor, Joann Williams, consulted Roger Baker of XYZ's information systems division on what could be done to alleviate the workload.

BACKGROUND

XYZ Corporation, established in 1912, is the manufacturer of a number of household products: paper towels, soap, toothpaste, and so on. The company employs roughly 16,000 people in its headquarters in metropolitan New York. There are offices and plants located throughout the United States and Europe.

The employee information division, of which payroll and personnel are a part, has the responsibility of maintaining documentation on employees at corporate headquarters. All the documents are either payroll- or personnel-related, such as employee applications, payroll control vouchers, and employee change notices. A sampling of these documents is presented in Exhibit 1. Originally, the documents were kept for three reasons: to fulfill a legal requirement; to verify the signatures that authorized the action; and to perform certain payroll and personnel related functions based on the information taken from the document.

XYZ CORPORATION
Payroll Change Voucher

| MR MRS MISS | LAST NAME | FIRST | MIDDLE | SOCIAL SECURITY NO. | EMP. NO. | ☐ MALE ☐ FEMALE | TRANSACTION DATE / /19 |
| STREET | | CITY | | STATE | ZIP | HOME TELEPHONE NO. | |

EMPLOYEE CHANGE

| DATE EMPLOYED / /19 | BIRTH / /19 | MARITAL STATUS ☐ SINGLE ☐ MARRIED ☐ DIVORCED ☐ WIDOWED | SEND PAYCHECK TO ☐ OFFICE ☐ HOME ☐ OTHER SPECIFY |

☐ NEW EMPLOYMENT—REGULAR
☐ NEW EMPLOYMENT—CASUAL
☐ REHIRE DATE OF PREVIOUS SEPARATION / /19

☐ RESIGNATION
☐ TERMINATION
☐ RETIREMENT
☐ DECEASED
☐ LAYOFF
☐ ADDITIONAL RATE

☐ MEDICAL LEAVE
☐ PERSONAL LEAVE
☐ MILITARY LEAVE
☐ MATERNITY LEAVE
☐ RETURN FROM LEAVE
DATE OF LEAVE FROM / /19 TO / /19

☐ PROMOTION
☐ MERIT INCREASE
☐ SALARY ADJUSTMENT
☐ TRANSFER

☐ TITLE CHANGE
☐ NAME CHANGE
☐ ADDRESS CHANGE
☐ MARITAL STATUS
☐ OTHER (Explain in Remarks Below)

DEPARTMENT OR DIVISION	ACCTG UNIT	LOCATION		DEPARTMENT OR DIVISION	ACCTG UNIT	LOCATION
CENTER NAME	CENTER NO.	TYPE OF EXPENSE		CENTER NAME	CENTER NO.	TYPE OF EXPENSE
FIELD OR HEADQUARTERS LOCATION				FIELD OR HEADQUARTERS LOCATION		
JOB TITLE OR CLASSIFICATION				JOB TITLE OR CLASSIFICATION		

SALARY RANGE MINIMUM $ MAXIMUM $ POINTS
EVALUATION PROGRAM JOB DESC. NO. FLSA ☐ EXEMPT ☐ NON EXEMPT
POSITION STATUS ☐ ADDITION TO STAFF IN EXISTING POSITION ☐ NEW POSITION
☐ REPLACEMENT (EMPLOYEE REPLACED)
PREVIOUS POSITION ☐ ELIMINATED ☐ RETAINED
VACATION DAYS CREDIT (IF ANY) TO EFFECTIVE DATE OF THIS CHANGE: DAYS

SALARY RANGE MINIMUM $ MAXIMUM $ POINTS DATE CHANGE EFFECTIVE / /19
EVALUATION PROGRAM JOB DESC. NO. FLSA ☐ EXEMPT ☐ NON EXEMPT
MR MRS MISS LAST NAME FIRST MIDDLE
STREET CITY STATE ZIP

SALARY CHANGE

HOW PAID ☐ WEEKLY ☐ SEMI MONTHLY	BASE HOURS PER WORK WEEK	SHIFT NO.	TWO PREVIOUS INCREASES		
RATE			DATE	TYPE	AMOUNT
FROM $ PER			/ /19		$
TO $ PER			/ /19		$

| ESTIMATE OF TIME WORKED IN EACH STATE (for calculating State and Local Taxes) | % OF TIME SPENT | | % | % | % | % |
| | STATE/LOCALITY | | | | | |

SEPARATION STATUS:

| ADVANCE NOTICE GIVEN ☐ YES ☐ NO TERMINATION ALLOWANCE ☐ YES ☐ NO PAY IN NOTICE_____ WEEKS LIEU OF VACATION _____ WEEKS | CHARACTER OF SERVICE VERY SATISFACTORY SATISFACTORY UNSATISFACTORY | WORK ☐ ☐ ☐ | ABILITY ☐ ☐ ☐ | CONDUCT ☐ ☐ ☐ | ATTENDANCE ☐ ☐ ☐ | DUE FROM EMPLOYEE (Explain how settled in Remarks) TRUST ACCT NOTES FUND $ _____ REC. $ _____ REC. $ _____ AIR TRAVEL CARD ☐ YES ☐ NO CREDIT CARD ☐ YES ☐ NO |

REMARKS	ENTER CODE
	POSITION
	SALARY
	DATE

RECOMMENDED / /19	APPROVED / /19	APPROVED / /19
APPROVED / /19	APPROVED / /19	MEDICAL DEPT APPROVAL (MED L/A ONLY) / /19
APPROVED / /19	APPROVED / /19	REVIEWED (PERSONNEL) / /19
PAYROLL DEPARTMENT (Indicate when salary action will be included on check) / /19		VOUCHER RECORDED IN PAYROLL BY / /19

EXHIBIT 1

In the mid-1960s the employee information division began microfilming the documents. This provided a more convenient means of retaining the documents without the bulk of paper. Prior to this, the original document was kept in an employee folder which, in turn, was stored in a file cabinet. The amount of space required for these folders was becoming overwhelming

XYZ CORPORATION   APPLICATION AND AUTHORIZATION TIP-1

TIP PR OFFICE	SOC. SEC. NUMBER		

TYPE OR PRINT IN INK ALL INFORMATION — LOCAL PAYROLL WILL FILL IN ALL SHADED AREAS

DO NOT KEYPUNCH

CC	EMPLOYEE'S LAST NAME	FIRST	I	DATE OF BIRTH	DATE OF EMPLOYMENT
1 1				/ /	/ /

CC	ADDRESS NUMBER STREET	CITY	STATE	ZIP CODE	RES CODE
1 2					

I Hereby Certify that I Understand the Thrift - Investment Plan and Its Regulations and that I Apply for Participation in the Plan in Accordance with Its Terms Effective the First Day of

MONTH	YEAR

I elect to contribute to each class the percentage of my annual base compensation rate circled below:

CIRCLE ONE

1	(2%)	*NOTE: Percentage automatically reduced to 6% on annual base compensation in excess of $15,000; up to $15,000 indicated % will apply.
2	(4%)	
3	(6%)	
4	(8%)*	
5	(10%)*	

and hereby authorize the necessary payroll deductions (calculated to the nearest whole dollar) under the Plan. I understand that the percentage specified will remain fixed until change is requested but not sooner than 6 months after the effective date of participation or change in investment formula.

I direct that my contribtions be invested by the Trustee(s) as indicated below in accordance with the provisions of the Plan. I understand that the investment formula specified below will remain fixed until change is requested but not sooner than 6 months after the effective date of participation or change in contribution rate

Insert % (must be multiple of 25%)

_____Stock Fund

_____Guaranteed Fixed Return Fund

_____Diversified Equity Fund

_____U.S. Government Securities Fund

100% Total

In accordance with the provisions of the Plan, I hereby designate as my beneficiary in the event of my death

LAST NAME	FIRST	INITIAL

RELATIONSHIP

ADDRESS	NO	STREET

CITY	STATE	ZIP CODE

WAIVER OF PARTICIPATION

☐ I do not wish to participate in the Plan but understand I may do so at a future date if I remain eligible.

CONTRIBUTION RATE

CC	ACTION CODE	CODE	MONTHLY DEDUCTION AMOUNT	INVESTMENT FORMULA CODE
1 3			$	

LOCATION:	SPOUSE'S SIGNATURE (COMMUNITY PROPERTY STATES)	PERSONNEL APPROVAL	PAYROLL APPROVAL
EMPLOYEE'S SIGNATURE			
DATE	DATE	DATE	DATE

TIP-1 (10-79)   CORPORATE EMPLOYEE INFORMATION CENTER

EXHIBIT 1 (Continued)
XYZ Corporation Employee Thrift-Investment Plan

for the department. Transferring to the process of microfilm greatly reduced the space needed. Although the images of the documents were still stored in the folders the size of the microimages afforded the storage of more documents per folder. The payroll specialists microfilmed the documents as they came in, and the microimages were cut and placed in the appropriate employee folders. The paper document was then destroyed. The folders were arranged in alphabetical order by the employees' last names. (Hereafter, microdocument will refer to the microimage of the original, unless otherwise specified.)

As in the original process, whenever a particular document for an employee was required, the payroll specialist went through each microdocument on file for the employee to locate the one requested. When the user was finished with the microdocument, it was placed back in the appropriate folder and the folder returned to its position in the file cabinet.

All of the folders were kept in any of ten file cabinets in a room within the payroll area. A layout of this room is shown in Exhibit 2. The room also had two film developers, two microscopes (to test the quality of the developed

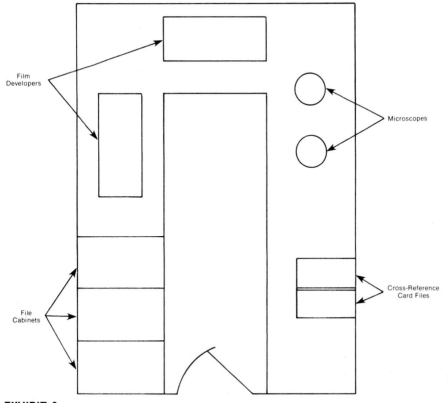

EXHIBIT 2
XYZ Corporation Room Layout

film), and a small file drawer containing a cross-reference for employees who may have changed their last names.

In 1970, the payroll department devised a new method of maintaining the documents which is still in use today. A personnel jacket was created into which the microimages of each employee's documents were inserted. The collection of these microimages in one jacket constitutes what is called a "microfiche." An example of a microfiche jacket is shown in Exhibit 3. This eliminated loose images in the folders, although the documents for a particular employee are inserted in a random order. As with prior methods, the jackets are placed in the file cabinet in alphabetical order. This new method tremendously reduces the amount of space required, since the file cabinets used in the present method (7" x 4") are smaller than the former one (15" x 12").

In addition, this new system of maintenance easily lends itself to separating out active and inactive documents. In particular, only the most recently jacketed documents need to be in the active file; the others are kept in the

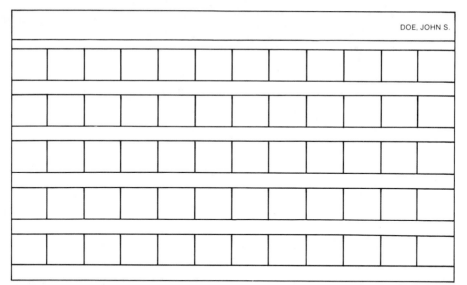

DOE, JOHN S.

EXHIBIT 3
XYZ Corporation Microfiche Jacket

inactive file. Jackets for employees who have retired are also kept in the inactive files. Both sets of files are arranged alphabetically.

Each employee has at least one microfiche jacket which can contain up to sixty frames. The documents are placed in the jackets in the order of their receipt (that is, the last frame inserted in each jacket is the most recent transaction document for that employee).

The present operation is completely manual. There are no process descriptions or written procedures for performing this function. As it exists today there are no reports or listings generated. Maintenance of the documents is as follows:

• The microfilm section of the payroll department receives the personnel or payroll document after it has been validated.

• The forms are sorted into alphabetical order before filming. Normally, the documents are batched into groups of 300 (the capacity of a roll of film).

• The sorted documents are filmed and the film developed. Usually filming occurs within one to three days after receiving the documents in the microfilm section. During peak periods backlogs occur so that sorting and filming are not completed until at least one week after the document is received.

• Particular employee microfiche jackets are pulled from the file cabinets after matching against the documents, and are held aside waiting for the film to be developed.

- The developed roll of film is then inserted into the proper jackets and cut at the end of the frame(s) making up the appropriate document.
- The jackets are copied for back-up purposes. Therefore, in case of microfiche destruction at headquarters, the entire file cabinet of documents can be replaced.
- The original employee microfiche jackets are then refiled in the file cabinets in alphabetical order.

A diagram of the above process is presented in Exhibit 4.

The retrieval process is a tedious frame-by-frame search conducted by the payroll specialists. In particular:

- The file cabinet at headquarters is accessed by employee last name and all the jackets for that employee are withdrawn from both the active and inactive files.
- The most recent employee jacket for that particular employee is placed in the reader. Since there is no index of documents for the jacket, the payroll specialist goes to the most recent document (the latest frame) and searches frame by frame through each jacket for the required document.
- At the completion of the search and use of the jacket, it is returned to the file cabinet along with the other jackets for that employee.

A diagram of this process is found in Exhibit 5.

The copied jackets (back-up) are stored in file cabinets at another XYZ plant. However, they are not interfiled. Consequently, they retain an association with the jackets at headquarters, but are not accessible alphabetically or by social security number. In addition, since a copy of the jacket is made every time a document is added, there are multiple copies of the documents in the jackets within the back-up file.

If anything should ever happen to the jackets at headquarters, the payroll specialists would have to search through all the back-up jackets until they found the most recent copy of each of the original jackets. These copies would, in turn, be copied for a new backup and the old backup filed alphabetically in the file cabinets at headquarters. All older copies of the original jackets could be discarded. From this point on, the process of document maintenance would resume the way it was before the disaster. The time to recreate the jackets is estimated at one day to two weeks. Thus far, no such incident has occurred.

Presently, the system includes approximately 30,000 jackets with a document count approaching one million. On average, there are 25 documents per employee. The greatest number of documents for any employee is 300. Each jacket can hold up to 60 frames. A document may take up any number of frames, where each frame represents one page of a document. Usually, the documents are only one page. Projected growth figures for fiscal year 1982 are 20,000 employees, or 25 percent. Progression of this growth since 1960 is shown in Exhibit 6. On average the microfilm section receives 1500 docu-

Time Line	Steps	Flow

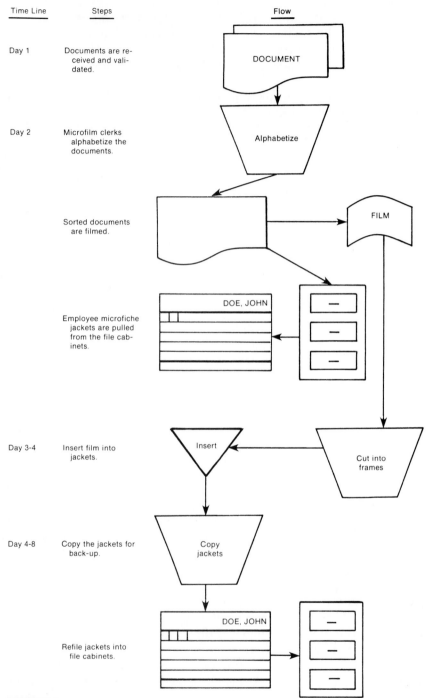

Day 1 — Documents are received and validated.

Day 2 — Microfilm clerks alphabetize the documents.

Sorted documents are filmed.

Employee microfiche jackets are pulled from the file cabinets.

Day 3-4 — Insert film into jackets.

Day 4-8 — Copy the jackets for back-up.

Refile jackets into file cabinets.

EXHIBIT 4
XYZ Corporation Current Microfilm Processing

Steps   Flow

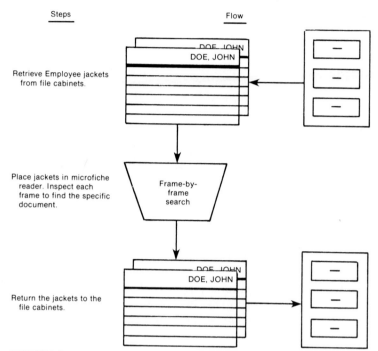

Retrieve Employee jackets
  from file cabinets.

Place jackets in microfiche
  reader. Inspect each
  frame to find the specific
  document.

Return the jackets to the
  file cabinets.

EXHIBIT 5
XYZ Corporation Current Microfiche Retrieval

EXHIBIT 6
XYZ Corporation Growth in Personnel since 1960

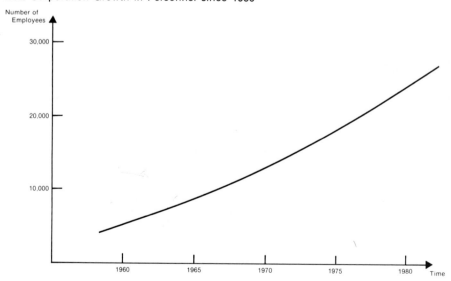

ments per week to be processed. Cost elements for the present system are given in Exhibit 7.

PLANS FOR CHANGE

Recently it has become clear that improvements on the present procedures are necessary if the payroll specialists are to maintain the microfilm records in a cost-effective and timely manner. In particular the current process is often time consuming without an accompanying increase in efficiency. In addition, the cost of materials, as well as those of labor and file cabinet security, are very high. Finally, and most important, there is a projected growth factor of more than 25 percent over the next three years. If operations continue as they are today, the only possible solution to accommodate this growth would be to add to the personnel already handling the maintenance function, which would in turn compound the cost problems.

As a result, Baker has undertaken a project to alleviate the workload of the document maintenance function and has initiated research into the background of that problem. As a preliminary step he has sought information from the ultimate users through interviewing. In an attempt to define the scope and direction of this project, excerpts of Baker's conversations with Johnson, the manager of the payroll department, and his supervisor Williams, were recorded.

Williams: The system we have now consists of segregating the incoming documents by employee. Since there is not necessarily a relationship among a particular employee's documents for our purposes, we now propose microfilming these documents and storing the microimages in the order in which they are received, without preliminary sorting. In order to keep track of where the particular docu-

---

EXHIBIT 7
XYZ Corporation Costs of the Current System

Personnel	Annual Cost
2 payroll specialists	$28,000 (including benefits)

Equipment & Supplies	Annual Cost
Microfilm	$ 200
Chemicals	500
Microfiche jackets	750
Diazo copy process materials	5,000
Total cost	$34,450

ments are located in the file cabinets, an index to these locations could be developed.

Bill Johnson and I have studied at some length a new microfilm system that would achieve this end with computer assistance. The purpose of the new system is to replace the present employee document microfilm function. We would like to reduce the labor intensity of the function of maintaining the documents. Although we would continue the microfilming of the documents, we feel that by creating an index which retains a close association with the file cabinet, we would eliminate some of the present tedium of the function. In particular, both maintenance and retrieval would be easier and faster. We are hopeful that a new system might be developed to be an extension of our other on-line systems. However, we realize that this may not be feasible.

Response time is not crucial since requests are so infrequent (on average, five per week). We would like to at least maintain, if not upgrade, the present level of integrity and security.

Johnson: First of all, we should install a microfilm index system on the corporate computer. This will streamline the entire operation. Documents can be filmed and inserted by the payroll specialists as they are received in the microfilm section without sorting. Information, such as name and document type, and the location of the document, can be entered into the computer. By consulting the index it is a simple matter to find any document in the file cabinet. We could use a software package that has been developed by U.S. Data Corporation: the Index Management System (Exhibit 8).

Second, we don't need to convert all the old files to the new system. We can maintain the current microfiche jackets for historical purposes only.

Third, installing a new microfilm camera would speed up operations considerably. There's one available with an automatic feed, dual lens, rotary camera that will create, in one pass, the master and back-up copies of the original document. This will shrink material costs to under 2¢ per document.

Finally, we should upgrade the position of payroll specialist. This is not a simple file clerk operation. It is a record-keeping responsibility requiring well-organized, highly motivated staff. Upgrading the position will permit us to attract and keep competent people.

The way I see it we could design the screens for the on-line system something like this (Exhibit 9). It would be on-line for easy updating and instant response. The operator entering the information could do data entry directly from the jacket. That is, he/she could have the jacket in a reader on one side and a CRT on the other. We should get a listing every day of all the transactions that were entered into the system the day before. These would be checked against the actual jacket to ensure correctness. In addition, an index of all the entries could be generated in hardcopy once a week to be used in an emergency when the computer is unavailable.

With the material presented, Baker, the programmer/analyst, set out to design the new microfiche index system. As his analysis of the situation progressed, Baker acknowledged a number of obstacles.

Baker: I think I understand the situation as described by Williams and Johnson. However, there are a few problems that have come to my attention. Specifically, my boss has made the decision to install a new IBM software package which is

---

EXHIBIT 8
Index Management System

The Index Management System (IMS),* developed by Datacorp, provides a method of maintaining indexed information on COM microfiche. The actual master index is kept on one or more microfiche while the supplementary data is maintained on a separate set of fiche. The master fiche which is updated periodically consists of identifying information to the rest of the associated data along with the locations within the remaining fiche. For example, if a customer's account number is considered to be key to the other information kept on the customer, then the master fiche would have each customer's account number along with pointers to the other fiche containing information on that account. The user is allowed the option of either retaining all occurrences in the files of a particular account or erasing outdated occurrences and pointing only to the most current information.

Another feature of IMS is the capability of managing more than one data file. Therefore, a report may be created based on a series of independently maintained files. As an example, if the account number from the above example points to customer name in one file and inventory in another, a report may be generated listing the names of all customers who purchased a specific item of inventory. This thereby ties the customer file to the inventory file.

Still another feature of IMS is the ability to cross-index information with many look-up sequences. In other words, rather than cumbersome sorting of the database, IMS allows the user to sort the index. Using this sorted index the job of locating a file in a sequence other than the original key is made possible.

Finally, the IMS master index may be used as a database. By including vital information, the IMS index becomes a mini-database. Often-used information is detailed in the index to a level which precludes the necessity of further search. Information needed less often or in more detail may still be found in the supplementary data fiche via the index.

In effect, IMS affords greater flexibility in the utilization and application of information maintained on COM microfiche. This frees the programmer from regimentation in designing an information system.

---

*This should not be confused with Information Management System (IMS).

---

designed to perform update and retrieval functions. This package, Application Development Facility (ADF) seems to be well-suited for the payroll department's problem. My boss feels it would be a good test project for the new system. The only alternative which could be considered is foregoing the ADF package and using pure IMS (Information Management System) to program all the necessary functions. (The two alternatives are costed out in Exhibit 10.)

Johnson's index management system was discarded primarily because it would be too "project specific." That is, it would be created solely for the use of the microfilm section and would probably not be usable in other areas of the company.

In addition, I see some problems developing with Johnson himself. Prior to his present position in the payroll department, Johnson worked with the information system representative for client services. That is, he dealt directly with the programmer analyst who developed systems for payroll. With this experience, Johnson appears to feel qualified to design the needed system on his own. Some of his

---

EXHIBIT 9
Microfiche Index System Input Screen

Social security number	Document type	Effective date	Location
012-10-1234	ECN	4/14/79	102234
013-20-5678	ECN	4/12/79	102235
014-30-9012	PCV	4/15/79	102236
015-40-3456	ECN	4/09/79	102237
016-50-7890	TAX	4/14/79	102238
017-60-1234	APP	4/13/79	102239
018-70-5678	PCV	4/11/79	102240
019-80-9012	ECN	4/15/79	102241
020-90-3456	ECN	4/13/79	102242
021-00-7890	PCV	4/07/79	102243
022-10-1234	TAX	4/10/79	102244
023-20-5678	MEM	4/01/79	102245
024-30-9012	TAX	4/07/79	102246
025-40-3456	APP	4/13/79	102247
026-50-7890	ECN	4/14/79	102248
027-60-1234	ECN	4/01/79	102249
028-70-5678	PCV	4/13/79	102250
029-80-9012	ECN	3/30/79	102251
030-90-3456	ECN	4/17/79	102252
031-00-7890	PCV	4/11/79	102253

---

preliminary designs seem workable. However, I don't think he really needs all that he wants.

Based on the information he collected, Baker went on to design and develop the required system.

EXHIBIT 10
Application Development Facility VS.
Information Management System Developmental Costs

	Amount	Man Days
Application Development Facility	$32,500	154.1
Information Management System	$35,200	167.1
Total Difference (IMS - ADF)	$ 2,700	13

EXHIBIT 10 (Continued)
Application Development Facility (ADF)

The basic concept behind the Application Development Facility (ADF) is to standardize application development for the programmer. In effect, there are a limited number of tasks any program will perform. ADF provides an environment for the programmer to incorporate these tasks with minimum effort, to produce the application. ADF is in essence application software to the Information Management System (IMS) database management system. It enhances the IMS environment and ultimately minimizes the amount of time required for application development.

This is done primarily with the use of standardized screens. These screens are formatted with specific information by the individual designer. This along with the application logic is the major ingredient to application development with ADF.

The application logic is most often specified to ADF with the use of "rules." There are two basic types of rules: static and dynamic. Static rules, as the name implies, are enumerated at the start of the application design and remain unchanged. They dictate what the batabase and screens look like as well as what functions will be performed in the particular application.

On the other hand, dynamic rules determine the action flows in the application. For instance, they specify who is authorized to perform which functions and reject any unauthorized users. They also specify what should happen if an error occurs in input or processing.

The database is designed by means of a series of statements: SYSTEM, SEGMENT, and FIELD. The format of these statements is dictated by ADF. The SYSTEM statement defines the parameters which are used throughout the application. In effect, it identifies the application. The SEGMENT statements outline the segments to be used in the hierarchical design unique to IMS databases. The FIELD statements detail the variables contained in each segment. The basic sequence of these statements is:

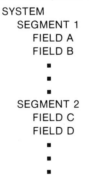

```
SYSTEM
  SEGMENT 1
    FIELD A
    FIELD B
      ■
      ■
      ■
  SEGMENT 2
    FIELD C
    FIELD D
      ■
      ■
      ■
```

Based on the information found in the dynamic and static rules and in the SYSTEM, SEGMENT, and FIELD statements, the ADF screens are tailored for the application. Specifically, there are five major screens provided with ADF: Sign-On, Primary Option Menu, Secondary Option Menu, Key Selection Screen, and Segment Display. The sign-on screen is the first screen the user sees. The user enters his/her ID and the appropriate project and group code. This is checked against a database which maintains authorizations for all users. If all the information is correct the next screen to appear is the primary option menu. This allows the user to select the transaction he/she wishes to process. If the user is authorized to perform the function he/she has selected, the next screen, the secondary option menu, appears. This screen displays all the segments the current user is allowed to manipulate. Once a segment is chosen, the key selection screen appears. On this screen the user specifies which occurrence of the particular segment he/she

EXHIBIT 10 (Continued)

wishes to see. For example, if the segment type is employee, Jones may be a desired occurrence. Finally, the segment display screen for the specified segment occurrence is made available to the user. Once all processing is complete, the user returns to the primary option menu and ultimately signs off the system. Although there is a standard format for each screen provided with ADF these screens may be redesigned to suit the user in his/her application.

The ease with which programming may be accomplished with ADF is the primary benefit of using the system. To an extent, it eliminates the need for a programmer to be trained in a high-level language.

THE CATTANI COMPANIES (A)

Lee Gremillion

Billie Cooper, office manager for the Cattani Companies, had just finished reviewing Cattani's accounting procedures for Francine Newton, an independent data processing consultant. "If we can put our accounting on a computer," she concluded, "we can take care of a number of concerns we have. For one thing, it should relieve the awful crunch we've been having at harvest time and again at year-end with the payrolls. And it could relieve me of some drudge work if it would take care of the payables. But the real payoff, for Arnold and me both, would come in the ledger accounting. If I'm understanding you correctly, a computer would let us keep the books by individual ranch and crop, and still produce statements for each crop across all ranches. That would be worth a lot. I will be very interested to see what you come up with."

THE CATTANI COMPANIES

The Cattani Companies refers collectively to four legally separate but related farming enterprises: A. Cattani & Son; WRA, Incorporated; Switchback Citrus Company; and Arnold Cattani, Jr., Farm Account. Although separate companies, all four were managed by and at least partly owned by Arnold Cattani, Jr. All four were engaged in farming a variety of crops in the southern San Joaquin Valley near Bakersfield, California. Headquarters for the companies are located just outside Arvin, California, a small town at the southeast tip of the Valley.

The original company, A. Cattani & Son, had evolved from a dairy farm established in the early part of the century by the Cattani family, immigrants from Yugoslavia. As the years passed, the business shifted away from dairying to cotton production, and then to a mix of cotton, row crops, and vineyards. Units of land, or "ranches" as they were called in the valley, were bought (or leased) and sold periodically, with the overall size of the company steadily increasing.

Arnold Cattani, Jr., was the third generation of the family to manage the company. After graduating from the M.B.A. program at the Harvard Business School in the early 1970s, Arnold, Jr., began to take over the active management as Arnold, Sr., gradually retired. At the same time he started getting involved in other farming ventures which became the other companies in the Cattani Companies group. Exhibit 1 shows the ranches making up each company, and the crops being grown on the ranches in 1979.

In 1973, Billie Cooper was hired to assist with the accounting and adminis-

---

EXHIBIT 1
Cattani Companies—Ranches and 1979 Crops

A. Cattani & Son

Crites	Cotton
Bock Place	Spring onions, fall onions, table grapes, cotton
Adobe & Teale	Alfalfa, cotton
Moore 1	Alfalfa, Garlic
Calciano	Grain, winery grapes
Logrecco	Winery grapes, cotton
Hog Ranch	Table grapes
Home Place	Cotton, watermelons
Canal Bank	Spring potatoes, cotton
Guerra Place	Alfalfa, cotton
Peters Place	Plums, barley
Mom's Place	Grain
Lundquist Ranch	Grain, cotton

W.R.A., Inc

Walker Ranch	Table grapes, winery grapes
D.R. Ranch	Table grapes, winery grapes

Switchback Citrus

Switchback	Oranges

A. Cattani Jr. Farm Account

Ranch 115	Table grapes, raisin grapes, winery grapes
Ranch 117	Table grapes, winery grapes
Ranch 126	Raisin grapes, kiwis
Ranch 134	Table grapes, winery grapes
Ranch 106	Almonds, winery grapes
Ranch 129	Almonds
Wilson Road Ranch	Alfalfa

trative functions, which previously had been largely handled by Arnold, Jr., himself. Billie rapidly proved herself very capable, and steadily assumed more and more responsibility for managing the administrative side of this business. As the companies grew, it became necessary to add a person working half time to handle the payroll, and a few clerical duties. Supervision of the actual field operations was in the hands of several foremen and supervisors, as shown in Exhibit 2.

ACCOUNTING

By 1979, Billie was handling all the administrative and accounting functions for the four companies. This basically involved keeping the books for four separate companies. Billie described the accounting functions as falling into three major areas: payroll, accounts payable, and general ledger accounting.

Payroll is one of the major administrative functions for the Cattani companies. Overall, labor expense amounts to about 35 percent of the total operating expense, although this varies considerably by crop. The size of the labor force fluctuates with the season. The peak comes during the period from mid-August through late-October each year, when the grapes, and then the cotton, are harvested. At that time, the payroll for each company swells to several hundred workers. A lesser peak occurs early in the year when the labor force is expanded to handle pruning in the vineyards. During the slackest work periods, however, the payroll size shrinks to under fifty workers.

EXHIBIT 2
Cattani Companies Organization Chart

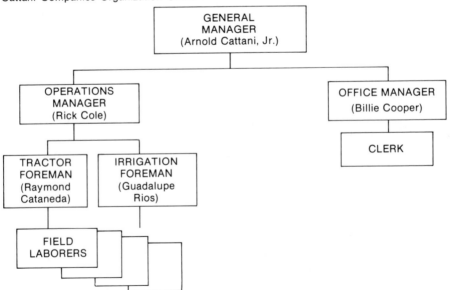

There is also considerable volatility in the work force—new persons are employed and others quit every week. Over the course of a year, each of the companies would typically have employed for some period of time (and therefore have to provide W-2s for) up to 1000 individuals. Because of the transient nature of the labor force, only a handful of these individuals would be back to work for Cattani next year.

All employees (with the exception of those management and clerical personnel shown on the organization chart) who work during a week are paid at the beginning of the next week. Standard practice in the valley is to have the paychecks to the workers within seventy-two hours of the end of the period for which they are being paid. During most of the year, this is no particular constraint. During the harvest time, however, this has meant long hours for everyone in the office, and they still didn't always meet the deadline. There have been no repercussions from paying employees up to a day late. Preparation of the W-2s at the beginning of the year also involved tedious, time-consuming work for the office staff.

Weekly payrolls are prepared from the timecards filled out by each employee and approved by his or her supervisor. (Exhibit 3 shows a sample timecard.) If the work the employee performed was paid on an hourly basis, then hours and the hourly rate are filled in on the card. If the work was paid on a piece rate basis, then the timecard line would show the number of pieces (of whatever) and the piece rate. (Hours and pieces are filled in by the workers in the fields; rates are filled in by the office staff after the timecards are turned in.) Gross pay for an employee is simply the sum of the extensions of the lines.

All work done in the fields is identified as to the ranch and crop on which it is performed, and as to the exact nature of the work. The different types of work are referred to as labor functions. Exhibit 4 shows the various labor functions used on the Cattani Companies. It was necessary to classify labor expenses by crop, ranch, and function so that Billie could maintain the general ledger accounts properly.

State Disability Insurance (SDI) is deducted from the pay of all employees at the rate of 1 percent of gross pay. However, the law forbids withholding SDI from an employee's paycheck until that employee has earned at least $150.00 total since the beginning of the year. For some workers, particularly children who only work a few hours a week on an irregular basis, it may be well into the year before they reach the $150 mark, if ever. Social Security Tax (FICA) is deducted from the pay of all employees, at the rate of 6.13 percent of gross. However, once a total of $1403.77 FICA for the year was reached, this tax was no longer withheld. State and federal income tax deductions are made for only a few employees who request that a specific amount be withheld.

A record is kept for every employee who receives a paycheck of any size at any time during the year. This record contains the employee's year-to-date totals for gross pay, and for deductions for SDI, federal income tax, state

A.CATTANI & SON

Employee's Signature _____ Period Ending ___10/1/79___

Check No. ___10113___

Employee's Number ___(305)___

Tues.	Wed.	Thur.	Fri.	Sat.	Sun.	Mon.	Ranch Name	Ranch Code	Crop Code	Function Code	Tractor Code	Implement Code	Total	Rate
10						10							20	3.10
	6	6	6	6									24	3.00
	500 vines	480 vines	300 vines	100 vines									1380 vines	.10

A.M.	Time Start	
	Time Finish	
P.M.	Time Start	
	Time Finish	
	Hrs Worked	

Total		272.00
Total Overtime		
Gross Wages		272.00
Less Deducts	State D.I.	2.72
	Soc. Sec.	16.67
	Fed. W/H Tax	
	State W/H Tax	
	Misc'l	
Net Earnings		252.61

Approved _____

EXHIBIT 3
Timecard Used by Cattani Companies

EXHIBIT 4
Cattani Companies Labor Functions

Pruning	Brush Disposal
Tying	Cultivating
Suckering	Tractor Work
Girdling	
GIB Application	Harvesting—Hand
Thinning	Harvesting—Mechanical
Trellis Repair	Repair & Maint.—Pipeline
Training	Road/building
Layering	Pump & well
Vineyard Repair & Maint.	Mech. Hrvstr.
	Sprayer
Irrigation—sprinkler	Tractor
Irrigation—row	Auto/truck
Fertilizer Application	Implement
Soil Amendment	Shop wages
Weed Control—Mech. spray	Misc.
Weed Control—Hand spray	
Weed Control—Hand	Supervision
Defoliation	Office wages
Pest & Disease Control	Miscellaneous

income tax, and social security tax. All of this had to be kept separately for each company for which the employee worked, since each was a legally distinct employer. Exhibit 5 shows a sample of the payroll ledger form on which this information was kept. Additionally, the employee's original application for employment, which contains his address, social security number, and other personal data, is filed in the office. This information is necessary to produce W-2s at the end of the year.

Accounts payable refers to the process of paying vendors for goods and services purchased by the companies, and then charging the expenses to the proper accounts. As bills came in during the month, Billie coded them as to the company, crop, and account to which they applied. Often a particular bill would have to be allocated across several companies and crops.

Periodically, she wrote checks to pay the invoices and posted the amounts to the ledgers. Each company, of course, had its own checking account, and in all cases the same account was used for both payroll and payables. The checks themselves were written using a system known as Safeguard, which used multiple copy paper to produce a check register as a by-product of actually writing the check. By 1979, Billie was writing about 300 checks per month, and was spending about 15 hours per week in handling the payables. During the times when payroll processing became particularly heavy, she helped with that function, which sometimes resulted in the bills' being paid late.

NAME: IROGD, MANUE'L   DEPT. 4009

STREET: PO BOX 327

CITY: ARVIN, CA

CLOCK NUMBER:

SOC. SEC NUMBER: 569-02-4009

PHONE NO.:

DATE STARTED / DATE LEFT:

MARITAL STATUS: ☐ M. ☐ OF.   NO. OF EXEMPT:

RECORD OF PAY RATE CHANGES — DATE / RATE: 3.00/hr.

PAY PERIOD ENDING	TIME WORKED	REGULAR EARNINGS	TOTAL PAY	SDI	FICA	INS.	OTHER	NET AMOUNT	CHECK NUMBER
		EARNINGS				DEDUCTIONS			
1/1	60 hours		216.00	2.16	13.44	25-		175.40	8009
1/7	41 hours		147.42	1.48	9.03	25-		112.02	8014
1/15	55½ hours		199.82	2.02	12.25	25-		160.55	8024
1/22	40 hours		144.00	1.44	8.83	25-		108.73	8038
1/29	54½ hours		196.20	1.96	12.03	25-		157.21	8059
2/4	56 hours		201.60	2.02	12.36	25-		162.22	8066
2/11	73 hours		262.60	2.63	16.21	25-	SP.15	160.42	8745
2/18	63½ hours		228.60	2.29	14.01	25-		187.30	8204
4/24	49 hours		176.40	1.96	10.82	25-		138.83	8242
3/3	44½ hours		160.20	1.60	7.82	25-		123.78	8268
3/11	67½ hours		243.00	2.43	14.90	25-		200.03	8272
3/18	49 hours		176.40	1.76	10.82	25-		138.89	8292
3/25	47 hours		169.20	1.65	10.82	25-		132.74	8320
QUARTERLY TOTALS			2521.00	25.22	154.57	325.00	53.15	1959.84	
4/1	31 hours		111.60	1.12	6.84	25-		78.64	8352

EXHIBIT 5
Earnings Record

General ledger accounting involved keeping a set of books for each company which recorded revenues and expenditures by crop. Exhibit 6 shows the general chart of accounts used by the Cattani Companies. Entries were posted to the books as each payroll was processed, and when the payables checks were written. Entries were also made to record receipts, corrections, and charges not part of payroll or payables. In general, however, payroll and payables transactions accounted for the bulk of the ledger entries. Billie spent an average of one half day per week posting to the ledgers.

At the end of each year these ledgers became the basis for financial statements prepared for the investors, and for tax reporting. (Income tax accounting for agricultural enterprises is done on a cash basis, much like individual income tax.) Billie also prepared a statement at the end of the season for each crop, after the crop was sold and all activities were completed. These reports showed the expenditures and receipts by account for a crop on all the ranches for a particular company. Ledgers were not kept for each individual ranch/crop combination because that level of detail would be too much for Billie to take care of in the time she had.

Occasionally, Arnold would need a financial statement for a particular ranch/crop combination, to respond to inquiries by a lender or for management purposes. In such a case, Billie would have to go back through past transaction data to obtain the information. This could be a time-consuming task, particularly if late in the crop season. So far, however, the requirement for these ranch/crop statements had not come often enough to justify maintaining all the ledgers by individual ranch/crop.

COMPUTERIZED FARM ACCOUNTING

Billie had been aware for some time that computers could be used to automate farm accounting. A few of the very large farming corporations in the valley in fact had computers, but, since these were all machines costing $100,000 or more, neither she nor Arnold had given much thought to computerizing Cattani's operations. In early 1979, however, Billie became aware of the existence of smaller, lower priced computers when a nearby family-operated farm of similar size to Cattani's, acquired an IBM 5100 system to do their payroll. She had seen a demonstration of this system which she had found very interesting. She was particularly impressed with the speed with which a payroll could be done, and with the error prevention features built into the system. For example, when an employee number was entered from a timecard, the 5100 displayed the employee's name, allowing the operator to see if it was the right person.

Shortly after the demonstration, Billie ran into Francine Newton, a friend from high school, who, after graduating from Cal State/Bakersfield, and then working for a computer vendor, had gone into business for herself as a consultant. Billie mentioned the demonstration she had seen of a computer used to do farm payrolls. She was very interested to hear Francine mention that the

EXHIBIT 6
Cattani Companies—Chart Of Accounts

Crop Sales Revenue Accounts

Alfalfa
Almonds
Barley
Beans
Beets—sugar
Carrots—spring
Cotton
Figs
Garlic
Grain
Grapes—unspecified
Grapes—raisins
Grapes—table
Grapes—winery
Kiwis
Lettuce
Onions—spring
Onions—fall
Oranges
Peaches
Plums
Potatoes—fall
Potatoes—spring
Tomatoes—fresh
Tomatoes—processing
Watermelons

Other Income Accounts

Government program payments
Interest earned
Gas tax refunds
Rental income
Water sold
Machine hire
Miscellaneous income
Patronage dividends

Direct Proration Expense Accounts

Taxes—payroll
Taxes—property
Insurance—Workers Compensation

Dollar Proration Expense Accounts

Bad debts
Bank charges
Cash short (over)
Dues, subscriptions, advertising
Interest
Legal & accounting

Supplies
Taxes—other
Insurance—ranch
Insurance—general

Management Value Proration Expense Accounts

Employee benefit pmts. (vac., etc.)
Foreman's supervisor's wages
Office salaries
Office expenses & supplies
Public relations
Travel & entertainment
Telephone & radio
Miscellaneous repair & maintenance
Insurance—group medical
Miscellaneous expense

Crop Production Expense Accounts

Commissions
Miscellaneous crop purchases
Equipment rental
Equipment rental—R & M
Hauling & freight
Land rent—alloc. for double crop
Seed
Utilities
Water
Pipe rental
Land preparation
Planting
Cultivating
Tractor work
Irrigation—sprinkler
Irrigation—row
Irrigation—drip
Fertilizer—application
Fertilizer—material
Herbicides—application
Herbicides—material
Fungicides, etc.—application
Fungicides, etc.—material
Weed control—mechanical spray
Weed control—hand spray
Weed control—hand spray
Pruning
Tying
Suckering
Girdling
GIB application

EXHIBIT 6 (Continued)

Thinning
Trellis repair
Training
Layering
Vineyard repair & maintenance
Turning canes
Miscellaneous expenses
New crop setup

Equipment Maintenance Expense Accounts

Equipment parts & supplies
R & M—pipeline
R & M—sprinkler pipe
R & M—roads/building
R & M—pump/wells
R & M—mechanical harvesters
R & M—sprayers
R & M—tractors
R & M—auto/truck
R & M—implements
R & M—shop wages
R & M—general
Trailer & gondola expense
Fuel, oil, etc.
Fees & licenses

Hauling & freight
Insurance—equipment
Miscellaneous expenses
Leasing—auto/truck

Harvest and Shipment Expense Accounts

Harvest labor—equip operators
Harvest labor—hand contract
Harvest labor—hand self
Harvest labor—machine self
Harvest—mechanical
Harvest labor—machine contract
Packing containers
Inspections & assessments
Harvest equipment rental
Harvest equipment R & M
Materials & supplies
Harvest & packing charges (contract)
Harvest—miscellaneous labor
Hauling—self
Hauling—contract
Miscellaneous expenses

Sales Expense Accounts

Selling expenses
Packing charges
Miscellaneous

IBM 5100, while a good machine, was much more expensive than comparable computers generally referred to as small business systems (SBS). In fact, Francine declared machines with functions similar to the 5100 were now on the market for around $10,000.

Billie returned to the office and told Arnold about the demonstration and her conversation with Francine. She felt that if the computer could do the payroll so quickly, then it could be used to perform other accounting functions as well. In particular, she thought the computer might have the potential to keep ledgers by individual ranch/crops, and to produce statements quickly and easily when needed. Accordingly, they decided to engage Francine to do a preliminary study of the feasibility of using a computer at the Cattani Companies. It was this possibility that Francine was now considering.

FRANCINE'S ANALYSIS

Francine knew from the start that total-system cost would be a very important factor in Cattani's decision whether or not to use a computer. She also knew that the only option they would seriously consider would be to have their own hardware in-house. They had tried a Los Angeles service bureau once for payroll processing, but had discontinued it after six months of completely unsatisfactory operations. The IBM 5100 which the neighboring farm had acquired had cost about $25,000, including a standard payroll package, and Billie had indicated that Cattani probably wouldn't be willing to spend much more than that. Francine saw her first task then as being one of determining whether she could find a hardware/software combination which met Cattani's needs and fell into that price range.

As a possible hardware system to consider, Francine was very interested in Infotecs Corporation's Infotecs Miniprocessor, or IMP. This system, which had become a best seller almost as soon as it was introduced, featured 24K bytes of main memory, two million bytes of on-line diskette storage on two drives, and a 115 cps bi-directional matrix printer. A built-in video display and keyboard was used for data input as well as for system control. At a total price of just over $10,000, Francine felt that this was a remarkably economical system. At any rate, she knew that the functions, features, and cost of the IMP were typical of a large number of SBSs.

The IMP would be programmed in HIBOL, a high-level language which resembled a streamlined version of COBOL. To input data into the system, a program written in HIBOL would accept entries from the console keyboard. All access to disk records on the IMP are made by relative record number.

As part of the system software, the IMP featured a text editor for entering and maintaining HIBOL source programs, and, of course, the HIBOL compiler. It also had a SORT utility program which would sort any diskette data file on any field or set of fields in the record. A general utility program offered diskette data file handling functions such as COPY, RENAME, ALLOCATE, and DELETE. In general, since the IMP was based on a PDP-8 processor chip, it was able to utilize software originally developed for the widely-used PDP-8.

Francine knew that perhaps the biggest decision Cattani would have to make concerning the computer would be on system development—should they attempt to buy a turnkey system, hire an outside programmer/analyst to develop a tailored system for them, try to train or hire an employee of their own to do it, or what? Nevertheless, she felt that before considering that question she should rough out a systems design which would allow some estimates of hardware and software requirements. In particular, she wanted to see if the job could be done on the IMP, or some other similar SBS.

After a couple of days' worth of detailed interviews with Arnold and Billie about Cattani's accounting system, Francine went back to her office to work on the problem. She promised a response within two weeks.

THE CATTANI COMPANIES (B)

Lee Gremillion

Francine Newton, data processing consultant, was in the midst of preliminary design for the computerized payroll system for the Cattani Companies. Her proposal—that Cattani acquire an INFOTECS IMP small business computer and contract with her for systems design and programming—had been accepted, and she had launched into the project. The first system up would be payroll, since automating it would provide the largest and most immediate payback.

Because of the fact that Cattani would be running, in effect, four separate payrolls for essentially the same employees, Francine decided to segment the data concerning employees. There would be one "Employee Master" file which would contain a record for each individual employed by one or more of the companies. Exhibit 1 shows the layout of this record. This record would contain all of the nonvolatile information about an individual, such as name, address, birthdate, and social security number.

For each company (which, as a separate legal entity, had to keep separate books) there would also be a "Payroll Master" file. In this file there would be a record for each individual who had worked for that company, as shown in Exhibit 2. There would be four of these payroll master files, and, if an individual worked on all four companies (as many did), that individual would have a record in each file. Because of the extremely high turnover in the largely migratory labor force, it was decided that these files would simply be started over from scratch each year.

EXHIBIT 1
Layout For The Employee Master Record

Item	Type	Length
Employee Number	N	5
First Name	A	10
Last Name	A	14
First Line of Address	A	20
Second Line of Address	A	20
ZIP Code	N	5
Birthdate (MMDDYY)	N	6
Telephone Number (with area code)	N	10
Social Security Number	N	9

The primary key for the records in both files would have to be the five-digit employee number. This number was derived by taking the last four digits of the employee's social security number, and prefixing it with a fifth digit in order to prevent duplicates. This numbering scheme had been in use for several years, and Billie Cooper (the office manager) had expressed a strong desire to retain it. Francine had pointed out that numbering employees sequentially from one each year would facilitate the design of the computerized system, but Billie concluded that renumbering would cause too many problems in interfacing to old records.

EXHIBIT 2
Layout For The Payroll Master Record

Item	Type	Length
Employee Number	N	5
Company Number	N	2
Year-to-date Gross Pay*	N	8
Y-T-D FICA Tax Withheld*	N	6
Y-T-D SDI Tax Withheld*	N	6
Y-T-D Federal Income Tax Withheld*	N	6
Y-T-D State Income Tax Withheld*	N	6
Y-T-D Misc. Deductions*	N	6
Y-T-D Repayment Deductions*	N	6
Month-to-date Gross Pay*	N	6
Month-to-date Hours Worked	N	4
Quarter-to-date Gross Pay*	N	6
Number of weeks worked this quarter where gross pay exceeded $20	N	2

*These monetary figures have two decimal places implied.

Francine was now considering how to organize these files onto the physical diskette storage of the IMP. As the Cattani system was configured, there were two on-line drives, each of which would hold a removable diskette capable of storing approximately one million characters of data. The IMP software supported files made up of fixed-length records of any size, automatically mapping logical records into and out of the sectored diskette. All record addressing, however, was by relative record number—there was no software support for indexing. The READ command (which made a logical record from the diskette available to the user's program) and the WRITE command (which took a logical record set up in the user's program and placed it on the diskette) both required as an argument the proper relative record number. An APPEND command created new records in a file by adding them to the end of the existing records.

Francine realized that if the system could be designed for all sequential processing, then the storage structure would be simple. The employee and payroll master files could be loaded and maintained by APPENDing new records, and then sorting (the software contained a SORT utility) the file back into employee number order. Batches of transactions (weekly timecard data, journal entries) would also be sorted by employee number, and check writing, file updating, and report writing could be done via normal sequential batch processing.

There seemed to be a need, however, for direct access to individual employee records in some cases. The most important of these was in conjunction with the entry of weekly timecard data. This would be accomplished by running a program which systematically prompted the operator for the data items to be entered. This program would build a transaction file on the diskette from this data. Each record would contain the employee number, the ranch, crop, and function applicable to the labor, the hours or pieces for which the employee was being paid, and the pay rate.

Both Francine and Billie felt very strongly that this data entry should be made as foolproof as possible, in order to minimize the chances of error. One foolproofing feature which Billie especially wanted would be to have the program look up each employee number as it was entered, and then flash up the employee's name on the CRT. The operator would check to see if this matched the name on the timecard. Ranch, crop, and function would be similarly checked as they were entered.

This required direct access to the records in the employee master file, and Francine was considering how to best effect that. One way would be to make the employee master a hashed file, using an algorithm to convert employee number to relative record number. This, she realized, might have implications for any sequential processing done later in the payroll system. The other alternative seemed to be to do some sort of homemade indexing on the employee master.

To get a better idea of what the file characteristics would be, Francine examined past payroll records. The file would be small in January (when there was little activity in the fields and vineyards) and grow to about 1000 records by the end of the year. Most of the growth would take place in August, September, and October, when hundreds of workers were employed briefly for harvest. No deletions would be made during the year, since a W-2 would have to be written for every employee who worked any time during the year. In prior years, Francine saw each company had written about 2500 weekly paychecks over the course of a year. Discussions with Billie, however, revealed that the number of persons paid any one week could vary from a few dozen to several hundred.

To get a person paid with the computer system, Francine estimated, would take at least three retrievals of his/her employee master file record—one when the timecard data was entered, one when the check was printed, and one when the check register was printed. Of these, the retrieval by timecard entry program was the only one which had to be direct. Each record would also have to be retrieved for the monthly insurance report, quarterly state of California report, and annual W-2 printing, as well as for periodic listings of the file.

Francine felt that there ought to be a way to determine what the best file organization would be. To try to get a better idea of the diskette performance characteristics, she ran some timing tests, described in Exhibit 3. Finally, gathering all her data together, she set to work on the problem.

DISCUSSION NOTE*

This case is designed to be used as the basis for a class discussion or exercise on file design and record search mechanisms. One issue in file design revolves around the decision to "normalize" or segment the data about the employees. The alternatives to this design should be explicitly considered.

At one extreme, one file could have been used, in which there was a record for each employee who worked for any of the companies. This record would have personnel data (name, address, etc.) for the employee, and a space for the year-to-date pay and deductions figures by each company. A drawback with this approach would be the waste of disk space used for employees who don't actually work for all four companies during a year. More seriously, this approach would be rather inflexible—if a new company was added, the files would have to be redesigned to accommodate slots for it in the employees' records. (Note: these problems would not exist on a system which supported variable-length records in indexed files, which the IMP does not.) The advantage to this approach would be simplicity—all the data for an employee would be stored in one record, retrievable with one access.

At the other extreme, the data would be put in four separate, unrelated files. In this case there would be a file for each company, and the records in it

*This teaching note was prepared by Assistant Professor Lee L. Gremillion of Indiana University.

EXHIBIT 3
Diskette Timing Tests

The IMP diskette is a single-sided, soft-sectored, 8-inch floppy disk, the surface of which is divided into 77 tracks. Each track is divided into eight physical sectors of 1536 characters each, and a physical sector is the unit of transfer during a diskette I/O operation.

To try and get an idea of diskette I/O timings, Francine ran two test programs. The first of these merely alternated reading the first and then the second record of a diskette file repeatedly, so that it was performing only local accesses. The second program repeatedly read two records which were deliberately located 38 tracks apart (about one-half the diskette width), so that an arm movement (seek) was involved on each read. Using a stopwatch to time the programs, she observed the following results:

Number of Records Read	Total Time	
	Local Access Only	Random Accesses
50	5 seconds	8 seconds
100	10 seconds	16 seconds

---

would contain both the personnel data for the employee and his/her payroll data for that company. The problem here is redundancy. Each employee's personnel data would be repeated for each company for which he/she worked. Not only would this require more disk space, but it would also mean updating multiple files whenever a change occcured. On the other hand, it would be relatively simple, with all the data required to do payroll processing for an employee within a given company retrievable with a single access.

The approach taken—one employee master file and four (or *n*) payroll files—is a compromise. It trades off simplicity for efficient processing and use of disk space. There is neither wasted space nor redundant data stored, but two accesses to two different files are required to get the information to process each employee in the weekly payroll. An area for class discussion might be how this solution would look in a different hardware/software environment—say an IBM System/370 with VSAM.

The other issue is how to organize the files, particularly the employee master, to facilitate record retrieval. The user wants interactive error checking—that is, she wants to be able to enter the employee number from a timecard and have the system immediately display the employee name from the diskette file. This means that there will have to be some sort of direct access to individual employee master file records, using employee number as the search key.

Using the Infotecs IMP hardware/software combination, a number of organizations and access strategies are possible. These include

• Storing the file in employee number order and performing a binary search to find the record with a given employee number value.

- Storing the file in employee number sequence and then building, as a separate file, an index which contains key values and record addresses. This homemade index could be a full index, a block index, or a hierarchic block index, with a variety of search strategies.
- Storing the file in employee number sequence, and building a block index in main memory dynamically when the file is opened. The employee number of each nth record would be placed in an array. When an employee number from a time card was entered, the array would be searched to determine which block of n records on the disk to search. (Note: this is the strategy that was actually employed at the Cattani Companies installation.)
- Storing the file according to a hashing algorithm, using the employee number as the hash key. Records would be retrieved when the timecard data is entered by transforming the employee number to a record address. Bucket sizes, transformation algorithms, and overflow techniques are all issues with this method.

And there are other methods as well.

The problem can easily be modified to be set in any hardware/software environment the instructor prefers. Disk characteristics are given for the Infotecs IMP. These are important in two respects. First, the 1536-byte sector size suggests bucket size of 15 for storing the file to make data transfers most efficient. Second, the timings allow at least rough evaluation of each of the search strategies. To do this evaluation, the student must convert the timings given in Exhibit 3 to times per local access (100 ms.) and per random access (160 ms.). These can be used to see how long a particular search would take to find a record, considering only disk access time. For example, a binary search in a file of 600 records would be expected to take about $\log_2 600$ (=9) random accesses to find a particular record. Thus, using this technique would mean 9×.16 seconds, or about 1½ seconds of disk time to find the record.

UNITED FARM WORKERS ORGANIZING COMMITTEE AND ROBERT F. KENNEDY MEMORIAL HEALTH PLAN (A)*

Rodney B. Plimpton
Henry C. Lucas, Jr.

The Dusenberg Foundation
1753 Michigan Avenue
Falls Church, Virginia 11007

Systems Group
This is obviously
an important
opportunity to
show the Dusenberg
Foundation
what we can do in
the non-profit
sector. Please give
it your best effort!
JB

August 28, 1970

Mr. James Bosworth, President
Superior Consulting Services
700 Welch Road
Palo Alto, California 94305

Dear Mr. Bosworth:

 Mr. John Trauth of the A.U.A. informed me recently of the excellent job your systems group has done on the Association of
University Accountants project. Based upon his recommendations
we are inviting your firm to sumbit a proposal for a study of
the data processing requirements of the United Farm Workers and
Robert F. Kennedy Memorial Health Plan to be funded by the
Dusenberg Foundation. Details of this project are provided in
the attached request for proposals.

 Final selection of a consulting firm for the project will be
made by a joint committee from the Union, Health Plan and the
Foundation. Since we hope to award the initial contract by September 30th, we would appreciate having your proposal in hand no
later than September 16th. If you have any further questions
after reading the request for proposals please do not hesitate
to call me.

Sincerely yours,

Peter A. Lake
Director, Dusenberg Foundation

PAL:lr

*This case was made possible by a grant from the Donaldson, Lufkin & Jenrette Foundation.

**THE DUSENBERG FOUNDATION REQUEST FOR PROPOSALS
UNITED FARM WORKERS ORGANIZING COMMITTEE AND
ROBERT F. KENNEDY MEMORIAL HEALTH PLAN
DATA PROCESSING STUDY**

Introduction

The Dusenberg Foundation has recently set up a special fund to improve the management practices in nonprofit organizations. A grant from this fund has been jointly awarded to the United Farm Workers Organizing Committee and the Robert F. Kennedy Memorial Health Plan of Delano, California, for a study of their data processing requirements. If this study shows that a computer-assisted data processing system is feasible and desirable, it is anticipated that the grant will be extended to include the system design and implementation. Proposals are being solicited at this time for the Phase I study of the Union and Health Plan data processing requirements.

The Need for the Study

The United Farm Workers Organizing Committee (UFWOC), led by Cesar Chavez, has been attempting to secure better working conditions and greater economic security for farm workers through collective bargaining. The union provides several services and benefits to its members, including union hiring halls, a death benefit plan, and a credit union. The RFK Health Plan also provides medical and death benefits for farm workers. To administer these services efficiently, the union must keep accurate records for each member, including his dues history and membership status. The union must collect and account for dues, voluntary donations, and growers' contributions to an economic development fund for retraining members. The union also administers credit union accounts, and keeps track of contract provisions and job availability. The RFK Plan must maintain records of hours worked, beneficiaries and process benefit claims.

These data processing tasks are difficult because:

- The majority of union members are migrant workers who move from job to job over a large geographic area.
- Many members are not fluent in English and have little formal education or experience with union membership.
- Almost all of the record keeping is being performed manually by staff members, who are volunteers receiving a small living allowance.
- The union is supported in large measure by contributions from sympathetic individuals. It does not have the financial resources to hire a large staff or invest in expensive equipment.

In recent months the union and health plan have experienced a sharp increase in membership resulting from the successful conclusion of a nationwide grape boycott and the signing of union contracts with major grape growers. Further increases in membership are anticipated from negotiations currently being conducted with producers of lettuce, strawberries, and other crops. This growth in membership has placed a serious strain on the capacity of the union and health plan to maintain timely and accurate records using their current procedures. The purpose of the proposed study, then, is to determine:

- How long the union and health plan can expect to keep up with the increasing paperwork using current methods
- Whether there are better manual methods which could be used to process the paperwork more efficiently
- Whether the union and health plan should plan now to change to some form of automated record keeping using a computer or other device
- If the union and health plan should use computer processing, what kind of a computer is necessary, what should it do, and what will various alternatives cost?

Proposed Requirements

Your proposal should be for a study of the information processing requirements of the United Farm Workers and RFK Memorial Health Plan, to be completed by December 31 of this year. Output from the study should be in the form of a written report recommending whether or not the union and health plan should proceed with the development of a computerized data processing system. The report should include sufficient detail on all of the present data processing activities so that the initial design of such a system could be completed by working solely from the report.

Special consideration should be given to the fact that the union is dependent upon volunteers to staff the union headquarters. Many of these volunteers have been field workers, and, while they may have had little or no previous contact with EDP, they do have a spirit and dedication to the union's cause which is vital to its continued success.

Specifically, your proposal should include:

1 What data you plan to collect, and how you plan to collect them.

2 A research plan showing a time schedule for each step in the study.

3 What demands the study would place upon union personnel and/or facilities.

4 The number of people from your firm who would be involved in the study.

5 An estimate of the total number of worker-days required for the study, and estimated expenses.

Some further background information about the United Farm Workers Organizing Committee and RFK Health Plan is attached to assist you in preparing your proposal.

OVERALL ORGANIZATION

The overall organization of the union and health plan is shown roughly in the accompanying organization chart.

The board consists of all of the officers of the union and meets as necessary to decide all matters of policy. The union's administrative headquarters are in Delano, California. The Delano headquarters has several departments, shown in Exhibit 1. In addition there are boycott representatives in seventy cities in the United States. Directing the work of these representatives is the responsibility of the boycott office. Budgets for these activities are administered by the accounting department. There are also eleven hiring halls in various other locations which essentially serve three functions:

1 As membership offices where new members may join and old members may pay dues, ask questions, etc.

2 As hiring halls, dispatching members who are available for work to jobs which are available at ranches in that area.

3 As administrative centers for the ranch committee at each ranch.

A ranch committee consists of union members from each ranch who are elected by all of the members working at the ranch. The function of the ranch committee is to decide questions of seniority, handle grievances, distribute information to union members, and ensure that the contract is being enforced.

The Robert F. Kennedy Health Plan is an independent entity administered by a board of union and employer trustees. The plan is financed primarily by employer contributions, and members not covered may participate by paying a small fee.

Union Membership Office

The central membership office in Delano is responsible for maintaining a current dues history for every union member. This is done by manually posting the amount of dues paid on an 8½″ × 11″ master card which is filed by Social Security number (Exhibit 2). Members who are not working under a union contract pay their dues in person at Delano or one of the regional postings, and a yellow dues card which the member carries is updated. Members working under union contracts have dues deducted monthly from their paycheck by the growers. The growers in turn remit these dues to Delano, along with a list of the workers and the amounts deducted for each one. Posting is done manually from these lists.

A member working under union contract and whose dues are checked off by the grower can only have his or her yellow dues book updated by taking a check stub showing the dues deducted to the local hiring hall. Since a member must have back dues paid up and/or must sign an authorization for dues to be deducted before he or she is dispatched to a job, it is important

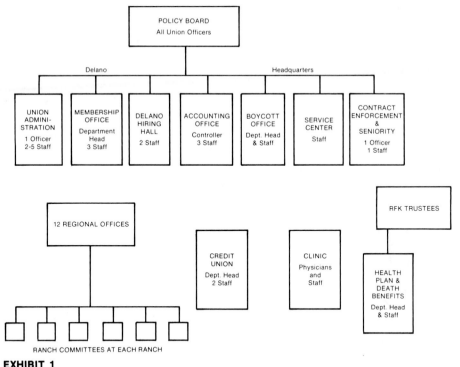

EXHIBIT 1
UFWOC & RFK Memorial Health Plan (A)

that the dues history be accurate. Problems sometimes occur because a grower is late in submitting a list of dues and/or the member does not retain his or her check stubs to prove that he or she is up to date with payments.

An alphabetical cross-reference file is maintained to locate members when the social security number is not known. At the present time there are about four full-time workers in the Delano membership office. Physical space is limited, and members of the department must answer questions about member status and receive dues payments as well as post dues from the growers' lists.

Union Accounting

The accounting office is primarily responsible for administering the union's budgets. The accounting office receives and verifies all incoming funds, keeps track of deposits and bank reconciliations, prepares and administers budgets, processes bills and issues checks, and prepares all necessary state and federal reports. All of the bookkeeping and accounting is done manually by the union controller and three other workers.

Social Security Number

Date of Birth

Cross Reference

Last Name   First   Middle

Home Address   P.O. Box   City

Membership Date
Initiation Date
Application File

Suspension   Reinstatement

RECEIPTS

CASH			CHECK OFF			Dues	Asses-ments	Initi-ation	Reinsta-tement	Fines	Other
Amount	Rct.No.	Date	Amount	Ranch	Date						

DUES MONTHS

19	19	19	19	19	19	19
Jan	Jan	Jan	Jan	Jan	Jan	Jan
Feb	Feb	Feb	Feb	Feb	Feb	Feb
Mar	Mar	Mar	Mar	Mar	Mar	Mar
Apr	Apr	Apr	Apr	Apr	Apr	Apr
May	May	May	May	May	May	May
June	June	June	June	June	June	June
Jul	Jul	Jul	Jul	Jul	Jul	Jul
Aug	Aug	Aug	Aug	Aug	Aug	Aug
Sept	Sept	Sept	Sept	Sept	Sept	Sept
Oct	Oct	Oct	Oct	Oct	Oct	Oct
Nov	Nov	Nov	Nov	Nov	Nov	Nov
Dec	Dec	Dec	Dec	Dec	Dec	Dec

ASSESSMENT MONTHS

Jan	Jan	Jan	Jan	Jan
Feb	Feb	Feb	Feb	Feb
Mar	Mar	Mar	Mar	Mar
Apr	Apr	Apr	Apr	Apr
May	May	May	May	May
Jun	Jun	Jun	Jun	Jun
Jul	Jul	Jul	Jul	Jul
Aug	Aug	Aug	Aug	Aug
Sept	Sept	Sept	Sept	Sept
Oct	Oct	Oct	Oct	Oct
Dec	Dec	Dec	Dec	Dec

NOTES

DoD-1c   10/69

EXHIBIT 2
UFWOC & RFK Memorial Health Plan (A)

Union Seniority and Contract Enforcement

This office has the general responsibility for seeing that all contract provisions are met, and for determining questions of seniority. At the present time most seniority questions are settled at the ranch committee level. The details of a unionwide seniority plan are still being worked out.

Service Center

The service center, which is supported almost entirely by voluntary contributions, provides additional services to farm workers, such as legal and consumer advice.

Credit Union

Membership in the credit union is available to union members for maintaining savings and obtaining low-interest loans. It is administered in compliance with state laws governing all credit unions, and all of the record keeping and processing is done manually by three members of the union staff.

ROBERT F. KENNEDY HEALTH PLAN AND DEATH BENEFITS PLAN

The union has negotiated a health plan which pays for certain medical costs incurred by eligible members, and a death benefits plan which provides a payment to the family of an eligible member in the event of death. Eligibility for health benefits is determined by the number of hours a member has worked under union contract during the previous quarter. The health plan office maintains a record of these hours for each worker which is updated by posting hours to an 8½" x 11" master card from lists submitted by the growers (Exhibit 3).

The health plan is funded by contributions from the grower based upon the total number of hours worked at his ranch by all union employees during the month. The plan is jointly administered by six trustees, three of whom are growers and three of whom are union officers. The health plan office is responsible for receiving and accounting for all payments by the growers, and for processing all claims made under the plan. The office also processes all claims made under the death benefits plan. (The union maintains a separate death benefit plan for workers not covered by the Kennedy plan.) At the present time there are four full-time workers in the health plan office who do all of the posting, claim processing, and answering questions about the plan and members' eligibility.

CLINIC

A medical clinic has been established in Delano to provide outpatient care to union members in the area. The clinic is run by physicians and registered

Social Security Number | Code | Code | Code | Last Name | First Name | Middle Name | Card Date

Home Address | P.O. Box | City | State

Birthdate | Married | Number of Children

Month	1 Balance	Hours	2 Balance	Wdrwl	Bank	Over	Category	Eligibility	Notes

6/23/69 1c

EXHIBIT 3
UFWOC & RFK Memorial Health Plan (A)

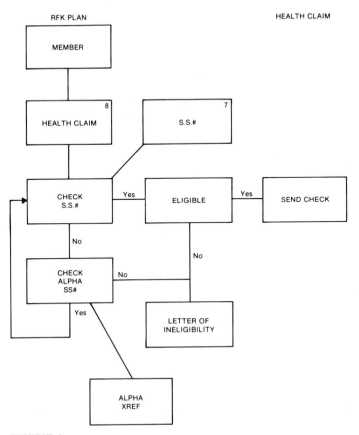

EXHIBIT 6
UFWOC & RFK Memorial Health Plan (A)

EXHIBIT 7
UFWOC & RFK Memorial Health Plan (A)

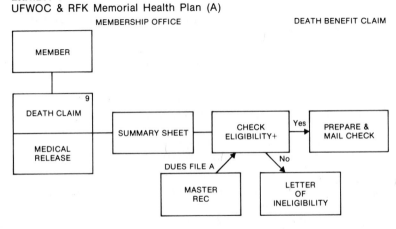

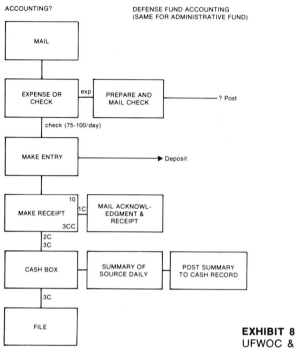

ACCOUNTING?

DEFENSE FUND ACCOUNTING
(SAME FOR ADMINISTRATIVE FUND)

EXHIBIT 8
UFWOC & RFK Memorial Health Plan (A)

nurses, and other assistants. If the medical service provided is covered under the health plan, the clinic files a claim with the health plan and receives payment from the plan. All medical records are maintained manually by the clinic staff. The clinic itself does not keep any record of members' eligibility under the health plan, but relies on the record kept by the health plan office.

FLOWCHARTS

High-level flowcharts of the major data processing activities are presented in Exhibits 4-8.

QUESTIONS

The situation described in this case is real, but it took place in the early 1970s when the technology was far different than today. Given *today's technology:*

1 How would you attempt to help the farm workers?

2 What kind of technology, if any, would be the most appropriate for this type of organization?

3 What approach to system analysis and design would you recommend if a system appears feasible for the union?

4 How does the technology help you in your approach in 3 above?

PERKINS AND STERN FINANCIAL SERVICES

Arnold Schron

INTRODUCTION

Perkins & Stern is currently a major financial services firm headquartered in downtown New York. Founded in the early 1900s by three enterprising young businessmen, it built its early success by providing access to investment opportunities and financial services for the small investor. While the competition continued to focus on the traditionally large individual and institutional investors, as well as portfolio management, Perkins & Stern introduced special products and services to attract the small investor.

Clients were encouraged to allocate fixed percentages of their weekly income to securities investment while Perkins & Stern would package their products and services so that these clients could purchase small amounts, or even partial shares, of blue-chip securities. Perkins & Stern prided itself on being the friend of the small investor while providing the same quality of service to all their clients.

A young, aggressive sales force was recruited and trained in sales techniques, product information, as well as the normal New York Stock Exchange (NYSEC) and National Association of Securities Dealers (NASD) examination preparation. Account executives were encouraged to open as many new accounts as possible and were evaluated on their total sales (production), as well as the number of new accounts opened. The firm supported the account executives' sales efforts by using mass media techniques to bring the message of stocks and bond investment opportunities to the small investor.

During the stock market boom years of the early and mid 1960s, when many firms (as well as the New York Stock Exchange) were overwhelmed by back-office paperwork, senior management at Perkins & Stern recognized that automation was the only way to control the paper crunch and sky-rocketing back-office overhead. Computers and computer specialists were added to the service divisions and thus began a new era in the brokerage back office. The introduction of computer professionals to back-office operations gave impetus to the eventual development of computer-based financial products and services.

In the mid- and late 1950s, Perkins & Stern senior sales management determined that some form of uniform system was necessary to analyze and evaluate account executive sales performance. A special committee of outstanding branch office managers was appointed to develop an overall strategy for a sales planning and analysis function. Members of this group introduced the now famous Quartile Evaluation System.

The original concept of the Quartile Evaluation System was (and still is) quite simple. Broker trainees are required by NYSE regulations to spend their first ninety days in a fully-recognized sales office before they can begin formal classroom training for the NYSE and NASD exams. During this time, they are permitted to work with study-at-home materials and other courseware, but they must spend the 10 a.m. to 3 p.m. part of the day (NYSE trading hours) in the sales office. At the end of this 90-day period, they can begin formal classroom training for the Series 7 Registered Representative certification exam.

The formal classroom training will vary from one firm to another. At Perkins & Stern, this phase of sales training consists of exam preparation, sales skills, and product knowledge. Over the years, the training program has been gradually reduced from 15 weeks to 4 weeks as higher costs and improved techniques (computer assisted instruction) have contributed to an environment where the account executive can be licensed and selling within 4 months of joining the firm.

THE QUARTILE SYSTEM

When the Account Executive trainee receives notice that he/she has passed the licensing exams, the firm assigns the trainee an internal sales number. This number is affixed to all sales records and is essentially an internal license to sell. The sales number is a nine-digit code consisting of a two-digit region code, a three-digit office code, and a four-digit sales ID code:

XX	XXX	XXXX
REGION	OFFICE	A/E ID

This sales number is different from the internal employee (or payroll) number, and also different from the social security number. Account executives are grouped into one of five major categories by product specialization:

1 Retail
2 Institutional

3 Commodity
4 Government Securities
5 Mutuals

In addition, account executives are grouped by a length of service (LOS) code. All trainees are grouped together in the LOS 0 class until the first January 15 after they receive their license. At this time, their LOS is increased to 1. Similarly, other brokers in LOS 1,2,3, and so on, are moved up 1 LOS unit annually on January 15. Brokers in the LOS 9 category are moved to LOS 10, which is the designated category for all account executives with 10 or more years of experience.

Using this scheme, each account executive has now been assigned a unique code for product specialization (retail, commodities, etc.) and a unique experience code (LOS 0,1,2, etc.). Each month, on a monthly and year-to-date basis, brokers are computer-ranked from high to low against account executives in their specialization (same product code) and equivalent LOS. These rankings are performed for total sales (monthly and YTD), as well as the number of new accounts opened (monthly and YTD).

Within each product code/LOS grouping, the high-to-low sales ranking is further partitioned into 25 percent groupings or quartile rankings. In essence, a retail account executive with quartile 1 rank and LOS = 5 ranks in the top 25 percent of all Perkins & Stern retail account executives throughout the continental United States, Hawaii, Alaska, and Puerto Rico with 5 years experience. A separate quartile ranking exists for commodity account executives (who compete against all commodity account executives) and a third set of quartile rankings exists for institutional account executives (who compete against all institutional account executives).

Sales commission data for each account executive are recorded on the account executive sales file as a product of the confirmed trade message which is returned from the NYSE computer to the Perkins & Stern computer. In Exhibit 1 the transaction is traced from the initial customer phone call to the Perkins & Stern account executive through the NYSE and back to the original Perkins & Stern sales office operations area. Step 7B highlights the recording of commission data on the account executive's sales record.

The account executive sales record was used to record and analyze sales and new account data. Up to 5 years of sales and new account data was entered on this record along with the production number, date of license, competitor code, and other miscellaneous data. (The competitor code is a three-character numeric code designated for NYSE members. This was used when an account executive went to, or was recruited by, a competitor firm.)

Data for new account executives joining the firm and terminating account executives were manually entered from various reports which were generated by payroll and/or the sales branches. Account executives with previous experience at competitor firms were usually assigned an LOS which was 2 years *less* than their total experience at the competition. This formula was based on Perkins & Stern's belief that changing firms had a temporary impact

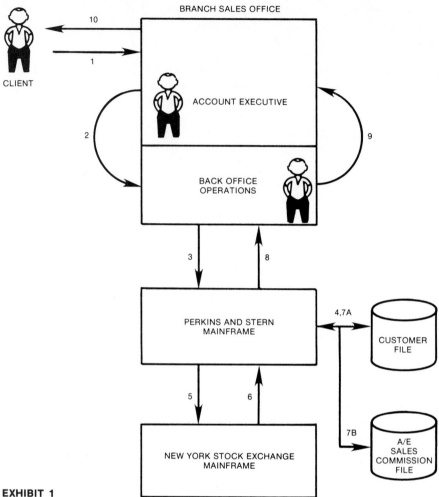

EXHIBIT 1

on an account executive's client book, thus the experienced account executive recruited from the competition should be put into a less experienced LOS group.

Originally, the account executive sales file was a sequential tape file keyed to production number. Payroll data was kept on a separate payroll master file sequenced on Perkins & Stern ID number. When necessary, data from the payroll file was generated as hardcopy output. Individual forms were then completed from these reports and converted to keypunch cards to be used as input to the account executive sales file. In the early 1970s, the account executive sales file was converted to a sequential disk file and several in-house programs were developed to update new and terminating account executive data on the account executive sales file. An extract was generated from the payroll master once per sales month (usually 4 or 5 weeks depending on the particular month) and this was processed against the account executive sales file. Several query languages, including Quick Query, were used to analyze the account executive sales file for sales performance by office and by region, as well as various reports highlighting the relationship of sales to product training, and recruiting from the competition, among others.

In the early 1970s, Perkins & Stern management felt the need for an overall human resource system which would provide good control and feedback data on the entire workforce, including the account executive sales staff. This system would have a common interface with payroll and all payroll changes would be driven by a standardized person profile record (PPR) completed by the employee's manager and forwarded to a central editing and validation department in New York. The payroll system currently in use would be abandoned and the payroll department would migrate to the new payroll system several months prior to implementing the new human resource system. During this period, several conversion programs would be used to reformat the payroll file so that it would be acceptable to the new system. The account executive sales file would also be linked to the new human resource system via a series of extract programs. In essence, the update schedule will follow the guidelines below:

Human Resource Update 1/week (Saturday mornings)
Payroll Update 1/every second Monday
A/E Sales Update 1/4 or 5 weeks

Each function, however, continued to maintain its separate files: there was a separate human resources file; payroll file; and sales analysis file. When an account executive terminated, or received a compensation increase, this information had to be updated to three separate files. As a result, each year at planning time, when senior management would forecast sales revenues and product mix for the new fiscal year, and then try to link these projections to the sales force population, and sales training needs for new and experienced account executives, several data inconsistencies resulted.

Sales Revenues
Product Mix --▶ these determine the required sales force
Required Sales Force
 – Current Sales force
 _____
Difference
 + Turnover
 _____
New hires

The hire number can be further broken down into trainees and experienced account executives. When workforce numbers for the current sales staff are requested from the human resource system, they are never in agreement with the current sales force numbers supplied by the account executive sales file or the payroll file. Even if the sales force numbers from all three files were equal, there is no guarantee that the same people are being counted in each file.

QUESTIONS

Perkins & Stern clearly needs a change of data-processing philosophy to eliminate data inconsistencies and the duplication of data storage.

1 Comment on an overall strategy you would recommend to the Perkins & Stern EDP department to address the problems described above. Be sure to include any relevant changes required on the user's side.

2 Develop a data flow diagram (DFD) describing the EDP changes you are recommending to Perkins & Stern. Also develop a record layout for each new file and include the file organization (ISAM, data base hierarchical, data base network, etc.) in your recommendation.

HIRSCH INDUSTRIES

MEMO TO: Mr. William Robbins, Vice President - Packaging Products
Division
FROM: Charles Garrard, Director - Business Systems
DATE: October 5, 1982

At your request, this memo sets forth the terms and conditions under which business systems proposes to assist the packaging products division in the development of a feasability study and plan of action for a new data processing system.

BACKGROUND

For several years packaging products has been using a well known service bureau for payroll, invoicing, accounts receivable, and accounts payable. Expenses for the service bureau are now approaching $30,000 per month. The variety and flexibility of reports is considered limited and the timeliness of the information is poor.

Therefore, you believe that an in-house computer system can give you what you want in response time and versatility, and provide an opportunity to expand data processing to the sales service department and upper management.

You believe an in-house system will allow you to put your California sales and warehouse on-line, improve the turnaround time on invoicing, improve cash flow, increase the efficiency of order processing, control your inventory turnover, and make better use of your customer base for advertising, mailing, marketing, and sales purposes.

You have currently assumed a budget level for the hardware and software of $400,000 to $600,000. Final installation is designated for November, 1983.

You believe the feasability of installation hinges on two aspects:

- A viable, effective order entry system.
- The ability of upper and middle management to be trained in query and report generators.

At this point, you are seeking a study of the feasability of installing an in-house computer system.

The following sections of this memo describe the objectives, scope, and expected results of the proposed feasability study, followed by a discussion of our approach to producing these results.

STUDY OBJECTIVES AND SCOPE

The four major objectives of the proposed study are:

- To generally describe the functional and technical requirements for an initial in-house data processing system.
- To develop and analyze alternative conceptual approaches for satisfying the initial system requirements.
- To determine the feasibility of alternative in-house and expanded services bureau systems for the division, and recommend the best solution.
- To develop options and plans for proceeding.

The scope of the study would include describing general requirements for the six applications modules under consideration, including:

- Accounts receivable and cash receipts
- Accounts payable and cash disbursements
- General ledger/financial reporting
- Order entry/invoicing
- Sales analysis/commission report
- Inventory Control
- Payroll

The study would also identify potential future interface requirements, but would not define detailed requirements for potential future additions such as manufacturing costing and material resources planning (MRP).

STUDY RESULTS

The results of this study will be documented in an oral presentation and a report of five major sections. The results will be discussed and reviewed with relevant division personnel at various points throughout the study. The five sections are expected to be as follows:

- Management Summary
  Background
  Approach and Scope
  Findings and Conclusions
  Recommendations
  Structure of this Report
- Business Analysis
  Business Environment, Need, and Objectives
  Functional Requirements
  Technical Requirements
  Economic Considerations
  Management Risk and Other Factors
- Systems Requirements
  Conceptual Requirements
  General Requirements
- Description of Alternatives Examined
  Hardware
  Software
  Staffing
  Cost Estimates
- Appendices

STUDY ACTIVITIES

The proposed study will consist of five major activities and will build on the work already done by Bernie Smith and other divisional personnel. The major study activities will be as follows:

1 Interview members of senior divisional management to determine the scope and direction of strategic business objectives, and management's plans for future growth and diversification. Also, determine the manner in which senior management expects information systems to support management decision making and control in the future.

2 Interview key user personnel to become familiar with functional and technical requirements for the seven applications you have identified, and assess the probable growth and diversification of volumes and applications in the future.

At the conclusion of our fact-finding activities we will conduct an interim project status review with divisional management to summarize our intitial findings and to highlight problem areas.

3 Evaluate the feasability of alternative approaches to satisfying the data processing requirements. Possible alternatives will include:

- Remaining with a service bureau for one or all applications
- Employing in-house computer services which are furnished and administered on-site by a service bureau
- Installing a divisional computer system and implementing purchased or custom-built software wherever appropriate

The feasability of each alternative will be assessed by estimating a likely range of costs, benefits, risks, and practicality for the components of each approach. These components will include:

- Hardware, systems software, and network architecture
- Available application packages
- Custom design and programming services
- Internal staffing requirements
- Alternative service bureau costs and processing services

4 The alternatives will be compared and ranked in order of desirability according to agreed-upon evaluation criteria, such as:

- Costs, including capital, lease/rental, start-up, service, interest, and depreciation
- Internal wage and salary expenses
- Benefits, including direct cost savings, better information, improved support to senior management, timeliness, and accuracy
- Adaptability, including the flexibility to grow and diversify with the company
- Risks, including vendor stability, functional and techical feasibility, and obsolescence factors

5 Should the evaluation of alternatives indicate that a change is not advisable, we will present our findings and recommendations in a written report and conclude our study.

Should a change be indicated, we shall outline the steps to be undertaken, and present a plan of action and timetable for implementation under the next work phase.

BACKGROUND INFORMATION

Packaging products division expects to continue its industry lead as a manufacturer and distributor of shipping room supplies and industrial packaging products. The approximate size of the division is 2400 employees with a projected sales volume of $200 million for 1982. Sales volume is expected to double within the next 5 to 7 years and the ratio of manufacturing to wholesaling volume will grow from 75 percent : 25 percent to 85 percent : 15 percent. Approximately 50 to 60 percent of the manufactured products are and will continue to be custom-made.

About 75 percent of divisional marketing is to industrial paper merchants and forms dealers throughout the United States. The other 25 percent of sales are direct to end users or the United States government. The 1100 forms dealers and 3500 industrial merchants are serviced either by a group of fifty independent sales representatives, paid on a commission basis, or by the division's own salesmen, who are responsible for warehouses in Illinois, Massachusetts, Georgia, and California. Direct sales to industrial and commercial accounts are handled either through one of twenty full-time local company salesmen, by internal sales/service personnel on a house account basis, or by sales management for special large accounts. The direct salesmen work on a salary/expense/incentive arrangement.

There are 7000 customers in the divisions's customer base, 2500 to 3000 of whom are active. Approximately 30 to 40 percent of the active base are wholesale customers and the rest are end users. On average there are two to four line items per order, including freight, handling, plate, and artwork charges. The division's vendor list consists of 750 companies.

The company is composed of five product lines:

- PRES-FAST pressure sensitive envelopes
- ZIP-TOP zippered poly bag
- AUTO-STICK pressure sensitive computer labels
- Industrial & commercial packaging products
- GUMME gummed tape dispensers

The division has four warehouse/sales offices and three production plants. The Atlanta and Essex facilities will continue to coat raw materials for several products and/or perform printing on polyethylene and paper.

Several changes are currently anticipated to occur within the next six months: The Atlanta plant will develop a graphic arts department for artwork, typesetting, and plate making. The Berkeley plant will assume responsibility for R & D evaluations of new equipment.

Future Work

In the event that acquisition of an in-house computer facility is recommended, we would normally expect to convert our previous requirements study into a request for proposal document (RFP) and assist you in soliciting and evaluating vendor proposals. Due to the uncertain outcome of the feasibility study, however, this activity is considered to be beyond the scope of this proposal.

Staffing

Adam Corliss will be the project manager. George Sullivan is a likely candidate to work with him on this project from the system development staff, and he will be assisted by members of the corporate MIS staff as their specific expertise is required.

In addition, it is planned that divisional personnel will also participate in the study. It is our understanding that you will serve as our principal point of contact within the division for all reporting and substantive matters.

Study Duration

We currently estimate that the study will require ten weeks to complete. Based on our present staffing commitments, we can begin this work at an early, mutually agreeable starting date.

Study Costs

Professional services will be charged according to standard policy, and are currently estimated at $23,000.

In addition to professional fees, we will charge for out-of-pocket expenses including transportation, hotel, meals, secretarial charges, printing, and report production as reasonably required for the performance of this work. These expenses are currently estimated at 20 to 25 percent of professional staff costs.

Divisional Participation

The estimates, costs, and schedules discussed above assume the availability and participation of divisional personnel, primarily in the financial, sales order, and inventory control areas, at various stages throughout the study.

It is understood that failure of divisional personnel to provide this agreed upon involvement in a timely fashion may lead to additional costs, extended schedules, or both.

I will call within the next several days and arrange for us to meet and further discuss this proposal. We are looking forward to working with you on this study.

ANALYSIS OF SYSTEMS

AIR TRAFFIC CONTROL COMPUTER FAILURES

Committee on Government Operations, U.S. Congress

INTRODUCTION AND SUMMARY

Beginning with a near mid-air collision during an air traffic control computer failure in October 1979 and continuing through 1980, there was extensive public and congressional concern over the potential threat to safety posed by breakdowns in automated data processing equipment used for air traffic control. Following up on and reopening an investigation begun in 1976, the Committee on Government Operations investigated this matter through the Subcommittee on Government Activities and Transportation. The subcommittee held two days of hearings on June 30 and August 15, 1980.

One of the primary purposes for which the Federal Aviation Administration was created in 1958 was to establish and operate a unified air traffic control system. Today, that system has grown into a very large, complicated, and highly automated complex to accommodate vastly increased traffic by much faster and larger aircraft. Great progress has been made in reducing the danger of mid-air collisions. But the consequences of mid-air collisions have also grown far greater.

Allegations that the computerized radar data processing on which air traffic controllers rely is not sufficiently reliable and may be getting worse instead of better raised the specter of an increase in mid-air collisions. FAA employees who operate the system (air traffic controllers, specialists, technicians, and their organizations) made a number of strong criticisms, including:

The automated data processing equipment is much more prone to failures—termed outages—than FAA management is willing to admit and this does pose a threat to safety.

267

The computer performance data on outages used by FAA management does not accurately describe the reality of the situation controllers experience with the equipment.

Presumably based on this unreliable data, the agency has made budget, staffing, procurement, and planning decisions which are making air traffic control problems worse.

The FAA repeatedly denied that these allegations were true. Then under the threat of a funding cut-off by the Appropriations Committees, it established a plan to correct these problems.

The committee's investigation revealed that the criticisms of the FAA's air traffic control automation system were not without foundation and did reveal significant problems. The committee finds that:

Computer outages pose a threat to safety, especially during peak traffic periods.

Because FAA's computer and facility performance reporting system and data are of dubious validity it is impossible to reach conclusions on computer reliability.

FAA is not doing an effective job of alleviating problems caused by automated data processing equipment failures or planning for replacement of the equipment.

The committee makes three general recommendations for improvement.

BACKGROUND

The Advent of the Current Air Traffic Control Computer System

The FAA began planning for the automation of its air traffic control radar in the early 1960s. As this acquisition planning proceeded at a slow pace, the volume of air traffic surged in the latter part of the decade, causing a severe strain on the existing system, which relied on primary or broadband radar. This radar displays aircraft to the controller as anonymous "blips" on a screen. The controller must establish the plane's identity, altitude, heading, speed, and other variables by radio contact and record it on a small movable marker called a "shrimpboat" to identify the "blip." The justification for going to computerized radar data processing (RDP) was to automate a significant number of these time consuming steps and thereby provide an increase in controller productivity by allowing the controller to handle more traffic.

After some prodding in the late 1960s and early 1970s,[1] the FAA went ahead with automation by acquiring the current Air Route Traffic Control Center (ARTCC) computers in one of the largest computer purchases in history,

---

[1]"Federal Aviation Agency Air Traffic Control Operations." Hearings before the Subcommittee on Government Activities. Committee on Government Operations, Apr. 26-27, 1966; 89th Congress, 2d session. "Emergency Problems Confronting the Air Traffic Control System." Hearings before the Subcommittee on Government Activities. Committee on Government Operations, Aug. 1, 1968; 90th Congress, 2d session. "Problems Confronting FFA in the Development of An Air Traffic Control System For the 1970's." Hearings Jan. 27, 1970; H. Rept. No. 1308; 91st Congress, 2d session. "Air Traffic Control Facilities and Equipment Requirements To Meet The Needs Of The 1970's." H. Rep. No. 92-757; Dec. 16, 1971; 92d Congress, 1st session.

involving twenty-two IBM 9020 model machines of various configurations. The IBM model 9020 is unique to the FAA, and essentially consists of an agglomeration of IBM 360 models hooked together. The basic IBM 360 model was designed in the late 1950s and is based on transistor and circuit board technology. Alongside this came secondary or beacon radar, which receives coded messages from aircraft mounted transponders giving aircraft identity, altitude, and other information including a more precise location.

With this equipment commissioned in 1974, controllers no longer work traffic from images of actual primary radar scanning, but from displays of purely relevant information generated by the computer, called narrowband. Each plane (and only those planes the controller is responsible for) is presented on a screen along with a data block giving the plane's identity, altitude, track, speed, and other information. The computer does a great deal more, such as matching aircraft with flight plans on file, presenting weather information, passing planes off from one controller to another, and monitoring for potential dangers. All of this relieves controllers of a great deal of peripheral work and allows them to concentrate on maintaining separation between more aircraft. This in turn has allowed the FAA to accommodate a substantial increase in air traffic during the 1970s with a relatively static workforce of controllers.

Obviously, increasing the capacity of the air traffic control system through automation means the capability of the system to meet greater demand is dependent on the reliability of the machines. The 9020 center computers were designed, to some degree, to be internally redundant and self-correcting in order to be reliable, although the debate over just how reliable is the subject of this report. The back-up for narrowband radar data processing in the event of failure or scheduled "down time" is the broad-band, primary radar system in use before 1974.

Subcommittee hearings in 1976 Within 2 years of the new RDP system being commissioned in 1974, a number of problems surfaced and were examined at a field hearing held by the subcommittee in Indianapolis, Indiana, on October 19, 1976. Controllers complained that the computers were not as reliable as they should be: that they were prone to sudden failures which left controllers in awkward and very tense situations of not knowing whether or not to make the transition from narrow-band to the broad-band back-up. Controllers pointed out a number of difficulties encountered in making the transition including:

1 The substantial gap or difference between narrowband and broadband presentations made the transition more difficult than FAA admitted, and presented a danger that aircraft could be overlooked.

2 The transition required a considerable period of time to fully accomplish; depending on traffic, up to 10 minutes, or more than 50 miles of a jetliner's travel distance.

3 There was little or no training being provided for making this transition, and many new controllers had little or no experience or training on the broadband system.

4 When the computer failed during high traffic periods, the system became instantly overloaded.

5 The computers were failing more than FAA's management realized or acknowledged because the many performance reporting systems did not accurately reflect the controllers' experience.

FAA's position was that the computers were, in fact, reliable despite occasional problems at individual centers. While better outage reporting was promised, FAA asserted that outages did not affect safety. Agency witnesses conceded that more and better training in the use of broadband and making the transition to it was a good idea, but argued that controllers should be able to handle a traffic situation no matter what system was used. Furthermore, and most important, the agency stated that it was in the process of developing and buying a more advanced back-up system to replace broadband, called Direct Access Radar Channel (DARC). The DARC system was scheduled to be completed for operational use in 1981, and would provide a redundant back-up to the 9020 primary computer to resolve most of the problems described by the controllers.

Events Leading to the Present Investigation

Beginning with a near mid-air collision between two large aircraft over North Carolina during an outage in October 1979, press coverage and public concern about ATC computer failures began to mount. Once the occurrence of ATC computer outages became newsworthy, the frequency of their occurrence startled the public, who could not understand how expensive installations like enroute control centers, on which so many people's safety depended, could be expected and allowed to fail more than twice per month.

Public concern was not lessened by the highly contradictory statements to the press about outages by controllers and FAA management. Controllers described computer outage occurrences as being very tense situations with a high potential for precipitating danger. Agency spokesmen, on the other hand, consistently described the failures as routine problems that presented no threat to safety. Typical of the latter kind of reassurances from the FAA was the following statement by the then administrator of FAA before the Subcommittee on Aviation of the Committee on Public Works and Transportation on December 11, 1979:

> Recently, there have been blanket charges made that system interruptions pose a hazard to aviation safety. It is the exception when such interruptions pose any significant threat to safety. While it is understandable that interruptions might raise concerns about safety, the reality is that the system itself, as well as air traffic procedures, is designed to accommodate interruptions without creating safety

problems....Once a controller has decided that a transition to broadband is necessary, all he needs to do is to push a single button to get broadband data displayed.

Matters continued to escalate with the agency's management and its employee unions trading accusations that one side was attempting a cover-up of falsified records and that the other side was attempting to use public fear as a tool in upcoming collective bargaining.

In June 1980, the automated system in the air traffic control tower at O'Hare airport in Chicago failed for an entire week, and the previously reliable ARTCC in Oakland, California, began experiencing a rash outages at the rate of about one a week. Public concern peaked and the subcommittee announced hearings for June 30, 1980. After the first hearing, the Oakland ARTCC continued to experience highly publicized outages, and amid rumors and hints that sabotage might be involved, FAA dispatched a special study team to try to resolve the problems there. The subcommittee held a field hearing in San Francisco on August 15, 1980, to focus on the Oakland problems.

The Controversy

Criticisms of the system by controllers and technicians (FAA employees who maintain the equipment) can be grouped into three catagories, as follows:

Management   One of the fundamental complaints by both controllers and technicians was that the national reporting systems for gathering data on RDP equipment interruptions did not accurately reflect the actual performance of the equipment. This data was nonetheless being used as the basis for management decisions on vital matters concerning staffing, budgeting, procurement planning, and the setting of performance goals.

Controllers asserted that their actual experience with the equipment did not match up with the picture of system reliability painted by FAA headquarters. They noted that partial failures of the system which often increased their workload or affected safety did not show up at all in national performance data. They also stated that partial or total outages, which were sudden and unexpected to the on-duty controllers often later showed up on the records as scheduled outages because someone else anticipated or authorized them.

Technicians and specialists stated that they felt they were under significant pressure from management to minimize and under-report equipment failures and that the reporting system allowed this to be done. The pressure on them came through an implied or explicit condition that their job performance would be evaluated to some degree on the basis of how well the equipment they were responsible for could be shown to have worked rather than strictly on how well they did their jobs. This condition in turn derived from pressure on facility, sector, and regional managers not to be singled out as poor performers for being too far below the regional or national norms constructed from the outage reporting data.

The net result alleged was a situation in which FAA headquarters was presented with a rosy view by its management information system while controllers and technicians in the field faced a grimmer reality of frequent equipment failures that didn't get management attention.

A second major complaint by FAA employee groups was the poor, ineffective, or simply nonexistent planning for an interim cure for outages or for the ultimate replacement of the enroute computer system.

Controllers pointed out that the long awaited DARC equipment which was supposed to provide a backup to the 9020 computers would not be much better than the old broadband system it was supposed to replace. Controllers would still have to pull their screens down into a horizontal position and make up and manipulate "shrimpboats," perpetuating rather than curing many of the problems controllers experienced in making the transition between systems. It was also pointed out that DARC was not wholly redundant to the primary system but shared some common elements that could cause both to fail; that as delivered, DARC could not be used by a single controller display position (as broadband can) without five other display positions having to make the transition also, thus potentially propagating an outage; and that DARC was to a certain extent mutually exclusive with the broadband system in that DARC would not have the capability the 9020 has to "punch in" a broadband display, that is, intermittently present a primary radar picture a controller can use to verify the machine-generated display and to check weather. In sum, after 4 years of work and 70 percent cost escalation DARC would be at best a half step of progress that would be of little help to controllers without years more work and expenditure. Nonagency witnesses believed this typified FAA's planning and procurement problems.

FAA's plan for replacing the primary enroute computers was also heavily criticized. The major criticism was that the acquisition plan stretched out over more that 10 years, envisioning operational completion in roughly 1991. This would virtually guarantee that the agency would once again be buying equipment well behind the state-of-the-art, as computer design and fabrication has been advancing through generational cycles about every 10 years. In other words, the plan calls for FAA to replace equipment designed before 1960, by buying equipment designed roughly in the early 1980s, for installation in the early 1990s, making one advance while the industry made three or four. Most disturbing, a 10-year acquisition plan means the air traffic control system would have to depend on 1960 vintage transistor technology for another decade and not take advantage of the substantial increase in reliability and cost savings available from existing modern solid-state chip technology.

Questions were raised as to whether the existing 9020 computers could be made to last and perform adequately until replaced in 1991. A number of allegations were made that shortages of parts and skilled labor for what is now a 20-year-old computer design were rapidly becoming critical and would become more so in the next decade.

Most disturbing, one witness raised the suspicion that implementation of a collision avoidance system was being delayed or held in abeyance pending the 10-year program for replacing the agency's primary computers.

A general and pervasive criticism of FAA by its employee organizations is simply that the agency has such poor management-employee relations that sincere and serious safety concerns may not be heard or addressed.

Agency employees indicated that the perceived internal avenues for raising problems, such as the unsatisfactory condition report system (UCRs) or facility safety committees, were often dead ends, used not to resolve problems but to "keep the lid on." In some cases, these internal systems were used for punitive purposes, to identify and thwart individuals who complained. In at least one case the committee received information that at one ARTCC, matters had reached such an impasse that management and the union safety committee hadn't been able to even meet for almost a year.

This criticism is, by its nature, susceptible to subjective evaluation, especially since the material on this point received by the committee during its investigation is anecdotal. Nevertheless, the very quantity and regularity of such criticism and anecdotal examples must be given some weight.

Operations Individual air traffic controllers and their organization repeated virtually all the operational problems they had described at the subcommittee's 1976 hearing, and pointed out that matters had only been made worse by the estimated 38 percent increase in traffic since then. They stated that the radar data processing equipment was still not as reliable as it should be, that equipment malfunctions or failures threatened safety, that there was still no satisfactory redundant back-up system in sight, and that the agency was trying to downplay the problems rather than resolve them.

Controllers emphasized that the most stressful and potentially dangerous time was at the beginning of an RDP interruption, whether it was a short startover or developed into an outage. Even though management statistics treated them separately, repeated startovers of less than 60 seconds were just as bad as an outage of more than 1 minute. In both cases, controllers had to distrust the validity of the display generated by their equipment, not knowing when or if it would rectify itself or fail totally. They also complained that there were no uniform, clearly-stated procedures for managing outages, with the result that sometimes notification and coordination of the transition to broadband was haphazard or sprung as a surprise.

Most controllers acknowledged that once a rhythm of traffic control had been reestablished with broadband, traffic could be handled safely, but it took much longer to reestablish than rhythm than FAA admitted, generally 10 minutes or more. If the outage occurred during peak traffic periods, the system was perilously overloaded during the transition.

On top of this, controllers stated that they still were not receiving adequate training on making a transition to broadband, nor even receiving much training in the basic use of the old system. This allegation was substantiated to a degree by a number of signed statements submitted to the committee by journeymen controllers saying they had received little or no training or experience on broadband in years. This somewhat contradicted the allegation that RDP outages were not an uncommon occurrence, since a working controller would therefore be expected to encounter the need to use broadband with some regularity. Controllers countered that it was the luck of the draw as to who encountered an outage, and in any event, on-the-job training was not a substitute for formal training in correct procedures.

Controllers dismissed the contention by FAA that they were receiving regular training in the use of broadband during late night shifts when narrowband was turned off. They pointed out that there was very little traffic during these night shifts which simply didn't replicate conditions during an outage. And many controllers could go for years without being assigned to a graveyard shift.

As confirmation that a problem existed, controllers pointed out that FAA headquarters, in the midst of the mounting controversy, had issued a new national notice to establish a program of refresher training in making the transition between narrowband and broadband. The committee notes that this program was initiated almost 4 years after its 1976 hearing, and was self-cancelling on March 1, 1981.

Air traffic controllers expressed not just concern and disagreement, but outrage, that during the 1976 to 1980 period when they estimated that traffic had increased roughly 38 percent, the number of air traffic controllers had actually remained static. The result was described in one controller's testimony as a situation in which some positions were being "bludgeoned" by the traffic load foisted on them. The anger over this situation was rubbed raw by the fact the FAA had substantially increased its supervisory staffing during the same period. The committee notes the following language from the report of the Senate Committee on Appropriations to accompany the fiscal year 1981 appropriation for FAA:

The committee is concerned that as of April 30, 1980, the total employment under this appropriation was only 51,217 personnel, a level that is more than 750 positions below the estimated end-of-year staffing level contained in the January budget. Within this level of personnel the Committee notes that air traffic controller positions are only slightly above September 30, 1979, levels even though Congress provided 200 new controller positions for the current year. The Committee strongly recommends that FAA expedite the hiring of controllers and other safety related personnel and intends to carefully monitor the progress made in that regard for the remainder of the year.

In providing the full budget level of 24,341 air traffic controller positions, the committee notes that the number of aircraft handled by en route traffic control centers using instrument flight rules is expected to increase from 30,700,000 in fiscal year 1980 to 31,800,000 in 1981. The Committee shares the concerns expressed in the House report that many of the air traffic controller positions requested by FAA and approved by Congress are not, in fact, either full-performance controllers or trainees. For fiscal years 1974 through 1979, the total increase in team supervisors and other personnel was 893 positions compared to an increase of only 372 positions in the full-performance and trainee controller category. This allocation of resources is contrary to the Committee's intent to provide increased controller staffing at the Nation's busiest centers and towers.

Maintenance   As stated above, the major criticism by representatives of FAA technicians and specialists who maintain the massive complex of air traffic control equipment was what they viewed as unfair and self-defeating pressure on them to under-report the true status of malfunctions and failures. Mixed in with this criticism was the serious allegation that agency supervisors or managers were altering actual equipment maintenance logs to change the coding of corrective maintenance to the more favorable, less scrutinized category of scheduled maintenance. To substantiate this charge, the technician group pointed to the wide variations between the figures produced by FAA's own data gathering systems for the number and duration of RDP outages and interruptions. The group also submitted a few examples of altered logs.

The criticism that FAA's management information system for facility performance is not, because of its design, producing consistent performance data is supported by substantial evidence, as is discussed at a later point. However, neither a review of some 14,000 pages of facility logs by FAA headquarters nor an audit by the Office of Inspector General of the Department of Transportation were able to substantiate the allegation of a pattern of actual alteration of documents. The mixing together of a powerful criticism regarding the inadequacy of the reporting system and an as yet unproven allegation of wrongdoing was confusing and distracting, and deterred the committee's investigation.

The second major criticism in the area of maintenance was that technician staffing had been and was planned to be further significantly reduced, at times to a skeletal level despite a steady 15 percent annual increase systemwide in the time it takes to repair malfunctioning equipment (mean-time-to-restore). Technician representatives stated that they believed the staff reductions were being accomplished by changing from a preventive maintenance regimen to one of reactive corrective maintenance. While reductions in maintenance routines on some automated systems, including the enroute center computers, might be justified, the technicians asserted that there hadn't been such a dramatic change in the overall equipment inventory of the whole ATC system as to justify the prior and planned reductions in personnel. They countered that in some cases, the aging of the equipment required more maintenance. As an example of this latter case they cited the broadband system itself, parts of which date from the 1950s and for which FAA now faces a severe shortage of qualified maintenance personnel.

The Agency's Response

The FAA's response to these criticisms and complaints was diametric opposition. While agency spokesmen conceded in general terms that their system was not perfected beyond improvement, they gave little other ground.

On the question of the validity of national computer interruption reports, then administrator Langhorne Bond told the subcommittee on June 30, 1980:

> There have been statements made that the FAA has intentionally misrepresented the numbers of interruptions experienced in the air traffic system. Those statements are incorrect. I know because we have specially checked into them....
>
> As for the representation that we have attempted to suppress the accurate reporting of data, that too is incorrect.

Ant on the questions of safety and staffing:

> To sum up, Mr. Chairman, we have not misrepresented data concerning system performance. The performance of our air traffic system has improved, not decreased, in the past 5 years. Significant threats to safety are not posed by system interruptions. And we have worked diligently to better the performance of the system and to reduce the potential impact of system interruptions on our controller work force.

The agency persisted in framing the criticisms in terms of labor-management or representational disputes, implying that such criticism was a ploy to gain the advantage of public support in collective bargaining. For example, the following exchange took place before the subcommittee on aviation of the Committee on Public Works and Transportation at a hearing on December 11, 1979:

> *Mr. Anderson.* We have heard many challenges to the accuracy of FAA's data on outages. It has been claimed that outages are not reported, that outages are misrepresented as scheduled when they are really unscheduled, and that supervisors pressure technicians to not report, or to misrepresent, outages.
>
> I wonder whether the same representations have been made to your agency and, if so, whether you have undertaken any investigations of the problem?
>
> *Mr. Bond.* Well, as you must be aware, Mr. Chairman, there is a union organizing fight that is going on within the FAA. The air traffic controllers union has sponsored another offshoot union, trying to replace the other union within our maintenance fleet. A great many charges and countercharges have flown back and forth during the heat of this battle, and this is one of them.

Discussion

Safety Aspects of Computer Outages

One of the central disputes examined during the committee's investigation was whether, and to what degree, ATC computer outages pose a threat to safety. The FAA clearly believed they do not. Air traffic controllers believed they do.

The basis of the agency's case was statistical. Specifically, the following figures were cited:

> With the introduction of automated systems, outages and all, the number of mid-air collisions involving domestic transport category planes had been reduced to only one in almost a decade compared to four in the preceding decade. Mid-air collisions between general aviation planes have not increased.
>
> There was actually a negative correlation between reported "system errors" (a term of art meaning the loss of aircraft separation minimums) and the transition to or use of broadband radar, i.e., there were fewer errors with broadband than would be expected as the proportionate share for the time the backup was in use. The actual numbers were twenty-six system errors, while broadband was in use (4%) out of a total reported 3-year sample of 649 errors.
>
> Reported computer service interruption data showed a steady downward trend.

The only fly in FAA's statistical ointment was the rapid increase in the number of near mid-air collisions being reported, which has increased 83 percent in 5 years.

The FAA cited the figures above to show that there was no persuasive, empirical trend to support claims that ATC computer outages posed a threat to safety. There are at least three flaws in this line of argument. First, the use of statistics derived from relatively small numbers to show the absence of a factor (prove a negative) is highly suspect if not dubious. Similar thinking, though on a much more sophisticated level, led another agency to the similar claim: "None of the test subjects for swine flu vaccine had adverse reactions, so the vaccine has no harmful side effects and is safe for mass precautionary inoculation." The reduction of three transport aircraft mid-air collisions could just as easily mean that we're overdue for a spate of them as it could mean the ATC system is improving, especially in view of the dramatic increase in reported near mid-air incidents.

Second, the nature of the FAA's system error reporting and investigation system is not conducive to reliable correlation of errors to outages. FAA Form 8020-7 simply has yes-no boxes to check to indicate whether equipment was working at the time of the error at that position. The only other way to determine from these reports if or how an equipment outage substantially contributed to the errors is if it is mentioned in the narratives or conclusions written by various individuals.

Third, a statistical argument such as FAA's assumes the validity and completeness of the supporting data and correlations. As is discussed below, the FAA's basic equipment failure reporting system lacks the necessary credibility to support this statistical argument.

Assertions by FAA's top management that outages do not compromise safety must therefore stand by themselves and be weighed against the extensive, sworn testimony of air traffic controllers who stated that outages did threaten safety.

In weighing these two conflicting assertions, the committee could not avoid the commonsense perception that the increased traffic allowed by automation must cause problems when it is suddenly thrown back onto the broadband system. As one controller described it:

All the time aircrafts are moving, and there is a lot of confusion.

We must lower the RDP scope to horizontal position and make up shrimpboats. We use those as an aid to maintain the identity of our traffic.

Usually during light traffic periods, this represents no problem, but when we are faced with moderate to heavy traffic, sometimes the situation just becomes chaotic, and that is when the potential exists for either system errors, mid-airs, or anything you can think of.

FAA's own mid-level management is aware of the potential problems, as indicated by a memorandum of January 21, 1980 from the Chief of the Air Traffic Division, Great Lakes Region, which responded to questions from headquarters as follows:

1 What operational impact do you encounter due to the present level of broadband maintenance?

The present level of maintenance allows the broadband to deteriorate during a shift even though it is checked at the beginning of the shift. The broadband is not being used, therefore, the deterioration is not detected and continues until the broadband is needed.

2 Does raising and lowering the PVDs cause a problem?

Yes, in all cases. Unless the controllers are certain it will be a long outage, they avoid lowering the PVDs and work with them vertical as long as possible.

3 [Deleted.]

4 After an unscheduled RDP outage, how long does it take for the broadband system to be working and effective? Does this impact the operation?

Generally, the following things occur after an outage:

1 First, the controller waits 1 or 2 minutes, depending on traffic, for the RDP to return.

2 He then brings up broadband, but remains in the vertical position for a period dependent upon traffic—probably another 2 minutes.

The full transition takes at least 5 minutes, but not usually more than 10 minutes.

This time can be shortened if the A/C or other responsible person makes the decision quickly that a transition to broadband must be made. In any event, the transition will take at least 5 minutes.

Many of the tasks, such as reidentifying aircraft, verifying handoffs and verifying flight data are duplications of tasks already performed. Additionally, the controller must begin performing manual coordination, preparing shrimpboats and notifying adjacent facilities. All of this adds up to a very sudden increase (at least double) in workload. This confusing traffic situation is further complicated by confusion over whether or not to change to broadband.

These conditions impact the operation by creating a situation where the system is prone to operational errors.

Just how tightly timed or precarious air traffic control can be and just how dependent the system is on the ability of human controllers to cope, was illustrated by an incident on October 7, 1980, over Atlanta, Georgia. A controller at the Atlanta Tower made a single error in turning a plane which precipitated six system errors within roughly 5 minutes in a domino-like progression. In that case, a supervisor was able to step in and straighten out the situation. A traffic condition can degenerate that fast with the automation system working. This does not comport with FAA's assertion that when the automation system fails and a transition to broadband must be made that this should be a cool, controlled occurrence, no matter what.

Given the weight of evidence that outages do pose a threat to safety in heavy traffic conditions, the committee is very disturbed that there is no current means to reduce the threat with an adequate back-up RDP system. As discussed below, the new DARC equipment has severe operational short-comings that make the transition to it from the primary computer just as wrenching as the transition to broadband. The controllers must still move the screen to horizontal, make up shrimpboats, and verbally reidentify planes.

As traffic increases, dependence on the reliability of the primary 9020 computers will be greater as there is a developing, critical shortage of trained technicians to maintain the broadband system in working order. If DARC was adequate to replace broadband, as intended, this would now be of little concern. But the committee was shocked to see the following quoted statement or admission by then administrator Langhorne Bond, published by Aviation Week and Space Technology in an interview (November 3, 1980, page 200): "We took the position that DARC was a substitute for broadband," Bond said. "In retrospect, that was wrong."

In short, problems in ATC computer reliability were identified before this committee in 1976, but after more than 4 years and the expenditure of $18 million, we are no further along toward solving the basic problems than we were then.

Computer Outage Reporting Program

During the course of the committee's investigation it was inundated with data generated through FAA's facilities-performance reporting programs. The agency maintains automated records on the performance of a tremendous number of equipment items, systems, and subsystems. The FAA also has multiple (at least three) systems for reporting outages and other performance parameters nationally. Despite this quantity and complexity, as a management information system the program is—in the words of a report by the investigations staff of the Senate Committee on Appropriations—"almost wholly worthless."

The inability of the FAA's performance data program to truly reflect actual performance has a number of causes, discussed below. But the fundamental problem is that the system is faulty in and by design. Given the size and complexity of the air traffic control apparatus and the large number of people involved, some inaccuracy and marginal error is to be expected. The committee is not suggesting that seamless perfection is expected. The committee is disturbed, however, that large amounts of data, paper, and expense are devoted to a system which simply does not give FAA management—or Congress—a clear picture of what is happening in the field, and that system does not do so because the basic orders and procedures from headquarters which govern reporting do not elicit or require the proper information.

Order 6040 FAA Order 6040.5A Facility and Service Outage Report sets out the requirements, definitions, and procedures for collecting performance data on FAA report Form 6040-3, which parallels and uses data from FAA Facility Maintenance Logs (FAA Form 6030-1). The data collected in the Facility and Service Outage Reports is the agency's broadest and most detailed performance data set and is used as the basis for determining reliability, setting goals, and gauging performance both locally and nationally. That order not only allows, but to a certain degree encourages, misreporting.

One of the fundamental distinctions made within Order 6040 is between scheduled and unscheduled outages. The distinction is important becasue the agency only counts unscheduled outages in preparing facility reliability reports (FAA Forms 6040-8 monthly, and 6040-49 biannually). However, the terms "scheduled" and "unscheduled" do not have their common usage meanings, but are specially defined in four places in Order 6040 § 11 as follows:

> c. Cause Code. A two-digit code used to most closely describe the reason for the facility or service outage.... For reporting purposes, outage causes are classified as scheduled or unscheduled. The following is a list of assigned cause codes and their definitions:
> 1. Scheduled Causes:
> Cause Code: 60—Scheduled Maintenance. A scheduled outage for routine and nonroutine activities such as equipment performance checks, adjustments, calibration, troubleshooting, repair, cleaning, painting, lubrication, and general upkeep of a facility. This code is applicable for electronic, plant structures, or ground maintenance....
> 2. Unscheduled Causes:
> Cause Code: 80—Equipment Failure. Any malfunction or failure of electronic equipment or plants and structures item (other than engine generator) to provide satisfactory performance because of breakdown or degradation.
> k. Scheduled Outage. The removal of a facility/service from the air traffic system with prior approval from Air Traffic.
> l. Unscheduled Outage. A condition in which there is an unanticipated interruption of a facility or service, or Air Traffic approval cannot be obtained for an extension of a scheduled outage.

A careful look at these four definitions quickly reveals that the terms "scheduled" and "unscheduled" really mean "momentarily authorized" and "wholly and suddenly unanticipated." A scheduled code 60 outage can be properly logged for "nonroutine adjustments, troubleshooting, repair" under these definitions as long as some "prior approval" is obtained, however hastily granted or verbal it is. In other words, if the ATC computers or components begin to show signs of trouble or failure, they can be shut down and a corrective repair applied without this showing up—or being required to be reported—as an unscheduled outage or failure of any kind, and without it being listed on any schedule of routine maintenance. If the sign of imminent equipment failure is a series of 30-, 40-, or 50-second interruptions for "startovers," after which the system is shut down for repair, the whole incident will not be factored into FAA's reliability calculations.

FAA's outage reporting system under Order 6040 therefore covers only sudden, unforeseeable, total, and enduring failures. It does not elicit information on a number of ATC automation equipment failures which could compromise safety or the ability of controllers to do their jobs. For instance:

> It does not cover gradual failures of equipment since "prior approval" would be obtained to shut down the equipment, however quickly, and for however long.
> It does not cover outages required for corrective repair or "trouble shooting," even though such maintenance is not on any schedule.
> It does not cover partial outages in which one or more components of the automated system is not operating. FAA stated this in writing to the committee, in effect admitting that even though one or more controllers might find themselves staring at a blank or frozen screen, this would not qualify as a "CRAD" (composite radar data processing) outage if other controllers' positions remained useable. This would therefore not show up in the computer reliability reporting system.
> Brief outages are not reportable as such because the term outage has been more or less arbitrarily defined as a lack of function for more than 60 seconds. Failures under 60 seconds are called "interruptions" or "startovers" and are not used in computing reliability.

All of these could or would have an impact on the ability of controllers to handle their workload or their confidence in their equipment. Yet, none are required to be factored into FAA management's system performance and reliability measuring programs. Data on these kinds of problems must be dug out of the raw records, if it is there at all. This does not constitute a useful management information tool, and the basic headquarters order perpetuates the situation.

Reporting System Accuracy   The committee was initially loath to believe that a Federal agency would expend so much time, effort, and money on internal data collection without some assurance that what was obtained was not an example of the old computer programmers' axiom, "garbage in, garbage out." In addition to the testimony at the subcommittee's hearings, a number of documents were received which cast serious doubt on FAA's basic bookkeeping.

A large-scale management information system should have, if at all possible, a self-checking system built in to validate the data generated. Optimally, this should be an automatic feature so that management information that begins to deviate from what is verifiable must come to management's attention. FAA has three separate airway facility performance reporting systems which should be cross-checking each other. However, in an "Action Plan for Improving NAS ARTCC Computer Performance," issued on May 12, 1980, the directors of the Airways Facilities and Air Traffic stated:

> The existing 6040 NASCOM and NASNET reporting systems were created for different purposes, and their reports sometimes conflict with each other. AAF-700, the organization best equipped to monitor system performance, does not receive NASNET reports.

It should be noted that these same conflicts were addressed at the subcommittee's 1976 hearing, and the "action plan" containing this statement was issued in the middle of a series of agency statements to Congress that its outage reporting data was valid.

Perhaps the most compelling evidence that FAA's outage reporting may be worthless was directly placed in the committee's lap by the events surrounding its field hearing in San Francisco on outages at the Oakland ARTCC. As stated earlier, a spate of outages lasting through June and July of 1980 caused FAA to send a special "operations analysis group" to the Oakland ARTCC to try to resolve problems there. That group drafted a report to FAA management which the subcommittee demanded and received the day of its hearing on August 15, 1980.

The operations analysis group had focused on the computer outage of July 10, 1980. The report states that the group did so for the following reasons:

> This outage was significant for several reasons. The cause of the interrupts leading to the eventual shutdown of the system had been quickly identified as a software problem, which would require a system shutdown and "cold start" to correct. However, in checking the broadband radars in preparation for the shutdown, broadband was found to be unusable on several factors. The narrowband system was kept operational until the broadband system could be made operationally usable. Planned shutdown was accomplished approximately one and one-half hours later after a total of ten unscheduled interrupts. Once shutdown was initiated, 52 minutes elapsed before the system was returned to operation. The time to restore the system was felt to be excessive even for an uncoordinated outage, and in view of the planning time preceding the shutdown was inordinately prolonged.

A narrative summary of this July 10, 1980, outage is given in another part of the report as follows:

> No problems were noted until approximately 1430. At that time, some aircraft were being assigned non-discrete codes, especially Code 3200. At 1445, it was recognized to be a problem with CPF111 (beacon code assignment). We tried to do an on-line correction, but, due to the type of patch, we could not correct it on-line. At 1451, we encountered the first solid error hit on a CE—couldn't see any connection with software (CPE111) causing the hardware problem. The only way to correct it was to do a FLOP, run a diagnostic test of CCC hardware, and correct the beacon code recovery recording problem. At 1500, the broadband radar was discovered unusable and corrective action began on this problem. By the third start-over, at 1507, it was agreed that the problem had been defined, but the system could not

be shut down for correction due to the broadband outage. The broadband problem came about from a PG & E power surge that the broadband system is not protected from. A 10-volt change in power will cause the engine generators to turn on, and this in turn requires approximately 45 minutes to adjust the new mappers. The PG & E power surges caused the maps to bloom, which the technicians tried to adjust. The monitoring device did not receive a strong enough surge to turn on the engine generators. As the power returned to normal, the newly-adjusted mappers began to return to normal intensities and again had to be readjusted. The systems engineer kept the computer system active during this period so that the controllers would continue to have some sort of system, even though it continued to have ten startowners. During this period, response time was slow and the computer reliability was degraded. At 1630, broadband became usable and a computer shutdown was scheduled for 1700 to repair the automated system. The 52 minute down time covered: Core dump—6 min.; planned shutdown to cover FPs—18 min.; determine no hardware problem via diagnostic tape—12 min.; DSS staff takeover to remove problem of CPF111 patch—6 min.; re-certify system—10 min. System reported operational and usable at 1752.

What this dry prose does not say is that two and possibly three aircraft separation system "deviations" occurred over the San Francisco area during this midafternoon outage. FAA witnesses went to some pains to explain that a "deviation" is defined, in this case, as aircraft flying in controlled air space which are not under positive air traffic control because they had not been reidentified after the computer failure, but which nevertheless luckily had not come close enough to other planes to violate aircraft separation minimums. A "system deviation" becomes a "system error" under these definitions if the radar recording tapes show that separation minimums were broached.

The committee is of the opinion that the difference between a "system deviation," a "system error," and a mid-air collision in this event was controlled more by the grace of God than by FAA definitions.

With all of this in mind—that the agency's own team had described this outage as "significant" and "inordinately prolonged," that the broadband backup also failed, and that aircraft safe separation might have been compromised but for good luck—the committee was incredulous to discover that this outage had been entered into FAA's reporting system as a code 60 scheduled outage.

From December of 1979 until August 15, 1980, FAA management repeatedly and explicitly told various committees of Congress that the agency's outage reporting system and the data it produced were valid and accurately described system performance. On August 28, 1980, however, W.B. Rucker, Chief, Airways Facilities Division for the Southern Region, sent the following notice internally to his subordinates, which deserves extensive quotation:

Department of Transportation,
Federal Aviation Administration,
Southern Region,
August 28, 1980

Notice

Subject: Integrity of reporting scheduled outages.

1 *Purpose.*—This notice advises Sector personnel to be more rigorous in their review of outage reports.

2 *Distribution.*—This notice is distributed to the Regional Airway Facilities Division, section level; Area Airway Facilities, branch level; and all Airway Facilities Sectors, Sector Field Offices, and Sector Field Units.

3 *Background.*—(a) The validity and integrity of the outage reporting system depend upon reliable Sector personnel providing accurate reports of all required and applicable outages. Discrepancies in any outage report cause a fallacious disparity among similar facilities which invites criticism and skepticism of the outage reporting system as a whole. It is reasonable to expect all facilities of a similar type to have approximately the same number of scheduled maintenance outages (cause code 60) during a 12-months period. Additionally, a survey of the required periodic maintenance schedules shows that almost all facilities have periodic maintenance tasks which require a facility shutdown. Most facilities should have at least one scheduled maintenance outage within a 12-months period, and all facilities of a similar type should have approximately an equal number of scheduled maintenance outages.

(b) Analysis of the outage report data for calendar year 1979 shows that 219 facilities reported zero outages for scheduled maintenance (cause code 60). A majority of facilities reported a total number of outages significantly below the regional average for that facility type. These conditions indicate that required periodic maintenance was not completed, or that errors were made in reporting the maintenance outages. Failure of the two records to agree casts doubt upon the integrity of both systems.

As is discussed below, there are disincentives built into FAA's outage reporting system for accurately recording unscheduled outages. These disincentives should not apply to scheduled outages. Yet, as the above notice states, even the records on scheduled outages cannot be rectified. This raises substantial doubt not only about FAA's outage reporting but also about the agency's basic maintenance log data that purportedly validates the reported information.

The final breach in the dike of the committee's reservoir of credulity was made by two documents from within FAA. They clearly indicated just how meaningless the carefully crafted definitions in FAA's performance evaluations can be and just how open the system is to abuse.

Both of these documents are monthly reliability reports for 1980 (FAA Form 6040—8): One for distance measuring equipment (DME) and the other for a very high frequency omnidirectional range (VOR) located together at Ponce, Puerto Rico. Both reports show these vital navigational equipment items to have been 96.8 percent reliable for the month of July 1980.

The committee was informed that, in fact, both these facilities were completely destroyed by a fire bomb in July of 1980.

Careful examination of the instructions in FAA Order 6040 for completing the monthly reliability reports reveals that the dedicated civil servant who completed these two reports followed his instructions to the letter. Since the facilities had (and probably could only have) one unscheduled outage for the month, albeit that one outage involved total destruction, he faithfully entered "one" into the conversion tables supplied by headquarters to derive a reliability figure of 96.8 percent. No false entry was made. No rule violated. The system looked great. Except that it wasn't even there, much less working.

Reporting System Disincentives   Witnesses at the subcommittee's hearings stated that there were pressures within FAA to under-report computer and other equipment outages, describing it as an unwritten but understood situation. These witnesses alleged that in many cases, if you didn't make the facility performance look good but insisted on recording the actual failures critically, the agency would subtly retaliate.

The committee spent considerable time trying to substantiate these allegations and identify the source of such pressure to under-report outages. The union representatives who testified were unable to supply sufficient documentation to make a conclusive case, purportedly because their members feared reprisal.

Nevertheless, there clearly is an incentive to under-report outages built into FAA's reporting system. The data generated by the system is used to rank each facility by its performance as measured by the number of unscheduled outages. These rankings, by percentile, are regularly published as Facility Performance Reports (RIS: AF 6040—4e) under FAA Order 6040.4A. If a facility such as a route center computer shows up as a "poor performer," a "performance improvement evaluation requirement" (PIER) report must be done, and it becomes a candidate for an investigation by regional or headquarters personnel. In other words, if a field office reports too many outages it generates paperwork for its supervisors and automatically draws an investigation or evaluation of its operations down upon itself.

Clearly, performance data indicating problems in a particular area is needed and should be acted upon. The disturbing aspect of this system, however, is that performance is being gauged by a single variable, unscheduled outages, and the distinction between the performance of people and that of machines is left vague. Compounding this is the reliance of the system upon individuals voluntarily acting against their own interest by fully reporting on their own problems while in competition with others. No one can be expected to like writing reports about their failures to their superiors. No one can be expected to be enthusiastic about identifying themselves for an outside investigation or evaluation. Yet this evaluation system depends on people voluntarily doing exactly that in a situation in which there appears to be almost no chance of being caught out if you don't.

What is most disturbing is the vulnerability of FAA's whole reporting and performance evaluation system under this arrangement of being corrupted in a cascade-like fashion by a few individuals willing to cut corners. Once a few people or a few offices start under-reporting, the system begins rewarding them and punishing those who honestly and accurately report outages. Those who fully report outages to accurately portray equipment performance are rapidly singled out to their superiors as having problems. Those who cut corners escape attention. In any organization, such "punishment of the innocent; praise for the guilty" is very quickly understood as an expression of what is really wanted by management, and even the most loyal and dedicated employee will become inured to playing the game.

Reporting Categories The whole purpose of a national systemwide outage reporting system is to provide FAA's management, especially headquarters, with useful information on performance that can serve as the basis for seeing trends and allocating resources. Neither FAA headquarters nor Congress should have to dig for information. The categories by which FAA groups outage reports do not, however, provide this kind of information. In addition to the abuse of the scheduled versus unscheduled distinction discussed above, even those outages clearly coded as unscheduled are not easily evaluated.

The committee began its investigation by reviewing the portions of FAA's Monthly Management Reports that graphed unscheduled ARTCC computer outages. This proved largely futile since these outages are presented on the same graphs as communications outages, and in order to accommodate both sets of data the graph scales compress the computer outage rates into meaningless marginal lines.

Next, the committee requested unscheduled computer outage data for each enroute center for the 5-month period from January 1 through May 31, 1980. FAA provided the computer printouts for all eighty series (unscheduled) outages for each of the twenty centers, with each outage categorized under one of nine cause codes.

The committee reviewed these and discovered the outages had been reported under cause codes listed as follows:[2]

Code and cause	Number of outages
80 Equipment failure	60
81 Line outage	—
82 Commercial power failure	—
83 Standby engine generator	—
84 Propagation conditions	—
85 Weather effects	—
86 Software	19
87 Self correcting; cause unknown	16
89 Other	200

Despite the specific admonition in FAA Order 6040.5A against overuse of cause code 89, over two-thirds of the almost 300 reported unscheduled outages were categorized as caused by "other." This obviously tells FAA management little or nothing except that the agency's reporting categories

[2]Numbers of outages not exact due to some data illegibility.

may not fit the actual problems with the computers. When questioned about this at hearings, agency witnesses said they could find the outage causes if they needed to be backtracking through the reporting data. This misperceives the purpose of a reporting system. Management should not have to dig for this kind of information, rather the reporting system should bring it to the front.

In further explaining the roughly 200 outages caused by something "other," FAA witnesses stated that these outage reports actually reported on "services" provided to the controller, and that a service outage could be caused by equipment or facilities other than the main route center computer. These explanations were difficult to follow because the content of the agency's terminology and categorizations kept shifting. The computer performance reporting system doesn't report on the computer but on the service it provides, even though the reports are supposedly generated (and validated) by hardware equipment maintenance logs. A "facility" can refer to either people or machines or part of a machine that provides a service. The meaning of what constitutes the enroute computer itself becomes blurred by dismemberment of the system into a list of acronyms and boxes, each with its own outage reporting, so that a CRAD outage would be reported if the CCC didn't interface with a DDC but not if a DGU failed to drive a PVD, even though in both cases controllers would have to abandon the computer and go to their back-up system.

The remaining ninety reported unscheduled outages listed in the 5 months of data provided to the committee were in three of the remaining eight categories: equipment, software, and unknown. This again, doesn't give headquarters management useful information. For example, the agency describes this computer system as the largest data processing effort of its time, involving millions of programmed words. Yet only one category, labeled software, is available to say something went wrong with the programming. If the agency's management had useful information on this huge system, it cound avoid committing blunders such as denying, in writing, to the committee that its 9020 computers have a capacity saturation problem, when its own field personnel are having to curtail diagnostic work because of limited computer capacity, and "this (saturation) problem has continued to be on the airway facilities list of 'Ten Most Wanted' problems to be resolved for several years," according to the Oakland Operations Analysis Group Report.

FAA's Response to Outages and Reliability Problems

FAA's consistent response to congressional and public concern over air traffic control computer reliability has been alternately to placate with statements that there is no problem, and to say it is studying or reviewing those problems that exist. Over a month before the administrator testified before the subcommittee "without reservation that performance has been steadily improving, not getting worse," the agency issued an "Action Plan for Improving NAS ARTCC Computer Performance" on May 12, 1980. One part of this plan stated "startover and outages have tended to increase as new system tapes (software) are made operational in field facilities."

After the subcommittee had reviewed the report of the Oakland Operations Analysis Group, a joint majority-minority letter to the administrator suggested that similar analyses be done at a portion of other route centers. Administrator Bond replied on October 31, 1980. His letter stated that since "similar local evaluations are routine," additional analyses would be redundant and unneeded. This letter also stated, however, that "the local analysis and evaluation is not always formally documented." The committee is disturbed that this may indicate a lack of institutional memory for sharing solutions between the various FAA offices. After all, this is an agency where internal memoranda are not addressed to people of offices but solely to location identifier numbers, indicating a degree of turnover.

After the Senate Committee on Appropriations issued a highly critical report on October 28, 1980, recommending a funding freeze, the agency again responded with "a plan for improvement" on January 14, 1981. The list of 11 "actions" in this plan are as follows:

1 Establish rigid control over system configuration of all NAS facilities.
2 Establish ATF evaluation function.
3 Complete staff work on organizational options.
4 Improve reporting system.
5 Revise and update automation directives.
6 Review manpower and skills requirements.
7 Assure that cost accounting and logistics data is available to support decision making.
8 Merge Air Traffic and Airway Facilities performance improvement programs.
9 Improve modeling and machine performance measurement.
10 Proceed with basic direct access radar channel (DARC).
11 Complete offloading and backup studies (including those required by the Senate).

While all of this is laudable and the committee is pleased at the increased attention being focused on ATC computer performance, it can't help but notice how many of these "actions" consist of working up options, revising and updating, reviewing, studying improvements, proceeding, and completing studies. This may be an overly jaundiced view. FAA is capable of responding rapidly and competently to real problems. Descriptions of FAA personnel working round the clock to restore service are not hard to come by. But as the agency conducts its plan of studies, events may be overtaking it.

First, it is faily clear that system maintenance, especially preventative maintenance, is being reduced because the maintenance staffing is being reduced. This may be a justified saving to the extent that more reliable equipment is in place. The committee received inconsistent testimony on whether in fact this is the case. Preventative maintenance routines were said to have been greatly reduced at the Indianapolis ARTCC, but not reduced at all at the Oakland, California ARTCC.

FAA technicians pointed out that some equipment they have to maintain is very old and in need of more maintenance as it ages, and additional, new equipment items were being added which will require some attention, however reliable.

No one had a concrete explanation why the total systemwide figure for the mean time to restore all FAA facilities was increasing at 15 percent per year, when the system is supposed to be still improving.

The committee received extensive testimony that programs for FAA technician training were in serious trouble. Obtaining training for a work-force which is experiencing reductions would not be an attractive prospect. The withering of FAA's technical training capability while the agency takes advantage of a temporary worker surplus to save funds could have serious future repercussions, especially if urgent retraining needs surface. Most disturbing was the comment made by a number of individuals from the industry that it is the skill and motivation of the individual maintenance technician that matters most and it is very difficult to attract or retain the best technicians if they cannot work with state-of-the-art computers.

What all this may portend is a developing situation in which FAA management, lulled by unreliable outage statistics, continues to implement budget cuts in maintenance at the same time the aging system is being stretched and extended to accommodate increasing traffic and workloads awaiting a replacement for 10 years. At some point the rubber band may snap and FAA will have a difficult time recovering. The agency may already be in this position with the broadband back-up system. After 5 years of announcements that broadband would be phased out, the realization that it is still needed suddenly finds the agency with very few individuals qualified to maintain it.

A similar situation exists with the users of the equipment, air traffic controllers. There appears to be deep confusion within the agency about staffing needs for controllers. At subcommittee hearings in June 1980, Administrator Bond stated that he believed the controller staffing standard was too high and more controllers weren't needed. In an interview published in October of 1980, he was quoted to exactly the opposite effect, that the standard was correct. A number of sources stated to the committee during its investigation that there was a real shortage of air traffic controllers coming in through the long training pipeline.

Advance planning to deal with these kinds of problems is essential. But such planning can only be meaningful if it is based on reliable information and accurate historical data. FAA's erratic responses to its own facilities performance data and the challenges to the system that produces it cast serious doubt on the agency's whole planning process. At this point, the committee can only accept the testimony of Gerald Thompson, FAA Director of Airways Facilities Service, in giving the most forthright, unvarnished assessment the committee received.

> There have to be troubles. We have problems. We list them here, we have listed them there.
> The issue that I think is at hand is whether or not there is an imminent collapse of the system as a result of those.
> I don't think, and the agency doesn't think, that that is imminent. Are there problems that we must pursue, address?
> Yes, we are trying to do that.
> I, for one, would be willing to accept whatever counsel these or others have on how we could do that better, but I do not think that it is reasonable to say that this system is imminently collapsing. That is not fair. It is not true.
> That is all I am saying.

Equipment Procurement Plans

The committee's confidence in FAA's 10-year plan to replace the main enroute computers is not strengthened by the history of the DARC system. At the subcommittee's 1976 hearings on ATC computer performance, DARC was described as the solution to the technological or perceptual wrench between the primary 9020 system and the broadband backup. Ideally it was to eliminate the need for broadband shrimpboats, and the lengthy transition process. Almost 5 years later it has not done this.

Although DARC is now being billed as an interim back-up system to be used until the new main frame computer is operational in 1992, it will require expensive enhancements during this interval. Along with DARC, a number of other interim, add-on data processing items and functions are to be procured while the 9020 is still in use, such as Electronic Tabular-Display System, and the Discrete Address Beacon System, while at the same time plans are being made to shed functions from the primary computer to preserve capacity for handling increased traffic. It is difficult, if not impossible, to determine whether all of this is being properly coordinated or will result in waste. Certainly the cost of all of the DARC enhancements, now estimated at upwards of $100 million for a system originally budgeted at $11 million, are difficult to justify if the system is to be replaced by a new primary computer.

A planning and procurement cycle to buy a new primary computer that runs from 1977 to 1992 virtually guarantees that the new computer will be way behind the state-of-the-art when completed. What is more troubling, and suspicious, is that a number of FAA's other major procurement completion schedules are slipping to coincide with the 1988-1991 time frame for installation of the new primary computer. Either everyone will get well at this milestone, marking a new age in air traffic control, or chaos could result with multiple new systems all being delivered and requiring coordination and debugging at once.

What is extremely disturbing about these schedule slippages, however, is at least one strong piece of evidence that FAA itself does not believe its own long-range plans and that this is, as one witness testified, delaying implementation of a Collision Avoidance System.

The FAA has committed itself to a collision avoidance system consisting of the Discrete Address Beacon System in conjunction with the Automatic Traffic Advisory and Resolution System, called DABS/ATARS. Greatly simplified, this concept calls for a combination of on-the-ground computers and aircraft equipment which would monitor air traffic, searching for potential conflicting flight paths. When the DABS/ATARS computer spots a potential conflict, it will advise the pilot and air traffic controller of the problem and devise a correction (reportedly there is still some dispute as to whether the controller will be informed). The original schedule for DABS/ATARS implementation that was publicly announced and given to Congress called for installation from 1983 to 1986 or 1987. Although not formally stated, it is widely admitted that this schedule has slipped roughly 5 years to the 1988 to 1992 time frame. And it was inevitable that this delay would occur because DARC is not compatible with DABS/ATARS and there is no firm plan or intention to make it so.

In other words, the back-up system for the 9020 to be used during outages and at night until 1992 would not have accepted the collision avoidance advisory messages that were to be introduced in roughly 1985. This would have increased the gap between the primary and back-up air traffic control system and left the controller in the dark as to what evasive manuevers the ATARS computer was directing to the pilots at the time the controller might most need to know. FAA's own planning and procurement schedule called for two different, new air traffic control system components to be introduced and operational during a 7-year period in which they were to be mutually incompatible.

The committee considers this to be evidence of either a breakdown in rational planning of major expenditures or cynical bad faith in informing the public and Congress about the agency's true intentions.

It appears that FAA has yet to correct the long-standing planning and management problems identified by the committee through the years. Until this is done, FAA will continue to experience (1) prolonged system development cycles, (2) significant cost overruns and (3) unnecessary or non-cost effective systems development efforts. Given the critical need for an effective air traffic control system, it is essential that FAA take decisive steps to correct these deficiencies.

Two important actions can be taken immediately by the agency. First, FAA should establish strong centralized management over the planning and development of all computer-based information systems, including air traffic control data processing. Under Public Law 96-511, the Paperwork Reduction Act, every agency including FAA is required to establish a Central Information Resources Mangement Office by July 1, 1981. The head of this office will report to the agency head and is responsible for planning and management of all major information systems. FAA's full compliance with this statute will ensure that the appropriate high-level attention will be given to the critical information management problems facing the agency. Another important step that can be taken is a comprehensive study of FAA's long-term automated data processing requirements. Such studies are fundamental to comprehensive planning for any future air traffic control system and are specifically called for in Public Law 96-511.

FINDINGS AND CONCLUSIONS

A Failures in the primary radar data processing computers must constitute a threat to safety, especially during the transition to the back-up system during peak traffic periods.

B It is impossible to reach final conclusions about the computerized radar system's reliability because the records and reporting system are of dubious validity.

   1 The reporting system does not collect reliable, relevant data because of its design.

      a The computer outage reporting systems only demand reports of wholly unanticipated, sudden, total, and enduring outages, not all outages which could affect safety.

      b The system contains disincentives for accurate reporting.

      c The failure reporting information is collected at the wrong level since it cannot be separately verified.

      d The reporting system lacks guidance for common sense application that would prevent a completely inoperative system or component from being reported as almost perfectly reliable.

   2 FAA assurances based on statistical conclusions drawn from questionable reported data are not persuasive.

C FAA is not doing an effective job of alleviating problems caused by computer outages or planning for replacing the computers.

   1 The DARC system has not lived up to expectations as a truly redundant, workable back-up system.

   2 Current software improvements may be causing outages.

   3 FAA planning for replacing the enroute computers and associated plans for staffing requirements are constantly shifting and lacking firm substantiation.

RECOMMENDATIONS...

NORAD COMPUTER SYSTEMS ARE DANGEROUSLY OBSOLETE

Twenty-Third Report by the Committee on Government Operations

SUMMARY

Beginning in October 1979, a series of computer failures occurred at the North American Aerospace Defense Command's (NORAD) missile warning center at Cheyenne Mountain, Colorado. These highly publicized failures led to our nation's strategic forces being placed unnecessarily on alert and caused many to question the credibility of our country's premier missile warning and attack center. Concern was also raised by Congress and the public that such failures could have far-reaching and catastrophic consequences, particularly in the age of nuclear confrontation. The reassurances coming from our military leaders that these events were isolated cases and the situation was under control did not allay the deep concern expressed throughout the country.

While several investigations were subsequently conducted by DOD, little effort was made to identify the underlying weaknesses in the NORAD system which were the root causes of the false alerts. Instead, these studies continued to maintain that the failures were merely the result of faulty computer components and that these problems had been corrected. A Senate study concluded that the component failures were the result of outdated equipment and found that Federal ADP procurement regulations had prevented NORAD from obtaining more modern computer systems.

Hearings conducted by this committee clearly revealed that the Federal ADP acquisition process was in no way responsible for the false alerts at the NORAD facility. Further, it was found that the NORAD facility had been mismanaged over the last decade by the Air Force, the Joint Chiefs of Staff, and the Department of Defense, resulting in obsolete computer systems which do not satisfy the requirements of NORAD's sensitive mission. These obsolete systems, coupled with poor management practices and human error, were directly responsible for the false alerts.

The underlying cause of the obsolete systems was the failure to complete a computer modernization program initiated by the Air Force in 1966. By May of 1981, it was more than 6 years behind schedule and about $150 million over budget. More importantly, the system only has, at best, an information processing capability of the 1966 system it replaces.

A major factor which contributed to the failure of the modernization program was the 1970 decision by the Joint Chiefs of Staff to force NORAD to use the computer equipment of the World Wide Military Command and Control System (WWMCCS) which was inadequate for NORAD's requirements. This decision was made despite strenuous objections from the NORAD commander. Like the NORAD modernization program, the WWMCCS project has been plagued by Air Force and Joint Chiefs of Staff mismanagement. The failure has resulted in the expenditure of more than $1 billion in a command and control system that has been judged by the GAO as incapable of meeting a crisis condition.

The committee believes that the problems at NORAD have reached a critical stage and that priority attention is needed at the highest levels of the Defense Department. Without this emphasis, it is unlikely that this country will have an up-to-date and effective attack warning system.

The failure of the NORAD modernization program and the past mismanagement of the NORAD facility culminating in the false alerts underscore the ADP management failures that have occurred throughout DOD during the 1970s. The department's attempts at large-scale systems development projects are habitually plagued by excessive cost overruns, schedule slippages, and unacceptable performance levels. The repeated failures of these projects are caused by poor planning, fragmented management, and a lack of accountability and leadership.

The situation is further exacerbated by DOD's reluctance to accept or even seriously consider valid criticisms of these projects. Instead of taking needed corrective actions, it all too often chooses to blame its problems on "unwarranted instrusions" by Congressional committees and outside oversight agencies.

The condition of our defense establishment is of great concern to all Americans. To ignore DOD's internal management weaknesses invites serious and far-reaching deception. Strong central management and oversight are urgently needed to ensure that these failures are recognized, and that corrective action is taken. Without such oversight, more billions will be wasted and our defense capabilities will be seriously undermined.

THE NORAD FAILURE

Introduction

NORAD, a functional partnership between the United States and Canada, has the responsibility for (1) providing warning of attack on North America by bombers and/or ballistic missiles, (2) surveillance of space to keep track of all objects of human origin orbiting the earth, (3) maintaining, in peacetime, a surveillance of North America capable of detecting and identifying unknown aircraft, and (4) providing a limited defense against bombers in the event of an attack on this continent.

To accomplish this mission, NORAD relies on a complex system of satellites and ground-based radar around the world to provide early warning of enemy missile and bomber attacks and to permit accurate and timely assessment of potential threats to the security of the North American continent. These satellites and radar installations are linked to our military commanders by a sophisticated computer and communications network. Basically, the Aerospace Defense system is composed of three major segments: (1) sensors to detect incoming missiles, (2) communications links and computer centers to transmit and analyze data from those sensors, and (3) command posts where the data are assessed and appropriate actions are addressed.

The critical focal point of this worldwide tracking communications system in which all essential information is processed and evaluated is located at Cheyenne Mountain, Colorado. Each year the NORAD command post receives numerous sensor warnings which must be assessed. According to OMB, over 3700 such warnings were received between January 1, 1979, and June 30, 1980. Most of these sensor readings were judged to pose no threat to our national security. However, starting in October 1979, a series of computer failures at the Cheyenne Mountain facility generated several false warnings of mass enemy missile attacks against the United States. Because of these false alerts, the U.S. strategic forces were unnecessarily placed on alert, causing considerable concern throughout the country. Not only are these failures disturbing due to their potentially serious and far-reaching consequences, but they also directly affect the credibility of our entire defense capability.

Because of concern by the Government Operations Committee about the failure of our defense warning system and the committee's jurisdiction over federal computer activities, the chairman of the committee requested the GAO to undertake an immediate investigation to (1) review NORAD's acquisition and use of ADP and telecommunications, and (2) determine what corrective actions are needed by the Air Force and other agencies to ensure that these failures do not recur. The results of this investigation are contained in GAO's report entitled "NORAD's Missile Warning System: What Went Wrong?" dated May 15, 1981.

On May 19 and 20, 1981, the Subcommittee on Legislation and National Security of the House Committee on Government Operations conducted hearings on the failures of the NORAD computer system. Testimony was presented on May 19 by the acting comptroller general, U.S. General Accounting Office (GAO); the commander-in-chief of NORAD; and the Office of Management and Budget (OMB). Further testimony was presented on May 20 by representatives from the Department of Defense (DOD), the Joint Chiefs of Staff, and the General Services Administration.

Cause of the False Alerts

There seems to be no disagreement as to the immediate causes of the most serious false alerts. The GAO reported the following:

1 On November 9, 1979, test data was inadvertently fed into the online missile warning computers. It generated false alerts.

2 On June 3 and 6, 1980, missile warning system failures occurred when a faulty component in the communications system began writing numbers into blank spaces in the missile warning messages sent out live to various command posts. The blank spaces during an attack indicate the number of attacking missiles and usually contained zeros, but in this case the erroneous numbers generated by the computer indicated a mass attack.

Opinions vary widely, however, as to the root causes that led to these occurrences. Lt. Gen. Hillman Dickinson of the Joint Chiefs of Staff and Under Secretary of Defense for Research and Engineering, Richard DeLauer, blamed the alerts on a faulty chip and the "inadvertent" use of a test tape on a live machine. At no time did they acknowledge that these failures were a manifestation of much larger problems plaguing NORAD's computer systems.

A report prepared by Senators Gary Hart and Barry Goldwater alluded to the Federal ADP acquisition process as contributing to the failures.[1] This position was also taken by certain Air Force officials in opposing passage of the Paperwork Reduction Act of 1980. During consideration of S. 815, the DOD authorization bill for 1982, it was again asserted that a primary factor in the false alerts was P.L. 89–306, the law governing the acquisition of automatic data processing (ADP) equipment for federal agencies, including DOD.[2]

In direct contrast, the GAO found that NORAD had been mismanaged for more than a decade by the Air Force, the Joint Chiefs of Staff and the Defense Department. This has resulted in the waste of hundreds of millions of dollars and has led to the installation of obsolete and inadequate computer systems which cannot satisfy the requirements of NORAD's sensitive mission. These obsolete systems, coupled with highly questionable management practices and human error, were directly responsible for the false alerts. The acting comptroller general testified that the problems at NORAD had reached a critical stage and that priority attention is needed at the highest levels of DOD.[3]

The committee agrees that the basic problems are with the Air Force's management and that the failures cannot be attributed to the federal government's acquisition process or tossed aside as an "inadvertent" accident. The committee is not in the least reassured by DOD's claims that the problems

---

[1]"Recent False Alerts From the Nation's Missile Attack Warning System," prepared by Senators Hart and Goldwater. Committee on Armed Services, U.S. Senate, October 1980.

[2]Congressional Record. May 14, 1981. S. 5047–5050.

[3]Hearings on "Failures of the North American Aerospace Defense Command's (NORAD) Attack Warning System," before the Subcommittee on Legislation and National Security of the House Committee on Government Operations, 97th Congress, 1st session, May 19 and 20, 1981 (hereinafter cited as "Hearings"), p. 95.

which caused the false alerts have been corrected. NORAD's current computer systems are severely deficient, and DOD's efforts to upgrade these systems over the last 15 years have been largely unsuccessful. The committee is alarmed that NORAD's critical capabilities have been allowed to deteriorate during this period.

Further, the committee is appalled that Air Force procedures could allow test data indicating a mass missile attack to be fed undetected into the NORAD computer system, with the consequence of placing the entire system in a position of high alert and almost activating our nuclear retaliatory forces. To use standard communications messages which could be taken for an actual missile attack is extremely irresponsible, considering the potential consequences.

The committee is heartened by the actions of the present NORAD commander, who appears to be trying to correct the problems at NORAD and to upgrade the facility to enhance its performance capabilities and reestablish its credibility. To correct the immediate causes of the false alerts, the following actions have been taken:

> **1** An offsite test facility was installed at a cost of $16 million to prevent recurrence of the problems that occurred on November 9, 1979. The implementation of this offsite test facility allows software development and testing to be performed outside of the on-line missile warning facility. Since testing is no longer performed on the live system, this type of false alert should not recur.
>
> **2** Computer programs have been added that, in effect, allow the tracing of a message through the entire message preparation phase to ensure that the transmission reflects the original message.
>
> **3** A display was added in the NORAD command post which shows what is being transmitted to other command posts. Further, all outgoing warning messages are now released only by the commander of NORAD.
>
> **4** The test messages being transmitted from NORAD to other command posts for communications line checks have been changed in format from blank warning messages to standard communications test messages.

The committee is also encouraged by the decision of the Secretary of Defense to restore the commander of NORAD's position to that of a full general. Clearly, the importance of NORAD to our nation's defense capabilities warrants the assignment of top military commanders.

While these actions are significant, the weaknesses inherent in our nation's missile warning system defy quick and simple solutions. The deficiencies in the current system have developed over more than a decade. Without a concerted effort by the highest levels of DOD, it is unlikely that this country will have an up-to-date and effective attack warning system.

The Failure of NORAD's Computer Improvement Program

The NORAD complex at Cheyenne Mountain became operational in 1966. At that time it relied primarily upon a combination of computer systems that were considered state-of-the-art processors and were specifically built for mission requirements. Although they were adequate at that time, they could not meet the expanded requirements of the next decade.

Almost immediately, the command began planning for an improved computer system to meet the mission needs of the 1970s. This activity was known as the 427M Computer Improvement Program.[4] The basic objective of the program was to enhance NORAD's mission effectiveness by providing greater and more reliable information processing capabilities than could be accomplished with the older equipment. Basically the 427M system is composed of three major segments: (1) the Communications System Segment (CSS) which provides essential communications support for NORAD headquarters, (2) the NORAD Computer System (NCS) which provides critical missile warning information, and (3) the Space Computational Center (SCC) which detects and tracks all manufactured satellites in space.

Despite the critical nature of the NORAD facility and the increased emphasis on upgrading its capabilities, the 427M upgrade program is not yet completed. It has been subject to schedule delays, excessive cost growth, and reduced mission performance capabilities. In fact, the 427M program is more than 6 years behind schedule and has cost overruns of almost $150 million over the projected cost of the computer upgrade. More importantly, the upgraded system will only have an information processing capability essentially equivalent to that of the 1966 system that it replaces.

GAO reported that there were two basic reasons for the failure of the 427M upgrade.[5] First, NORAD was directed in 1970 by the Joint Chiefs of Staff to use the World-Wide Military Command and Control System (WWMCCS) computer equipment and software, which does not have the capabilities necessary to handle NORAD's information processing requirements. The commander of NORAD at that time strenuously objected to the Joint Chiefs of Staff, but was overruled.

Second, program management was divided between the Air Force Systems Command and NORAD. GAO reported that fragmented management made it exceedingly difficult to establish and maintain effective administrative control over the program and contractor operations on a daily basis.[6] NORAD's attempts to resolve the problems inherent in the WWMCCS equipment and software and the divided management resulted in the development of an information system that will not improve NORAD's operational capability over that which it has had since 1966.

The GAO reported that after 7 years of effort and millions of dollars spent, the Air Force, in 1977, recognized that the NORAD project was in trouble. The Air Force, acknowledging that the system would not reach its full opera-

---

[4]See Appendix III for a chronology of events on the 427M Computer Improvement Program.
[5]U.S. General Accounting Office report, "NORAD's Missile Warning System: What Went Wrong?" MASAD-81-30, May 15, 1981.
[6]Responsibility was divided among two commands, eight contractors, and four Air Force contract control officers.

tional capability, redefined the criteria for acceptance. The new criterion for acceptance, according to the Air Force's redefinition, termed "equivalent operational capability," occurred when the new system matched the capability of the obsolete system being replaced.

Under the new criterion, the Air Force accepted the upgraded system as "operational" in September 1979, apparently to reduce the criticism over its system development failures. The first false alert occurred only a month later, in October, and succeeding false alerts occurred with increasing frequency thereafter.

Both Under Secretary DeLauer and Lieutenant General Dickinson attempted during the hearings to downplay the effect that the WWMCCS program had on the NORAD facility.[7] General Dickinson asserted that an exemption had been given for NORAD and the relationship with WWMCCS was "minimal." This attempt to deemphasize the effect that the Joint Chiefs of Staff decision had on NORAD could mislead the public about the severity of the problem. In fact, the WWMCCS computers used at NORAD are the central processors comprising the heart of the Tactical Warning and Attack Assessment System. The effect of such a "minimal" relationship could have far-reaching consequences on this country's defensive capabilities.

After the hearings, Chairman Brooks requested that General Dickinson provide specific documents showing an exemption was granted for NORAD from the WWMCCS program. The general did not provide the requested information. Instead of responding directly to the chairman's request, the general asked and answered his own version of the chairman's question. The chairman's question and the general's response follows:

Chairman Brooks. Additionally, the committee would also like to receive the specific January 9, 1981, document exempting NORAD from the World Wide Military Command and Control System requirement.[8]

General Dickinson. I would first like to address the issue of the exemption of NORAD from the World Wide Military Command and Control System requirements. As I stated in testimony to the committee on May 20, 1981, the Joint Chiefs [sic] of the exemption of NORAD from the World Wide Military puters [sic] in the future. However, the area of computers in WWMCCS is one which has distinct problems in which semantics is a barrier to clear communication; i.e., "WWMCCS," "WWMCCS ADP," "Standard WWMCCS ADP System," "New Standard WWMCCS ADP System," "WWMCCS Intercomputer Network," "WWMCCS Information System." So, in order to avoid any confusion on this issue, I would like to restate the question thusly: "Will NORAD be allowed to acquire computer hardware and software for the Tactical Warning and Attack Assessment (TW/AA) function without being constrained in its approach, solution, or acquisition by other areas of the command, control, and intelligence community?" The answer is unequivocally yes. This position was affirmed by the Joint Chiefs of Staff in a January 9, 1981, Memorandum for the Secretary of Defense, JCSM-4-81; subsequently clarified by

---

[7]Hearings, p. 323.
[8]Letter from Chairman Brooks to General Dickinson, dated May 20, 1981.

ASD(C31) in the Modernization of the WWMCCS Information System (WIS), January 19, 1981, prepared in response to House Report No. 96–916, which specifically directed that the ADP requirements of the strategic warning system were to be included in this DOD response; and then the exclusion was again explained by the Joint Chiefs of Staff in MJCS 15–81, February 2, 1981. Further discussion of this issue is provided at Enclosure A.[9]

The misstatement of the chairman's question and the subsequent reference to documents not provided to the committee has only served to muddle this important issue. What is clear, however, is there appears to be no document containing a specific exemption.

Further, the NORAD commander who specifically requested the exemption, and who testified the day before General Dickinson, was not aware of any such exemption,[10] even though General Dickinson asserted it was given on January 9, 1981. If such an exemption exists, surely the NORAD commander would be told that his request for an exemption had been granted. In fact, about 2 months after the committee's hearings and 7 months after the supposed exemption was granted, the commander of NORAD requested clarification from the Joint Chiefs of Staff on the status of the exemption. The committee believes that a matter of this importance should not be kept vague and consequently recommends that the Secretary of Defense immediately direct the JCS to provide a clear and certain exemption for NORAD from WWMCCS for all current and future WWMCCS standard equipment and software. In today's technology, it is no longer necessary for each site within WWMCCS to have the same computer system. Instead, there should be standard communication protocols connecting the sites.

GAO testified that it alerted the Department of Defense in September 1978 to the serious problems associated with the NORAD development program and recommended: (1) that NORAD be exempted from using future standard WWMCCS computers, (2) that a redesign effort be initiated to replace the major system with state-of-the-art equipment, and (3) that the faulty power system be upgraded to protect critical computers. GAO stated that despite continued warnings the Department of Defense, the Joint Chiefs of Staff, and the Air Force repeatedly failed to take effective action to implement GAO's recommendations.

After a comprehensive review, the Air Force inspector general confirmed GAO's findings and classified the NORAD upgrade program as a failure due to mismanagement and the inability of WWMCCS to meet NORAD requirements. The inspector general further indicated that there was no relationship between NORAD's missile warning failures and the ADP acquisition process. He blamed the problems on fragmented management and internal regulations. In assessing the 427M program, the inspector general stated that:

---

[9]Letter from General Dickinson to Chairman Brooks, dated May 29, 1981.
[10]Hearings, p. 324.

The 427M was 200–300 percent ($80–100 million) over the original System Management Directive (SMD) budget (scope was changed several times), was over 3 years late, and had marginal performance when accepted. By the standard stated earlier in this report, this was an unsuccessful acquisition...In the final analysis, the overriding criterion for determining the success of a program is whether the final product meets the needs of the user.[11]

The inspector general went on to state that by this criterion, the 427M program was a failure.

WWMCCS—A BILLION DOLLAR FAILURE

Problems with the World Wide Military Command and Control System (WWMCCS) are not limited to NORAD. WWMCCS is an integral part of our nation's defense forces providing warning and intelligence information in support of the President, the Secretary of Defense and the Joint Chiefs of Staff. This essential system, like the NORAD facility, has been continually mismanaged over the last decade and is at a point where its continued effectiveness is being questioned by GAO and the Congress. Poor planning and fragmented management which led to the failure of the NORAD program also contributed to the serious problems being experienced by WWMCCS.

The GAO began reviewing the WWMCCS program in 1970. At that time, it determined that the proposed acquisition of up to eighty-seven computers was not adequately planned nor supported by valid cost and savings estimates; that specifications were not based on need; and that management responsibilities for the planning and direction of the acquisition program were fragmented. Since the project's initiation in the mid-1960s, a billion dollars has been spent. GAO reported that there has been little if any improvement realized by the department since the WWMCCS program's inception.[12]

GAO's evaluation showed that the existing WWMCCS management structure is so complex and fragmented that no one organization or individual has a complete overview of the program or the centralized responsibility for its funding, budgeting, and management. As a result, the WWMCCS program:

Is unresponsive to stated requirements;
Is unreliable;
Lacks economical and effective growth potential;
Is incapable of transferring data and information efficiently;
Makes the exploitation of ADP technology extremely difficult and costly; and
Impairs each command's operational backup capability.

[11]"Special Management Review of USAF Support to the Tactical Warning/Attack Assessment System." Inspector General of the Air Force. September 1980.
[12]U.S. General Accounting Office report, "The World Wide Military Command and Control System—Major Changes Needed in Its Automated Data Processing Management and Direction," LCD-80-22. Dec. 14, 1979. *Note:* See Appendix IV for a chronology of events on the development of the WWMCCS project.

Since WWMCCS is an essential element of United States national security, the mismanagement of this project by the Air Force and the Joint Chiefs of Staff over fifteen years has seriously jeopardized our defense capabilities.

This committee was concerned over the viability of the WWMCCS program as early as February 1969 when the present chairman of the committee wrote to Secretary Laird expressing his concerns over the WWMCCS project. The principal areas of his concerns were as follows:

1 Despite the magnitude of the proposed expenditure, there is no one office or individual in the entire department, to the subcommittee's knowledge, having overall jurisdiction over the processing of this proposed procurement. Over a period of several months, every official in the department the subcommittee has contacted responded to some important aspect of this proposed procurement by saying that the matter was beyond his jurisdiction. Surely, when a sum in the magnitude of between $100 million and $500 million is involved, there should be overall coordination of the entire project at some level within the department with firm responsibility to evaluate the need and to maintain control over all aspects of the project.

2 The subcommittee has not been able to obtain or to determine the existence of any feasibility study or any other substantive evaluation of the equipment now in use that supported the immediate need for the acquisition of new hardware. It is not suggested that such a requirement does not exist, but to the extent the subcommittee has been able to determine, the requirement is of an abstract type based upon a letter or memorandum simply directing that the new procurement be made, rather than supporting in factual and logical terms the need for a new procurement.

3 During several years of investigating computer procurement in the government, most experts coming before the subcommittee have urged that acquisition of computer hardware come after completion of the basic design of the system in which it is to be used. The "World-Wide System" is probably the largest of its kind and has more built-in problems and demanding requirements than any other system ever developed. Yet, it is apparently the decision of the department to select and acquire hardware in anticipation of system development under this procurement. Only the most definitive and persuasive reasons should allow this procurement to be an exception to what otherwise has become a generally-accepted rule in efficient computer system procurement.

4 From information obtained from the department, it would appear that the principal increase in computer compatibility expected from this procurement would correspond to a high level of hardware performance. There is no indication that the procurement proposes a new computer system significantly better in capability or versatility as compared to its present output.[13]

As noted by the GAO some 10 years later in its December 1979 report, these are the same factors which contributed to the failure of the WWMCCS project. At that time, GAO stated that the department's planned future expenditures to continue this program will not resolve the most outstanding

[13]Letter from Chairman Jack Brooks to the Secretary of Defense, Melvin R. Laird, February 17, 1969.

problems of the project unless the department initiates major changes in the program's management structure and direction. GAO then recommended that Congress withhold funds from the project.

In an October 1981 report, the GAO evaluated the Air Force's new plan to upgrade WWMCCS.[14] The upgrade originally was expected to be completed in 1989 at a cost of untold billions of dollars. GAO's evaluation of the department's WWMCCS upgrade shows that these efforts have been slow, do not address the fundamental issues, and will not lead to a timely responsive solution to known WWMCCS problems.

After 14 years, many hundreds of studies, and the expenditure of more than $1 billion, DOD has failed to develop a responsive, reliable, survivable design or provide a firm and detailed planning document describing how to achieve such a design. The performance of the current WWMCCS is so poor that rapid improvements are necessary to minimize continuing critical shortfalls in capability, particularly during times of crisis. But the WWMCCS upgrade planning is proceeding far too slowly to be responsive to these deficiencies. An already unnecessarily long acquisition process scheduled for completion in 1989 may slip repeatedly because of poor management by the department. Specifically, after 13 years since the start of the WWMCCS program and after more than 2 years since the start of the recent WWMCCS upgrade, the department:

> Has only recently approved a concept of operations for WWMCCS upon which detailed information requirements must be based;
> Did not plan to properly define the detailed information requirements necessary as a cornerstone for a successful system acquisition;
> Has prematurely selected a computer design, before defining requirements; and
> Has only recently established a central manager for WWMCCS.[15]

In spite of numerous studies, which essentially contain the same or similar information and recommendations, DOD persists in an unrelenting pursuit of additional funds to support further studies. This commitment to study at the expense of decisive action prolongs the operation and maintenance of antiquated and dangerously inadequate hardware and software, seriously impairing DOD's ability to provide responsive, reliable support to the National Command Authorities, the Joint Chiefs of Staff, and the Unified and Specified Commands.

The committee is concerned that this country will lack a viable command and control system in the 1990s if the Air Force and the Joint Chiefs of Staff

---

[14]U.S. General Accounting Office report, "The World Wide Military Command and Control Information System—Problems in Information Resource Management," MASAD–82–2, Oct. 19, 1981.

[15]Note: Recently DOD established a central manager for WWMCCS called the Joint Program Management Office (JPMO). However, GAO reported to this committee that it is concerned that this office may not have adequate financial control and program accountability over the WWMCCS upgrade.

continue to refuse to modify their methods of operation and management. If this pattern continues, we can be certain that many more billions of dollars will be wasted in a futile attempt to develop a command and control system which meets our needs.

THE PROBLEM: THE FEDERAL ACQUISITION PROCESS OR DOD MANAGEMENT?

In 1965, the committee, anticipating the key role that computers would play in the operations of government, recommended, and Congress enacted, Public Law 89–306 (Brooks Act), which established a framework for the central management and procurement of the government's ADP resources. The act is grounded upon two basic objectives: (1) ADP resources should be procured as economically and efficiently as possible; and (2) only those resources should be procured which are needed and which can assist the management of government programs. The Department of Defense as well as other federal agencies fall under the provisions of the Brooks Act and are required to follow the policies and procedures established by it.

Since its passage, the Brooks Act has opened the government market more widely to the ADP industry, thereby providing private sector innovations to federal agencies. Additionally, the act has encouraged increased competition within the computer industry itself. In 1965, almost half of Federal ADP procurements were supplied by one vendor. Today, many ADP firms supply their products to federal agencies. As a result of increased competition, $5.2 billion has been saved by the government since the act's passage.

Charges have been made that the acquisition process established under Public Law 89–306 was responsible for the computer system failures at NORAD. Testifying before the committee, Under Secretary DeLauer and General Dickinson even went so far as to assert that the implementation of Public Law 89–306 was harming national security.[16] When requested by the committee to support this allegation, these two officials did not supply any studies or analyses performed by DOD to back up their assertion.

However, they did submit highly selective and misleading quotes from studies performed outside DOD. For example, the President's Reorganization Project (PRP) was cited as a principal study supporting this charge. On the contrary, that study, like the other studies cited, concluded that Public Law 89–306 is a viable and effective law.

The response also contained thirteen examples of DOD computer procurements dating back to 1976 where unnecessary delays were alleged to be caused by Public Law 89–306. However, most of the cases involved sole-source or limited competitive acquisitions in which the delays in the procurement process occurred when justifiable questions about the legality of such procurements were raised.

---

[16]Hearings, pp. 227–283, 290.

General Dickinson cited as a specific example of unnecessary and costly delay the Army's program to replace the computers at the U.S. Army Finance and Accounting Center at Fort Benjamin Harrison (JUMPS). The actual facts of this case, uncovered by an extensive GAO review, showed that the project suffered from serious deficiencies in planning and design and was not properly justified. Based on the GAO recommendations, the chairman of the House Government Operations Committee recommended that the procurement be cancelled. The project was subsequently cancelled and later redirected at considerable savings to the government.

The lack of substance to DOD's allegation compels the committee to conclude that the federal acquisition process itself has not been responsible for the inability of DOD to successfully acquire and develop computer systems. The problem is the lack of proper management.

WWMCCS and NORAD are not the only examples of DOD computer system failures during the past decade due to deficiencies in management. The Advanced Logistics System, Phase IV, and Project MAX[17] are other examples where billions of dollars would have been wasted by the military departments if Congress had allowed them to continue.

The GAO testified that they had issued over 100 reports since 1965, and that the department, the Joint Chiefs of Staff, and the military services have historically:

> Failed to effectively plan for ADP procurement and implementation;
> Failed to adequately identify user requirements;
> Failed to develop functional specifications;
> Failed to provide centralized acquisition management;
> Failed to make effective use of the competitive process; and
> Failed to establish adequate accountability.[18]

Over the last 10 years, DOD ADP management has been the subject of many critical studies. Conclusions from the most significant of these studies follow.

President's Reorganization Project (PRP). This study was initiated in 1977 by OMB to identify potential improvements in the Federal Government's acquisition, management, and use of computer resources. Extensive comments were received from members of Congress, federal agencies, industry representatives, and the public. The PRP identified a considerable number of problem areas in DOD, including the following:

> The role of computers in the area of national security is a vital one and is not receiving attention within DOD commensurate with this importance.

---

[17]The Advanced Logistics System (ALS) was an effort to acquire computer systems to support the Air Force's Logistics Command. After approximately $250 million had been wasted, the Congress directed the Air Force to cancel this effort. Despite this direction, the Air Force went forward with substantial parts of this system under the name of Project MAX. This project was subsequently cancelled as a result of actions by the House and Senate Appropriations Committees.

[18]Hearings, p. 5.

The uneven level of competence in employment of information technology is symptomatic of the management problems within the department in dealing with this technology.

A great many competent DOD personnel have been lost at the periods when their productivity and value are at their peaks.

Computer resource management is fragmented in DOD.

The President's Reorganization Project examined many procurement and management issues and concluded that long acquisition times experienced by DOD are often self-generated. For example, the PRP reported that "a great deal of time is spent in reviews of proposed systems and computer acquisition at many different levels of the various military organizations... most of the reviews add very little to the project being considered and the entire process stifles innovations by creating an atmosphere of over-control and counter-productivity."[19]

The PRP criticized OMB and GSA for exercising insufficient oversight to correct ADP management problems. The responsibility for the mismanagement of these critical resources, however, lies solely with the operating agencies. For example, the PRP report states that "the Department of Defense (DOD) is encountering difficulties in the management and direction of its information technology resources." After listing six internal management problem areas, the report concluded that "the problems listed above are impeding the efficient and effective use of information technology within DOD." The report further states that "a range of serious management problems requires extensive attention to ensure that the effectiveness of Defense information technology support is returned to the highest practical levels" and that "the lack of computer resource management from an overall perspective has been an important source of the technical deterioration of the computing equipment throughout DOD."

Finally, the PRP stated that Public Law 89–306 remains a viable and effective policy and called for the exercise of stronger leadership by OMB and GSA.

Study of Management-Automation/Communications, February 12, 1979, Part I, page 9: "The most significant conclusion of this study group was that a policy statement which encompasses all automation within the Army is needed. Current automation policy is fragmented...."

Report of the Navy Automatic Data Processing Acquisition Review Committee, pages 1 and 2: "Navy instructions in many cases are outdated and do not reflect current policy....Users have trouble putting together requirements packages which are adequate... further users neither plan sufficiently in advance of their anticipated needs, nor provide adequate advance information of those needs to higher levels of management. The results of these problems are extended time to meet ADP needs...."

Air Force Preliminary ADP Acquisition Study, September 21, 1979, pages 2

---

[19]President's Reorganization Project, "Federal Data Processing Reorganization Study," October 1978, p. 4.

and 8: "It was the unanimous opinion of AFCAC personnel that specifications received during the last several years *were of poor quality and were the cause of significant delays in the acquisition cycle* ... ADP acquisition time can be reduced. *Some of the acquisition lead time* experienced by the *Air Force is self-imposed* by the Air Force, MAJCOM, and AFCAC procedures and tradition. Acquisition lead times can be reduced, to some degree, *without changes to law,* OMB directives or FPR/FPMRs." (Italic supplied.)

Memorandum Report—Review of DOD Acquisition of ADPE, May 1981 Institute of Defense Analysis. This report, commissioned by Dr. DeLauer, found no reason to fault Public Law 89–306 but goes on to cite the main problem within DOD as being their own internal review and approval process. For instance, it states:

> The number of DOD acquisition directives has multiplied in the past ten years showing particular growth in the past four years.[20] No attempt has been made to merge these directives into a reasonable number ... a system manager confronts a considerable array of overlapping, sometimes reinforcing, sometimes supplementary, documents when he seeks guidance in acquisition. p. 22.

This study was a two-week review which was contracted out at a time when DOD had already begun its efforts in the Senate to gain an exemption from Public Law 89–306. Nonetheless, the body of the report is surprisingly objective and seeks to identify the problems with DOD's ADP acquisitions process. Admittedly, the report recommends some form of broad delegation for DOD from outside management and oversight. However, the body of the report clearly does not support these conclusions, suggesting that the recommendations were added to the report without regard to the content.

The committee believes improvements can be made to the acquisition process which can reap large benefits once DOD corrects its managerial problems. The most logical starting place is DOD's own voluminous regulations, which are one of the main reasons for the lengthy procurement cycle within the department. DOD's internal regulations and lengthy review and approval process stifle innovative thinking and reward the cautious and indecisive at a tremendous cost to the taxpayer. Under Secretary DeLauer testified during the subcommittee's NORAD hearings that it takes as many as 135 coordinating signatures within DOD for an approval of a DOD procurement, a process which results in delaying projects anywhere from six months to seven years. In contrast, Public Law 89–306 requires only one signature—that of GSA's ADTS commissioner—which takes an average of only 30 days.

The Air Force, in particular, has experienced serious problems in its ADP management over the last decade. Starting in the early 1970s, a series of massive and debilitating failures of large Air Force information systems have occurred. Most recently, the Air Force was severely criticized for a project

---

[20]As noted in the Institute of Defense Analysis Report, there were 15 DOD acquisition directives (with related instructions) in 1970, 25 in 1976, and there are 114 at present.

called Phase IV, the world's largest computer project to date. Warnings sounded by the GSA, along with oversight hearings conducted by this committee, resulted in an admission by the Air Force in March 1980 that the proposed procurement was deficient and could have resulted in unnecessary costs of $800 million.

In a letter to Chairman Brooks dated March 28, 1980, Secretary of the Air Force Hans Mark stated:

> Dear Mr. Chairman: After publication of the House Government Operations Committee report of December 19, 1979, entitled, "The Department of the Air Force's Phase IV Program Should be Redirected," I asked the Air Force to completely review the Phase IV Program in light of the committee's recommendations ...I believe the redirection of Phase IV—which I will outline in detail in this letter— will satisfy the concerns raised by the General Accounting Office and your Committee....I expect this program redirection to achieve substantial savings, with total cost avoidances of about $800 million. OSD has reviewed our revised approach and has agreed to support it through the newly created Life Cycle Management Review process. I believe this redirected Phase IV Program now responds to the major concerns of the committee and will enable us to move ahead expeditiously with the critical modernization of our base level computer systems. The attachment to this letter describes other actions the Air Force is taking to strengthen its management of the ADP requirements and acquisition process in response to specific recommendations in the committee report.

Some commanders in the Air Force have begun to recognize the seriousness of its ADP management problems. In a letter, dated February 13, 1981, to the Air Force Chief of Staff, Gen. Lew Allen, Jr., the then commander of the Strategic Air Command (SAC), Gen. R.H. Ellis, stated that:

> The Air Force has heeded neither the RAND nor the President's Reorganization Project Report by failing to establish a high-level focus for management in the Air Staff. Little action has been taken to strengthen the Air Force ADP management organization as a result of ALS, Phase IV, or problems in the missile warning system. The obsolescence of our computers and the personnel overhead associated with old technology continues. There remains little career progression for senior ADP personnel in the Air Force, hence their exodus to civilian positions. There is no high-level focus in the Air Force to correct either managerial or technical deficiencies in our systems or to insure that new systems meet requirements.

The problems highlighted by General Ellis are indicative of the management deficiencies within the military services and DOD. This committee is encouraged by General Ellis's recognition of the problems and hopes that forceful action can be taken expeditiously to resolve them. If this is done, the Air Force could once more become the leader in the use of ADP technology.

DOD'S RESISTANCE TO OVERSIGHT

The Department of Defense has an apparent entrenched resistance to oversight of its activities by other government agencies. In his May 29 response to

Chairman Brooks on the exemption, General Dickinson stated that there "is a lack of *value added* to DOD's acquisition process by the oversight agencies. In fact, in many instances, attempts to make efficient acquisitions are actually thwarted through the oversight process."[21]

General Dickinson's view masks the real problems facing DOD in its ADP management. No outside authority has forced DOD to mismanage its project over the last decade. Nor did an outside agency insist that NORAD use inadequate computers to perform its highly complex scientific calculations. Clearly, the responsibility for these decisions rests on the Air Force and the Joint Chiefs of Staff.

Commissioner Frank Carr of GSA's Automated Data and Telecommunications Service (ADTS) has repeatedly offered to work with DOD in resolving its acquisition problems. In fact, Mr. Carr testified in May that he had written to the department a year and a half ago renewing a previous offer to make his staff available to DOD when they were ready to revise their cumbersome and time-consuming procurement policies. The DOD never took Mr. Carr up on his offer.

Equally disturbing to this committee are documented reports by GAO showing a distinct lack of cooperation toward GAO personnel, particularly by the Joint Chiefs of Staff. The Joint Chiefs of Staff have often displayed an adversarial relationship toward GAO's auditors who are performing work at the request of Congress. In its report on WWMCCS in December 1979, the GAO documented its problems in obtaining material required for its evaluation:

> We were unable to fully discharge our statutory responsibilities and be totally responsive to the chairman, Subcommittee on Research and Development, House Committee on Armed Services, and to Congressman Thomas J. Downey because the Joint Chiefs of Staff denied us complete access to documents we considered to be pertinent to this evaluation. These documents, which included internal surveys, reviews, draft reports, military exercises, operational plans, and future ADP plans, are materials to which we have a statutory right of access under section 313 of the Budget and Accounting Act, 1921 (31 U.S.C. 54). In our view, the department's denial, without legal justification to provide us with complete access to the documents, had an adverse impact on our ability to complete our review of the WWMCCS ADP program in a timely and efficient manner.[22]

Denial of access to needed information is unfortunately consistent with the department's refusal to implement recommendations not in line with their own desires. GAO has stated repeatedly that its recommendations in both the NORAD and the WWMCCS projects have been largely ignored by the Air Force and the Joint Chiefs of Staff.

[21]Hearings, p. 300.

[22]U.S. General Accounting Office report, "The World Wide Military Command and Control System—Major Changes Needed in Its Automated Data Processing Management and Direction," LCD-80-22, Dec. 14, 1979.

GAO recommended in 1978 that NORAD be exempted from the requirements of the WWMCCS system. Yet in 1981, NORAD was still not exempt despite the vigorous objections of past and current NORAD commanders.

GAO also recommended in 1978 that NORAD initiate acquisition of an Uninterruptable Power Supply (UPS) in the NORAD Combat Operations Center to provide protection for critical information processing equipment. The GAO reported that the center does not have a system that protects data integrity against power fluctuations or disturbances developing in either the commercial power or their self-sustained generator system.

As GAO noted,

> UPS not only provides protection against prolonged power outages, but also protects the system against slight fluctuations in power. These more subtle, split second failures can have an equally devastating effect on an information processing system's reliability. For example, industry studies have shown that 98 percent of the power outages causing a computer to break down are those lasting less than half a second. Also, almost any power outage will cause a disk storage device to be electronically interrupted or disconnected from the computer. This can result in loss or alteration of data being transferred to or from storage.[23]

In its response in July 1981 to the GAO report, Under Secretary DeLauer agreed with GAO's recommendation that NORAD should have a UPS and that the Air Force was programming the money for the project in the fiscal year 1982 budget. Further, the NORAD commander testified that NORAD was rebuilding powerplant and was going to install a UPS. However, the money budgeted for the project was cut from the fiscal year 1982 budget and was proposed for fiscal year 1983, 5 years after GAO first recommended a UPS for NORAD.

While the present NORAD commander fully agrees with the need for a UPS, it appears that he has not been able to get full departmental support for obtaining a UPS, despite the fact that over the past years various power outages have interrupted computer and communications operations, causing degradation of tactical warning and attack assessment capability. As was noted during this committee's hearings, the Air Force considers the UPS essential at the Air Force Finance Center, which has a UPS installed, but apparently not at the critical NORAD facility. The Air Force would seem to have its priorities reversed when it ensures continued operations of its payroll system, but not the critical attack warning system at NORAD. This committee believes that immediate action should be taken to install a UPS at NORAD.

The outright refusal to effectively and immediately implement GAO's recommendations, even ones as critical to the operation of the NORAD facility as the UPS, illustrates the resistance the department has manifested toward oversight, including Congressional oversight. Apparently, some DOD

---

[23]U.S. General Accounting Office report, "NORAD's Information Processing Improvement Program—Will It Enhance Mission Capability?" LCD-78-117, Sept. 21, 1978.

officials are fearful of exposure when multibillion dollar projects for which they are responsible come under close scrutiny. The committee is concerned that without proper Congressional oversight, billions of dollars will continue to be wasted on unjustified and poorly managed projects. The attitude that Congress should just give DOD money and not review the efficiency of its expenditures will not guarantee an effective defense. More likely, the result will be a weakened national security posture at great expense to the taxpayers.

CONCLUSION

The severe and potentially catastrophic deficiencies found in the nation's missile attack warning system are a result of significant and long-term management failings within the Air Force and the Joint Chiefs of Staff. Continued inability to correct these failings by the highest levels within the Department of Defense will continue to perpetuate past mistakes, and will undermine any chance that an effective attack warning or command and communications system can be installed by 1990.

When Under Secretary DeLauer testified before the subcommittee, he acknowledged the problems that are prevalent within the department. He agreed with Chairman Brooks's statement that the department had failed to effectively plan ADP equipment procurements and implementation, failed to identify user requirements, failed to develop functional specifications, failed to provide centralized acquisition management, failed to make effective use of the competitive process, and failed to establish adequate accountability.[24] The committee believes that no significant improvements will be forthcoming unless the under secretary pursues solutions to these problems.

After a decade or more of poor planning and mismanagement, our nation's missile warning center is seriously deficient. Urgent attention must be given to resolving the problems at NORAD by the Secretary of Defense. However, the problems at NORAD are not easily resolvable now. In the short run, even if NORAD received the most modern technology, it would be incapable of using it for at least another 2 years. Given the past mismanagement, implementation of longer range solutions will be difficult to achieve. While the present NORAD commander is attempting to implement most of GAO's recommendations, continued resistance is being exerted by the Joint Chiefs of Staff and the Air Force. The committee is not reassured that adequate consideration will be given within the military structure to make a strong commitment to a modern, effective missile attack warning system at NORAD. If this situation continues, this committee doubts the ability of DOD to provide this country with a timely, effective missile warning system. The Secretary of Defense must take decisive action to ensure that NORAD receives the highest priority within the department in its modernization program.

[24]Hearings, p. 270.

FINDINGS

1 The false missile alerts which were reported by the North American Aerospace Defense Command were not in any way related to the Federal acquisition process as governed by Public Law 89–306.

2 The NORAD computer failures were a result of mismanagement by the Air Force and the technical difficulties associated with the use of WWMCCS computers as directed by the Joint Chiefs of Staff.

3 The NORAD upgrade program which began in 1966 is 6 years behind schedule and $150 million over budget. Due to the failure of this program, NORAD has obsolete computer systems which, at best, offer the same capability as the 1966 computer system.

4 The serious deficiencies in NORAD's computer system have developed over a number of years and defy quick and easy solutions.

5 The current WWMCCS program has failed to meet its mission objectives as a result of continued mismanagement by the Air Force and the Joint Chiefs of Staff.

6 The computer problems plaguing both the NORAD and the WWMCCS projects are symptomatic of broader management problems that exist throughout the Department of Defense.

7 The lack of cooperation with GAO auditors and DOD's continued resistance to oversight shields the department from legitimate and con-structive criticism.

8 Unless the Secretary of Defense takes immediate and decisive action to correct the problems with NORAD, WWMCCS, and other major critical computer systems, the nation's defense capability will be weakened.

RECOMMENDATIONS ...

Appendix III   NORAD Chronology of Events

June 1966—NORAD Cheyenne Mountain Complex computer systems (425L and 496L) become operational, planning begins for replacement system, known as 427M.

December 1968—NORAD completes master plan for 427M system expected to replace existing system by 1975.

March 1969—Joint Chiefs of Staff and Air Force approve NORAD Master Plan, Air Force commences planning for acquisition.

June 1970—Secretary of the Air Force approves competitive procurement of standard World Wide Military Command and Control System computers (WWMCCS) for all Unified and Specified Commands. This includes NORAD.

August 1970—The Commander in Chief of NORAD, realizing that computers described in benchmark statements of WWMCCS Request for Proposals are inade-quate for his mission, complains to the Chief of Staff Air Force.

August 1970—The Air Force replies, through the Vice Chief of Staff, telling the NORAD Commander in Chief that he will use WWMCCS standard hardware and software.

October 1971—Contract for WWMCCS awarded to Honeywell Information Systems, Inc.

September 1972—The Air Force, executive agency for the 427M acquisition, establishes December 1975 as the Initial Operational Capability target for 427M.

March 1974—As a result of cost growth and schedule slippages, the Air Force analyzes the 427M program. It finds that the hardware is inadequate and NORAD is given another Honeywell 6080 computer.

June 1976—NORAD's general system specifications are down-graded to meet WWMCCS computer capabilities.

March 1977—NORAD Deputy Commander for Operations complains that 427M computer system is inadequate for his mission requirements.

April 1977—An Air Force Independent Review Group evaluates 427M program. They conclude that 427M will never reach Full Operational Capability and Initial Operational Capability is too far off. They invent another term called Equivalent Operational Capability (EOC) as the point the computers will be accepted by the Air Force. This was defined as that point when the 427M was operationally equivalent to the 425L and 496L.

June 1977—GAO begins first investigation.

January 1978—The requirements of the 427M program are again reduced to meet WWMCCS computer capabilities.

March 1978—The MITRE Corporation reports that the 427M system processing capability [is] limited in stress situations.

September 1978—GAO issues first report on NORAD, "NORAD's Information Processing Improvement Program—Will It Enhance Mission Capability?" (LCD78–117) September 21, 1978. GAO recommends replacing total 427M system; centralizing acquisition and implementation management; procuring uninterruptible power supply for critical equipment; and exemption of NORAD from the requirement to use WWMCCS standard hardware and software.

September 1979—The 427M system is declared to be at EOC by the Commander in Chief of NORAD.

November 1979—Major Missile Warning System failure due to using operational system for 427M software development.

March 1980—GAO issues report "Review of Department of Defense Strategic Missile Warning Systems" (C–LCD–80–3), March 14, 1980. GAO generally restates 1978 recommendations and additionally reports that there is no overall missile warning plan.

June 1980—Missile Warning System failure due to faulty communications computer sending out warning messages.

September 1980—The Air Force Inspector General reviews NORAD Missile Warning System and concurs with GAO that the causes of 427M problems are mismanagement and attempting to use inadequate WWMCCS computers.

October 1980—A Senate report suggests that NORAD's problems are related to the acquisition process. Further, it suggests that a blanket delegation of procurement authority be given NORAD to replace its computers.

May 1981—GAO reports "NORAD's Missile Warning System: What Went Wrong?" (MASAD-81-30), May 15, 1981. Reiterates that the problems of the 427M are related to mismanagement and use of inadequate WWMCCS computers as reported in 1978. GAO also reports that there is no connection between NORAD's problems and the acquisition process and that NORAD needs no Delegation of Procurement Authority to replace its computers.

Appendix IV WWMCCS Chronology of Events

November 1969—DOD announced a plan to acquire up to eighty-seven standardized computer systems for use in the World Wide Military Command and Control System.

December 1969—House Committee on Appropriations directs GAO to review WWMCCS.

June 1970—Secretary of the Air Force approves competitive procurement of World Wide Military Command and Control System (WWMCCS) computers for all Unified and Specified Commands. This includes NORAD.

December 1970—GAO reports that the WWMCCS program ignored the fact that many sites already had modern computers that would be unnecessarily replaced; did not consider advances in technology; was not based on a thorough study of requirements; planning and direction of the acquisition program was fragmented; and estimates of cost and savings were questionable.

April 1975 and April 1978—GAO reports on WWMCCS software deficiencies.

December 1979—GAO reports that WWMCCS existing management was extremely complex and fragmented. As a result it was not responsive to national or local requirements; unreliable and inefficient. In addition, the equipment is not installed in survivable facilities and generates excessive maintenance costs.

October 1981—GAO reports that WWMCCS modernization plan will take another 10 years to upgrade equipment and may result in a system no better than what currently exists.

SOCIAL SECURITY NEEDS TO BETTER PLAN, DEVELOP, AND IMPLEMENT ITS MAJOR ADP SYSTEMS REDESIGN PROJECTS

U.S. General Accounting Office

INTRODUCTION

The Social Security Administration's (SSA's) primary responsibility in administering its benefit programs is providing prompt and meaningful service—including timely and accurate benefit payments—to the public. The quality of that service depends largely on how well the agency's automatic data processing (ADP) systems function in supporting its daily operations. Significant deficiencies in these systems during the last several years have caused erroneous program benefit payments totaling many millions of dollars, inaccurate data in automated program beneficiary records, and inaccurate notices to beneficiaries regarding their benefit status. These problems have stimulated concern by the public and by members and committees of Congress.

In response to congressional requests, we have reviewed the design, development, modification, and operation of several of SSA's primary ADP systems, including the Supplemental Security Income system and the Retirement, Survivors, Disability, and Health Insurance (RSDHI) system. We reported the results of our Supplemental Security Income system review in two reports to the Secretary of Health, Education, and Welfare.[1] We found that SSA did not(1) adequately involve key field office users in planning system

---

[1] "Flaws in Controls over the Supplemental Security Income Computerized System Cause Millions in Erroneous Payments" (HRD-79-104, Aug. 9, 1979).

"The Social Security Administration Needs To Develop a Structured and Planned Approach for Managing and Controlling the Design, Development, and Modification of Its Supplemental Security Income Computerized System" (HRD-80-5, Oct. 16, 1979).

changes, or (2) properly validate system changes before implementing them. In addition, the department's audit agency had neither (1) participated in the design and development of the computerized system, nor (2) reviewed the automated controls placed in the system.

This report discusses the results of our review of SSA's efforts to redesign the RSDHI automated system. The review was requested by the chairman, House Committee on Government Operations, based on his concern that SSA's failure to successfully implement major ADP systems initiatives would be extremely costly while undermining the agency's ability to fulfill its mission to the public. The chairman directed us to make an extensive investigation of SSA's total system development plans. We identified the RSDHI redesign as a major SSA systems initiative to be analyzed. Other agency systems activities we reviewed in response to the chairman's request are discussed in three other reports—two issued to the secretary of Health, Education, and Welfare[2] and the other to the commissioner of Social Security.[3]

Our primary objectives in reviewing the redesign were to determine whether it was warranted and whether it was characterized by significant system development/modification deficiencies similar to those identified during our review of the Supplemental Security Income system. Although the redesign appears to have been properly directed toward solving RSDHI system problems, it had deficiencies similar to those identified in our earlier review, leading us to conclude that they represent agencywide system development/modification problems. This report presents recommendations for correcting these deficiencies and other management weaknesses we identified.

The Social Security Program

The Social Security Act (42 U.S.C. 301 et seq.), enacted in 1935, established one of the world's largest insurance programs. Nine out of ten American workers—more than 110 million people—pay social security taxes to fund key social insurance programs established by the act and related laws. These programs—Retirement and Survivors Insurance, Disability Insurance, and Health (hospital and medical) Insurance for the aged and the disabled—have the basic objectives of providing (1) an income for taxpayers and their dependents when the taxpayers' earnings are curtailed or stopped because of disability, retirement, or death; and (2) comprehensive health insurance protection to the aged, disabled, and those suffering from chronic kidney

[2]"The Social Security Administration Needs to Continue Comprehensive Long-Range Planning" (HRD-79-118, Sept. 20, 1979). Letter report to the secretary of Health, Education, and Welfare questioning certain aspects of the proposed computerized National Recipient System (HRD-79-88, May 29, 1979).

[3]"Improving Social Security Administration Procedures for Acquiring ADP and Telecommunications Resources" (Mar. 31, 1980).

disease. The Department of Health and Human Services[4] has overall responsibility for administering these programs.

Retirement, survivors, and disability insurance benefits in fiscal year 1979 totaled $101 billion—an 11 percent increase over 1978. Benefits paid to 30.1 million retirement and survivors insurance beneficiaries rose to $87.6 billion, and benefit payments to 4.8 million disability insurance recipients totaled $13.4 billion. In addition, over $28 billion in hospital and medical insurance payments were made on behalf of more than 16 million health insurance beneficiaries.

SSA's Responsibilities, Activities, and Structure

Within the Department of Health and Human Services, SSA has direct administrative responsibility for the Retirement and Survivors Insurance and Disability Insurance programs. In 1977 the Health Care Financing Administration relieved SSA of administrative responsibility for the Health Insurance program. Nevertheless, SSA has continued to provide major operational support to that program, primarily in the form of ADP services and use of its extensive network of field offices to serve beneficiaries.

In administering these programs, SSA handles enormous workloads and delivers a wide range of services to the public. Although SSA provides more than 400 individual services, the following broad categories of services generally describe the bulk of SSA's workload: (1) assignment and maintenance of social security numbers, (2) earnings records maintenance, (3) claims processing, (4) postentitlement event processing, (5) payments and settlements, (6) appeals, (7) services for and from other agencies, and (8) general inquiries and information.

To deliver these services, SSA has about 75,000 full-time permanent employees in its Baltimore headquarters and field offices throughout the country. The field offices include ten regional offices, over 1300 full-time district and branch offices serving the public in their local communities, and 6 program service centers. These service centers review claims prepared by district and branch office personnel, certify retirement and survivors insurance benefit payments, and maintain beneficiary records.

SSA's ADP operations, centrally located at its headquarters, serve a crucial supporting function for SSA-administered programs. SSA carries out daily program operations on eighteen large-scale computer systems and a number of medium-to-small-scale special-purpose computers used to perform a wide variety of tasks, ranging from microfilm production to communication network control. SSA also maintains an extensive nationwide communications network giving field offices access to automated beneficiary data stored

---

[4]Effective May 4, 1980, a new Department of Education was established, and the remaining components of the Department of Health, Education, and Welfare became the Department of Health and Human Services.

in the headquarters computer complex. Thus, the quality of SSA's service to the public depends largely on how well its ADP systems operate.

Background on the RSDHI Redesign

The RSDHI system is an ADP system used to maintain records for all RSDHI beneficiaries and to process initial program benefit claims, postentitlement actions, and other transactions affecting those records. An essential record maintained by the system is the Master Beneficiary Record (MBR), which contains for each beneficiary the basic account, benefit, and payment data necessary to issue benefit checks. Over the years, however, several significant operational deficiencies have hampered the RSDHI system's overall effectiveness. Among these are (1) system limitations, which precluded reducing response timelags and automating substantial manual functions and computations, (2) inadequate software modification, which allowed major processes to become large, cumbersome, and inflexible, and (3) inability to provide SSA field office personnel with timely access to centrally stored and processed beneficiary data.

History of the Redesign In mid-1974, SSA's commissioner approved a proposal authorizing agency systems personnel to redesign the ADP systems supporting RSDHI processes. These personnel undertook an extensive examination of then-existing ADP processes, and in June 1974 they finalized the broad system design philosophies intended to guide detailed system design and implementation planning. Using these basic conceptual design plans, they developed and implemented several system improvements during the following 2 years.

Despite successful implementation of these improvements, SSA felt that the lack of a consolidated approach to system development was hampering overall RSDHI system effectiveness; the large number of independently developed, overlapping systems projects complicated the planning and management of developmental activities. Thus, in October 1976, after reexamining their earlier redesign effort in relation to other developmental activities supporting RSDHI processes, SSA systems personnel formally established the redesign project to consolidate RSDHI systems development efforts.

The redesign represented a major overhaul of existing computerized case processing capabilities, under which SSA established a limited number of system improvements as basic redesign objectives. Each objective was assigned a relatively short-range target date for implementation, and redesign activities were to be geared toward selecting alternatives that would enable these objectives to be realized by the specified dates. SSA designated a project manager for the redesign and established several small teams to assist him with RSDHI system modification planning, design, and coordination activities. Actual software development was to remain the responsibility of systems operations personnel. SSA described the redesign's scope, objectives, requirements, timing, individual projects, and expected impact in its May 1977 "Functional Requirements Document," which also contained a development plan for the use of developers and users. SSA revised the development plan in September 1977, July 1978, and November 1978.

SSA expected the RSDHI redesign to improve service to the public by increasing both the timeliness and accuracy of case processing activities and to substantially reduce personnel costs through the automation of required manual actions. The Functional Requirements Document outlined ten major categories of individual systems changes planned by SSA—five representing improvements to existing systems capabilities and five representing new capabilities. The major new features included:

• Implementing the automated job stream, the principal transaction processing segment, which involved new software combining about two dozen RSDHI application subsystems and designed to expand benefit rate determination capabilities while linking the processing of various claims and postentitlement transactions into one logical operation.

• Expanding the online RSDHI data base to include certain data from the MBR and several other records and benefit estimate data, thus improving data retrieval capabilities needed by field personnel.

• Using mass storage and microfilm technology to retain complete transaction history data, eliminating the need to produce hard-copy documentation of transaction history filed in individual claims folders.

• Developing new software designed to perform several updating functions, such as preparation of updated MBR data for delivery to the RSDHI on-line data base.

• Developing new software to direct interrelated transaction control functions, such as input editing and management information collection, through interaction with the on-line data base.

Current Status of the Redesign   Although the RSDHI redesign was scheduled to be completed by December 31, 1978, SSA had not fully implemented many of the planned individual systems changes at the time of our review, and some of those which had been implemented were not successful. As of November 1980, only one of the five major new features discussed above—expanding the on-line data base to include such information as summary MBR data and benefit estimate data—had been substantially implemented with success.

During our review, SSA reassigned the redesign project manager to other duties and disbanded the user liaison committee, originally formed to communicate user comments to redesign management. Work on key redesign activities, although only partially completed, was suspended, and SSA was reevaluating resumption in light of time and resource constraints and changing agency priorities. As of November 1980, SSA was planning to resume work on certain redesign-related systems enhancements during fiscal years 1981 and 1982. However, sources within the agency indicated that a renewed SSA commitment to pursuing redesign activities would be required before they could be resumed.

Lack of systematic planning and consistent management of the redesign and deficiencies in SSA's system modification process—discussed in chapters 2 and 3—appear to be the primary factors that precluded completion of the redesign.

Objectives, Scope, and Methodolgy

We made our evaluation of the RSDHI redesign at SSA headquarters and the following field offices:

- The Kansas City Regional Office and Mid-America Program Service Center, Kansas City, Missouri.
- The Southeastern Program Service Center, Birmingham, Alabama.
- The Atlanta Regional Office, Atlanta, Georgia.
- Local offices in Kansas City and Independence, Missouri, and in Atlanta, East Point, and Decatur, Georgia.

We examined various documents, correspondence, and reports about the redesign to determine the scope, objectives, and anticipated and actual results of individual systems enhancements making up the total project. In addition, to obtain comments about the usefulness of the project and the management of redesign activities, we discussed individual redesign efforts with knowledgeable personnel at various levels in the agency.

In developing our findings, conclusions, and recommendations, we compared information on procedures SSA used to manage the redesign with generally accepted systems development/modification criteria, as discussed in enclosure II of our October 16, 1979, report on the Supplemental Security Income computerized system. (See footnote 1.)

RSDHI REDESIGN SUFFERED FROM LACK OF SYSTEMATIC PLANNING AND CONSISTENT MANGEMENT

As noted in our October 1979 report on the Supplemental Security Income system, and in earlier reports, planning the development or modification of an ADP system involves following a series of sequential steps, each of which must be completed before the next can begin. First, the users are to define the needs and objectives to be met by the system, which systems analysts use to develop conceptual system designs. Once these design alternatives are found to be technically and operationally feasible, a cost/benefit analysis is needed to identify the particular system or modification proposal which should produce the desired results most economically. After reviewing the results of these planning steps, the users should decide whether and when to proceed with detailed development of the selected system design. Throughout these activities responsible communications among users, systems analysts, programmers, and management—such as the sharing of information on the status of system development—should be promoted.

In planning the RSDHI redesign, however, SSA did not sufficiently involve users (particularly its field offices) and failed to adequately measure project costs and benefits, thus inhibiting the development of key data needed for determining proper system design and monitoring system development/ modification progress. During the redesign, SSA never achieved adequate user involvement or complete, up-to-date cost/benefit comparisons. As discussed in section 1, many of the individual system changes planned for the redesign were not completed. In our view, it is doubtful that these changes— even if completed—would have met actual user needs, and some may not have been cost beneficial. The lack of consistent SSA management of the redesign apparently contributed substantially to these planning and monitoring weaknesses.

Key Users Not Sufficiently Involved

The first step in planning the development or modification of an ADP system is for the user to identify the need for the system or change. Because the user is also responsible for making sure that this need and related objectives are achieved by the final operational system, he or she must actively participate in all phases of system development. The user should always be the final authority on whether the system meets his or her needs. Thus, it is the user who is responsible for deciding whether and when to proceed on to the next stage of system development, including the final decision to implement the system. However, field users of SSA's ADP systems generally were not adequately involved in the planning and design of RSDHI redesign projects and often were not kept up to date on the development status of individual projects, even though the systems changes making up those projects directly affected their operations.

Field Users Not Adequately Involved Although key redesign projects were validated and/or pilot tested in the Mid-America and Southeastern Program Service Centers, and thus directly affected RSDHI claims and postentitlement activities at the centers and at certain local offices, in only one instance did field office users play a significant role in the planning and design of a redesign project—the accelerated claims project, discussed below. Instead, most of the input to the redesign came from program bureau systems analysts at the central office rather than from personnel at the program sevice centers and local offices, where most beneficiary services are provided, or from regional staff, who are most familiar with common systems problems and needs in local offices. A user liaison committee, composed of central office program bureau representatives, was formed to plan and evaluate redesign actions, coordinate problem resolution, and communicate user comments to project management. This committee, however, did not actively solicit field user comments or disseminate information about redesign activities.

Limited Regional Office Involvement   Regional office personnel in Atlanta and Kansas City agreed that they generally were not given the opportunity to provide input to the design of individual system projects. SSA's Atlanta regional office did play a major role in planning, designing, and implementing one element of the RSDHI redesign, the accelerated claims project, a systems change designed to allow local office personnel to process benefit claims more quickly. Initial planning and design of all other redesign projects, however, was done exclusively by central office personnel before soliciting regional office input, according to Atlanta and Kansas City regional staff. They added that their regional offices received drafts of proposed systems from headquarters for comment, but only after the plans had been formulated.

Regarding their ongoing knowledge of individual projects once undertaken, personnel in the Atlanta and Kansas City regional offices indicated that from time to time headquarters had provided them with information on the status of redesign projects.

Inadequate Program Service Center Involvement   Staff of SSA's Southeastern Program Service Center in Birmingham and Mid-America Service Center in Kansas City told us they had no involvement in the initial planning and design of individual redesign elements and generally were not kept informed about the status of projects. No formal input for project planning purposes was solicited from the service centers, although, according to the redesign project manager, field users were asked for their opinions on projects informally. In this regard, an operations official at one service center we visited acknowledged that on several occasions central office personnel visited the center to obtain such opinions from service center officials once the systems design was completed, but noted that service center personnel were not given an opportunity to provide input to systems design or to comment on design alternatives.

To inform selected field personnel about redesign projects to be pilot tested in the Atlanta region and the Southeastern Program Service Center, central office staff held a 3-day seminar in July 1978 at the Southeastern center. This was the only such conference held during the project. Representatives from the Mid-America and Southeastern service centers and the Atlanta and Dallas regional offices attended the conference, but no local office personnel were included, even though they were also affected by the pilot tests.

Personnel from both program service centers stated that, after the conference, they were not kept informed on the status of specific redesign activities. At one center we noted that some of the most current data available on redesign activities were out of date. When we requested operations analysts at that center to provide data on additional activities discussed in a revision to the redesign development plan, we found that key analysts were not aware of some of these activities. Service center personnel explained that the center had not received key redesign documents, including that particular development plan revision and several status reports. When asked about this, the redesign project manager explained that he stopped sending status reports to the service centers because center personnel lacked enthusiasm and support for some redesign projects. At the other service center we visited, operations analysts who had been deeply involved in validating major redesign changes told us they subsequently received no feedback from SSA headquarters regarding any system modifications made to correct errors identified by the validations.

Insufficient Involvement of Local Office Users   Like regional office and program service center personnel, staff of local offices we visited in the Atlanta and Kansas City regions did not have the opportunity to provide input to redesign project planning and design. Local office staff, a major segment of the SSA users to be served by the redesign, were not included in the July 1978 conference at which the redesign was discussed with users. In addition, although the local offices we visited received some information on redesign activities—often in the form of implementing instructions for specific projects—from both SSA headquarters and their regional offices, they did not always receive subsequent information on the status or results of specific projects affecting their operations.

SSA Should Do More to Increase User Involvement   Under SSA's January 1979 structural reorganization, a newly created Office of User Requirements and Validation became responsible for identifying and requesting needed new and revised ADP systems and representing users during systems planning activities. Systems changes requested by that office were to be reviewed and approved, disapproved, or modified by an ADP steering committee before being implemented by the Office of Systems, which assumed responsibility for detailed systems design, development, and implementation. Although the Office of User Requirements and Validation quickly recognized the need to increase user involvement in the overall system development/ modification process and began developing specific plans and procedures for accomplishing this goal, these plans and procedures had not been finalized at the time of our review. In addition, as discussed in the following sections, the limited action SSA has taken thus far to increase user involvement may not be resulting in systems initiatives that are responsive to current user needs.

Procedures for Communicating with Users Not Finalized In its role as user representative, the Office of User Requirements and Validation planned to give all users of agency-automated systems a greater opportunity to participate in defining how the systems development/modification process would work. In this regard, early office goals included:

- Bring all members of the user community more deeply into the entire systems development and change process
- Provide all users with a clear understanding of systems direction in nontechnical language
- Establish appropriate mechanisms to ensure direct and responsive user feedback
- Describe monitoring and control mechanisms aimed at promoting timely and accurate responses to users

To attain these goals, the office developed preliminary procedures for communicating with users both in field offices and in headquarters components. These procedures gave detailed directions for using such mechanisms as specific documents, user conferences, and onsite reviews of the operational environment to support users in systems planning and development. The procedures also described how various other communication channels, such as telephone calls and written correspondence, might be used not only to be highly responsive to user inquiries, but also to disseminate timely information to all users. In July 1980, however, SSA replaced top management of the Office of User Requirements and Validation. The new management told us in August 1980 that, although the office's early goals had not changed, top SSA management had not yet approved specific procedures for attaining those goals. As of November 1980 the office had not formally adopted the preliminary procedures previously developed. According to office management, many of these procedures were being successfully used anyway in communicating with users, and the office was expecting its new form for requesting systems services (still being finalized at that time) to serve as its primary formal communication mechanism.

SSA Should Periodically Reassess User Needs The Office of User Requirements and Validation has acted to implement one of its preliminary procedures for communicating with users by providing advance notice of major systems proposals being initiated. In its formal response to our October 1979 report on the Supplemental Security Income computerized system, SSA restated its intent to begin circulating periodic notices of systems proposals for the review and comment of all users, including field staff. We noted that the office did this in November 1979 while assembling data for assessing agency ADP budget needs for fiscal years 1981-85. At that time, the office invited field users to describe system projects or improvements they would like to see SSA undertake in addition to the proposal summaries being circulated. The thrust of this effort, however, was to obtain user comments on systems projects already proposed and reviewed by headquarters components. This approach, in our view, may not result in systems projects that respond to current user needs.

The office's approach has been to establish a project control system for needed systems improvements and changes by compiling an inventory of user needs, helping the ADP Steering Committee assign priority to those needs and identify necessary projects to meet them within available resource limits, and then notifying users of planned projects to obtain their comments, as discussed above. The office planned to regularly reassess established needs and adjust priorities and planned projects accordingly. However, we found no indications that the office has periodically reassessed its existing inventory to make sure it represents current and actual user needs. Office officials stated they have not been further soliciting current needs from field users.

In this regard, SSA headquarters personnel had already defined enough user needs during the past several years to keep the office busy for the next five years, and the systems project proposals circulated for user comments have been based on this "pipeline" of user needs, according to office sources. Thus, since those needs have not been periodically updated and, according to office sources, primarily represent the perceptions of SSA headquarters personnel rather than the current views of field users, the resulting systems proposals may not reflect field user needs. All users, but especially those from field offices, could be better served if their role in the systems planning process was to provide a reliable basis for initial development of project proposals, rather than commenting later on proposals that may not reflect their needs.

Inadequate Cost/Benefit Analysis

Once users have defined their needs and objectives to be met by a proposed ADP system or system change, and operationally and technically feasible system design alternatives for meeting those needs and objectives have been developed, a cost/benefit analysis should be made. By comparing the costs and expected benefits of each alternative system or change proposal, managers can select the particular configuration which will produce the desired results most economically. Such economic comparisons are an integral part of the overall systems planning process.

SSA included a cost/benefit analysis of the redesign as part of the May 1977 Functional Requirements Document. It showed total annual costs of $3.4 million for equipment and software development, but total annual savings of $9.2 million due to reductions in manually processed transactions, files maintenance costs, and micrographic production costs—resulting in a net annual cost reduction of $5.8 million. The analysis allocated $1.9 million of this total cost reduction to SSA's proposed telecommunications upgrade/expansion project and the other $3.9 million to the redesign. This analysis, however, was inadequate because it did not account for all required hardware resources, did not include certain personnel costs, contained questionable savings projections, and was not updated to reflect the many changes in redesign activities and resource requirements.

Costs Understated The cost/benefit analysis in the Functional Requirements Document presented the estimated cost of acquiring direct access storage devices, mass storage equipment, communications linkages, and main memory for the redesign. According to that document, these would be the only equipment acquisitions required for the redesign. Specifically, the document noted that redesign objectives had been "deliberately set at a level that avoids dependency on the acquisition of additional ADP resources," and that, therefore, "the RSDHI redesign is not dependent on the acquisition of major new ADP resources, although additional improvement in efficiency and cost-effectiveness may warrant such acquisitions." We believe this presentation was misleading, thereby precluding top agency management from fully understanding how crucial specific ADP resource acquisitions actually were to project success and how much such acquisitions would cost.

The November 1978 revision to the redesign development plan pointed out the need to acquire additional direct access storage and main memory capacity, acknowledging that the earlier stated requirements for this equipment had been underestimated. SSA systems officials also indicated that, to successfully carry out redesign activities, SSA would have to replace card reader equipment and upgrade certain ADP equipment, not only in the headquarters telecommunications complex, but also in the program service centers—acquisitions not included in SSA's cost/benefit analysis.

SSA's telecommunications upgrade/expansion proposal called for providing all district and branch offices and program service centers with modern telecommunications equipment. The cost/benefit analysis for the redesign allocated most of the anticipated reduction in files maintenance costs to the telecommunications project, recognizing that such savings depended on SSA installing telecommunications equipment in all program service centers. Later SSA discussions of redesign status made it clear that key project benefits, such as reduced file maintenance costs and decreased micrographic production costs, could not be fully realized until the agency upgraded and expanded its telecommunications capabilities in field offices. However, the costs associated with acquiring and installing this equipment were not presented in the redesign cost/benefit analysis. In our view, since SSA acknowledged that upgrading and expanding telecommunications capabilities in the field, as proposed under the telecommunications project, would be required before SSA could fully achieve anticipated redesign savings, the costs of such upgrade and expansion should have been recognized in the cost/benefit analysis and allocated between the two projects.

The cost/benefit analysis also failed to reflect all personnel costs associated with the redesign. Software development costs, for example, were based on an average of seventy-five systems development personnel employed over a one-year period, at a per capita cost of $32,400. According to the redesign project manager, however, the time required to develop the software greatly exceeded one year. This would have increased the total personnel costs associated with software development, although specific figures were not available. Personnel costs for other than software development activities such as testing, validation, and training directly related to redesign activities, were not included in the cost/benefit analysis, even though such costs were apparently substantial. SSA did not maintain an accurate record of such costs, but SSA staff involved with redesign projects indicated that considerable time and effort were required to test, implement, and refine redesign changes.

Projected Savings Questionable   As the redesign progressed, the savings projections contained in the cost/benefit analysis became questionable. For example, the cost/benefit analysis projected that the redesign would ultimately save 290 staff-years annually by reducing handling of claims folders at program service centers. SSA tested this concept by conducting a 6-month folderless processing experiment in six operations modules at its Southeastern Program service center. This experiment showed that SSA would have to solve numerous operational problems, including on-line data base limitations and poor telecommunications response time, before the folderless approach to processing RSDHI transactions at service centers could be considered practical.

Folderless processing during the experiment was slower and in some cases less accurate than traditional processing procedures, required significantly more manual actions, and created work backlogs. Although SSA records we examined did not contain precise data on how large the manual workload increase was, the managers of one participating module estimated that, in processing cases under the folderless approach, their staff spent almost 13,000 more hours than would have been required using traditional processing procedures. In addition, service center management had to assign additional staff—more than 2000 staff-hours—to the participating modules to maintain satisfactory workload processing levels.

Cost/Benefit Data Never Updated   Unless top management of a federal agency can compare expected system development/modification costs to expected benefits, either of which may change during a prolonged development/modification process, it will have no assurance that the resulting system or change will be cost beneficial. Therefore, cost/benefit analyses regarding the development or modification of an ADP system, especially one of substantial size and complexity, should be updated periodically to enable top management to make such comparisons and, when changes occur, to decide whether system development/modification should be continued, revised, or terminated. To reflect the increases in resource requirements for the redesign, as well as events having the potential to reduce projected benefits, as discussed above, SSA should have updated the initial cost/benefit data when such changes became known. However, during the project SSA neither updated its initial cost/benefit analysis nor maintained any ongoing record of redesign-related costs. In essence, the only redesign cost/benefit data SSA prepared during the project were those included as part of the May 1977 Functional Requirements Document.

SSA did not track redesign costs either from an overall perspective or for each individual system change. According to the redesign project manager, this was because the agency generally considered redesign activities to be part of normal RSDHI system operations. Savings data projected for the redesign, like cost data, were not adequately updated. An SSA budget official explained that identifying savings specifically attributable to redesign activities would be difficult because field offices and agency headquarters components either did not distinguish redesign activities from other changes to normal systems operations or did not consider redesign activities as distinct projects for accounting purposes.

Fragmentation of Management Duties

As shown above, SSA did not sufficiently involve field users in the redesign and failed to adequately measure redesign costs and benefits. Such deficiencies occurred, at least in part because SSA did not provide consistent management of the redesign.

In the system development/modification process, as discussed in our October 1979 report on the Supplemental Security Income system, the project leader should represent top management and be responsible for controlling and coordinating the system project. The project leader is normally given the authority for making decisions on personnel resources, scheduling, cost and budget, and most technical matters. As the leader of a team comprising persons with mixed skills, he or she should provide a well-defined, structured environment within which system development/modification can progress in an orderly manner. The project leader should also serve as the interface between users, system programmers and analysts, system validators, and top management. These responsibilities and associated duties clearly require full-time attention. They should be established at the outset of the project and provide for performance and management accountability, enabling management to effectively control the development/modification process.

Although SSA appointed a redesign project manager in January 1977, the agency later chose the same person to also manage key daily systems operations activities, thereby reducing the time and effort he could spend on redesign activities. Similarly, other systems staff also worked simultaneously on normal daily systems operations as well as redesign activities. According to the project manager, these personnel sometimes gave priority to daily systems operations and maintenance and worked on redesign activities when time was available. On the other hand, he indicated that they may on occasion have been reluctant to make minor modifications to existing computer programs if such programs were eventually to be replaced as part of the redesign.

In the project manager's view, assigning responsibility for both ongoing daily systems operations and redesign projects to the same staff is appropriate since the systems staff responsible for daily operations must maintain those operations even after they have been redesigned. Such a rationale, however, contradicts a basic organizational concept described in two of our prior reports discussing SSA systems activities.[5] This concept implies that, to be effective, ADP systems planning, design, and development at SSA should be performed by a separate group freed from interruptions caused by day-to-day operations. In our view, this concept applies as well to systems modification activities like the redesign. The project manager and systems personnel assigned to the redesign should have been able to devote all their time to planning, designing, and implementing the system changes associated with the project.

INADEQUATE VALIDATIONS PREVENTED SUCCESSFUL IMPLEMENTATION OF RSDHI REDESIGN CHANGES

As discussed in our October 1979 report on the Supplemental Security Income computerized system, validation, or acceptance testing, of ADP system changes, whether the result of initial system design or later modifications, requires thorough testing of the system's performance, functional specifications, documentation, outputs, operating procedures, and user procedures. The entire system should be validated before implementation begins and audited after implementation in order to maintain its integrity, even when the program or system modification is minor. System validation is needed to test whether the entire system will function as required by the user and as designed by the systems analyst; postimplementation audit is needed to assure that the system continues to function in this manner after becoming operational.

Nevertheless, SSA did not perform adequate validations before beginning implementation of major RSDHI redesign segments, and Department of Health and Human Services internal auditors never audited these system changes. In attempting to validate major segments of the automated job stream, a series of system changes designed to increase and improve automated processing of RSDHI claims and postentitlement actions,[6] SSA (1) did not select program test cases adequately, (2) failed to fully perform validations throughout the entire system, and (3) began implementing major systems

---

[5]"The Social Security Administration Needs To Continue Comprehensive Long-Range Planning" (HRD-79-118, Sept. 20, 1979).

"Increased Efficiency Predicted If Information Processing Systems of the Social Security Administration Are Redesigned" (B-164031(4), Apr. 19, 1974).

[6]Discussed in Section 1.

changes prematurely. Consequently, significant system deficiencies in the automated job stream were not detected and corrected, resulting in many social security beneficiaries receiving incorrect benefit payments and payment notices that were confusing. SSA field offices had to spend considerable staff time helping beneficiaries resolve these payment and notice deficiencies.

These validation shortcomings and the resulting automated job stream deficiencies apparently occurred primarily because SSA (1) had not developed formal validation standards and procedures, (2) may not have allocated enough staff time to testing system changes, (3) failed to ensure that the validation group could control all program and system modifications, and (4) had not established adequate system performance criteria upon which to base validations.

Shortcomings in SSA's Approach to Validating The Automated Job Stream

Inadequate Case Selection SSA officials connected with the RSDHI redesign defined validation as the use of a test file to verify that a computer program processed correctly. In addition to test data, SSA also used live processing (pilot runs) to test the accuracy of some redesign changes. According to SSA, pilots of certain redesign changes were run live, but only on a small scale, such as at one program service center, to identify possible errors not detected by using test data. Such pilots were used to verify that a redesign change was ready to be implemented nationwide.

Although some problems can be expected when varied complex transactions are processed, use of adequate test data should identify serious problems before program implementation begins. SSA's selection of cases for validating redesign changes, such as those comprising the automated job stream, however, did not always provide adequate data for testing the programs' ability to process complex transactions correctly.

Number and Types of Cases Insufficient Test criteria for validating a system should be as comprehensive as possible. As a minimum, the test data should include all combinations of valid transactions in order to test their acceptance and proper processing by the system. However, SSA's test file for validating the annual retirement test segment[7] of the automated job stream was not sufficiently comprehensive.

Although beneficiaries ultimately submitted nearly one million annual earnings reports for 1978, SSA program officials provided for a test file of only 2000 cases in their detailed plan for validating the annual retirement test

[7]The Social Security Act requires that certain beneficiaries have their benefits reduced if they work and have earnings that exceed an annual exempt amount. These beneficiaries must file an annual report of earnings with SSA to facilitate the required benefit adjustments. This procedure is known as the annual retirement test. A major element of the automated job stream was to handle the automated processing of annual earnings reports and related benefit adjustments and beneficiary notices.

segment of the automated job stream. That number was based on the work-load SSA believed its validators could handle, rather than the number needed to adequately test the system change. An SSA official closely associated with validation activities told us that SSA program officials wanted the test file to include a variety of transaction types that the new program would need to process, especially difficult types. Accordingly, their validation plan provided for including in the test file cases requiring specific types of actions. When the test file was prepared by SSA's systems personnel, however, it consisted of less than half of the requested 2000 cases and did not adequately represent all the specific types of cases required. According to an August 1979 report by SSA's Office of Assessment, test file cases were selected without regard to the characteristics of the case situations, and as a result, deficiencies in the system were not identified and corrected promptly, causing serious processing errors.

Similarly, in selecting test file cases for validating the recomputations portion[8] of the automated job stream, SSA again based the number of test cases on the perceived capacity of its validation staff. SSA program staff believed it was nearly impossible to represent every potential case in the test file because of the number of variables and types of payment situations. In addition, they referred to difficulties in getting the systems staff to provide adequate numbers of test cases and to provide such cases promptly.

Before SSA began implementing the annual retirement test segment of the automated job stream nationwide, program service center personnel verified the results of two pilot runs of the program. The results convinced SSA officials to proceed with nationwide implementation because the payment accuracy rate shown was equivalent to that in prior years using the unmodified ADP system. Program service center personnel informed us that the pilot runs included some of the more difficult types of cases. They added, however, that verification, both before and after nationwide implementation, was primarily directed toward the easier cases. Thus, the verification of pilot runs did not give SSA a complete projection of how accurately the job stream would process annual retirement test cases, including the more difficult ones.

Invalid Test Cases Not Used   Validation is supposed to verify processing accuracy, and one method is to compare processing results with predetermined test results. The test files should contain data to test both valid and invalid conditions as well as a predefined set of input and output transactions.

However, test data for validating both the recomputations and annual retirement test portions of the automated job stream consisted primarily of actual case records selected from SSA files; no erroneous case data were included. While actual case data could be used to verify a program's ability to process valid cases correctly, these data were not able to test program con-

[8]Another element of the automated job stream was established to handle certain other benefit payment adjustments applicable to working beneficiaries, such as the annual recalculation of benefit payments to reflect additional beneficiary earnings.

trols for identifying and rejecting erroneous or invalid data. Although SSA validators did create data for about 15 percent of the test cases associated with the annual retirement test programs, these data had valid rather than erroneous case characteristics. Thus, such data were created apparently in order to include additional specific types of actual cases in the test files, not to test program controls for handling invalid data.

Validations Not Adequately Performed   For proper validation, a program change should be tested throughout the entire system to determine its impact on other system aspects. This was not adequately done for RSDHI redesign changes. For example, in validating the annual retirement test segment of the automated job stream, SSA did not fully test how these changes might affect other portions of the RSDHI system, even though output from the annual retirement test segment also serves as input for updating other RSDHI system elements, such as the MBR and the Recovery of Overpayments, Accounting, and Reporting Subsystem. Improper updating of the MBR could, in turn, result in erroneous benefit payments.

MBR data deficiencies would result either if the system added erroneous annual retirement test data to the MBR or if the system failed to carry out the updating function correctly. Both of these conditions may have existed during the redesign. For example, both program service center personnel and local office staff expressed doubt about the reliability of data produced by the annual retirement test segment of the job stream. In addition, an operations analyst at one service center told us that the MBR was not properly updated when certain changes were made to the annual retirement test program. This may have resulted in payment errors when MBR data were used for later transaction processing. The automated job stream rejected some cases where MBR data needed by the system for computing benefits were missing or questionable, thus requiring extensive manual verification. However, program service center personnel could not determine how often the system was computing program benefits using inaccurate or out-of-date MBR data.

Premature Implementation   Validation of computer program changes is preimplementation activity. Before beginning implementation, procedures needed for converting to the new programs and for building new files should be prepared. After conversion procedures are completed, the entire system should be validated to make sure that it performs in accordance with all functional and performance specifications, meeting user needs and objectives. Only after the system has been certified to be accurate and complete should it be placed into operation. However, SSA began implementing certain major redesign changes, even though they had not been validated to the validators' satisfaction.

Under the annual retirement test requirements of the Social Security Act, beneficiaries must report their earnings for the year by April 15 of the following year, SSA generally begins processing the earnings reports as they are received and adjusts benefits accordingly. The 1977 amendments to the act changed the annual retirement test operation in 1979, requiring SSA to decide whether to modify the existing annual retirement test computer program or to incorporate the required program changes into the automated job stream. SSA did not reach its final decision to pursue the job stream approach until August 1978, substantially limiting the time available to develop, validate, and implement the annual retirement test segment of the job stream. As a result, SSA did not complete its validation activities before beginning to process beneficiary earnings reports. Although SSA emphasized validating certain types of actions, such as automated computations and deductions, it did not fully validate other actions, such as month of election adjustments[9] and final MBR annotations. The completed validations identified numerous problems, some of which SSA did not correct.

Initial validation of the recomputations segment of the automated job stream identified certain program problems requiring correction. According to SSA validation personnel, however, the resulting program changes made to correct these problems were never validated because of pressure to move quickly on to new redesign activities.

Automated Job Stream Processing Errors Demonstrate the Need for Improved Validations

SSA began implementing the recomputations and annual retirement test segments of the automated job stream without correcting system deficiencies that proper validation should have identified for correction. These deficiencies caused many beneficiaries to receive erroneous benefit payments and confusing payment notices, the resolution of which required substantial additional work by SSA field offices.

Processing by Recomputations Segment Not Accurate   Although the recomputations segment of the automated job stream was able to automate about 65 percent of annual recomputations previously processed manually, validations have demonstrated the need to improve the program's accuracy. The processing accuracy rate ranged between 59 percent and 68 percent before nationwide implementation in October 1978, according to initial validation results.

We found no precise data on the degree of processing accuracy by the recomputations segment after SSA implemented it nationwide. However, a program service center analyst closely involved with validating the recom-

---

[9]This generally refers to certain cases involving reduced benefits in which the RSDHI system is to automatically adjust the month of entitlement while processing the beneficiary's earnings report for the year of application. As a result of the 1977 Social Security Act amendments, SSA cannot complete these adjustments until beneficiaries have reported their earnings for the year of application.

putations segment told us the programs had problems not only when SSA began implementing them, but also when SSA revised them to accommodate changes required by the 1977 amendments to the Social Security Act. In fact, some changes required by the amendments—such as rate adjustments for widows who remarry—did not work at all, according to the analyst, and cases had to be processed manually.

Although the analyst believed that most initial program problems with the recomputations segment of the job stream had been corrected, she noted that the program still was generally unable to process the more difficult, error-prone cases, such as widows' cases. She added that it was also unable to process certain cases containing pre-1972 data, because of limitations in the previous computer program that had been incorporated into the job stream. In addition, cases involving such factors as readjusted benefit rates and partial-month payments were often processed inaccurately, according to the analyst.

SSA headquarters personnel told us that the agency has continued to make program corrections to the recomputations segment of the job stream. However, a revalidation of the annual recomputation program in late 1980 showed that it was still unable to correctly process certain cases and would sometimes generate incorrect payments.

Annual Retirement Test Segment Caused Problems   SSA began implementing the annual retirement test segment of the automated job stream nationwide in March 1979. In August 1979, personnel from the Mid-America Program Service Center advised SSA headquarters of their concern over the apparent inability of the job stream to process large numbers of annual retirement test cases accurately. They indicated that the annual retirement test segment of the job stream contained at least sixty-eight separate program problems, some affecting many cases and others extensively affecting future processing. In addition, they noted that, although the system identified for follow-on manual review many cases having questionable or incomplete data elements that might affect benefit payments, it had issued checks, updated the MBR, and generated beneficiary notices, even though the follow-on case reviews had not been made. About 25 percent of the annual retirement test cases processed were in this postreview category, and the results of later program service center case reviews indicated that a large percentage of transactions processed by the job stream were incorrect, requiring complete reworking of the cases.

For example, a program service center sample of processed dual entitlement[10] cases showed that only one-third of the cases were totally correct, having no payment, documentation, or notice errors. The program service

---

[10]This generally refers to instances in which one beneficiary is entitled to more than one program benefit at the same time, such as a widow entitled to survivors insurance benefits because of her deceased husband's earnings and to retirement insurance benefits because of her own earnings.

center recommended to SSA headquarters that further job stream processing of postreview cases be suspended until after completion of such reviews. According to an SSA headquarters official, the agency took no action on this recommendation, but instead directed program corrections at the source of such errors.

Erroneous Benefit Payments Although numerous underpayments and overpayments of RSDHI benefits apparently occurred as a result of program problems in the annual retirement test segment of the job stream, SSA could provide no precise data quantifying such payment errors. According to SSA officials, the agency made no comprehensive effort to identify payment errors before May 1979, when it began a review of all annual retirement test processing output. Although this review identified certain individual erroneous payments, SSA prepared no comprehensive erroneous payment statistics. After reviewing a sample of annual retirement test cases processed during 1979, however, SSA's Office of Assessment projected that system errors had caused about $3.6 million in overpayments and $3.9 million in underpayments to beneficiaries.

Individual payment errors were sometimes brought to SSA's attention by beneficiaries themselves or were identified by later reviews or actions at the program service centers. One center reported overpayments as high as $1500 to individual beneficiaries because the system incorrectly handled certain cases involving readjustment of the benefit rate. Such overpayments increased SSA's recovery workload and resulted in SSA requesting numerous beneficiaries to return checks. Similarly, system-caused underpayments not only delayed payments due to beneficiaries, but also required SSA to incur the administrative costs of making payment adjustments.

We noted one instance where program problems resulted in the annual retirement test segment of the job stream generating substantial overpayments. While implementing program changes made in response to the 1977 Social Security Act amendments, SSA estimated that overpayments totaling between $10 million and $15 million would be paid to some beneficiaries. Because of the administrative cost of collecting the overpayments and the resulting inconvenience to beneficiaries, SSA waived recovery of all such overpayments. In some of these cases, the annual retirement test program correctly computed the amount to be waived but, instead of waiving it, considered it an underpayment and issued a check for the amount, resulting in a second overpayment to some beneficiaries. Explanatory notices generated by the system and sent to the beneficiaries indicated that the checks represented "benefits due." Based on its sample case review, the Office of Assessment projected that the system processed as many as 3000 cases of this type incorrectly. Program service center personnel reported that the amount of the second overpayment was as high as $4000 in certain cases. The redesign project manager told us this type of case was not well represented in the test file used to validate the program.

Confusing Beneficiary Notices   SSA designed one element of the annual retirement test segment of the job stream to automatically generate a beneficiary notice explaining any upcoming benefit adjustments based on the annual earnings data the beneficiary had submitted. The notices generated by the system in early 1979, however, were frequently erroneous, confusing, and unintelligible. For example, the first eleven lines of one such notice contained the following statements:

> We received your work report showing that you worked in January through December and earned $3,765.00 in 1978 and that you expect to earn $2,227.00 in 1979.
> Because you did not earn more than $3,240.00 in 1978, we are not required to withhold any benefits for that year.
> Because you do not expect to earn more than $4,500.00 in 1979, we are not required to withhold any benefits.
> The amount of the overpayment will be recovered by withholding $47.00 a month from your benefit payments beginning May 1979.

As shown above, this notice not only contained contradictory information regarding the amount of the beneficiary's earnings for 1978, but also informed the beneficiary that future benefit payments would be reduced to recover an overpayment, even though earlier statements indicated that no such benefit withholding was required.

In some cases, even local office personnel were unable to interpret the notices and had to request assistance from program service center personnel before responding to beneficiary inquiries. One local office estimated that as many as 50 percent of the notices were erroneous.

The Office of Assessment reported in August 1979 that its staff identified one or more notice defects in about 15 percent of the completely automated annual retirement test actions. Common errors identified by the staff for such cases not subject to manual review after system processing included:

- The beneficiary was advised that the correct amount of benefits had been withheld for the year when, in fact, he or she had received an underpayment or overpayment.
- The beneficiary was advised that an adjustment had been made for increases in benefits due when there were no such increases.
- The beneficiary was not advised of the reason for a benefit rate change when such change was made to give credit for benefits not paid due to work.

The erroneous notices had a tremendous impact on RSDHI beneficiaries, and as a result, SSA received a lot of adverse publicity. In August 1979 the commissioner initiated a special high-priority effort to "clean up" the notices. As part of this effort, SSA awarded a consultant contract to a private software development firm in October 1979 for assistance in correcting the systems problems causing the erroneous notices. Under this contract, as later modified, the private firm had received over $320,000 as of November 1980. At that time, SSA was internally processing a contract amendment to provide up to an additional $200,000 to cover remaining contractor services. These contract costs are in addition to administrative costs incurred by SSA to develop software performance specifications, monitor contractor activities, and validate the software developed by the contractor.

Additional Work Imposed on SSA Field Offices   Both local offices and program service centers felt the impact of faulty processing by the annual retirement test segment of the automated job stream. Because of the overpayments, underpayments, and confusing notices generated by the computerized system, local office personnel were "swamped" with beneficiary inquiries. A service representative at one local office we visited stated that the automated job stream caused twice as much work in handling the annual retirement test operation in 1979 as compared to the year before. Field office personnel told us they did not receive adequate training, procedures, or alerts concerning the increased workload and what was received was not timely. For example, several weeks after beneficiaries began coming to one local office with questions on their notices, that office received a teletype from SSA headquarters indicating that the notices would not be accurate.

The impact of annual retirement test problems on the program service centers went beyond responding to beneficiary inquiries. As of March 1979, when SSA began implementing the annual retirement test segment of the job stream nationwide, over 900,000 earnings reports were awaiting processing at the service centers. Because of the magnitude of later program problems, SSA's commissioner required a review of all annual retirement test processing output. The service centers began this review in late May 1979. Because of substantial case backlogs, the two service centers we visited initially established full-time special work groups to perform the review. One service center assembled a group of fourteen full-time and twelve as-needed staff, which spent 163 staff-days on this project. Their review identified that about 32 percent of the cases required additional work, such as corrections to notices or preparation of a notice. Personnel at the other service center spent about 175 staff-days on similar work. SSA discontinued the review in March 1980 even though about 35 percent of the notices continued to contain errors. SSA indicated it had corrected major notice deficiencies, such as garbled language and disjointed paragraphs, and that continuing the review would make it difficult for the service centers to handle upcoming workloads.

In summary, the annual retirement test segment of the automated job stream was described by one program service center official as the "most traumatic of programs," hurting the morale of service center staff immeasurably because it caused large work backlogs, program problems, and complaints from local offices and beneficiaries.

Status of Annual Retirement Test Processing by the Automated Job Stream   According to an SSA official involved in annual retirement test processing operations, the agency began correcting identified system problems in late 1979 and began processing the 1979 annual retirement test workload in January 1980. At that time, however SSA's Office of Assessment reported that it was unable to determine whether identified system problems had been corrected. As of November 1980, SSA had essentially completed this processing but had not completed analyzing processing accuracy. We noted indications that overall processing had improved compared to 1979. However, SSA acknowledged in September 1980 that a number of "processing anomalies" in the annual retirement test software remain to be corrected, noting that this software has yet to be perfected to the point of being operationally stable.

SSA Weaknesses Leading to Inadequate Validations

As shown above, SSA's failure to properly validate the automated job stream resulted in uncorrected systems flaws that created substantial hardships for SSA and beneficiaries. In identifying potential causes of SSA's validation shortcomings, we noted that the agency (1) had not developed formal validation standards or procedures, (2) may not have allocated enough staff time to testing redesign changes, (3) failed to ensure that the validation group could control all program and system modifications, and (4) had not established system performance criteria upon which to base validations.

Lack of Validation Standards or Procedures   According to SSA staff involved with validating automated job stream segments, SSA had not developed formal validation procedures. As a result, SSA did not employ generally accepted techniques in attempting to validate these systems changes. For example, as noted, SSA personnel based the number of test file cases to be selected on the workload they believed the validating staff could handle, and they specified the types of cases to be used for test purposes primarily on the basis of the validating staff's knowledge of case types to be processed, rather than on specific guidelines for selecting test cases. Similarly, rather than developing processing accuracy standards for determining when validation was complete and full-scale implementation could begin, SSA adopted a "hurry-up" approach to project implementation.

In May 1980, SSA's Office of User Requirements and Validation, the structural component with responsibility for validating systems changes, issued interim validation guidelines that prescribed very general procedures for conducting such validation activities as selecting test cases, identifying the impact a given systems change may have on other program applications or subsystems, and determining the processing accuracy required for implementation. According to an office representative, these guidelines were to establish parameters and ranges to help validators perform these activities, and the agency expected to incorporate more detail into future versions. It is too soon to tell whether the guidelines are bringing about improvements in these validation areas.

Not Enough Staff Time Allocated to Validations   Validations of RSDHI redesign projects were performed by SSA central office personnel and program service center staff. We found no SSA data showing precisely how many staff were performing project validation activities at any time or how much time the validators spent testing system changes. However, as stated, SSA program personnel restricted automated job stream test files to a case level they felt the validators could handle, resulting in test files that were not sufficiently comprehensive. The amount of staff time allocated to validation should be determined in part by the number of test cases needed to adequately test a system change, not vice versa. Thus, SSA may not have allocated sufficient staff time to validating system changes.

Validators Not Controlling All Program and System Changes   Because validation tests all aspects of a system, including its performance, functional specifications, documentation, outputs, operating procedures, and user procedures, to assure that each aspect and the total system function as required by the user and as designed by the systems analyst, systems validators must control all planned changes so that no changes can be made without their approval. In this regard, validation team members must also maintain independence from those responsible for implementing the system changes, in this case, SSA systems personnel.

However, SSA systems staff not only had responsibility for developing redesign changes, but also played a major role in validating those changes. They supplied the test data, ran the tests, and sometimes maintained more control over certain aspects of the validations than did the validators. For example, as noted, systems staff did not meet the validator's specifications in selecting test file cases for the recomputations and annual retirement test segments of the automated job stream, according to SSA program personnel. In addition, despite contentions by the validation staff that the recomputations segment was not ready, the redesign project manager (a member of the systems staff), and the user liaison committee made and then carried out the decision to begin its implementation. Placing responsibility for validations within the Office of User Requirements and Validation—achieved during SSA's 1979 structural reorganization—may eventually promote greater independence of the validation staffs from those involved with the design and development of systems changes.

Lack of Baseline System Performance Criteria   As previously defined, validation is to assure that a system functions as required by all key users. However, as noted in Section 2, SSA never effectively solicited the requirements of certain key users regarding proposed RSDHI system changes. As a result, SSA had no comprehensive user criteria describing desired system performance against which to validate redesign changes. Thus, SSA apparently would still have been unable to adequately validate RSDHI system modifications, even if proper validation procedures had existed and validators had been given sufficient staff time and authority to properly test redesign changes.

In May 1980, SSA issued revised standards for developing functional requirements for proposed system modifications. SSA expected these standards, in conjunction with the interim validation guidelines discussed above, to facilitate users' providing the required system performance criteria. The standards appeared to be directed primarily toward users in agency headquarters. However, it is too soon to tell whether these standards are resulting in the development of comprehensive system performance criteria to be used during validation.

Internal Audit Staff Not Involved in RSDHI Redesign

The internal audit staff of a governmental organization should participate actively in reviewing the system design and development/modification process in order to verify that application systems being developed or modified comply with development and operational standards and include adequate automated controls and audit trails. Once ADP system changes have been implemented, the internal auditors should also review the entire system to assure that it performs satisfactorily and that it is meeting its objectives. This audit, in part a postimplementation validation, should measure the effectiveness of any automated controls and audit trails built into the modified system and assess the system against the goals and objectives previously established for it.

In our October 16, 1979, letter report (HRD-80-5) to the Secretary of Health, Education, and Welfare concerning weaknesses in SSA's Supplemental Security Income computerized system, we noted that the department's audit agency had reviewed neither the process SSA used in designing and developing system modifications nor the effectiveness of automated controls built into the system. This finding also applies to the RSDHI redesign. A department auditor assigned to ADP reviews at SSA told us in July 1980 that the audit agency had yet to become involved in the design and development of new ADP systems at SSA, but planned to do so in the future. He added that, although audit agency staff have performed ad hoc evaluations of how well certain SSA ADP systems function, they have not performed any review work specifically aimed at assessing systems changes implemented under the RSDHI redesign or any other system redesign activities at SSA. In responding to the recommendations contained in our earlier report, the department explained that the audit agency has performed limited work in these specialized audit areas because of a lack of qualified staff. The department added that, although it was undertaking an intensive training program and employing several computer systems analysts, comprehensive ADP evaluations at SSA remain a long-range goal.